Horizons

Preschool

Teacher's Guide
Part 2
Lessons 91-180

Authors:
Alan L. Christopherson, M.S.
Alpha Omega Publications

Original Interlock Curriculum by
Rebecca L. Avery

Adaptation/Revision for Horizons Preschool by
Marilyn Zent Schlitz
Alpha Omega Publications

Editor:
Jeannie Burrus, B.S.

Illustration & Layout:
Jennifer Davis

Alpha Omega Publications, Inc. • Rock Rapids, IA

Table of Contents

Horizons Preschool Scope and Sequence

The following list gives a breakdown by lesson groupings of the concepts that are covered in the pre-school program. This list is certainly not exhaustive and primarily serves to illustrate the depth and progression of concepts as they are presented.

Lessons 1-30

- Day 1 – Day 3 of Creation
- God, Jesus, Holy Spirit, light, darkness, air, clouds, dry land, rocks
- Finger and action activities, spatial concepts, lists, names, sort, compare, rhyme, describe, classify
- Letter recognition Aa-Ii
- Numerals 1-6
- Oral counting 1-10
- Recognize red, green, blue, black, white, yellow
- Identify triangle, circle, and square
- Recognize first name, read an illustrated schedule
- Trace first two letters of first name
- Color, glue, stamp, draw, shape, fold, trace, cut, paint
- Self space, general space, ball activities, ribbon sticks, rhythm, run, skip, jump

Lessons 31-60

- Day 3 – Day 4 of Creation
- Soil, plants, grasses, seeds, trees, fruits, vegetables, sun, weather, day, night, seasons, hour
- Sort, solve puzzles, finger activities, label, vocabulary development
- Letter recognition Jj-Ss
- Numerals 7-10, 0
- Oral counting 0-10
- Recognize purple, orange, gray
- Identify rectangle, star
- Trace letters of first name
- Write the first letter of first name
- Glue, shape, paint, draw, solve puzzles, construct, color, stamp
- Jump, crawl, ribbon sticks, hopscotch, stretch, exercise

Lessons 61-90

- Day 4 of Creation
- Seasons, earth's rotation, earth's tilt, moon, stars, constellations, astronomy, planets, comets, meteors
- Action rhymes, stories, finish stories, complete sentences, verbalize concepts, answer questions, rhyme, naming, comparing, vocabulary development, grouping
- Letter recognition Ss-Zz
- Letter sounds Aa-Bb
- Numerals 10-12
- Oral counting 0-20
- Tell time to the hour

- Addition 1 + 1
- Identify star, heart, oval
- Review colors
- Write first name with a guide
- Cut, shape, glue, draw, interpret, cut, assemble, trace
- Walk, skip, hop, balance beam, launch board, ballet
- Fire safety

Lessons 91-120

- Day 5 – Day 6 of Creation
- Fish, climate, ocean creatures, amphibians, eggs, birds, animals, mammals
- Comparison, action rhymes, role play, imitate, describe, finger play, rhyme, classify, vocabulary development, alphabetical order
- Letter sounds Cc-Ii
- Blend letter sounds Aa-Hh
- Write first name without a guide
- Addition 2 + 1, 3 + 1, 4 + 1
- Identify diamond, pictograph
- Shape, color, cut, glue, label, draw
- Catch, jump, ribbon dance, throw, fine motor skills

Lessons 121-150

- Day 6 of Creation
- Reptiles, insects, man, cells, senses, bones, digestion, breathing, muscles
- Size relationships, comparison, guessing, role play, describe, alphabetize, chart, vocabulary development, classify, sort
- Letter sounds Jj-Rr
- Blend letter sounds Aa-Rr
- Write home address and phone number
- Addition 5 + 1
- Subtraction 2 – 1, 3 – 1
- Review shapes
- Type one's name
- Mold, string, shape, paint, draw, stamp, cut, glue, trace
- Crawl, walk, jumping jacks, bowling, crouch & jump, ride tricycles, ring toss

Lessons 151-180

- Day 6 – Day 7 of Creation, Noah's flood
- Blood, circulation, brain, body parts, occupations, health & safety, music, work, rules, helpers, friends, family, promises, flood
- Letter sounds Ss-Zz
- Blend letter sounds Aa-Zz
- Write home address and phone number
- Initial sound of shape words
- Subtract 4 - 1, 5 – 1, 6 – 1
- Cut glue, shape, draw, color, paint, decorate
- Ring toss, swinging, bowling, dribble, kick, throw, rhythm sticks, ball rolling, tag, tumbling

Introduction

A preschool program is now a part of the Horizons product line. This program will serve as both as a complement and an introduction to the other fine Horizons products. Give your preschoolers a foundation that will help them to be successful in kindergarten with this flexible and comprehensive curriculum choice from the Horizons series.

Our goal in early childhood education is to develop the best style of education, the optimum learning environment and to establish within the child the correct foundation emotionally, intellectually, socially, and spiritually.

Horizons Preschool is based upon the most perfect source available, the Bible. You and your students will be studying the world around you from the viewpoint of the Creator. Lessons begin with a Bible concept and flow into activities and academic subjects including social studies, language arts, math, phonics and science. Arts and crafts, music, story times, outdoor excursions, and other exciting learning activities enhance the student lessons. The Teacher's Guides contain daily lesson plans making learning and teaching fun and easy. *Horizons Preschool* helps students gain the important knowledge that God is the beginning of all things. It gives them a perspective of the world which can be gained in no other way.

The *Horizons Preschool* program is adaptable to many school situations, the home school, a daycare setting or the traditional school classroom. Five days a week are provided, with the understanding that any number of days per week may be used successfully. New concepts are introduced on days 1, 3, and 5 of the week. Days 2 and 4 have activities that expand and further practice those concepts. You will be given a variety of learning experiences from which to choose in the material. Students coming into this program with preschool exposure will be more successful with the fine motor skills required to complete some of the worksheets. Students with less background may need more time writing letters in corn meal, sand or whipped cream. The great thing is that you will have lots of ideas to choose from in running a program that fits your situation.

Understanding the Young Child

As teachers and parents, we desire the best for our students. We go to great lengths to assure that they receive a good education. We want an environment where a child can freely explore the world using the five senses, feelings, and intellect to encompass the world. This type of a learning environment is rarely found in any school. What then, are the factors that give a special quality to the learning that will take place?

A young child is not at a mental distance from his world. A child will put his hand flat on the summer turf, feel it, and give a little shiver of private glee at the elastic firmness of the globe. He is not thinking how well it will do for some game, or to feed the sheep upon, he has an ecstatic sense of the thing's inherent characteristics. The image in the mind, and the actual object, are not clearly differentiated for the young child. The almost obsessive concern of some adults with reason and intellectualizing is not present in the young child. It isn't there to act as a barrier to the process of feeling deeply and gaining pleasure from sensual experience. A young child takes an element of our world and makes it his own. It is this personal relationship, this intermingling of self and experience that is characteristic of the development of understanding in young children. The knowledge is always acquired with personal sensual experience and it is in this way that a child gets close to the "inherent characteristics" of things.
An observant teacher will note that there is a world of difference between the learning experience in which the child is personally involved and one in which he is "going through the motions" with a task

regarded as "school learning." We desire for the child to be personally involved. This can only occur through real-life, hands-on, manipulative experiences; i.e., through the use of as many of the five senses as possible. What the child feels, he internalizes. And what he has internalized, he has learned, for learning is internalization.

We must also come to the realization that to the child there is no separation between the experience of the object at hand and himself. Knowing this, the teacher understands that while we may separate subjects in our mind and call them Social Studies and Science, they are not so to the child. Nor should they be presented as such. They are simply another part of his world, and rightly so, for in the integration of an experience into self true learning is achieved.

If we can grasp this understanding of a young child, we will save ourselves a tremendous amount of time and energy. The normal sequence of teaching involves the teaching of separation of subjects, and then, when the child has learned that, an attempt to integrate the subjects again. The resulting confusion is not necessary.

The *Horizons Preschool* has integrated the subject materials for you throughout the lessons. Although we have listed them in categories, you will want to flow between the lessons without notifying your students of a change in what you are teaching. Each lesson is formulated to flow smoothly, discussing the same subject throughout, and giving the child opportunities to explore, through various senses, the world about him. We do not desire to begin with a list of subjects, but rather with the child's relationship with his world. We desire to teach the child HOW to think rather than WHAT to think.

Following the teaching period, the child will also require a time period for internalizing what has been taught. An indication of internalization of teaching will occur when the child begins to play the subject that has been taught. The allowance for a play period is, therefore, very important to the school, as this is how the child learns. The concept is that the teacher should allow for a play period, and not expect the child to have internalized the materials presented before an adequate time span has passed.

In understanding and evaluating your student, you must decide when to make them a "student." How old should a "preschooler" be? All students are different at different ages so it makes sense that there is no hard and fast age to consider your child a preschooler. The usual age for starting *Horizons Preschool* is four years old. But there are three year olds that are more than ready, anxious to do school. And there are five year olds that simply aren't ready yet. This is a decision totally up to the parents and their observation of the child. If you just can't decide, try it. The child will let you know by complaint and disinterest if they aren't ready. The most important rule is "Don't Push." Let the child's actions and desires guide your decision, not their age.

The Environment of the School

The first step to successful education in early childhood is discipline. You need to discipline your students with a Godly perspective. Your students need to obey your voice command. They need to know the limits you have set. This gives them a sense of security, a sense of being loved.

There are many wonderful Christian books on the market about discipline. We suggest you read the books by Dr. James Dobson, Dr. Raymond Moore's writings on the subject, and *The Hurried Child* by David Elkind. Charles Stanley's book *How To Keep Your Children On Your Team* is also excellent. These books will give you an overall view of Godly discipline and how our society interacts with children. Godly discipline should be a priority in the home before formal education is begun.

The second step (but more important than the first) in successful education is the teacher's and/or parent's relationship with God. You cannot teach your students about someone whom you do not know. Throughout this course you will be using the Word of God in depth to teach about the world around us. You need to know the Creator on a personal level. When you do, you then have access to the wisest Teacher on earth from whom to learn.

The third step is the routine of your school. Students need to have a set routine which guides their days and nights. Without this, they lose their sense of judgment as to the time and the occurrence of things. A routine gives the child the security needed to expand his world. This is true for the home school and for the traditional school.

We suggest that the preschool student have no more than two hours of actual school. By interspersing action activities and meaningful play between the quieter academic sessions you will fill the time that is available. Morning time usually works better as the child is refreshed. Planning a schedule will benefit the teacher more than the child. Even though you retain a routine for school, let the teaching time be natural and flexible.

Knowing that the young child learns best by doing, you will want to plan the day to include times when everyone is working together at a task. In this way the child learns how to do a variety of things. Encourage the children to learn to do some of the jobs around the house and/or classroom. A four year old is quite capable of dusting, straightening books, or cleaning up toys. Give sufficient work so that the student realizes that he is a productive part of the society of your classroom or home. This type of scheduling alone will greatly improve his or her self-esteem.

As noted previously, internalization of what you have taught and what the child has experienced will only take place through play. The child needs to have sufficient unstructured time to play. It is only through play that the child relives, rethinks, and clarifies what he has seen and done. Following field trips and time spent "studying," give students the opportunity to verbalize and recreate their experience. Knowing this, the wise teacher not only allows for play time, but encourages it. If you will listen to your students while they play, it will give you an insight into what they have understood of the materials you have presented.

The Classroom

The environment at school needs to be clean and safe. Make it a school habit that everything is back in its place at the end of every day. Develop a routine of basic cleaning. Regularly spray and wipe any toys or manipulatives with disinfectant.

Consistency is the key to a smoothly running school. Make sure there is a big clock with large easy-to-read hands at the front of the room. Print out your basic schedule and post it in two or three places around the room. This said, remember that the schedule is your guide, not your task master.

We have scheduled the teaching lessons to cover five days a week. We suggest that if you want to do a three day school, that you chose Days 1, 3, and 5. If you are running a half day program you will want to select activities that can be completed in the time that is available. There are 180 lessons in this guide, so in some situations where a three day school is in session on a year long basis most of the lessons in this guide can be covered.

Set aside a special area where school supplies are kept. The child needs to know where supplies needed for creativity are kept and that he can reach them without your help. Include in this area glue, children's scissors, pencils, paper, color crayons, and colored markers. As the year progresses, add pets, plants, bulletin boards, and other items that will add to the educational environment. A supply list is included in this guide.

Younger children in the home may often distract you in the homeschool. Keep special toys for them to play with during your schooling time. This should be the only time they are allowed to play with these toys. Should the younger child be closer to the age of the preschool age child, you may use some of the preschool level with him. We caution you not to push the young child into work above his level. Rather, let him exist along with your teaching, gaining what he will. As the younger child grows he can be trained to sit still by gradually increasing the time he spends with you in a required quiet time. The home school works best if a special room is set aside as a classroom. At the least, have a bookcase set aside for school supplies, notebooks, and school work.

There are many wonderful books available for the Preschool age student. Try to provide good books in the classroom at all times. Purchase those that you can, then use the library regularly.

In the traditional school, make sure to provide a special cubby, drawer or cubicle for each student. Stacking plastic drawers work very well. Any personal items may be kept in the cubby. Notes for the parents have a better chance of success for reaching them if put in the cubby. Each student needs a small pillow or blanket for rest times.

Determining Your Type of Program

The *Horizons Preschool* program has been designed to meet the needs of two different types of preschool programs. We will call them an *activity*-centered program and an *academically*-centered program. What's the difference? An *activity*-centered program places a stronger focus on meaningful play. Students form letter shapes with their bodies, write letters in pans of sand and/or cornmeal, trace the shapes of large felt letters. They build letters out of sticks, toys or items glued onto paper. Oral counting is practiced by counting objects as they encounter them in their surroundings. In this setting you see more emphasis on social skills, speaking skills, large motor development and discovery.

An *academically* centered program places more emphasis on a structured classroom setting. Students not only learn to recognize letters of the alphabet, they also learn to write them and learn introductory phonics skills that teaches them to sound out and read words. In addition to counting objects, they learn to recognize and write numbers, and begin to practice addition and subtraction skills. These students are talking about stories that the teacher reads, acting them out and creating new endings. Fine motor skills of cutting, pasting, coloring, and writing are used to complete worksheets and projects. The teacher spends a short portion of each day "teaching" with lecture, demonstration, review, and group practice of the concepts.

What does this mean to you? Basically, it means that there is far more material presented in this teacher's guide than what some classes of students can cover. You as the teacher or school administrator must first decide the overall goals and objectives for your school. From there you can use this teacher's guide to pick out the specific activities that support your philosophy of education. If the emphasis of the school is focused on meaningful play, you will choose activities from the guide that support that focus. If the emphasis is academic, you will select activities that include the worksheets and a deeper study of the concepts. For either program this guide provides a basic structure and sequence of activities.

We have also tried to accommodate the various schedules of the typical preschool programs. Some are half-day programs, some are three-day programs and some are all-day programs. Obviously, if the guide contains enough material for an all-day program the others must pick and choose activities based upon their school's goals and objectives. Because some of the three-day and half-day programs may be either activity or academically focused, this guide makes no attempt to make the decision for you as to which activities are recommended for the various programs.

Another factor that will determine the selection of activities is the previous experience of your students. During the school year you will have to take the students from where they currently are with their skills and abilities to where your school has determined they should be by the end of the year. As the instructor you must bridge whatever gap exists between the student's previous "school" experience and the goals and objectives of your school. If your students come from a play centered three year-old preschool program and you wish to be more academically focused, the gap to bridge will be greater and the activities you choose from the guide will be different than those one would choose if their students came from an experience with more academic focus.

It has been necessary to assume in designing this teacher's guide that the preschool teachers who will be using it have experience, training or knowledge of how to run a preschool program. We have not gone into detail about learning center layout, schedules, procedures, strategies or methods. There is enough here in the guide to give you direction but not enough to dictate what is done every minute of the preschool day. The guide suggests the concept to teach. For example if you are to teach the letter M, whether you do board work, air writing, writing in sand/cornmeal, flashcards, felt shapes, body shapes or whatever to teach the concept has been left up to you. Through experience and practice a teacher "finds" her own methods of instruction that fit both her own personality and the needs of her students. Methods are a variable that each teacher must learn and develop on her own. If you are apprehensive about this issue there are plenty of methods resources available either from print resources or on the Internet. You will be amazed at the volume of preschool information available on the Internet. For some reason this group of people loves to share and display what they have learned about their preschool experience.

Components of the Horizons Preschool Program

This product has several distinctive components.

1. **Horizons Preschool Student Workbooks** contain the consumable student materials. Consumables are items that a student uses once either for arts and crafts or for practice in math, phonics or other academic topics.

    The 180 student lessons have been separated into two books. **Student Book 1** has lessons 1-90 and **Student Book 2** has lessons 91-180. These are 4-color; perfect-bound books with perforated pages for easy tear out. Most pages are front and back but some are 1-sided to be cut out for crafts.

2. **Horizons Preschool Teacher's Guide** is a detailed daily lesson planner that includes sufficient activities for a normal school day. The daily lesson planner includes an integrated selection of activities that as naturally as is possible flow from one to the other. All topic areas relate in some way to the themes examined in the Bible lesson for the day.

    The Horizons Preschool Teacher's Guide has 180 lessons. The 180 teacher lessons have been separated into two books. **Teacher's Guide Book 1** has the course introduction and lessons 1-90. **Teacher's Guide Book 2** has the course introduction and lessons 91-180. These are black and white books with a coil binding.

3. **Horizons Preschool Resource Packet** includes full-color **Teaching Aids** and **Black Line Masters** for reproducibles. The **Black Line Masters** include the **Memory Verse** cards, the **Alphabet Puzzle**, and other reproducible items for art and crafts. The **Teaching Aids** pages consist of **Flashcards** and colored pictures of animals, body systems, and other items found in nature that are used to demonstrate and illustrate lesson concepts. There are approximately 300 pages in this packet, of full-color loose sheets, that are shrink wrapped for shipping.

   a. **Memory Verse** cards are send-home reproducibles for the memory verses learned in the program. The teacher has the option of choosing either KJV or NIV to reproduce for the memory verses.

   b. **Alphabet Puzzle** is a manipulative to aid in teaching letters. The needed puzzle pieces are reproduced and cut out for the students.

   c. **Flashcards** are used as manipulatives for teaching concepts. These include **Numbers** (1-12); **Letters** (Aa-Zz); **Colors** (red, green, blue, black, white, yellow, brown, pink, purple, orange, gray); **Shapes** (triangle, circle, square, rectangle, star, heart, oval, diamond); **Time** (analog clocks, digital clocks, and o'clock time to the hour); **Seasons** (Fall, Winter, Spring, Summer); and **Months** (January-December).

   The **Numbers** cards have items on them for counting. The **Letters** cards have an animal or item that illustrate the sound that the letter makes. The **Colors** cards have a picture of a fruit or item that normally has the color. The Shapes cards are large geometric shapes, colored with the colors being taught in the program. The **Time** cards are very simple with both analog and digital clocks. The **Seasons** cards have illustrations that depict typical events for the season. The **Months** cards have illustrations that depict typical events for the month.

   The **Flashcards** include both a handi-size for individual or small class instruction and a display-size which is a full page for large class instruction or wall display. All of the flashcards are two sided. The front side of the card includes a picture clue with the letter or word for the concept. The back side has either the letter or a picture clue for drilling the concept.

4. Several **Multimedia** items are included in the curriculum package. These include:

   a. **Horizons Preschool Music CD** of the songs taught to the students that reinforce key topic areas. This has been recorded using some children's voices and serves as a sing-along instructional aid.

   b. **Horizons Preschool Multimedia Package** consists of Videos, CDs, and Software that fit the lesson themes from the AOP library of titles. These can be purchased as a package or by individual titles from AOP.

   c. **Suggested multimedia that is NOT part of the Package.** There are several recommended items that can be purchased or obtained from other sources.

The Lesson Structure of the Horizons Preschool Program

Each *Horizons Preschool* lesson is divided (for teacher purposes only) into subdivisions of Bible Reference, Bible Concept to Present, Bible Lesson, Social Studies, Science, Language Arts, Phonics, Reading, Writing, Memory Verse, Math, Shapes, Color, Story Time, Music, Health & Safety, Arts & Crafts, Outdoor Activity, Homework, and Physical Education. These divisions will be examined in the paragraphs that follow.

- **Bible Reference** is given for the purpose of going directly to the Scripture and researching any reference previous to teaching. We desire that you understand directly from the Bible what is being taught.

- **Bible Concept to Present** will give you an overall view of what we consider to be the objective of the lesson. This is presented from a nondenominational viewpoint.

- **Bible Lesson** is a format giving you the information that should be presented to the students. We suggest you do not read this directly from the book, but rather interpret it into your own terminology. Any illustration that can be used will supplement and reinforce your teaching.

- **Social Studies** is concerned with how the materials being studied affects the student's lives. Discussed under this subject will be items that have an impact on the child's lifestyle, those people around him, and how we use the Creation of God. Many of the suggestions are activity oriented.

- **Science** is concerned with the details of God's Creation. These are activity oriented ideas with specific subjects discussed. You will want to generally introduce the materials.

- **Language Arts** consists of the verbalization (expression) of ideas and preparatory materials for the teaching of reading. Language Arts in the *Horizons Preschool* includes word exercises, poems, verbalization, games, etc. Note: Reading should be taught only when the students are individually ready. Many of the action rhymes do not have specific actions given. This provides an excellent opportunity for you and the students to "create" actions to go along with the rhymes. Do them in an echo, response format, teacher says the verse, students repeat the verse. Some of these will become favorites of the students so repeat them more often than what is suggested in the lesson plan. They also can be dramatized as one group of students says the rhyme and another "acts" it out.

- **Phonics** initially focuses on letter recognition and alphabet order. Associating, differentiating, and blending the letters sounds comprise the remainder of the program. When the student reaches the Kindergarten level, we suggest *LIFEPAC Kindergarten Language Arts* or *Horizons Kindergarten Phonics and Reading*, both available from Alpha Omega Publications.

- **Reading** is an extremely important aspect to the entire program. One of the primary goals for the year is to increase the verbal skills of the students. This is a time when stories are read to the students and they work on listening and comprehension skills. After a story has been read, reviewed, and discussed it can be acted out by one or more students. This will help them learn and remember how to sequence events into a logical order.

- **Writing** is a section that contains general suggestions for building the skills a young child will need to be able to write. A developmental progression of activities is presented with the goal of enabling the student to independently write his first name.

- **Memory Verses** are suggested with ideas to illustrate them. The young child is very capable of memorizing verses of Scripture with the help of the teacher and repetition. The planting of the seeds of the Word of God now will aid the child greatly in the future. As it is common with young children to easily memorize, you will be surprised at the rapid rate with which they can learn the verses. Have them learn the verse, then the reference. Always insist that they add the reference to the end of their recitation. We give you the verses from the both the New International Version and the King James Version of the Bible. However, you may use whichever version your school prefers. There are reproducibles in the *Horizons Preschool Resource Packet* for both KJV and NIV. Make copies of the version that you wish to use for sending home with the students. We give you new verses almost every week, but the choice of how many to do is up to the teacher.

- **Math** lessons are planned to teach the fundamentals of number sense. They are multi-sensory experiences to aid the child in the acquisition of skills. Counting and number recognition are the initial focus with simple addition and subtraction concepts closing out the year. When the student reaches the Kindergarten level, we suggest *LIFEPAC Kindergarten Math* or *Horizons Kindergarten Math*, both available from Alpha Omega Publications.

- **Shapes** lessons will introduce and provide practice in identifying the basic geometric shapes that a student will need to be able to recognize in kindergarten. A new shape to study is introduced about every two weeks. Through the year the students will learn to recognize the circle, triangle, rectangle, square, star, heart, oval, and diamond shapes.

- **Colors** lessons will introduce and provide practice in identifying the basic colors that a student will need to be able to recognize in kindergarten. A new color to study is introduced about every two weeks. Through the year the students will learn to recognize the red, green, blue, black, white, yellow, brown, pink, purple, orange, and gray colors.

- **Story Time** is a wonderful time to generate an excitement for reading. In a very short time the preschoolers will begin to see letters as words, words as sentences, and sentences as stories. Stories create a visual image of an object or an event. Storybook reading is an effective means of helping the preschool child improve his vocabulary. With strong vocabulary skills a young child is better prepared to begin reading on his own. He then can focus on gaining skill in decoding words that already have meaning for him.

Story Time for the *Horizons Preschool* program has been left very open. We have provided a list of possible books to use but often do not give a specific book in the lesson plan. This gives you, the teacher, the opportunity to pick books from our list or use others that you like or have found work well with your students. We have included the list only to get you started in selecting the books that you will use with your program. There are many different opinions about what books are appropriate for preschool children. We have attempted to provide a balanced list that includes conservative, modern, classic, and traditional titles. We would recommend that you begin by borrowing books from a local library before you develop a list of titles that you would like to purchase and add to your classroom collection of resources. Any of the poems in this guide can be read again at a later time as part of the story time.

The books that you read during story time should be read several times. Each time you are helping the students to deepen their vocabulary skills. Spend time talking about and retelling the stories. Work on both listening and speaking skills during story time. Talk about the setting, the characters, and the sequence of events in the story. Stop at strategic times in the story to ask the students to predict what might happen next. Give the students an opportunity to use their imaginations to create a story based on the pictures or in creating a new ending for the story. Discuss the book format with title pages, illustrations, and story lines. Review the problem, conflict or question raised by the story, and how it is resolved in the sequence of events.

One day of the week could be used for story favorites. Allow the students to select books that have already been read or to bring books from home for this special day. Seeing what books are brought from home will give you an insight into what recommendations need to be given to parents. Encourage the parents to read to their preschooler on a regular basis. This will reinforce what they are learning in the classroom.

- **Music** is suggested for each lesson. You will find the tune to the songs suggested listed for you. Should they not be familiar tunes, the "Horizons Preschool Music" CD will have many of the songs for you. The songs are either character building songs or teaching songs that help to reinforce concepts. There is nothing wrong with making up a new melody for any of the teaching songs. Each new song appears in the lesson plan for seven lessons. This doesn't mean that you cannot use them any more, in fact some will become favorites of the students and they will ask to sing them very often. A few of the lessons do not specify any songs for the music time, on these days do any of the teaching songs that the students need or let them sing any of their favorites.

- **Arts & Crafts** are the process by which children create. We have given you the suggestion of the medium; the child will add the ideas. Note what he creates and praise him highly for work accomplished. Provide time for this activity to occur. Arts & Crafts are designed for sharpening the skills of observation in the child and for familiarizing them with various art tools. Do not expect perfect performance in these projects. The action involved will be of more value to the child than a perfect project.

- **Physical Education** is designed to not only be subject oriented when possible, but to develop the motor coordination needed in the child previous to the teaching of reading. Be certain your student is in good health prior to any exercise period. The physical education time should be used to develop the large muscle motor skills so the student can move with gracefulness and rhythm.

- **Outdoor Activities** are a time to observe the wonders of Creation and the responsibility for caring for it.

- **Creative Cooking** is the fun part to learning. It is a way to involve more of the senses in the learning process.

- **Health & Safety** is learning habits of hygiene and everyday safety skills.

- **Field Trips** are another way for the students to experience first hand what they have been learning. Suggestions are given for possible field trips. It is not necessary that the trip occur on the day that it is mentioned in a lesson. Look ahead so that you can be prepared. These do not need to be complicated or elaborate. Simply walking down the street and around the corner to visit a grocery store can serve as an excellent field trip. Make arrangements to have some parents help with the supervision of the students. As an alternative have an "expert" come in and to give a simple demonstration to the students. Use the ideas that are given in the lessons as a springboard to come up with your own plans for a field trip.

- **Homework** pages are provided in the *Horizons Preschool Student Books*. Traditional school teachers may send the pages home with students as directed. Homeschool teachers may use the pages as they choose. These pages might be done with dad in the evenings. The main goal of the homework pages is to involve parents in what the student is learning.

- **Catch Up** time is listed every six to eight weeks. When you don't have time to do a lesson, make a note to save it for a Catch Up day.

Things to do Before School Begins

Make *Name Plates* for each student. Several will be needed for each student. Themed or seasonal ones will add color and interest to the classroom and can be either made or purchased. One name plate for each child should be taped to the top of the table where you want him/her to sit. Another set of name plates should hang on a bulletin board as a class roster. Another set can be used for flash cards in helping the students learn to read the names of their classmates.

Make a simplified, illustrated *Daily Schedule* of activities. This can be a poster or section of a bulletin board. If the activities are put on individual cards the schedule can be easily rearranged. If you plan to vary the schedule for each day of the week a weekly schedule may be needed.

Purchase or make a *Monthly Calendar*. This should be a blank template where the name of the month and the numbers for the dates can be changed each month. Themed artwork for the month will make this colorful and interesting for the students.

Plan to have the *visuals* constructed well ahead of the time that they are needed. There may be ways in which you can involve the students in making some of these.

Scheduling Suggestions

The difficult thing about scheduling is that each day is different. Science might take ten minutes on Monday and forty minutes on Thursday. Wednesday might include music while Friday has no music. These schedule plans are merely to be guidelines or suggestions. Use them with much flexibility.

HALF-DAY SCHEDULE
9:00 Bible Time
9:20 Social Studies/Science/Language Arts
10:00 Snack
10:15 Recess/Play break
10:30 Phonics/Memory Verse
10:45 Music/Physical Education/Health & Safety
11:00 Math
11:30 Arts & Crafts/Outdoor activity
12:00 Dismiss

ALL-DAY SCHEDULE
9:00 Bible Time
9:20 Social Studies/Science/Language Arts
10:00 Snack
10:15 Recess/Play break
10:30 Phonics/Memory Verse
11:00 Music/Physical Education
11:30 Math
12:00 Lunch break
12:20 Recess/Play break
12:50 Reading
1:20 Arts & Crafts
1:40 Health & Safety/Outdoor activity
2:00 Dismiss

Preparing Ahead: *Horizons Preschool* helps you prepare ahead by *ITALICIZING* things that need to be done ahead of school time.

Naptime: Many preschool children will need a time to rest if they are involved in an all-day program. This is an excellent time to read a story to the children. You can also review the shapes of figures, letters or numbers by drawing them on the ceiling with a flashlight while the room is dark. Each student should have a rug, mat or blanket on which to lie down on the floor.

Cubbies: Each student should have his own cubby or box in which to store his crayons, scissors, counters, shapes, flashcards, etc. Students may need both a cubby and a pencil box. If the cubbies are large enough they can store sleeping mats, jackets, etc. in them.

Media Resources

The following resources will need to be obtained in advance of when they are needed for the Lessons. They can be used several times if desired.

Lesson 1:
"Love" from the *Character Builders Video Series*
"The Amazing Book" CD

Lesson 2:
"Music Machine: The Majesty of God" CD
"The Amazing Book" CD

Lesson 3:
"Bullfrogs and Butterflies: God Loves Fun" CD
"The Amazing Book" CD

Lesson 4:
"The Amazing Book" CD

Lesson 5:
"Music Machine" video
"The Amazing Book" CD

Lesson 6:
"Music Machine: The Majesty of God" CD
"Rev-Up for Learning: Reading, Writing, & Arithmetic" DVD
"Bullfrogs and Butterflies: God is Great" CD
"Horizons Preschool Music" CD

Lesson 7:
"Bullfrogs and Butterflies: God is Great" CD

Lesson 8:
"Music Machine: The Majesty of God" CD
"Sir Oliver's Song" CD
"Politeness" from the *Character Builders Video Series*
"Bullfrogs and Butterflies: God is Great" CD

Lesson 9:
"Joy" from the *Character Builders Video Series*
"Bullfrogs and Butterflies: God is Great" CD

Lesson 10:
"Bullfrogs and Butterflies: God Loves Fun" CD
"Sharing" from the *Character Builders Video Series*
"Bullfrogs and Butterflies: God is Great" CD

Lesson 11:
"The Amazing Miracles" CD
"Rev-Up for Learning: Reading, Writing, & Arithmetic" DVD
"Music Machine: The Majesty of God" CD
Where Does Electricity Come From?, Usborne Publishers

Lesson 12:
"Bullfrogs and Butterflies: I've Been Born Again" CD
"Music Machine: The Majesty of God" CD
A simple biography of Helen Keller

Lesson 13:
"Music Machine: The Majesty of God" CD
A simple biography of Helen Keller
"Horizons Preschool Music" CD

Lesson 14:
"Music Machine: The Majesty of God" CD
A simple biography of Helen Keller

Lesson 15:
"Music Machine: The Majesty of God" CD
A simple biography of Helen Keller

Lesson 16:
"Rev-Up for Learning: Reading, Writing, & Arithmetic" DVD
"Bullfrogs and Butterflies: God is My Friend" CD
"Horizons Preschool Music" CD

Lesson 17:
"Faith" from the *Character Builders Video Series*
"Bullfrogs and Butterflies: God is My Friend" CD

Lesson 18:
"Horizons Preschool Music" CD
"Bullfrogs and Butterflies: God is My Friend" CD

Lesson 19:
  "Bullfrogs and Butterflies: God is My Friend"
  CD

Lesson 20:
  "Bullfrogs and Butterflies: God Loves Fun" CD
  "Bullfrogs and Butterflies: God is My Friend"
  CD

Lesson 21:
  "Self Control" from the *Character Builders Video Series*
  "The Amazing Children" CD
  "Rev-Up for Learning: Reading, Writing, & Arithmetic" DVD

Lesson 22:
  "The Amazing Children" CD

Lesson 23:
  "Bullfrogs and Butterflies: God is Great" CD
  "Music Machine: The Fruit of the Spirit" CD
  "Horizons Preschool Music" CD
  "The Amazing Children" CD

Lesson 24:
  "The Amazing Children" CD

Lesson 25:
  "Music Machine: The Majesty of God" CD
  "The Amazing Children" CD

Lesson 26:
  "The Amazing Miracles" CD
  "Nathaniel the Grublet" CD
  "Rev-Up for Learning: Reading, Writing, & Arithmetic" DVD

Lesson 27:
  "Bullfrogs and Butterflies: God Loves Fun" CD
  "Nathaniel the Grublet" CD

Lesson 28:
  "Nathaniel the Grublet" CD

Lesson 29:
  "Nathaniel the Grublet" CD

Lesson 30:
  "Bullfrogs and Butterflies: God Loves Fun" CD
  "The Amazing Children" CD
  "Nathaniel the Grublet" CD

Lesson 31:
  "The Amazing Miracles" CD
  "Rev-Up for Learning: Reading, Writing, & Arithmetic" DVD
  "Horizons Preschool Music" CD

Lesson 32:
  "The Amazing Miracles" CD

Lesson 33:
  "Patience" from the *Character Builders Video Series*
  "The Amazing Miracles" CD

Lesson 34:
  "The Amazing Miracles" CD

Lesson 35:
  "Horizons Preschool Music" CD
  "The Amazing Miracles" CD

Lesson 36:
  "Bullfrogs and Butterflies: I've Been Born Again" CD
  "Rev-Up for Learning: Reading, Writing, & Arithmetic" DVD

Lesson 37:
  "Bullfrogs and Butterflies: I've Been Born Again" CD

Lesson 38:
  "Bullfrogs and Butterflies: I've Been Born Again" CD

Lesson 39:
  "Bullfrogs and Butterflies: I've Been Born Again" CD

Lesson 40:
  "Bullfrogs and Butterflies: I've Been Born Again" CD

Lesson 41:
  "Bullfrogs and Butterflies: God Loves Fun" CD
  "Music Machine: The Fruit Of The Spirit" CD
  "Rev-Up for Learning: Reading, Writing, & Arithmetic" DVD

Lesson 42:
  "Music Machine: The Fruit Of The Spirit" CD

Lesson 43:
"Music Machine: The Fruit Of The Spirit" CD
First Book of Nature, Usborne Publishers

Lesson 44:
"Music Machine: The Fruit Of The Spirit" CD
Planting a Rainbow, by Lois Ehlert

Lesson 45:
"Music Machine: The Fruit Of The Spirit" CD

Lesson 46:
"Sir Oliver's Song" CD
"Rev-Up for Learning: Reading, Writing, &
    Arithmetic" DVD
First Book of Nature, Usborne Publishers

Lesson 47:
"The Amazing Miracles" CD
"Sir Oliver's Song" CD

Lesson 48:
"Sir Oliver's Song" CD

Lesson 49:
"Horizons Preschool Music" CD
"Sir Oliver's Song" CD

Lesson 50:
"Sir Oliver's Song" CD

Lesson 51:
"Music Machine: All About Love" CD
"Rev-Up for Learning: Reading, Writing, &
    Arithmetic" DVD
"Horizons Preschool Music" CD

Lesson 52:
"Music Machine: All About Love" CD

Lesson 53:
"Music Machine: All About Love" CD

Lesson 54:
"Music Machine: All About Love" CD
Eating the Alphabet, by Lois Ehlert

Lesson 55:
"Music Machine: Benny's Biggest Battle" video
"Music Machine: All About Love" CD

Lesson 56:
"Bullfrogs and Butterflies: God is Great" CD
"Sir Oliver's Song" CD
"Bullfrogs and Butterflies: God Loves Fun" CD
"Rev-Up for Learning: Reading, Writing, &
    Arithmetic" DVD
"Horizons Preschool Music" CD
Rockets and Space Flight, Usborne Publishers

Lesson 57:
"Music Machine: The Majesty of God" CD
"Bullfrogs and Butterflies: God Loves Fun" CD

Lesson 58:
"The Amazing Miracles" CD
"Bullfrogs and Butterflies: God Loves Fun" CD

Lesson 59:
"Bullfrogs and Butterflies: God is Great" CD
"Bullfrogs and Butterflies: God Loves Fun" CD
"The Amazing Miracles" CD

Lesson 60:
"Horizons Preschool Music" CD
"Bullfrogs and Butterflies: God Loves Fun" CD

Lesson 61:
"The Birthday Party" CD
"The Gift" from the *Kingdom Under the Sea*
    adventure video series
"Rev-Up for Learning: Reading, Writing, &
    Arithmetic" DVD

Lesson 62:
"Thankfulness" from the *Character Builders
    Video Series*
"The Birthday Party" CD
"The Gift" from the *Kingdom Under the Sea*
    adventure video series

Lesson 63:
"The Birthday Party" CD
"The Gift" from the *Kingdom Under the Sea*
    adventure video series

Lesson 64:
"The Birthday Party" CD
"The Gift" from the *Kingdom Under the Sea*
    adventure video series

Lesson 65:
"The Birthday Party" CD
"The Gift" from the *Kingdom Under the Sea* adventure video series

Lesson 66:
"Once Upon A Christmas" CD
"The Gift" from the *Kingdom Under the Sea* adventure video series
"Rev-Up for Learning: Reading, Writing, & Arithmetic" DVD

Lesson 67:
"Joy" from the *Character Builders Video Series*
"Nathaniel the Grublet" CD
"The Amazing Children" CD
"Once Upon A Christmas" CD
"The Gift" from the *Kingdom Under the Sea* adventure video series

Lesson 68:
"Once Upon A Christmas" CD
"The Gift" from the *Kingdom Under the Sea* adventure video series

Lesson 69:
"Once Upon A Christmas" CD
"The Gift" from the *Kingdom Under the Sea* adventure video series

Lesson 70:
"Once Upon A Christmas" CD
"The Gift" from the *Kingdom Under the Sea* adventure video series

Lesson 71:
"The Birthday Party" CD
"The Gift" from the *Kingdom Under the Sea* adventure video series
"Rev-Up for Learning: Reading, Writing, & Arithmetic" DVD

Lesson 72:
"Peace" from the *Character Builders Video Series*
"Horizons Preschool Music" CD
"The Birthday Party" CD
"The Gift" from the *Kingdom Under the Sea* adventure video series

Lesson 73:
"Bullfrogs and Butterflies: I've Been Born Again" CD
"The Birthday Party" CD
"The Gift" from the *Kingdom Under the Sea* adventure video series
Rockets and Space Flight, Usborne Publishers

Lesson 74:
"The Birthday Party" CD
"The Gift" from the *Kingdom Under the Sea* adventure video series

Lesson 75:
"The Birthday Party" CD
"The Gift" from the *Kingdom Under the Sea* adventure video series

Lesson 76:
"Music Machine: The Majesty of God" CD
"Once Upon A Christmas" CD
"The Gift" from the *Kingdom Under the Sea* adventure video series
"Rev-Up for Learning: Reading, Writing, & Arithmetic" DVD
The Christian Mother Goose Book of Nursery Rhymes, by Marjorie Ainsborough Decker

Lesson 77:
"Once Upon A Christmas" CD
"The Gift" from the *Kingdom Under the Sea* adventure video series

Lesson 78:
"Once Upon A Christmas" CD
"The Gift" from the *Kingdom Under the Sea* adventure video series

Lesson 79:
"Once Upon A Christmas" CD
"The Gift" from the *Kingdom Under the Sea* adventure video series

Lesson 80:
"Once Upon A Christmas" CD
"The Gift" from the *Kingdom Under the Sea* adventure video series

Lesson 81:
"Rev-Up for Learning: Reading, Writing, & Arithmetic" DVD
"Music Machine: Benny's Biggest Battle" video

Lesson 82:
"Music Machine: Benny's Biggest Battle" video

Lesson 83:
"Music Machine: Benny's Biggest Battle" video

Lesson 84:
"Music Machine: Benny's Biggest Battle" video

Lesson 85:
"Bullfrogs and Butterflies: God Loves Fun" CD
"Music Machine: Benny's Biggest Battle" video

Lesson 86:
"The Amazing Book" CD
"Rev-Up for Learning: Reading, Writing, & Arithmetic" DVD
"Horizons Preschool Music" CD

Lesson 87:
"The Amazing Book" CD

Lesson 88:
"The Amazing Book" CD

Lesson 89:
"The Amazing Book" CD

Lesson 90:
"The Amazing Book" CD

Lesson 91:
"Bullfrogs and Butterflies: God is Great" CD
"The Red Tide" from the *Kingdom Under the Sea* adventure video series
"Rev-Up for Learning: Reading, Writing, & Arithmetic" DVD
"Horizons Preschool Music" CD
First Book of Nature, Usborne Publishers

Lesson 92:
"The Amazing Miracles" CD
"Bullfrogs and Butterflies: God is Great" CD
"The Red Tide" from the *Kingdom Under the Sea* adventure video series

Lesson 93:
"Bullfrogs and Butterflies: God is Great" CD
"The Red Tide" from the *Kingdom Under the Sea* adventure video series

Lesson 94:
"Bullfrogs and Butterflies: God is Great" CD
"The Red Tide" from the *Kingdom Under the Sea* adventure video series

Lesson 95:
"Bullfrogs and Butterflies: God is Great" CD
"The Red Tide" from the *Kingdom Under the Sea* adventure video series

Lesson 96:
"Bullfrogs and Butterflies: God is Great" CD
"Bullfrogs and Butterflies: God is My Friend" CD
"Music Machine: The Majesty of God" CD
"Rev-Up for Learning: Reading, Writing, & Arithmetic" DVD

Lesson 97:
"Sharing" from the *Character Builders Video Series*
"Music Machine: The Majesty of God" CD
The Rainbow Fish, by Marcus Pfister and J. Alison James

Lesson 98:
"Music Machine: The Majesty of God" CD

Lesson 99:
"Music Machine: The Majesty of God" CD
One Fish, Two Fish, Red Fish, Blue Fish, by Dr. Seuss

Lesson 100:
"Music Machine: The Majesty of God" CD

Lesson 101:
"Bullfrogs and Butterflies: God is Great" CD
"Music Machine: The Fruit of the Spirit" CD
"Bullfrogs and Butterflies: God is My Friend" CD
"Rev-Up for Learning: Reading, Writing, & Arithmetic" DVD
"Horizons Preschool Music" CD
First Book of Nature, Usborne Publishers

Lesson 102:
"Bullfrogs and Butterflies: God is My Friend" CD

Lesson 103:
"Bullfrogs and Butterflies: God is My Friend" CD

Lesson 104:
"Bullfrogs and Butterflies: God is My Friend" CD
Feathers for Lunch, by Lois Ehlert

Lesson 105:
"Bullfrogs and Butterflies: God is My Friend" CD

Lesson 106:
"The Amazing Children" CD
"Rev-Up for Learning: Reading, Writing, & Arithmetic" DVD

Lesson 107:
"The Amazing Children" CD

Lesson 108:
"The Amazing Children" CD

Lesson 109:
"The Amazing Children" CD

Lesson 110:
"The Amazing Children" CD

Lesson 111:
"Nathaniel the Grublet" CD
"Rev-Up for Learning: Reading, Writing, & Arithmetic" DVD
First Book of Nature, Usborne Publishers

Lesson 112:
"Nathaniel the Grublet" CD

Lesson 113:
"Nathaniel the Grublet" CD

Lesson 114:
"Nathaniel the Grublet" CD
Stellaluna, by Janell Cannon

Lesson 115:
"Nathaniel the Grublet" CD

Lesson 116:
"Gentleness" from the *Character Builders Video Series*
"The Amazing Miracles" CD
"Rev-Up for Learning: Reading, Writing, & Arithmetic" DVD

Lesson 117:
"Bullfrogs and Butterflies: God is Great" CD
"Bullfrogs and Butterflies: God Loves Fun" CD
"The Amazing Miracles" CD
Millions of Cats, by Wanda Gag

Lesson 118:
"The Amazing Miracles" CD

Lesson 119:
"Responsibility" from the *Character Builders Video Series*
"The Amazing Miracles" CD
"Babe" a Universal Studios video

Lesson 120:
"The Amazing Miracles" CD

Lesson 121:
"Bullfrogs and Butterflies: God is Great" CD
"Bullfrogs and Butterflies: I've Been Born Again" CD
"Rev-Up for Learning: Reading, Writing, & Arithmetic" DVD

Lesson 122:
"Bullfrogs and Butterflies: I've Been Born Again" CD
A, You're Adorable, by Buddy Kaye, Fred Wise and Sidney Lippman, illustrated by Martha G. Alexander

Lesson 123:
"Bullfrogs and Butterflies: I've Been Born Again" CD

Lesson 124:
"Bullfrogs and Butterflies: I've Been Born Again" CD

Lesson 125:
"Bullfrogs and Butterflies: I've Been Born Again" CD

Lesson 126:
"Music Machine: The Majesty of God" CD
"Goodness" from the *Character Builders Video Series*
"Music Machine: The Fruit Of The Spirit" CD
"Rev-Up for Learning: Reading, Writing, & Arithmetic" DVD
"Horizons Preschool Music" CD
First Book of Nature, Usborne Publishers

Lesson 127:
"Music Machine: The Fruit Of The Spirit" CD
Five of the following Eric Carle books: *The Very Hungry Caterpillar, The Grouchy Ladybug, The Honeybee and the Robber, The Very Busy Spider, The Very Quiet Cricket,* or *The Very Lonely Firefly*

Lesson 128:
"Bullfrogs and Butterflies: God is Great" CD
"Bullfrogs and Butterflies: God is My Friend" CD
"Music Machine: The Fruit Of The Spirit" CD
Five of the following Eric Carle books: *The Very Hungry Caterpillar, The Grouchy Ladybug, The Honeybee and the Robber, The Very Busy Spider, The Very Quiet Cricket,* or *The Very Lonely Firefly*

Lesson 129:
"Music Machine: The Fruit Of The Spirit" CD
Five of the following Eric Carle books: *The Very Hungry Caterpillar, The Grouchy Ladybug, The Honeybee and the Robber, The Very Busy Spider, The Very Quiet Cricket,* or *The Very Lonely Firefly*

Lesson 130:
"Bullfrogs and Butterflies: God is Great" CD
"Music Machine: The Fruit Of The Spirit" CD
Five of the following Eric Carle books: *The Very Hungry Caterpillar, The Grouchy Ladybug, The Honeybee and the Robber, The Very Busy Spider, The Very Quiet Cricket,* or *The Very Lonely Firefly*

Lesson 131:
"The Amazing Children" CD
"Sir Oliver's Song" CD
"Rev-Up for Learning: Reading, Writing, & Arithmetic" DVD
Five of the following Eric Carle books: *The Very Hungry Caterpillar, The Grouchy Ladybug, The Honeybee and the Robber, The Very Busy Spider, The Very Quiet Cricket,* or *The Very Lonely Firefly*

Lesson 132:
"Bullfrogs and Butterflies: I've Been Born Again" CD
"Bullfrogs and Butterflies: God Loves Fun" CD
"Sir Oliver's Song" CD
Five of the following Eric Carle books: *The Very Hungry Caterpillar, The Grouchy Ladybug, The Honeybee and the Robber, The Very Busy Spider, The Very Quiet Cricket,* or *The Very Lonely Firefly*

Lesson 133:
"Sir Oliver's Song" CD
The Little Engine That Could, by Watty Piper

Lesson 134:
"Music Machine: The Fruit of the Spirit" CD
"Sir Oliver's Song" CD

Lesson 135:
"Music Machine: The Majesty of God" CD
"Love" from the *Character Builders Video Series*
"Bullfrogs and Butterflies: God is My Friend" CD
"Sir Oliver's Song" CD

Lesson 136:
"The Story of Little Tree" CD
"Return of the King" from the *Kingdom Under the Sea* adventure video series
"Rev-Up for Learning: Reading, Writing, & Arithmetic" DVD

Lesson 137:
"The Story of Little Tree" CD
"Return of the King" from the *Kingdom Under the Sea* adventure video series

Lesson 138:
"The Story of Little Tree" CD
"Return of the King" from the *Kingdom Under the Sea* adventure video series

Lesson 139:
"The Story of Little Tree" CD
"Return of the King" from the *Kingdom Under the Sea* adventure video series
My Five Senses, by Aliki

Lesson 140:
"The Story of Little Tree" CD
"Return of the King" from the *Kingdom Under the Sea* adventure video series

Lesson 141:
"Bullfrogs and Butterflies: God Loves Fun" CD
"The Story of Little Tree" CD
"Return of the King" from the *Kingdom Under the Sea* adventure video series
"Rev-Up for Learning: Reading, Writing, & Arithmetic" DVD

Lesson 142:
"Music Machine: The Fruit of the Spirit" CD
"Bullfrogs and Butterflies: God is Great" CD
"Rack, Shack, and Benny," a Veggie Tales® movie by Big Idea. Or "Obedience" from the *Character Builders Video Series*
"The Amazing Miracles" CD
"The Story of Little Tree" CD
"Return of the King" from the *Kingdom Under the Sea* adventure video series

Lesson 143:
"Music Machine: The Fruit of the Spirit" CD
"Horizons Preschool Music" CD
"The Story of Little Tree" CD
"Return of the King" from the *Kingdom Under the Sea* adventure video series
Bread and Jam for Frances, by Russell Hoban (1993)
Gregory, the Terrible Eater, by Mitchell Sharmat
Oliver's Fruit Salad, by Vivian French

Lesson 144:
"Bullfrogs and Butterflies: God is My Friend" CD
"The Story of Little Tree" CD
"Return of the King" from the *Kingdom Under the Sea* adventure video series

Lesson 145:
"The Story of Little Tree" CD
"Return of the King" from the *Kingdom Under the Sea* adventure video series

Lesson 146:
"Music Machine: All About Love" CD
"Rev-Up for Learning: Reading, Writing, & Arithmetic" DVD

Lesson 147:
"Honesty" from the *Character Builders Video Series*
"Music Machine: All About Love" CD
Dem Bones, by Bob Barner, 1996

Lesson 148:
"Music Machine: All About Love" CD
Oliver's Milk Shake, by Vivian French, 2000

Lesson 149:
"Music Machine: All About Love" CD
Junie B. First Grader: Toothless Wonder, by Barbara Park

Lesson 150:
"Music Machine: All About Love" CD

Lesson 151:
"Bullfrogs and Butterflies: God Loves Fun" CD
"Rev-Up for Learning: Reading, Writing, & Arithmetic" DVD

Lesson 152:
"Music Machine: The Majesty of God" CD
"Bullfrogs and Butterflies: God Loves Fun" CD

Lesson 153:
"Horizons Preschool Music" CD
"Bullfrogs and Butterflies: God Loves Fun" CD

Lesson 154:
"The Amazing Children" CD
"Bullfrogs and Butterflies: God Loves Fun" CD
"Where's God When I'm Scared," a Veggie Tales® video from Big Idea

Lesson 155:
"Love" from the *Character Builders Video Series*
"The Amazing Book" CD
"Bullfrogs and Butterflies: God Loves Fun" CD

Lesson 156:
"Music Machine: Benny's Biggest Battle" video
"Rev-Up for Learning: Reading, Writing, & Arithmetic" DVD

Lesson 157:
"Kindness" from the *Character Builders Video Series*
"Music Machine: Benny's Biggest Battle" video
The Berenstain Bears and Too Much Junk Food, by Jan and Stan Berenstain

Lesson 158:
"The Amazing Book" CD
"The Amazing Children" CD
"Music Machine: Benny's Biggest Battle" video
Mike Mulligan and His Steam Shovel, by Virginia Lee Burton. Written in 1939

Lesson 159:
"Music Machine: Benny's Biggest Battle" video

Lesson 160:
"Music Machine: Benny's Biggest Battle" video

Lesson 161:
"Music Machine: The Majesty of God" CD
"Rev-Up for Learning: Reading, Writing, & Arithmetic" DVD
"Horizons Preschool Music" CD
Any one of the following: *The Tale of Peter Rabbit* by Beatrix Potter, *Frog and Toad Are Friends* by Arnold Lobel, *A Bear Called Paddington* by Michael Bond, *Winnie the Pooh* by A. A. Milne, *The Boxcar Children* by Gertrude Chandler Warner, any of the *Little House on the Prairie* books by Laura Ingalls Wilder, *Mr. Popper's Penguins* by Richard Atwater, *Sarah Plain & Tall* & its sequel,

Skylark, by Patricia MacLachlan, or *Black Beauty* by Anna Sewell

Lesson 162:
"Sir Oliver's Song" CD

Lesson 163:
"Joy" from the *Character Builders Video Series*
"Horizons Preschool Music" CD
"The Hallelujah Chorus," by George Frideric Handel from *The Messiah* audio CD

Lesson 164:
"Bullfrogs and Butterflies: God Loves Fun" CD
"Faith" from the *Character Builders Video Series*
"Dave and the Giant Pickle," a Veggie Tales® video from Big Idea

Lesson 165:
"Music Machine: The Majesty of God" CD

Lesson 166:
"Confidence" from the *Character Builders Video Series*
"Rev-Up for Learning: Reading, Writing, & Arithmetic" DVD

Lesson 167:
"Horizons Preschool Music" CD

Lesson 168:
a baby name book

Lesson 169:
"Bullfrogs and Butterflies: God is My Friend" CD
Stone Soup, by Marcia Brown

Lesson 170:
"Sir Oliver's Song" CD

Lesson 171:
"Kindness" from the *Character Builders Video Series*
"Rev-Up for Learning: Reading, Writing, & Arithmetic" DVD

Lesson 172:
"Nathaniel the Grublet" CD
"Obedience" from the *Character Builders Video Series*

Lesson 173:

"Nathaniel the Grublet" CD

"Josh and the Big Wall," a Veggies Tales® video by Big Idea

Lesson 174:

"Sharing" from the *Character Builders Video Series*

"The Amazing Book" CD

"The Amazing Children" CD

Lesson 175:

"Bullfrogs and Butterflies: God Loves Fun" CD

Lesson 176:

"Faith" from the *Character Builders Video Series*

"Bullfrogs and Butterflies: God is My Friend" CD

"The Amazing Book" CD or "The Amazing Sing Along" DVD

"The Amazing Miracles" CD or "The Amazing Sing Along" DVD

"Rev-Up for Learning: Reading, Writing, & Arithmetic" DVD

Lesson 177:

"Bullfrogs and Butterflies: God is My Friend" CD

"The Amazing Book" CD or "The Amazing Sing Along" DVD

"The Amazing Miracles" CD or "The Amazing Sing Along" DVD

Lesson 178:

"Bullfrogs and Butterflies: God is My Friend" CD

"The Amazing Book" CD or "The Amazing Sing Along" DVD

"The Amazing Miracles" CD or "The Amazing Sing Along" DVD

"Peace" from the *Character Builders Video Series*

"Horizons Preschool Music" CD

Lesson 179:

"Bullfrogs and Butterflies: God is My Friend" CD

"The Amazing Book" CD or "The Amazing Sing Along" DVD

"The Amazing Miracles" CD or "The Amazing Sing Along" DVD

"Fantasia 2000" a Disney video

The Honey Makers, by Gail Gibbons (1997)

Internet Links

Occasionally there are some suggested Internet links in the lessons. As with all materials found on the Internet, these materials need to be used with care and caution. The links were current when this material went to press but since web content is very dynamic the links may no longer point to the correct location. If a link is broken then do a search for keywords that fit the topic. You will find many other sites with good content that can be used to supplement the lesson material.

Reading Resources: Totally optional but very helpful.

The Big Book of Books and Activities: An Illustrated Guide for Teacher, Parents, and Anyone Who Works With Kids!, by Dinah Zike, Dinah-Might Activities, Inc., 1996
Creation Crafts, by Darlene Hoffa, Concordia, 1993
Nature Crafts for Kids, by Diehn and Krautwurst, Sterling Publishers Co., Inc., New York, 1997
Play and Find Out About Science: Easy Experiments for Young Children, by Janice VanCleave, John Wiley & Sons, 1996
Preschool Readiness, by Mary Ellen Quint, Alpha Omega Publications, 800.622.3070
Six-Minute Science Experiments, by Faith Hickman Brynie, Sterling Publishers Co., Inc., 1996
What is Inside You?, Usborne Publishers
What Makes It Rain?, Usborne Publishers
Why Do People Eat?, Usborne Publishers
The Usborne Big Book of Experiments, Usborne Publishers

Story Time Reading List: Optional but very helpful.

A Child's Garden of Verses, by Robert Louis Stevenson (illustrated by Tasha Tudor)
"A Hunting We Will Go," (Traditional Rhyme)
A Rainbow All Around Me, by Sandra L. Pinkney
A Story for Bear, by Dennis Haseley
Aesop's Fables
Agapanthus Hum and Major Bark, by Jennifer Plecas
Alfie Gives a Hand, by Shirley Hughes
Aloha, Dolores, by Barbara Samuels
Alphabet Under Construction, by Denise Fleming
America's Champion Swimmer: Gertrude Ederle, by David A. Adler
"An Old Person From Ware," by Edward Lear (Poem)
Apple Pie 4th of July, by Janet S. Wong
At the Edge of the Woods: A Counting Book, by Cynthia Cotten
"At the Seaside," by Robert Louis Stevenson (Poem)
"Bat, Bat," (Traditional Rhyme)
Beatrix Potter: The Complete Tales, by Beatrix Potter (Peter Rabbit, etc.)
Bedtime for Frances, by Russell Hoban, 1960 (Harper)
Blessings Every Day, by Carla Barnhill, Tyndale House Publishers, Inc.
"Bobby Shafto," (Traditional Rhyme)
Bonaparte, by Marsha Wilson Chall
Boundless Grace, by Mary Hoffman
Brown Bear, Brown Bear, What Do You See? by Bill Martin, Jr.
Cam Jansen and the Birthday Mystery, by David A. Adler

Caps for Sale, by Esphyr Solbodkina

Cinderella, Anonymous. Fairy tales, folk tales, and nursery rhymes

Clifford, the Big Red Dog, by Norman Bridwell

Corduroy at the Zoo, by Don Freeman

Corduroy, by Don Freeman, 1968 (Viking Press)

Curious George, by H. A. Rey

"Diddle, Diddle Dumpling, My Son John," (Traditional Rhyme)

"Doctor Foster," (Traditional Rhyme)

Dog Food, by Saxton Freymann

Dream Carver, by Diana Cohn

Duck on a Bike, by David Shannon

Eaglet's World, by Evelyn Minshull

Emily's First 100 Days of School, by Rosemary Wells

Everything to Spend the Night: From A to Z, by Ann Whitford Paul

Faraway Home, by Jane Kurtz

Farmer Brown Shears His Sheep: A Yarn About Wool, by Teri Sloat

Flower Garden, by Eve Bunting

Frog's Best Friend, by Marion Dane Bauer

Giant Steps for Little People, by Kenneth N. Taylor, 1985 (Tyndale House Publishers)

Go, Dog, Go, by Philip D. Eastman, 1961 (Beginner Books)

"Goldilocks and the Three Bears," Anonymous. Fairy tales, folk tales, and nursery rhymes

Goodnight Moon, by Margaret Wise Brown

Hamster Chase, by Anastasia Suen

Harry, the Dirty Dog, by Gene Zion

Henry Hikes to Fitchburg, by D. B. Johnson

"Here We Go Round the Mulberry Bush," (Traditional Rhyme)

"Hickety, Pickety, My Black Hen," (Traditional Rhyme)

"Higglety, Pigglety, Pop!" by Samuel Goodrich (Poem)

How Many? How Much? by Rosemary Wells

How to Catch an Elephant, by Amy Schwartz

Hunter's Best Friend at School, by Elliott, Laura Malone.

I Stink! by Kate McMullan

Ira Sleeps Over, by Bernard Waber, 1972 (Houghton Mifflin)

It's Just in Time, Amber Brown, by Paula Danziger

"Jack-o-Lantern," by Aileen Fisher (Poem)

"January," by Maurice Sendak (Poem)

"Jump or Jiggle," by Evelyn Beyer (Poem)

Just in Case You Ever Wonder, by Max Lucado, 1992 (Word Publishers)

King of the Stable, by Melody Carlson, Crossway Books/Good News Publishers

Letters and Sounds, by Rosemary Wells

"Little Red Riding Hood," Anonymous. Fairy tales, folk tales, and nursery rhymes

"Lucy Locket," (Traditional Rhyme)

Mad Maddie Maxwell, Zonderkidz, The Children's Group of Zondervan Stacie Maslyn

Madeline, by Ludwig Bemelmans, 1963 (Viking Press)

Make Way for the Ducklings, by Robert McCloskey, 1941 (The Viking Press)

Max and Jax in Second Grade, by Jerdine Nolen

Measuring Penny, by Loreen Leedy

Millions of Cats, by Wanda Gág, 1928 (Coward, McCann & Geoghengan)

Miss Nelson Is Missing! by Harry Allard

Mother Goose rhymes.

Mouse in King Solomon's House, by Mack Thomas, Questar Publishers, Inc.

Nicholas Pipe, by Robert D. San Souci

Noah's Ark, by Peter Spier, 1977 (Doubleday)

Old Thunder and Miss Raney, by Sharon Darrow

Oliver Finds His Way, by Phyllis Root

On My Way, by Tomie De Paola

"Once I Saw a Little Bird," (Traditional Rhyme)

"One for the Money," (Traditional Rhyme)

One Lighthouse, One Moon, by Anita Lobel

"One Misty, Moisty Morning," (Traditional Rhyme)

"Pat-a-Cake," (Traditional Rhyme)

"Pease Porridge Hot," (Traditional Rhyme)

Peekaboo Morning, by Rachel Isadora

"Peter, Peter Pumpkin Eater," (Traditional Rhyme)

Peter's Chair, by Ezra Jack Keats, 1967 (Harper & Row)

"Polly Put the Kettle On," (Traditional Rhyme)

Praise And Worship, by Ken & Angela Abraham, Tommy Nelson

"Pussy Cat, Pussy Cat," (Traditional Rhyme)

"Rain, Rain Go Away," (Traditional Rhyme)

Rainbow Fish to the Rescue, by Marcus Pfister

"Raindrops," by Aileen Fischer (Poem)

"Ride a Cock Horse," (Traditional Rhyme)

"Ring Around the Rosey," (Traditional Rhyme)

Ring! Yo? by Chris Raschka

"Rock-a-bye, Baby," (Traditional Rhyme)

"Singing Time," by Rose Fyleman (Poem)

Sixteen Cows, by Lisa Wheeler

Song of Night: It's Time to Go to Bed, by Katherine Riley Nakamura

Spaghetti Eddie, by Ryan SanAngelo

Stone Soup, by Ann McGovern, 1986 (Scholastic)

Stories Jesus Told, by Nick Butterworth and Mick Inkpen, Questar Publishers, Inc.

Tanya and the Red Shoes, by Patricia Lee Gauch

The Berenstain Bears, by Stan & Jan Berenstain

The Bravest Cat: The True Story of Scarlett, by Laura Driscoll

The Cat in the Hat, by Dr. Seuss, 1957 (Houghton Mifflin)

The First Thing My Mama Told Me, by Susan Marie Swanson

"The Gingerbread Man," Anonymous. Fairy tales, folk tales, and nursery rhymes

The Girl Who Spun Gold, by Virginia Hamilton

The Honest to Goodness Truth, by Pat McKissack

The Hosanna Bible, by Ken and Angela Abraham, Word, Inc.

The Kidderminster Kingdom Series - King Leonard's Celebration, by Christopher Lane, Victor Books

The Lion and the Mouse and Other Aesop Fables, by Doris Orgel

The Little Engine That Could, by Watty Piper, 1976 (Platt & Munk)

The Little House, by Virginia Lee Burton

The Little Red Hen, various authors since 1942

The Lorax, by Dr. Seuss

The Moffats, by Eleanor Estes

The New Bible in Pictures for Little Eyes, by Ken Taylor, Moody Publishers

"The Old Woman Must Stand at the Tub,Tub,Tub," (Traditional Rhyme)

"The Pancake," by Christine Rossetti (Poem)

The Parable Series (Set of 4), by Liz Curtis Higgs, Tommy Nelson

The Puppy Who Wanted a Boy, by Jane Thayer, 1958 (Morrow)

The Rhyme Bible Storybook for Toddlers, by Linda Sattgast, Zondervan Publishing House

"The Snowy Day," by Ezra Jack Keats

The Story About Ping, by Marjorie Flack

The Story of Babar, the Little Elephant, by Jean De Brunhoff

The Tale of Peter Rabbit, by Beatrix Potter (Public Domain, online versions available)

"The Three Little Pigs," Anonymous. Fairy tales, folk tales, and nursery rhymes (Public domain)

The Velveteen Rabbit, by Margery Williams (Public domain)

The Very Hungry Caterpillar, by Eric Carle

"The Worm," by Ralph Bergengren (Poem)

"There was a Crooked Man," (Traditional Rhyme)

"There Was a Fat Pig," by Arnold Lobel (Poem)

"This Is the Way the Ladies Ride," (Traditional Rhyme)

"This Little Piggy Went to Market," (Traditional Rhyme)

Three Cheers for Catherine the Great! by Cari Best

"To Market, To Market," (Traditional Rhyme)

"Tom, Tom, the Piper's Son," (Traditional Rhyme)

"Two Little Blackbirds," (Traditional Rhyme)

"Wee Willie Winkie," (Traditional Rhyme)

What's Up, What's Down? by Lola M. Schaefer

Where the Wild Things Are, by Maurice Sendak, 1963 (Harper & Row)

Willie's Birthday, by Anastasia Sue

Winnie-the-Pooh Series, by A.A. Milne

Yoshi's Feast, by Kimiko Kajikawa

Young Classics: Alice in Wonderland, by Julie Fior

Supply List

Though supplies are listed for each week, you will only need supplies for the activities you choose to do. We include this supply list to help you prepare in advance. Please plan your week at one time so you will know which activities you are doing and which supplies you need.

Student Supplies: Each student should be responsible for bringing some basic supplies. Develop a list prior to the school year that can be communicated as early as possible to the parents. Each student should bring an old shirt for Arts & Crafts time.

Room Supplies:

Abacus or a set of 20 beads on a wire, clothesline or dowel (for counting and addition/subtraction practice)

Alphabet blocks

Banner paper for the Creation Mural (the larger this can be the better)

Bulletin boards

Calendar (perpetual monthly, see instructions)

CD player

Chore list:
- clean white board
- change week of the year card
- empty trash
- turn off lights
- turn on lights
- hold door, etc.

Clock (analog, moveable hands)

Clock (digital, wipe off or one with changeable numbers)

Clock hour flashcards (o'clock time on top, clock face in center, digital time on bottom, analog clock only on back side)

Color dice (one color on each side)

Color flashcards: red, green, blue, black, white, yellow, brown, pink, purple, orange, gray

Color spinners (pointer points to color and number)

Computer for word processing

Counters (coins, seeds, sticks, tokens)

Counting Train (see the instructions)

Daily schedule

Days of the week chart (Sunday-Saturday, numbered 1-7)

Days of the week flashcards

Letter flashcards Aa-Zz

Months of the year chart (January-December)

Months of the year flashcards

Name plates

Number blocks

Number flashcards 1-20

Pop Beads

Rope

Shape flashcards: triangle, circle, square, rectangle, star, heart, oval, diamond

Recording device (phone or computer)

Television or computer with DVD player.

Week of the school year cards to hang on a peg, numbered 1-36. One of the classroom chores can be to have a student hang a new card each week of the school year.

White board

Wooden blocks of a variety of shapes and sizes

General Supplies: Always have on hand

Aluminum foil

Cardstock, all colors including white

Cellophane tape

Cotton balls

Craft sticks

Crayons (Keep the crayons nice. Nothing is more depressing than a big box of broken crayons. BUT keep the pieces for crafts.)

Construction paper, 8.5 X 11 and 11 X 17, all colors including white

Magnifying Glass: It would be beneficial if each student had a magnifying glass. But also have at least one high quality magnifying glass.

Masking tape

Markers (Test the markers occasionally to be sure they still have ink)

Paint brushes
Paint: Tempura washable
Pencils
Plain, white paper
Playdoh®
Poster board
Ribbon
Scissors (children's)
Stickers, a variety of shapes, characters, and sizes
Tacky Glue, glue sticks
Waxed paper

It is recommended that you purchase a roll of white freezer paper (butcher paper or banner paper), especially if you have more than one or two students. Paper with a plastic backing will be ideal for some of the activities.

Many usable supplies are thrown away in our trash each day. As a teacher, it is a good habit to save certain items through the year. If you have a large class, enlist parents to help you. Send a list home of item for them to save and send to school. Also keep cardboard boxes labeled "Paper scraps" and "Craft scraps." There will be many art and craft lessons that use bits and pieces of paper, yarn, chenille wire, pipe cleaners, etc.

Here is a brief list of usable items to save:

cardboard egg cartons	pieces of thin cardboard
clear lids, like coffee can	scraps of foil
film canisters	shoe boxes
foam deli food trays	small jars with lids
frozen dinner containers	toilet paper rolls
magazines	yarn scraps
old sponges	wrapping paper rolls
paper towel rolls	plastic berry baskets
fabric scraps	

Other Resources:
The Picture Rulebook of Kids' Games, by Roxanne Henderson and Michael Brown, McGraw-Hill/Contemporary Books; April 1, 1996
Hopscotch, Hangman, Hot Potato, & Ha Ha Ha : A Rulebook of Children's Games, by Jack Macguire, Fireside, August 1, 1990

Weekly Supplies:

Supplies for Week 1, Lesson 1-5

box of inexpensive small envelopes
world globe
lunch bags, the brown kind
old magazines and catalogs to cut pictures from
craft sticks
carpet squares (samples)
recording device (phone or computer)
11 X 17 colored construction paper
freezer paper (from a grocer or a food service supply)

narrow sponges
clothespins
tempera paint
liquid dish soap
puppet
glitter
cotton balls
contact paper

Supplies for Week 2, Lessons 6-10

pencil
peanut butter
honey
dry milk
rolling pin
cardboard
dull knife
contact paper or wallpaper
empty film canisters, one each, a small plastic water
    bottle will also work

stickers
various sizes of pom-poms
small wiggly eyes
fresh eggs, one each
little disposable bowls
large weed
rice
graham crackers

Supplies for Week 3, Lessons 11-15

alphabet cereal
magnetic alphabet letters
flashlight
candle and matches
lamp
9 x 13 pan
cornmeal
rice
science book on the workings of the eye
abacus or a simple set of 20 beads on a wire or string
    that can slide back and forth for counting exercises

stickers
number line
blindfolds
piece of board
flour, salt, oil: clay recipe
tissue paper
alarm clock
colored blocks
magazines

Supplies for Week 4, Lessons 16-20

yard stick
blackboard or poster board
flashlight
blocks
computer
number line
raisins or beans or dominoes
bright light
cut out numbers 1-9
sand paper
foil cookie sheets

large ball
shaving cream
prism
tempera paint-yellow, blue and red
classical music
any other music
lamp or large flashlight
long piece of string
several flowering plants
gardening tools
water colors

Supplies for Week 5, Lessons 21-25

bicycle pump
colored blocks
music recording
balloons, round and long
water colors with brush
drinking straw
blow dryer
two wet rags
paper triangle, circles and squares
ribbon sticks or ribbons glued to a plastic shower ring

cotton balls
stickers
ribbon
hula hoops
a fan
long skinny balloons, one each
a helium filled balloon
small glider airplanes

Supplies for Week 6, Lessons 26-30

globe
tub of dirt
magnifying glass
tweezers
9 x 13 pan
cornmeal
rice
room freshener
breathing mask
rolling pin
sand ball
celery

peanut butter
plastic spoons
raisins
heavy cardboard
masking tape
Fruit Loops® or Cheerios®
string
empty 2-liter soda bottle
paper towels
small amount of sand
charcoal

Supplies for Week 7, Lesson 31-35

large magnet
rolled cookie recipe
raisins
frosting
stapler
blocks
two planters or jars
several small plants, one each
ribbon sticks or ribbons glued to a plastic shower ring

sand
soil
dirt
bucket or pan
ground cover to plant in yard
clay
small planters, one each

Supplies for Week 8, Lessons 36-40

blocks
grass seed
waterproof glue
shoe box
garden seeds
3 x 5 cards

sponges, one for each
magnifying glass
high fiber wheat bread
margarine
plastic knives, one each
small paper plates

Supplies for Week 9, Lessons 41-45

number line
tomato
blackberry
potting soil
two pots
shapes previously cut from construction paper
seed catalog
seeds or pictures of fruit and seeds
gardening book
tray
baskets

blocks
whole cloves
orange
ribbon
vegetables
peanut butter
loaf of bread
ribbon pieces
plastic knives
zippered sandwich bags

Supplies for Week 10, Lessons 46-50

electric clothes iron
crayon shavings
stapler
raisins
colored pencils
dry beans
glass bottle
fruit patterns from week 9 day 3
basket
number line

pine cones
serrated knife or saw
mixed bird seed
a set of Lincoln Logs™
evergreen branch
dry corn or wheat kernels
small round rock
large flat rock
a variety of noodles

Supplies for Week 11, Lessons 51-55

vitamins found in fruits and vegetables
gardening magazines to cut up
old magazines with pictures of food
sidewalk chalk for marking hopscotch
sticks
grass
clay
encyclopedia
globe

recording device (phone or computer)
veggies
white foam meat trays
garment made of 100% cotton
blunt tip large embroidery needles
several colors of yarn
woven linen material

Supplies for Week 12, Lessons 56-60

oatmeal boxes
paper bags
yellow clay
breakfast bars
globe
flashlight
old magazines
sidewalk chalk
gold glitter
pieces of 4 x 4 wood

bananas
large wooden frame
cheesecloth
staples
artist's blade
brads
kitchen timer
shallow metal pan
shallow glass pan

Supplies for Week 13, Lessons 61-65

butcher paper
glitter
supplies for marshmallow topping
umbrella on a toothpick
small, green leaves from a tree
fall colored leaves from real trees or magazines
twig from a tree in the shape of a rake
old December, January, and February magazines

sand
popcorn
yellow tennis ball
candy corn
pipe cleaner
piece of terry cloth
plastic cling wrap
tape

Supplies for Week 14, Lessons 66-70

yellow and black pipe cleaners
short pencil
wiggly eyes
number line

house plant
glitter glue
pictures of heat sources
yellow and/or gold yarn

Supplies for Week 15, Lessons 71-75

globe
flashlight
small ball
blocks
cheese slices
9 x 13 pan

cornmeal
rice
laundry baskets
cardboard
chairs

Supplies for Week 16, Lessons 76-80

poems about stars
number line
cardboard
star stickers
yellow clay
cement blocks
rock
binoculars
2 x 4 that is 6 feet long with a brick for
    each end for a balance beam

cookie dough to roll out
cornmeal/rice box
hanger, one each
yarn
glitter
foil pie pan, one each
nails
string
chicken & stars soup

Supplies for Week 17, Lessons 81-85

poster or map of stars
cardboard tube
number line
glitter
musical instrument or pan lids

lively music
quiet music
calm music for ballet
gold star stickers
toilet paper tubes, one for each

Supplies for Week 18, Lessons 86-90
foam balls:
   1 - 10 inches in diameter
   1 - 8 inches
   1 - 6 inches
   3 - 1 1/2 inches
   2 - 7/8 inches
straight pin with a bright colored head
white or silver glitter glue

string and thumbtacks
masking tape
ball
tempera paint

Supplies for Week 19, Lessons 91-95
large map of U.S.
dowel rod
string
magnet
long piece of ribbon

classical music
globe
book on sea life
a whole fish
crab legs or a whole crab

Supplies for Week 20, Lessons 96-100
big plastic bag
chalkboard
chalk
multi-colored sequins
frog hatchery kit (optional)
fish eggs from a bait shop

sardines
small plates
plastic knives
craft clear varnish
small paint brushes

Supplies for Week 21, Lessons 101-105
active music
gliding, serene music
disinfecting solution, Lysol®
dark paint
string
adding machine tape

egg recipe for family
eggs for boiling
markers to use on eggs
library book on birds
real bird nest

Supplies for Week 22, Lessons 106-110
pine cone
bird seed
fat
globe
four pencils
chocolate chips

Chinese noodles
jelly beans and/or M&Ms®
balloons, one for each
flour
whisk
string and/or yarn

Supplies for Week 23, Lessons 111-115
magazine with animals in it
small carton of milk, one for each
plastic animals

a bathroom scale
a mammal pet

Supplies for Week 24, Lessons 116-120

book with pictures of mammals
straws
yarn

animal coloring books
baby animal video

Supplies for Week 25, Lessons 121-125

music
book with snakes
colored beads
string
fake fur
leather
piece of fish with skin
feathers (these may need to be purchased due to recent
    health problems associated with birds)

baby doll
glitter
fake eyes
a reptile pet
flour and salt
computer or old typewriter

Supplies for Week 26, Lessons 126-130

bug jar
cardboard or foam with pins
small jars, like baby food jars
small, lightweight rug
large tea jar
smaller jar
sand or soil
ants
the game Cootie®
spray paint
Chinese noodles
cream cheese
crackers
paper plates
plastic knives
sugar cookies, round or oval (vanilla wafers will work)

piece of real silk
magnifying glasses
tweezers
stamp pads with colored ink
paper towel rolls
bug eyes
small foam balls
pipe cleaners
magnifying glasses
lids or trays
red and/or black frosting
black licorice
black jelly beans
sliced black and green olives
computer or old typewriter

Supplies for Week 27, Lessons 131-135

mirror
paper plates
magazines
stamp pad
soapy sponge
clay recipe

computer
box of gingerbread mix
gingerbread cookie cutters
canned frosting
fine dirt

Supplies for Week 28, Lessons 136-140
two clear plastic 8 oz glasses
sugar
yeast
two liter bottle
a big deflated balloon
a dozen eggs
zippered sandwich bags
two pieces of bread

cinnamon
applesauce
wire
paper towel tube, one for each
pair of glasses
contact lenses
chicken skin

Supplies for Week 29, Lessons 141-145
8 oz foam cups
a hearing aid
all different scents
cinnamon
paper plates
ribbon
apples

onion
sugar free Jell-O®
gingerbread man cookie cutter
cheese
plastic knives
big bone

Supplies for Week 30, Lessons 146-150
large rubber bands
English muffins, cut in half and toasted
American or jack cheese
various fruits, cut into chunks
skeleton kit
food from the food groups or plastic food
instant pudding
milk

a set of dentures
toothbrush, one for each
poster on tooth brushing
clay recipe
vanilla or peppermint flavoring
balloons, one for each
small bottle
sponges, one piece for each

Supplies for Week 31, Lessons 151-155
stethoscope
cow heart
teddy bear shaped cookies or grahams

camera and film
large butcher paper

Supplies for Week 32, Lessons 156-160
cardboard egg cartons
bug eyes
pipe cleaners
string or ribbon
occupational accessories

detergent
medicine
some kind of good food
waffles
toaster

Supplies for Week 33, Lessons 161-165

a chapter book

dry noodles, several kinds

Handel's Messiah, or similar work

a set of eight glasses

teaspoons

musical instruments

whale songs CD

candy sprinkles/coconut/chopped nuts

envelopes

pretzels

candy melts

paper towels

pipe cleaners

wooden clip clothespins

compass, one for each would be great

magnet, one for each would be great

carrots

bottle of blow bubbles, one for each

Supplies for Week 34, Lessons 166-170

straws or toothpicks

cookie sheet

soil or dirt

toilet paper tubes

fake jewels

coloring book

cardboard egg cartons

clay recipe

green food coloring

a cake mix

egg

soil

Optional: chocolate chips, coarsely chopped semi-sweet chocolate, white chocolate chips, peanut butter chips, butterscotch chips, raisins, coconut, toasted-coarsely chopped nuts
cookie sheets

Supplies for Week 35, Lessons 171-175

paper plates

large brown grocery bags, one for each

plastic animals from Week 23

paper towel rolls, one for each

real or play phone

computer

ceramic praying hands, one for each

silver or gold ceramic paint

magnetic strip

foam board

Supplies for Week 36, Lessons 176-180

wood pieces, variety

a family tree

Noah's ark set

long piece of white butcher paper

Noah's Trail mix: popcorn, pretzels, raisins, sunflower
    seeds, almonds, walnuts, pecans, or coconut

rainbow party goods

rainbow rewards

party food and punch

glitter

Memory Verses

Week	Verse
Weeks 1 and 2	Genesis 1:1
Weeks 3 and 4	Genesis 1:3
Week 5	Genesis 1:6
Weeks 6 and 7	Genesis 1:10
Week 8	I Peter 1:24-25
Weeks 9 and 10	Genesis 8:22
Week 11	Review
Week 12	Genesis 1:16a
Week 13	Psalm 90:12
Week 14	Psalm 89:1
Week 15	Genesis 1:16 a and b
Week 16	Genesis 1:16 all
Week 17	Revelation 22:16
Week 18	Psalm 148:13
Week 19	Genesis 1:26
Week 20	Psalm 48:1
Weeks 21 and 22	Matthew 6:26a
Weeks 23 and 24	Genesis 1:24a
Weeks 25 and 26	Review
Weeks 27 – 30	Psalm 139:14-16
Week 31	Review
Weeks 32 – 33	Genesis 2:2
Week 34	Proverbs 17:17a
Week 35	Romans 3:23
Week 36	Review

Days of Creation Numbers

Many of the Bible Lessons use a set of the Days of Creation Numbers as a visual aid. These numbers have two functions:

A.   They aid in number recognition.

B.   They provide a visual summary of what God created on that day of the Creation week.

We suggest that the days of Creation be illustrated by making the numbers one through seven from cardboard, foam core, or poster board. A set of numbers that can be used as patterns is provided on the back pages of this Teacher's Guide. The size of the pattern numbers can be increased or reduced using a scanner or copier depending on your needs. To these numbers add:

#1.   Foil overlay for Day One

#2.   Blue paper with cotton ball clouds for Day Two

#3.   Rocks and various seeds for Day Three

#4.   Sun, moon, stars, comets, and planets for Day Four

#5.   Fish and bird stickers for Day Five

#6.   Mammal and people stickers for Day Six

#7.   Make Day Seven look like a bed, with a coverlet of material and a cotton ball for a pillow.

Use these numbers to both teach and review what God did on each of the seven days. Size the numbers appropriate for the number of students that you will be teaching.

During the Bible Lesson a number will be held by the teacher as they discuss the Creation events that occurred on that day. Eventually, all seven numbers will be posted on a bulletin board or on the wall for review.

Lyrics to The "Horizons Preschool Music" CD

I Know He Loves Me Too (# 1)
I love ____ (student's name) ____ .
I love ____ (student's name) ____ .
I love ____ (student's name) ____ .
And I know she (he) loves me too.

Note: Continue through the group, singing each student's name. Include the teacher's name. The last verse is:

We love Jesus.
We love Jesus.
We love Jesus,
And we know He loves us too.

I Have a Shadow (# 2)
Frank Hernandez / Copyright 2007 His & Hernandez
    Music

I have a shadow, (I have a shadow)
That follows me, (That follows me)
(Everywhere I go.)

I have a shadow, (I have a shadow)
If I go fast, (If I go fast)
If I go slow, (If I go slow)
It follows me, (It follows me)
(Wherever I go.)

I'm A Little Candle (# 3)
Frank Hernandez / Copyright 2007 His & Hernandez
    Music

I'm a little candle shining in the dark,
It's the light of Jesus shining in my heart,
I will shine,
I will shine,
Like a candle in the dark,
I will shine.

We are little candles shining in the dark,
It's the light of Jesus shining in our hearts,
We will shine,
We will shine,
Like little candles in the dark,
We will shine.

God Made You, God Made Me (# 4)
Frank Hernandez / Copyright 2007 His & Hernandez
    Music

God made you, God made me
God made us how we should be
Birdies fly
Fishes swim
God made you and me to love like Him

(Additional verses)
God made you, God made me
God made us how we should be
Bunnies hop
Fishes swim
God made you and me to love like Him

God made you, God made me
God made us how we should be
Horses prance
Fishes swim
God made you and me to love like Him

Heaven Is A Happy Place (# 5)
Frank Hernandez / Copyright 2007 His & Hernandez
    Music

Heaven is a happy place,
Heaven is a happy place,
Hallelujah, Hallelujah,
We will smile and see God's face,
That's why Heaven is a happy,
It's a happy place.

Heaven is a happy place,
Heaven is a happy place,
Hallelujah, Hallelujah,
We will smile and see God's face,
That's why Heaven is a happy,
It's a happy place.

My God Is So Big (# 6)
Karen Mitzo Hilderbrand & Kim Mitzo Thompson,
   1999 Twin Sisters IP, LLC

My God is so big, so strong and so mighty.
There's nothing my God cannot do. (clap, clap)

My God is so big, so strong and so mighty.
There's nothing my God cannot do. (clap, clap)

The mountains are His. The valleys are His.
The trees are His handiwork, too. (clap, clap)

My God is so big, so strong and so mighty.
There's nothing my God cannot do. (clap, clap)

He Plants Me Like A Seed (# 7)
Dave Huntsinger & Dottie Rambo, 1978
   HeartWarming Music (Admin. by Brentwood-
   Benson Music Publishing Inc.

He plants me like a seed,
And watches as I grow.
He waters me with love
And shields me from the cold.
My tender leaves may bend
Beneath the storms and wind.
But comes the morning sun
I'm growing strong again.

He plants me like a seed
Beneath the fertile land.
My roots grow strong and deep
While tended by His land.
And soon the plants will bear
The harvest sweet and fair.
The Master smiles to see
The fruit from one small seed.

Countdown (# 8)
Dorothy Montgomery, 1966 by Dorothy G.
   Montgomery

Somewhere in outer space,
God has prepared a place,
For those who trust Him and obey.
Jesus will come again,
And though we don't know when,
The countdown's getting lower everyday.

Ten and nine,
Eight and seven,
Six and five and four,
Call upon the Savior while you may.
Three and two,
Coming through the clouds in bright array.
The countdown's getting lower everyday.

Great Is Thy Faithfulness (# 9)
Thomas Obediah Chisholm & William Marion Runyan,
   1923. Renewed 1951 Hope Publishing Company

Summer and winter and springtime and harvest,
Sun, moon and stars in their courses above
Join with all nature in manifold witness
To Thy great faithfulness, mercy and love.

Great is Thy faithfulness.
Great is Thy faithfulness.
Morning by morning new mercies I see.
All I have needed Thy hand has provided.
Great is Thy faithfulness, Lord unto me.

He's Still Working On Me (# 10)
Joel Hemphill, 1980 Family & Friends Music (Admin.
   by Brentwood-Benson Music Publishing, Inc.

He's still working on me
To make me what I ought to be.
It took Him just a week to make the moon and stars
The sun and the earth and Jupiter and Mars.
How loving and patient He must be
He's still working on me.

Peter, James, and John In A Sailboat (# 11)

Peter, James and John in a sailboat.
Peter, James and John in a sailboat.
Peter, James and John in a sailboat,
Out on the deep, deep sea.

We are fishers of men for Jesus.
We are fishers of men for Jesus.
We are fishers of men for Jesus,
Out on life's big sea.

The Birds Upon The Treetop (# 12)

Hal Wright, Karen Hilderbrand & Kim Thompson,
   2002 Twin Sisters IP,LLC

The birds upon the treetops sing their song.
The angels chant their chorus all day long.
The flowers in the garden blend their hue.
So why shouldn't I, why shouldn't you
Praise Him too?

Skeeters And The Bed Bugs (# 13)

(Sometimes called "The Whipper Whopper" song or
   "Eener Meener" song)

I woke up Saturday morning
And looked up on the wall.
The skeeters and the bed bugs
Were playin' a game of ball.
The score was six to nothin'
The skeeters were ahead.
The bed bugs hit a home run
And knocked me out of bed, I'm singing ...

Eenie, meenie and a miny-mo
Catch a wiffle-waffle by his toe.
And if he hollers, hollers, hollers
Let him go, singing
Eenie, meenie and a miny-mo

The Wake-up Song (# 14)

Frank Hernandez / Copyright 2007 His & Hernandez
   Music

Wake up, wake up,
Wake up you sleepy head.
It's time, It's time,
It's time to get out of that bed.

There's lots of work and things to do,
There's lots of play and fun things, too.
Wake up, wake up,
Wake up you sleepy head!

(repeat)

God Put A Rain Cloud In The Sky (# 15)

God put a rain cloud in the sky.
And Noah was safe in the ark.
God put a rain cloud in the sky.
And Noah was safe in the ark.
Lions, tigers, and kangaroos,
Monkeys, zebras, and people too.
God put a rain cloud in the sky.
But Noah was safe in the ark.

God put a rainbow in the sky.
And Noah knew it was safe.
God put a rainbow in the sky.
And Noah knew it was safe.
He freed the animals, big and small.
And thanked God for saving them all.
God put a rainbow in the sky.
And Noah knew it was safe.

Head And Shoulders, Knees and Toes (# 16)

Head and shoulders, knees and toes
Knees and toes,
Knees and toes.
Head and shoulders, knees and toes.
Clap your hands and praise Him.

(repeat)

Say To The Lord I Love You (# 17)

Debby Kemer Rettino & Ernie Rettino, 1981
   Rettino/Kerner Publishing (Admin. by Word
   Music Group, Inc.)

Touch your finger to your nose,
Bend from the waist way down and touch your
   toes,
And when you come up slowly,
Start to sing,
And say to the Lord, I love You.

I love You, I love You
Say to the Lord, I love You
I love You, I love You
Say to the Lord, I love You.

Activities in this Lesson: Bible Lesson, Social Studies, Science, Language Arts, Phonics, Reading, Writing, Memory Verse, Math, Shapes, Story Time, Music, Arts & Crafts, Physical Education

Bible Reference: Genesis 1:20a and 1:21a.

Bible Concept to Present: On the fifth day of Creation God made fish. Fish live in the ocean, lakes, rivers, and ponds.

Bible Lesson: Let's review the days of Creation. Use the Days of Creation Numbers. (See the Table of Contents for the location of the instructions.) What did God make on Day One? On Day Two? On Day Three? On Day Four? Very good. On the fifth day of Creation, God said let the waters be filled with many, many living creatures. This is the day God made all the fish and living things that live in the water. On the fifth day of Creation, God made the eels, shrimp, seahorses, sea stars, and catfish. He made whales, dolphins, little tiny fish, and great big sharks. God made all fish to live in water. Fish must have water to live. If you take a fish out of water, it will die. Some fish like to live in the ocean. The water in the ocean is not like the water we drink. Ocean water is very salty; it would taste much like your tears do. Some fish can only live in salty water. Other fish like to live in fresh water that is not salty. These fish live in lakes, ponds, and rivers on land. (Show your student the location of the oceans on the globe and the locations of lakes and rivers on land.) Utilize the pictures on Lesson 91 Bible worksheet to illustrate this lesson. Talk about the different life forms, and then let the students color their page. Also, there is a chapter on fish in *First Book of Nature*, an Usborne book.

God made fish very special. This week we are going to be talking about some special fish, how fish are different than we are, and how fish live. I am happy God made fish. They help to make our world a fun place to be.

Multimedia Resources: Listen to the song "My Favorite Things" from the "Bullfrogs and Butterflies: God is Great" CD.

Social Studies: On a map of the United States show the students where they live. Then show them where the nearest ocean is located. Show them the nearest lake location on the map and the nearest river. Mark these locations with small paper fish cut out and taped onto the map.

Science: Fish are very different from people. Fish must live in water. We do not live IN water, do we? Fish have a backbone. They breathe through gills, instead of lungs. There is information on how fish breathe in *First Book of Nature*, by Usborne. Use Lesson 91 Resource page to find the gills on a fish and to show them to students. Fish have two pairs of fins in place of legs and toes. Their bodies are covered with hard scales. Do you have hard scales on your body? No. We have skin and little hairs. We are different from fish. Look at and identify the basic fish parts from the picture.

Language Arts: Perform the following action rhyme.

FIVE LITTLE FISHES:

Five little fishes were swimming near the shore. (Hold up five fingers. Starting with thumb,
    bend down one at a time as verse progresses)
One took a dive and then there were four.
Four little fishes were swimming out to sea.
One went for food, then there were three.
Three little fishes said:
"Now what shall we do?"
One swam away, and then there were two.
Two little fishes were having great fun.
But one took a plunge,
Then there was one.
One little fish said:
"I like the warm sun."
Away he went and then there was none. (Put hand behind back.)

Phonics: Teach the initial hard sound of Cc. Review the initial sounds of Aa-Bb. Review letter recognition Aa-Zz.

Write several initial Hard Cc words on the board: Cain, can, call, car, cap, cob, cog, etc. Underline the initial letter Cc and say the words. Ask the students for other words that start with the same sound. We will only cover the hard sound in this program. If necessary, explain that the letter also has a soft sound.

Continue to use the "A Was an Apple Pie" poem to review the letters of the alphabet and initial sounds.

Reading: Blend two parts of a compound word or two syllables. Represent "in written form," following an actual experience: directions for completing a recipe or craft, scientific observations of experiments, events.

Multimedia Resources: Review "Rev-Up for Reading" from the "Rev-Up for Learning" DVD to drill letter recognition and sound. The students should say each letter sound along with the presentation.

Writing: The students should write their first name freehand without using their Name Plates. If this is too difficult, continue to have the Name Plates available.

Writing Skill Builders: Keep these objectives in mind as you direct the class. Incorporate writing strokes wave, X, star, and zigzag line.

Multimedia Resources: Review "Rev-Up for Writing" from the "Rev-Up for Learning" DVD to review the writing of upper- and lowercase letters.

Memory Verse: Genesis 1:26.
Let [man] rule over the fish in the sea. Genesis 1:26 NIV

Let [man] have dominion over the fish of the sea, Genesis 1:26 KJV

Using Lesson 53 Resource page, make copies on cardstock so that each student has several fish. Attach a string somewhere at the front of the room. Each day that a student says his verse correctly, let him color a fish, cut it out and staple it to the fish line. Save this pattern for future projects. Let the students take home Memory Verse Card 14.

Math: Teach 2 + 1 = 3. Show the students a plus (+) sign. Tell them that it means addition. Addition is putting things together. Show the students an equal (=) sign. Tell them that it means equals. When things are put together, addition, it makes more. Have three students come to the front, put two together, a plus sign and the third student. Say, "Jane and Bill are two students and Dick is one student. If we add them together what does that equal?" Have three more students come to the front. Hold the equal sign after Jane, Bill and Dick and have the three new students stand in a group after the equal sign. Have the students count the number in the new group. Say "two plus one equals, three" and count the three students in the new group. Do this with several groups of students.

$$\text{👫} + \text{🧍} = \text{👪}$$

Do the Lesson 91 Math worksheet. Count the number of objects in the box with the number 4. Trace the number 4 following the proper strokes. Count the objects in each box at the bottom of the page. Color the set that shows 4.

Multimedia Resources: View "Rev-Up for Arithmetic" from the "Rev-Up for Learning" DVD to practice number recognition, counting and addition 1-20.

Shapes: Review the oval shape. Draw a large circle and a large oval in the sand on the playground or make shapes out of rope. Have a small group of the students stand between the shapes. When you sing the song below the children need to move into the correct shape and do the movement activity. Other movements can be used such as skipping, jumping, crawling, etc. Other shapes can also be used for this activity.

Hop, Hop, Hop in the Oval
To the tune of Skip, Skip, Skip to My Lou

Hop, hop, hop in the oval,
Hop, hop, hop in the oval,
Hop, hop, hop in the oval,
Hopping in the oval is funny.

(other verses)
Hop, hop, hop in the circle,
Hop, hop, hop in the circle,
Hop, hop, hop in the circle,
Hopping in the circle is funny.

Do the Lesson 91 Shapes worksheet. Name the shapes. Trace the shapes, count them, and trace the numbers.

Story Time: Read a story or stories of your choice.

Music: Review "He's Still Working On Me." Tell your student the story of Peter, James, John, Thomas, and Nathaniel and their fishing expedition in which they caught no fish, until Jesus came. This is found in John 21. After telling your students the story, teach them the song "Peter, James, and John In A Sailboat" on the "Horizons Preschool Music" CD.

Multimedia Resources: This week, listen and sing along to selections from "Bullfrogs and Butterflies: God is Great" CD. This week, watch *The Kingdom Under the Sea* adventure "The Red Tide" which teaches about trust and forgiveness.

Arts & Crafts: Make the fishbowl on Lesson 91b Resource page. *Copy the patterns on four pieces of cardstock: white, light green, light blue, and tan.* Do this for each student. Older students can cut out the appropriate pieces. Younger students might need help. Instruct students to assemble their fish bowls on the white paper, gluing pieces on well. Provide some small fish crackers to "swim" in the fish-bowls.

To prepare for tomorrow's arts & crafts activity, paint the bottom half of Day 5 on the Creation Mural with pale blue water colors. Paint a thin strip of brown above the water. The students will be adding fish and other sea creatures to the mural tomorrow.

Physical Education: Fish swim very well. Do your students know how to swim? Pretend to swim. Kick feet, wave arms, breathe deeply. How many laps around the room can you swim? What type of a fish would you like to pretend to be?

NOTES:

Activities in this Lesson: Bible Lesson, Science, Language Arts, Phonics, Reading, Writing, Memory Verse, Math, Shapes, Story Time, Music, Arts & Crafts, Outdoor Activity, Physical Education

Bible Reference: Genesis 1:20a and 1:21a.

Bible Concept to Present: God made vast bodies of water and seas. Some fish live in the colder climates and some live in the warmer climates.

Bible Lesson: Review yesterday's lesson. Discuss the vastness of the oceans and seas. Look at a globe to see how much of our earth is land and how much is water. There are so, so many kinds of animal life in the water, not just fish. Sea creatures live in different parts of the world, just like land creatures. There are whales and fish that live in the cold, cold arctic regions. There are tropical fish that live near the equator. Tropical sea life is much more colorful than arctic sea life.

Illustration: Give students their Lesson 92 Bible worksheet. The sea horse is one of the cutest tropical fish; yes, it is a fish. These creatures have a crested, curled tail and a tiny, horse-like head. Sea horses can be anywhere from an inch long to a foot long. Sea horses prefer a close environment with lots of vegetation because they are poor swimmers in open water. These little creatures stay attached to plant stems by their tails for most of the time. Only when they are hungry, do they swim about to find tiny, tiny little sea animals to eat. Talk about the body parts of the sea horse. Let the students color their page.

Science: *Buy a whole fish from the meat market, the bigger the better.* Bring it in for the students to observe. Let the students touch the scales. Pull the gills out and look inside. Use the picture on Lesson 91 Resource page and point out the body parts on the real fish. Let the students feel the teeth. Try to break off a gill. Talk about how God made the fish to be strong. If you can, cut the fish in half lengthwise, and look inside. Talk about the fact that after the Flood, when God gave man permission to eat meat, that also included fish. Have the student wash their hands after touching the fish.

Multimedia Resources: Listen to the song "The Master Shared His Love" from "The Amazing Miracles" CD.

Language Arts: Say, There are so many kinds of sea creatures. Let's have some word fun. I will say the sentence, and then you fill in the last word with a word that rhymes with "sea."
> My friend saw me running in circles because I didn't want to get stung by the _____.
> BEE
> I don't know how the little birds don't fall out, when they live way up in a _____. TREE
> It wasn't much fun when I tripped and skinned my _____. KNEE
> I'm glad I got glasses because they help me to _____. SEE
> In warm areas, they put little bags in a jar of water and set it out in the sun to make
> _____. TEA

Review the action rhyme from yesterday, "Five Little Fishes."

Phonics: Review the initial hard sound of Cc. Review the initial sounds of Aa-Bb. Review letter recognition Aa-Zz.

Do the Lesson 92 Phonics worksheet. The Hard Sound of Cc. Review the letter sound with the picture and words on the worksheet. Ask the students for other words that begin with the same sound. Discuss the position of the letters on the guidelines. Give them specific instructions for how the letter should be traced. Trace the letters and say the hard sound of Cc. Observe the students as they trace the letters and help them with the letter strokes. If you have the students do one row at a time, the worksheet can be carried over to various parts of the day or another day.

Reading: Blend two parts of a compound word or two syllables. Represent "in written form," following an actual experience: directions for completing a recipe or craft, scientific observations of experiments, events.

Writing: The students should write their first name freehand without using their Name Plates.

Writing Skill Builders: Keep these objectives in mind as you direct the class. Incorporate writing strokes wave, X, star, and zigzag line.

Memory Verse: Review the memory verse Genesis 1:26. Say the memory verse while working on the Creation Mural and making the ocean creatures.

Continue the fish activity from Lesson 91. Attach a string somewhere at the front of the room. Each day that a student says his verse correctly, let him color a fish, cut it out, and staple it to the fish line.

Math: Review time to the hour. Review 1 + 1 = 2 and 2 + 1 = 3. Give the students the dog bones that they cut out previously and a bowl to put them in. Have them place 2 bones in the bowl while saying "two plus one" and have them place another bone in the bowl, "equals" and have them count "one, two, three bones in the bowl." Do this several times. Reverse the order putting one in and then two.

Do the Lesson 92a Math worksheet. As they count the images have them say "one plus one equals two" and "two plus one equals three." Trace the numbers.

Do the Lesson 92b Math worksheet. Write the digital time for the analog clock.

Shapes: Review the oval shape. Thumbprints can be used to make oval shapes. Have the students draw branches on a sheet of construction paper and then add leaves by making thumbprints from green tempera paint that has been soaked into sponges.

Story Time: Read a story or stories of your choice.

Music: Review "Peter, James, and John In A Sailboat" and "He's Still Working On Me."

Multimedia Resources: This week, listen and sing along to selections from "Bullfrogs and Butterflies: God is Great" CD. This week, watch *The Kingdom Under the Sea* adventure "The Red Tide" which teaches about trust and forgiveness.

Arts & Crafts: Go to Day 5 on the Creation Mural. Today, add fish and other sea creatures to the water. Hand out Lesson 92 Arts & Crafts worksheet for some types of ocean life. Make sure students understand that there are many, many more things in the sea than fish. Have the students color the sea animals. Allow the students to draw some creatures and add them to the mural. Only put the animals in the water part of the day. Let the students take their colorful student page home.

Give the students playdough. Let them create a fish.

Outdoor Activity: Take a walk outside. Say, We breathe in air. But fish and sea creatures breathe in air, too. They just breathe in a different way. They breathe through their gills. Let's take a walk and see if we can walk like fish would swim. How do they move their mouths?

Physical Education: Catch a Fish. For this activity you will need a launch board and a fish shaped bean bag. A small ball, bean bag or koosh type ball will also work. The students will place the bean bag on the low end of the launch board. They will then go around and stomp on the high end of the launch board, sending the bean bag into the air where they can attempt to catch it. Instructions for constructing a launch board were given in Lesson 82.

NOTES:

Lesson 93

Activities in this Lesson: Bible Lesson, Social Studies/Science/Field Trip, Language Arts/Math, Phonics, Reading, Writing, Memory Verse, Math, Shapes, Story Time, Music, Physical Education

Bible Reference: Genesis 1:20a and Genesis 1:26.

Bible Concept to Present: After God made the fish, He gave man the ability to rule over them. Fish are subject to our control.

Bible Lesson: God made the fish on the fifth day of Creation. He made the fish for many reasons. Fish play a special part in our world. But when God made the fish, he made them so that man could rule over them. Men today have the ability to kill fish, to help fish, or to simply capture them. Fish that live in aquariums are fish that have been captured. We have caught these fish, and put them in an environment that will help the fish live well. God spent much time in making the fish. We need to be careful about the fish that we catch, and if we place them in an aquarium, we need to take good care of them.

Do the Lesson 93 Bible worksheet. Discuss the animal characteristics that distinguish a fish. Have the student color the fish.

Social Studies/Science/Field Trip: Take the students to a pet store that carries fish. Look at the aquariums. Why do they have air bubbling in the tanks? Why do they have rocks in the tanks? What kind of water is in the aquariums? Note the different kinds of fish. Discuss the people who work with fish and how they must provide food, clean living conditions and proper care for the fish. They must know the kind of fish well that they are taking care of. Some fish require different care than others. Look for the gills, fins, eyes, and scales on the fish.

Language Arts/Math: Make a fishing pole from a dowel rod. On the end of the dowel rod, place a string. On the end of the string, add a magnet. Use the patterns on the Lesson 93 Resource page to cut out several fish from cardstock. On the back of the fishes, place a magnet that will attract the magnet on the fishing pole. Place numbers 1 - 10 on the fishes. Circle a part of the fish on each fish pattern. (Examples: fins, head, eyes, scales) Let the children go "fishing." The students will tell you the number on the fish he catches and the part of the fish that is circled. Save these items for an activity in Lesson 99.

Phonics: Review the initial hard sound of Cc. Review the initial sounds of Aa-Bb. Review letter recognition Aa-Zz.

Do the Lesson 93 Phonics worksheet. The Hard Sound of Cc. Review the letter sound with the picture and words on the worksheet. Ask the students for other words that begin with the same sound. Give them specific instructions for how the letter should be traced. Allow time for tracing the letters and observe their progress. If you have the students do one row at a time, the worksheet can be carried over to various parts of the day or another day.

Reading: Blend two parts of a compound word or two syllables. Represent "in written form," following an actual experience: directions for completing a recipe or craft, scientific observations of experiments, events.

Writing: The students should write their first name freehand without using their Name Plates. Writing Skill Builders: Keep these objectives in mind as you direct the class. Incorporate writing strokes wave, X, star, and zigzag line.

Memory Verse: Review Genesis 1:26. Continue the fish activity from Lesson 91. Attach a string somewhere at the front of the room. Each day that a student says his verse correctly, let him color a fish, cut it out, and staple it to the fish line.

Math: Review 2 + 1 = 3. Review 2 + 1 = 3 by writing the problem 2 + 1 = 3 on the board. Under the 2 draw two objects under the 1 draw one object with a + sign between them. Write the = sign and then draw 5 or 6 objects under the 3. Have a student come to the board and circle the correct number of objects under the 3 to make the addition problem correct. Erase the extra objects and orally say the problem with the class. Repeat several times drawing simple objects such as dots or various shapes.

Do the Lesson 93a Math worksheet. Count the items and do the addition problem. Trace the numbers and say the addition problem. As they trace the twos and ones have them say "two plus one equals" and have them look at and read, "three."

Do the Lesson 93b Math worksheet. Count the number of objects in the box with the number 5. Trace the number 5 following the proper strokes. Count the objects in each box at the bottom of the page. Color the set that shows 5.

Shapes: Review the oval shape. Draw both ovals and circles on the white board. Tell the students that you have drawn "only" ovals on the white board. The students should correct you and tell you that some of the shapes are circles. Tell them that you need some help in getting rid of the circles because you only want ovals on the board. Point to each shape and ask if it is a circle or an oval. Erase the shapes identified as circles.

Do the Lesson 93 Shapes worksheet. Draw lines to match the pictures that are the same. Color as you wish.

Story Time: Read a story or stories of your choice.

Music: Review "Peter, James, and John In A Sailboat."

Multimedia Resources: This week, listen and sing along to selections from "Bullfrogs and Butterflies: God is Great" CD. This week, watch *The Kingdom Under the Sea* adventure "The Red Tide" which teaches about trust and forgiveness.

Physical Education: Pretend to go on a fishing trip today. Use the following dialogue as you go. Use the dowel rod fishing pole you made for Language Arts.

We are going on a fishing trip. Let's get a jacket, our fishing pole and a fishing box. Let's take our lunch and a bucket to place the water in to keep the fish fresh. Now, tell me what all we have with us. (Child repeats what you are taking). Ok. Let's go. We will shut the door to our home and lock it. Now we walk down to the river. Let's take this path through the woods. (Pretend to walk up a hill). Oh my, look at this hill. It is very steep. Let's climb up it. Watch out for the branch from that tree. Do you see the bird in the tree? Oh look! That fishing pole got caught in the bush, let's pull it out. (Pretend to pull out the fishing pole.) Wow! This is a long way to the river. Let's go down the hill now and then up this one. Ugh! I'm getting tired. Now let's go over this hill, around this bend. And Look! Here's the river. Let's take out our poles and put a worm on the end of it so the fish can eat the worm. (Pretend to do so.) Now let's cast the pole into the water. Oh Very good. Now SHHH! We must be quiet so the fish will not hear us and not come near. (Sit quietly) Oh! Quick! Reel your line in. You have caught a fish. He is a big one. He is fighting to get away. You have him. Pull him in. Very Good. Isn't fishing fun?

NOTES:

AOP's Commitment to Quality—Tell us how we are doing

As a publisher dedicated to providing high quality educational materials we invite you to tell us how we are doing. Please visit our website at www.aop.com to give us your comments, concerns, and/or compliments concerning Horizons Preschool. Contact information can be found in the support area for Horizons at the AOP website.

Activities in this Lesson: Bible Lesson, Science, Language Arts, Language Arts/Math, Phonics, Reading, Writing, Memory Verse, Math, Shapes, Story Time, Music, Arts & Crafts, Physical Education, Homework

Bible Reference: Genesis 1:20a and 1:21a.

Bible Concept to Present: Many of God's ocean creatures live at the edge of the oceans in tidal pools.

Bible Lesson: Review yesterday's lesson. God made so many kinds of fish! Why did He do that? How small is the smallest fish? How big is the biggest fish? (Let the students use their arms.)

Social Studies: Have any of you ever gone to the ocean or to a lake? What makes the ocean different from a lake? Remember we talked about the moon? What does the moon do to the water in the big ocean? Many animals live at the edge of the ocean, where the tides change all the time. They are made to live right there, where the water is sometimes high, and sometimes low. When ocean waves go out at low tide they leave pools of water all around the rocks. These are called tidal pools. There are some animals that only live in these tidal pools. Have any of you ever looked at tidal pools at low tide? It is so much fun. Many little crabs, sea urchins, and starfish live there. Let's pretend we are at the edge of the ocean looking in tidal pools. How do we have to walk? Very carefully, right? What do you see?

Science: Today, we want to look at crab legs. *Get a few from the meat department.* You can remove the meat ahead of time and use it in a recipe. *OR get a whole crab, in the shell.* Let the students see how the crab legs are jointed, and how thin yet strong the shell is on the legs. If you got a whole crab, look at how everything fits together. If you brought the crab meat to class, let the students try some.

Language Arts: Review the action rhyme, "Five Little Fish."

Language Arts/Math: Let the students play with their fishing poles and fish.

Phonics: Review the initial hard sound of Cc. Review the initial sounds of Aa-Bb. Review letter recognition Aa-Zz.

Have the students brainstorm words that begin or include the letter Cc. Write these words on the board. Model the correct letter formation as you write the letters on the board. The students should practice forming the letter Cc on a blank sheet of paper. Students who are ready can practice copying complete words from the board.

Do the Lesson 94 Phonics worksheet. The Hard Sound of Cc. Review the letter sound with the picture and words on the worksheet. Ask the students for other words that begin with the same sound. Trace the letters and say the hard sound of Cc. Observe the students as they trace the letters and help them with the letter strokes. If you have the students do one row at a time, the worksheet can be carried over to various parts of the day or another day.

Reading: Blend two parts of a compound word or two syllables. Represent "in written form," following an actual experience: directions for completing a recipe or craft, scientific observations of experiments, events.

Writing: The students should write their first name freehand without using their Name Plates.

Writing Skill Builders: Keep these objectives in mind as you direct the class. Incorporate writing strokes wave, X, star, and zigzag line.

Memory Verse: Review the memory verse Genesis 1:26. Write the words, plus the reference, on strips of paper. Lay them at random on the floor and help the students put them in order. Say the verse over and over.

Continue the fish activity from Lesson 91. Attach a string somewhere at the front of the room. Each day that a student says his verse correctly, let him color a fish, cut it out, and staple it to the fish line.

Math: Review time to the hour. Review 2 + 1 = 3. Give each of the students 10 counters. Have them count the objects to make sure that they have 10 objects. Have them make 2 + 1 = 3 addition problems with the counters. Have them point to the counters and say, "two plus one equals three." The students should draw the plus and equal sign with their finger between the counters as they say the words. Can they make another problem with the counters that remain? How many counters are left after making the second problem?

Do the Lesson 94a Math worksheet. The Addition of 2 + 1 = 3.

Do the Lesson 94b worksheet. Write the o'clock time for the analog clock.

Shapes: Review the oval shape. If you do activities such as a reading circle have the students form a reading oval today.

Story Time: Read a story or stories of your choice.

Music: Review "Peter, James, and John In A Sailboat."

Multimedia Resources: This week, listen and sing along to selections from "Bullfrogs and Butterflies: God is Great" CD. This week, watch *The Kingdom Under the Sea* adventure "The Red Tide" which teaches about trust and forgiveness.

Arts & Crafts: Hand out pale blue construction paper to all the students. Hand out poster pens. Let the students draw their version of a tidal pool. Explain that tidal pools are always in the rocks at the sea shore.

Physical Education: Jump the Fishing Stream. Have the students pretend that they are fishing and that they need to jump the stream to get to the other side. They will need something to jump over, lines on the floor, rope, hula hoop, etc. The students will stand on both feet on one side of the rope and then jump to the other side by swinging their arms from front to back and landing on both feet. This exercise will give practice in jumping and landing while keeping balance. Put together a course of streams to jump over.

Homework: Let the students take home Lesson 94 Homework worksheet, the Aquarium illustration. Instruct them to return the page to class tomorrow. This can be done in class if there is time.

NOTES:

Lesson 95

Activities in this Lesson: Bible Lesson, Social Studies, Science/Language Arts, Language Arts, Phonics, Reading, Writing, Memory Verse, Math, Story Time, Shapes, Music, Physical Education/Music

Bible Reference: Genesis 1:20a.

Bible Concept to Present: When God made the fish, He made many kinds of fish.

Bible Lesson: When God made the living creatures in the water, He made many kinds of them. Some are fish. We have talked about what a fish is. Can you tell me the body parts of a fish? God also put creatures in the water that have shells. Some of these are called mollusks. They are animals that live in shells. A snail is a mollusk. Snails have hard shells. Under their shell is a soft body. Snails have the ability to crawl on the rocks. God has made them with a special foot that moves. They only have one foot, not two feet like we have.

Some of the animals in the ocean have two parts to their shells. They are called bivalves. A clam is a bivalve. Clams have two parts to their shells. Oysters are a bivalve like clams. Some animals in the ocean have many parts to their shells. A shrimp has many parts to his shell. He has pinchers to help him obtain his food. Shrimp are called crustaceans.

The shells we find at the beach are from animals like these we have talked about. The animals that lived in them no longer need them. They wash up with the waves of the ocean onto the beach.

Some of the water animals God made are big. Some are small. The biggest water animal is the blue whale. The smallest is a tiny little creature we can't even see without a microscope.

God is so wonderful and talented to make so many different creatures in one day. Let's thank God now for what He made.

Illustration: Bring in any sea shells you might have. Craft stores have inexpensive bags of shells. If possible, get a live snail from the fish store. Ask if you can bring it back when you are done showing it to the students.

Social Studies: We use fish for many different things. We eat some fish. Some fish we use to help us grow plants. Other fish we use for the oil in their bodies. Cod liver oil is a product from fish that humans need. We use it in many health products. Whales are used for the fat in their body. Perfume is made from whales. Fish are very important to us.

Science/Language Arts: Review the various kinds of fish. Show students a nice picture book about fish and other sea creatures.

Language Arts: Read the following action rhymes.

> ### THE FISH
>
> I hold my fingers like a fish (Place one hand on top of the other)
> And wave them as I go. (Waving motion with hands)
> See them swimming with a swish (Swimming motion)
> So swiftly to and fro.

OCEAN SHELL

I found a great big shell one day
Upon the ocean floor
I held it close up to my ear
I heard the ocean roar!
I found a tiny shell one day.
Upon the ocean sand.
The waves had worn it nice and smooth
It felt nice in my hand.

Phonics: Blend sounds Aa-Cc. (ab, cab) Review the initial hard sound of Cc. Review the initial sounds of Aa-Bb. Review letter recognition Aa-Zz.

Continue to show the students that letter sounds can combine to make words. Use only the sounds covered so far to make the words. Begin with *ab*. Say the sound of *a* then the sound of *b*, then combine the two to say *ab*. Next say the *b* sound and add to the *ab* sound to say the word *bab*. Repeat by pointing to the *ab* and saying the sound, then point to *c* and say the sound *c* and add it to the *ab* to say the word *cab*.

As discussed previously, combine sounds to form words by following this procedure. Point under each letter and sound it out slowly – [c], then [a], then [b] – to make sure the students recognize each individual letter and know the sound. Then go back, point to each letter and read the sounds a little faster, giving each letter a longer sound than is normal, ccc-aaa-bbb. Finally, read the word without pausing between the sounds with yet a shorter sound for each letter. This should be quite close to the way the word should be read. Move your finger or pointer faster under the letters each time as you say the sounds faster.

To help with sounding individual letters write the words out twice as we have illustrated below. Words can be sorted into categories with common beginnings and endings to help illustrate the sounding out process.

b̲ a̲	b̲a̲	a̲ b̲	a̲b̲
b a	baa	a b	ab
B a b	Bab	B a b	Bab
		c a b	cab

Do the Lesson 95 Phonics worksheet. The Hard Sound of Cc. Review the letter sound with the picture and words on the worksheet. Ask the students for other words that begin with the same sound. Trace the letters and say the hard sound of Cc. Observe the students as they trace the letters and help them with the letter strokes. If you have the students do one row at a time, the worksheet can be carried over to various parts of the day or another day.

Reading: Blend two parts of a compound word or two syllables. Represent "in written form," following an actual experience: directions for completing a recipe or craft, scientific observations of experiments, events.

Writing: The students should write their first name freehand without using their Name Plates.

Writing Skill Builders: Keep these objectives in mind as you direct the class. Incorporate writing strokes wave, X, star, and zigzag line.

Memory Verse: Finish the verse for the week, Genesis 1:26. Congratulate students for all they have accomplished. Continue the fish activity from Lesson 91. Attach a string somewhere at the front of the room. Each day that a student says his verse correctly, let him color a fish, cut it out, and staple it to the fish line.

Math: Review time to the hour. Review 2 + 1 = 3.

Do the Lesson 95a Math worksheet. Circle the analog clock for the digital time and draw hands on the clock for the digital time.

Do the Lesson 95b Math worksheet. Circle the correct number of objects to answer the addition problems.

Do the Lesson 95c Math worksheet. Count the number of objects in the box with the number 6. Trace the number 6 following the proper strokes. Trace the numbers to complete the clock. Read the numbers on the clock.

Shapes: Review the oval shape.

Do the Lesson 95 Shapes worksheet. Draw a line to follow the ovals to the egg carton.

Story Time: Read a story or stories of your student's choice or ones they have brought from home.

Music: Review "Peter, James, and John In A Sailboat."

Multimedia Resources: This week, listen and sing along to selections from "Bullfrogs and Butterflies: God is Great" CD. This week, watch *The Kingdom Under the Sea* adventure "The Red Tide" which teaches about trust and forgiveness.

Physical Education/Music: Listen to classical music. Give your students several long pieces of ribbon or ribbon sticks and permit the students to "dance" to the music, moving the ribbon so that it creates various patterns in the air.

NOTES:

Lesson 96

Activities in this Lesson: Bible Lesson, Social Studies, Science, Language Arts, Phonics, Reading, Writing, Memory Verse, Math, Shapes, Story Time, Music, Outdoor Activity, Physical Education

Bible Reference: Genesis 1:20a and 1:21a.

Bible Concept to Present: God also made amphibians.

Bible Lesson: When God made the water creatures, He made fish. He made crustaceans. He made water mammals like the whales and dolphins. He made mollusks and bivalves. But God also made a wonderful surprise. God made an animal that can live in the water or on land. He made frogs. Since frogs live both in water and on land, some think they were created on Day 5 along with fish, while others think they may have been created on Day 6 along with the land animals. We don't know for sure. A frog is a special kind of creature called an amphibian. Amphibian means it can live in the water or it can live on land. A frog begins its life as an egg. It hatches in the water and it looks like a little fish. We call baby frogs "tadpoles." Tadpoles live in the water and then one day they begin to grow legs. Pretty soon, they lose their tails and they look just like a little frog. They grow bigger and can hop onto the land, and they spend part of their time on the land and part of it in the water. Frogs eat insects. A frog has a long tongue that sneaks out of its mouth very quickly and grabs the insect while it is still flying. Frogs are a wonderful water surprise.

Multimedia Resources: Listen to the songs "Oh Me Oh My," "My Favorite Things," "Floydd Frogg," and "It's Time To Let My People Go" from the "Bullfrogs and Butterflies: God is Great" CD.

Social Studies: Frogs are wonderful creatures. They help us very much by eating insects that could hurt our plants. Some people even eat frogs. Frogs are sometimes used to bait hooks to catch fish. We use frogs in many ways.

Science: Lesson 96a Resource page shows the life cycle of a frog. Review the process of a frog's life. Pretend to be the frog. Go through the stages with your students. Use the following poems as activity suggestions.

Language Arts: Read this little verse. Instruct the students on the motions.

LITTLE FROG

A little frog in a pond am I (Squat down)
Hippity hippity hop (Suitable action)
And I can jump in the air so high (High jump)
Hippity, hippity hop

Multimedia Resources: Listen quietly to the song "Bullfrogs And Butterflies" from the "Bullfrogs and Butterflies: God is My Friend" CD.

Read this action rhyme with suitable actions:

THE FROG

This little froggie broke his toe.
This little froggie said "Oh, Oh, Oh!"
This little froggie cried and was sad.
This little froggie thoughtful and good,
Ran to the doctor's as fast as he could.

You may also choose to tell students the story of *The Ox and The Frog*. It is an Aesop's Fable. The story and visuals are on Lesson 96b Resource page. Explain to students that some frogs have the ability to puff out their skin.

Phonics: Teach the initial sound of Dd. Review the initial sounds of Aa-Cc. Review letter recognition Aa-Zz.

Write several initial Dd words on the board: dab, dad, day, dim, dip, do, dog, etc. Underline the initial letter Dd and say the words. Ask the students for other words that start with the same sound.

Continue to use the "A Was an Apple Pie" poem to review the letters of the alphabet and initial sounds.

Reading: Blend two parts of a compound word or two syllables. Represent "in written form," following an actual experience: directions for completing a recipe or craft, scientific observations of experiments, events.

Multimedia Resources: Review "Rev-Up for Reading" from the "Rev-Up for Learning" DVD to drill letter recognition and sound. The students should say each letter sound along with the presentation.

Writing: The students should write their first name freehand without using their Name Plates. If this is too difficult, continue to have the Name Plates available.

Writing Skill Builders: Keep these objectives in mind as you direct the class. Incorporate writing strokes wave, X, star, and zigzag line.

Multimedia Resources: Review "Rev-Up for Writing" from the "Rev-Up for Learning" DVD to review the writing of upper- and lowercase letters.

Memory Verse: Psalm 48:1.
Great is the LORD, and most worthy of praise... Psalm 48:1 NIV

Great is the LORD, and greatly to be praised... Psalm 48:1 KJV

Talk about the memory verse. Explain each word, especially "worthy," "greatly," and "praise." Send home Memory Verse Card 15 with the students.

Math: Review 2 + 1 = 3. Use an abacus, pop beads, or beads on a wire, string, or clothesline to review 1 + 1 = 2 and 2 + 1 = 3. Move one bead over and say, "one plus one," and slide another bead over, "equals," and count "one, two" the beads you have slid over. Do the same for 2 + 1 = 3. Slide over two beads and say "two plus one," and slide over one more bead, "equals," and count "one, two, three" all the beads you have slid over. The same can be done with pop beads by snapping them together. Have students slide the beads as you do the problem. The students can practice this if they have their own pop beads or a string of beads.

Do the Lesson 96a Math worksheet. As they count the images have them say "one plus one equals two" and "one plus two equal three." Trace the numbers.

Do the Lesson 96b Math worksheet. Count the number of objects in the box with the number 7. Trace the number 7 following the proper strokes.

Multimedia Resources: View "Rev-Up for Arithmetic" from the "Rev-Up for Learning" DVD to practice number recognition, counting and addition 1-20.

Shapes: Review the oval shape.

Do the Lesson 96 Shapes worksheet. Have the students cut out the fish shapes and glue them on to the correct tank shape.

Story Time: Read a story or stories of your choice.

Music: Review "Peter, James, and John In A Sailboat."

Multimedia Resources: This week, listen and sing along to selections from "Music Machine: The Majesty Of God" CD.

Outdoor Activity: Talk a walk. If there is a pond nearby, hurrah! Go and find some frogs. If not, walk and recite the memory verse. After each time, yell out something you see that you are thankful for.

Physical Education: Use the song "Bullfrogs and Butterflies" and pretend to be a bullfrog, jumping and hopping as the song indicates.

NOTES:

Lesson 97

Activities in this Lesson: Bible Lesson, Science, Science/Arts & Crafts, Language Arts, Language Arts/Reading/Arts & Crafts, Phonics, Reading, Writing, Memory Verse, Math, Shapes, Story Time, Music, Arts & Crafts, Creative Cooking, Physical Education, Homework

Bible Reference: Genesis 1:20a and 1:21a.

Bible Concept to Present: God has unlimited power and imagination.

Bible Lesson: God made an amazing variety of creatures. Everything He made, whales, fish, starfish, eels, crabs, everything has many different varieties. When God made amphibians, He made them to produce thousands of different species, including true frogs, tree frogs, toads, and salamanders.

Social Studies: It would be wonderful if you could get some frogs for the students to observe and touch. Even better would be to get some tadpoles and watch them change. Tadpoles are perfect specimens because they change rapidly and obviously. Students can really see the stages of their life. Home Science Tools (formerly known as Home Training Tools) is a possible source for ordering a frog hatchery kit.

Science: There are 3,140 different amphibians! He made them in every color and with every kind of strange feature. Frogs have three thin eyelids that protect their eyes. One is transparent, like clear plastic, so they can see underwater. The others are like human eyelids. Some frogs have long, sticky tongues while toads have short, fat tongues. Some frogs have sticky feet that help them to climb trees. Frogs are some of the best jumpers around, jumping twenty times their length. Frogs can breathe and drink through their skin. And frogs are loud! They can croak loud enough to be heard for miles.

Science/Arts & Crafts: Start a Facts Poster that will be used for many weeks. On the poster today, write "Amphibians: 3,140." As you learn about different animals, add the numbers to the poster. The poster may be illustrated.

Language Arts: Let the students act out some of the things they have learned about frogs. Instruct them to call out the feature first, and then act it out. For example: "Some frogs have sticky feet and can climb trees." Student then acts like she is climbing a tree.

Read the following Aesop's fable about two frogs.

The Two Frogs

TWO FROGS dwelt in the same pool. When the pool dried up under the summer's heat, they left it and set out together for another home. As they went along they chanced to pass a deep well, amply supplied with water, and when they saw it, one of the Frogs said to the other, "Let us descend and make our abode in this well: it will furnish us with shelter and food." The other replied with greater caution, "But suppose the water should fail us. How can we get out again from so great a depth?"

Do nothing without a regard to the consequences.

Language Arts/Reading/Arts & Crafts: Get the book *The Rainbow Fish*, by Marcus Pfister and J. Alison James, from the library. Read it to the children. Discuss the importance of sharing. Complete the Lesson 97 Language worksheet. *Purchase multi-colored sequins from the craft store.* Let the students glue the sequins onto the fish, making patterns of gills. They will need to put just a touch of glue on each piece of sequins. As an alternative, have the students tear up small pieces of colored construction paper to glue onto the fish shapes.

Multimedia Resources: Watch "Sharing" from the *Character Builders Video Series*.

Phonics: Review the initial sound of Dd. Review the initial sounds of Aa-Cc. Review letter recognition Aa-Zz.

Do the Lesson 97 Phonics worksheet. The Sound of Dd. Review the letter sound with the picture and words on the worksheet. Ask the students for other words that begin with the same sound. Discuss the position of the letters on the guidelines. Give them specific instructions for how the letter should be traced. Trace the letters and say the sound of Dd. Observe the students as they trace the letters and help them with the letter strokes. If you have the students do one row at a time, the worksheet can be carried over to various parts of the day or another day.

Reading: Blend two parts of a compound word or two syllables. Represent "in written form," following an actual experience: directions for completing a recipe or craft, scientific observations of experiments, events.

Writing: The students should write their first name freehand without using their Name Plates.

Writing Skill Builders: Keep these objectives in mind as you direct the class. Incorporate writing strokes wave, X, star, and zigzag line.

Memory Verse: Review Psalm 48:1. Write the words on cards and have the students arrange them in the correct order.

Math: Review time to the hour. Review 2 + 1 = 3. Demonstrate addition of 1 + 1 = 2 and 2 + 1 = 3 with a clock with moveable hands. Set the clock at 1:00 and ask what time it would be if you added 1 hour. Have a student come and set the clock to 2:00. Ask if an hour is added to 2:00 what time will it be? Have another student come up and set the clock to 3:00. Return the clock to 1:00 and say, "1 o'clock plus 1 hour equals 2 o'clock, 2 o'clock plus 1 hour equals 3 o'clock." Move the hands of the clock to the new times as you say the addition problems.

Do the Lesson 97a Math worksheet. Write the o'clock time for the analog clock.

Do the Lesson 97b Math worksheet. Count the number of objects in each box at the top of the page. Color the set that shows 6. Count the objects in each box at the bottom of the page. Color the set that shows 7.

Shapes: Review the oval shape.

Do the Lesson 97 Shapes worksheet. Color the large ovals green and the small ovals orange. Color the rest as you wish.

Story Time: Read a story or stories of your choice.

Music: Review "Peter, James, and John In A Sailboat." *Obtain an audio recording of whale songs from the Internet or a library.* Play the music while the students rest. You may also allow students to paint while listening to the whale songs.

Multimedia Resources: This week, listen and sing along to selections from "Music Machine: The Majesty Of God" CD.

Arts & Crafts: Hand out Lesson 97 Arts & Crafts worksheet. Let the students color their frogs as they choose. Then cut out around the dotted lines. Glue the frogs on the Creation Mural, all along the water line. Some frogs can be on land and some in the water. It doesn't matter if they overlap, because that's what real frogs do.

Creative Cooking: Make a rainbow fish cake. Cut a sheet cake into a fish shape. Frost the cake with white frosting. Decorate the fish with colored candy wafers, gum drops, etc.

Physical Education: Review the Jump the Fishing Stream game. Have the students pretend that they are fishing and that they need to jump the stream to get to the other side. They will need something to jump over, lines on the floor, rope, hula hoop, etc. The students will stand on both feet on one side of the rope and then jump to the other side by swinging their arms from front to back and landing on both feet. This exercise will give practice in jumping and landing while keeping balance. Put together a course of streams to jump over.

Homework: Say, Who brought their homework to class today? What kind of things did you draw in your aquarium? Let the students share the things they remembered to draw.

NOTES:

Activities in this Lesson: Bible Lesson, Social Studies, Science, Language Arts, Phonics, Reading, Writing, Memory Verse, Math, Shapes, Story Time, Music, Arts & Crafts, Physical Education

Bible Reference: Genesis 1:20a and 1:21a.

Bible Concept to Present: On the fifth day of Creation, when God made the water creatures, He made them to lay eggs so that there would always be fish.

Bible Lesson: On the fifth day of Creation, God made the living creatures in the water. God made them each very special. He made some of the fish and water creatures to be fathers. He made some of the creatures of be mothers. God made it so that (usually) the Mommy fish will lay eggs. Mommy lays the eggs under a rock, or a plant, or in the sand of the ocean bottom. Some protect their eggs so that no one will bother them. Then one day, the eggs hatch to be baby fish. Almost all fish and water creatures lay eggs. The baby fish are much like their parent fish. They know how to swim from birth. They know what they like to eat. Some baby fish live with the parent fish and other fish in a big family called a "school." These fish help to protect one another. I am happy God made the fish and water creatures to lay eggs to have babies. Baby fish are very wonderful.

Social Studies: Fish eggs are used by man, too. Sometimes fishermen use fish eggs to bait their hooks so they can catch bigger fish. Sometimes people eat fish eggs. Caviar is fish eggs. Purchase some fish eggs from a sports or bait shop. Show the students what they look like. Let the students handle the fish eggs. Cut some open to see what is inside.

Science: Other fish sometimes eat fish eggs. They like the taste of them. Fish eat a variety of things. Some fish eat plants, some eat smaller fish, and some eat fish eggs. God provides food for all fish and living water creatures.

Language Arts: The following action rhyme may be done with your students. Add appropriate actions.

LITTLE FISH

Little fish goes out to play
He wiggles his fins
Then swims away
He swims and swims in the water bright
He opens his mouth and takes a bite.
MMMMM! Tastes good!

Little fish lays some eggs
And then she swims around and plays
The little eggs hatch
There's tiny fish around
SWISHHH! They go by without a sound.

Phonics: Review the initial sound of Dd. Review the initial sounds of Aa-Cc. Review letter recognition Aa-Zz.

Do the Lesson 98 Phonics worksheet. The Sound of Dd. Review the letter sound with the picture and words on the worksheet. Ask the students for other words that begin with the same sound. Give them specific instructions for how the letter should be traced. Allow time for tracing the letters and observe their progress. If you have the students do one row at a time, the worksheet can be carried over to various parts of the day or another day.

Reading: Blend two parts of a compound word or two syllables. Represent "in written form," following an actual experience: directions for completing a recipe or craft, scientific observations of experiments, events.

Writing: The students should write their first name freehand without using their Name Plates.

Writing Skill Builders: Keep these objectives in mind as you direct the class. Incorporate writing strokes wave, X, star, and zigzag line.

Memory Verse: Review Psalm 48:1. Continue to practice with the words cards.

Math: Review 2 + 1 = 3. Draw a strip of 10 squares on the board. Under the strip write 2 + 1 =. Have a student come up and color the first two squares, have another student come and color the next square using a different color. Say, "two plus one equals how many squares?" Point to the squares as you say this. Have a student give the answer to the addition problem and have another student write 3 after the = sign if they can. Repeat for 1 + 1 = 2 so that all students have a part in at least one problem.

Do the Lesson 98a Math worksheet. Count the number of objects in the box with the number 8. Trace the number 8 following the proper strokes. Read the time on each clock. Have the students trace the numbers for the time.

Do the Lesson 98b Math worksheet. Count the dots in the tiles and trace the numbers to do the addition problems.

Shapes: Review the triangle, circle, rectangle, square, star, heart, and oval shapes. Put shapes cut from cardboard, carpet, foam, or cloth into a touchy, feely box. See if the students can identify the shape only by touching it and not seeing it.

Do the Lesson 98 Shapes worksheet. Name each of the shapes. Color all of the rectangles brown and the other shapes any color that you wish.

Story Time: Read a story or stories of your choice.

Music: Review "Peter, James, and John In A Sailboat."

Multimedia Resources: This week, listen and sing along to selections from "Music Machine: The Majesty Of God" CD.

Arts & Crafts: Make an ocean mural. Using the patterns from all of our Resource pages with sea creatures, place them as directed below on a piece of blue construction paper with brown around the edges to indicate shoreline. Cover the blue paper with plastic wrap to indicate the water.

> Clam: Place by the seashore.
> Oyster: Place by the clam on a "rock" made from paper.
> Snail: Place by the clam and oyster on the "rock."
> Tuna: Place out in the "water."
> Shark: Place out in the "water."
> Sea star: Place on "rock."
> Seahorse: Place with its tail wrapped around a piece of paper cut to look like seaweed.

Physical Education: Continue singing and acting to "Bullfrogs and Butterflies."

NOTES:

Activities in this Lesson: Bible Lesson, Science, Language Arts, Language Arts/Reading, Phonics, Reading, Writing, Memory Verse/Music, Math, Story Time, Shapes, Arts & Crafts, Physical Education

Bible Reference: Genesis 1:20a, 1:21a, Job 40:15–24, and Job chapter 41.

Bible Concept to Present: There are sea creatures that we don't even know about yet. God still has some surprises for us.

Bible Lesson: Continue teaching about sea creatures. Talk today about the most unusual and largest creatures. There is actually a science that studies unusual sea creatures. "In our vast oceans, there are still possibly many creatures yet to be discovered. Often, unknown sea creatures are labeled 'sea monsters' and 'sea serpents' when there may actually be a plausible, explanation for what they are. Cryptozoology, the study of animals which do not exist according to science, attempts to make sense of some of these legendary sea creatures."*

When God made the sea creatures on Day 5, he also made the huge "dinosaurs" of the sea, like the ple- siosaur (**plee**-see-uh-sawr) and the mosasaur (**moh**-suh-sawr). The Bible talks about a huge sea creature in the book of Job. It is called the Leviathan (Job 41).

There are many stories and legends about unusual sea creatures. There are lots of deep, deep areas of the ocean, where man has never been. In the past few years, huge jellyfish have washed up on several beaches. A jellyfish has no brain, head, heart, or ears. Jellyfish float through the water, looking like open umbrellas. Blue whales can weigh as much as 150 tons. Giant squids have been reported by sailors, said to be 60 feet or more in length. Many lakes in the world have been reported to have sea creatures that we don't understand.

Science: *Bring a can of sardines (in water, not oil) to the classroom.* Give each student a sardine on a small plate and a plastic knife. Say, Many people like to eat sardines. These are little fish that have been cooked in salt water. You may cut them up to look at their body parts. You may even taste them if you want to. What do you notice about their smell? Most fish have a very strong smell when they are out of the water for a time. If you have been to an ocean wharf where fishing boats are kept, you have noticed the strong smell of fish. An interesting thing about fish is that fish eat other fish. Most animals don't do this. Tiny fish eat fish eggs. Small fish eat tiny fish. Large fish eat small fish, and very huge fish eat the large fish.

Language Arts: Continue learning "Little Fish" from Lesson 99.

Language Arts/Reading: *Get the book One Fish, Two Fish, Red Fish, Blue Fish by Dr. Seuss from the library. Copy Lesson 93 Resource page on several sheets of blue and red cardstock. Cut out each fish. Hot glue a piece of magnetic strip on the back of each fish. (If your students are old enough, they can cut out the fish themselves.)* Read the story. Then let the students go fishing with their magnet fish- ing poles from Lesson 93. Call out "Red Fish" and let them try to "hook" a red fish. Then call out "Blue Fish."

Phonics: Review the initial sound of Dd. Review the initial sounds of Aa-Cc. Review letter recognition Aa-Zz.

Have the students brainstorm words that begin or include the letter Dd. Write these words on the board. Model the correct letter formation as you write the letters on the board. The students should practice forming the letter Dd on a blank sheet of paper. Students who are ready can practice copying complete words from the board.

Do the Lesson 99a Phonics worksheet. The Sound of Dd. Review the letter sound with the picture and words on the worksheet. Ask the students for other words that begin with the same sound. Trace the letters and say the sound of Dd. Observe the students as they trace the letters and help them with the letter strokes. If you have the students do one row at a time, the worksheet can be carried over to various parts of the day or another day.

Do the Lesson 99b Phonics worksheet. Find the path through the maze that connects the letters of the alphabet in order.

Reading: Blend two parts of a compound word or two syllables. Represent "in written form," following an actual experience: directions for completing a recipe or craft, scientific observations of experiments, events.

Writing: The students should write their first name freehand without using their Name Plates.

Writing Skill Builders: Keep these objectives in mind as you direct the class. Incorporate writing strokes wave, X, star, and zigzag line.

Memory Verse/Music: Review Psalm 48:1. This is a wonderful verse for students to memorize. Let them shout the words "Worthy" or "Greatly" and "Praised!" Turn on some music and dance and sing to the Lord, praising Him by voicing the verse.

Multimedia Resources: This week, listen and sing along to selections from "Music Machine: The Majesty Of God" CD.

Math: Review 2 + 1 = 3. Have the students count off steps to practice addition. If they start from a wall or a line they can step toe-to-toe two steps and then step one more. Have them place a bean bag or some marker where their toe ends up. Have them back up to the wall or line and step forward again counting, "one, two, three," until their toe is again at the bean bag. Have them say, "two steps plus one step equals three steps." Do the same for 1 + 1 = 2.

Do the Lesson 99a Math worksheet. Count each color of blocks in the strip and say the addition problem and count all of the blocks to get the answer. (Ex. "1, 2, two red blocks plus 1 blue block equals, 1, 2, 3 blocks altogether.") Trace the correct number.

Do the Lesson 99b Math worksheet. Read the time on each clock. Have the students trace the numbers for the time.

Shapes: Review the triangle, circle, rectangle, square, star, heart, and oval shapes.

Do the Lesson 99 Shapes worksheet. Cut out the shapes and glue them to decorate the hot air balloon.

Story Time: Read a story or stories of your choice.

Arts & Crafts: *Buy little craft boxes made of brown cardboard for each student. Buy a package of little shells.* Give each student a box, some shells, and some tacky glue. Let the students glue the little shells to the tops of their boxes. They can arrange them in patterns if they choose. Let dry. Finish tomorrow.

Continue working on the ocean mural. Be sure to put the ocean creatures in the correct places.

Physical Education: Rainbow Trout. Divide your students into at least four families of trout. Assign each family a color; blue trout, green trout, red trout, etc. Each student will need a base that is in their color. Spread the bases out in an area with a boundary. Within the boundary is the water where the trout can live, outside the boundary is the sand where the trout cannot live. Put a hoop by the boundary on the sand. This is the fisherman's (teacher's) bucket. The activity starts with the students standing on their home bases. When you say GO the trout should swim around in the water and explore their space. After they have been swimming for awhile call out the word "FISHERMAN" and count "5, 4, 3, 2, 1." When the word FISHERMAN is called the students should run back to their home base for protection from the fisherman. Play the game again but this time the fisherman (teacher) should go out and catch one of the fish and put them in the bucket when the word FISHERMAN is called out and the countdown begins. Find out what color trout has been caught in the bucket. Find out who else is in that trout's family. The next time you say "GO" the trout family can rescue trout in the bucket by tagging them. Repeat the game making certain that a fish is caught from each family so that all of the families have the experience of rescuing a caught fish. The students should be imitating fish by wiggling their fins and tails while they explore the water. They should be moving in all of the available space, without bumping into one another, and should be happy to help rescue each other.

NOTES:
* http://www.floridasmart.com/subjects/ocean/animals_ocean_crypto.htm

Activities in this Lesson: Bible Lesson, Social Studies, Science, Language Arts/Reading, Phonics, Reading, Writing, Memory Verse, Math, Story Time, Shapes, Music, Arts & Crafts, Outdoor Activity, Health & Safety

Bible Reference: Genesis 1:20a and 1:21a.

Bible Concept to Present: God knew the fish would need water, air, plants, and the sun to warm the water. He made all those things before He made fish. God also intends for us to care for the fish.

Bible Lesson: When God made air, water, plants, and the sun, He knew that the fish would need all of those to live. The fish live in water, but need the air in the water to breathe. Fish need the plants in the water to eat and to keep them healthy. Fish need the warm sunshine to warm the waters so they don't freeze. God knew the fish would need all of these, so He made all of these previous to making the fish. At the beginning of creation, all fish ate plants. No fish ate other fish.

God has given us a very special gift in fish. Fish need clean water to live in. God gave us the fish, and we need to care for the fish. We need to be sure we don't put trash in the water. When people don't keep the oceans and rivers and lakes clean, fish die. We need to be certain we help to take care of what God has given us.

Social Studies: Fish give us many things. But if we don't take care of our bodies of water the fish will die. People who help to care for our water are called *ecologists*. Ecologists study the water in the oceans and lakes and make sure it is clean. They tell us we must not put our waste paper or trash in the water. We must throw our trash away in the trash barrels where it will not hurt the fish.

Science: Some fish are not safe for us to eat any more because they have eaten our trash. If we were to eat these kinds of fish, we would get very sick ourselves. People need to be careful of what kind of fish they eat. They also need to be careful as to what they do with their garbage. There are many laws now about what people can put into rivers and lakes. Large factories have to be very careful about their trash, because they have a lot of it. Factories and families have to be careful about what they pour down their drains. Where do you think the water goes when it goes down the drain into the sink? It is treated and eventually goes back into the river or lake water. So if someone puts oil-based paints or gasoline down the drain, eventually a fish in the lake can drink it. We need to protect our fish and be good stewards of what God has given us.

Language Arts/Reading: Review the book *One Fish, Two Fish, Red Fish, Blue Fish* by Dr. Seuss. Let the students go fishing with their magnet fishing poles again. Call out "Red Fish" and let them try to "hook" a red fish. Then call out "Blue Fish."

Phonics: Blend the sounds Aa-Dd. (ad, add, bad, cad, dad, bad, dab) Review the initial sound of Dd. Review the initial sounds of Aa-Cc. Review letter recognition Aa-Zz.

Continue to show the students that letter sounds can combine to make words. Use only the sounds covered so far to make the words. Begin with *ad*. Say the sound of *a* then the sound of *d*, then combine the two to say *ad*. Next say the *b* sound and add to the *ad* sound to say the word *bad*. Repeat by pointing to the *ad* and saying the sound, then point to *c* and say the sound *c* and add it to the *ad* to say the word *cad*.

As discussed previously, combine sounds to form words by following this procedure. Point under each letter and sound it out slowly – [b], then [a], then [d] – to make sure the students recognize each individual letter and know the sound. Then go back, point to each letter and read the sounds a little faster, giving each letter a longer sound than is normal, bbb-aaa-ddd. Finally, read the word without pausing between the sounds with yet a shorter sound for each letter. This should be quite close to the way the word should be read. Move your finger or pointer faster under the letters each time as you say the sounds faster.

To help with sounding out the individual letters write the words out twice as we have illustrated below. Words can be sorted into categories with common beginnings and endings to help illustrate the sounding out process. The word lists can be written on a series of flip charts for review and reinforcement as new letter sounds are added. New words can be added to categories as they are introduced.

<u>b</u>	<u>a</u>		<u>ba</u>		<u>a</u>	<u>b</u>	<u>ab</u>		<u>a</u>	<u>d</u>	<u>ad</u>
b	a		baa		a	b	ab		a	d	ad
B	a	b	Bab	B	a	b	Bab		a	d	add
				c	a	b	cab	b	a	d	bad
				d	a	b	dab	c	a	d	cad
								d	a	d	dad

Some of the words formed in these activities may not be common or real words. They are included because they illustrate blending concepts that may be needed for other words.

Do the Lesson 100 Phonics worksheet. The Sound of Dd. Review the letter sound with the picture and words on the worksheet. Ask the students for other words that begin with the same sound. Trace the letters and say the sound of Dd. Observe the students as they trace the letters and help them with the letter strokes. If you have the students do one row at a time, the worksheet can be carried over to various parts of the day or another day.

Reading: Blend two parts of a compound word or two syllables. Represent "in written form," following an actual experience: directions for completing a recipe or craft, scientific observations of experiments, events.

Writing: The students should write their first name freehand without using their Name Plates.

Writing Skill Builders: Keep these objectives in mind as you direct the class. Incorporate writing strokes wave, X, star, and zigzag line.

Memory Verse: Finish Psalm 48:1 today. Let the students recite and encourage them to do it enthusiastically.

Math: Review 2 + 1 = 3. Give each student 10 pennies to count 1-10. Have the students add pennies to practice the addition facts: 1 + 1 = 2, 2 + 1 = 3.

Do the Lesson 100a Math worksheet. Count the number of objects in the box with the number 9. Trace the number 9 following the proper strokes. Count the objects in each box at the bottom of the page. Color the set that shows 9.

Do the Lesson 100b Math worksheet, Addition with pennies. Count the first group of pennies in the row and say "plus one penny," then count all of the pennies to get the answer. Trace the correct number.

Shapes: Review the triangle, circle, rectangle, square, star, heart, and oval shapes. Get 7 boxes and draw one of the shapes on each of the boxes. Have the students sort and classify shapes cut from construction paper or toy shapes into the correct box.

Story Time: Read a story or stories of your student's choice or ones they have brought from home.

Music: Review "Peter, James, and John In A Sailboat."

Multimedia Resources: This week, listen and sing along to selections from "Music Machine: The Majesty Of God" CD.

Arts & Crafts: Give each student a small cup of clear craft varnish and a small brush. Let them paint their shell box tops with varnish. Explain that they can take their shell boxes home next week, when they are dry.

Outdoor Activity: Take a nature walk. Emphasize to the students that should we fail to pick up our trash, we are polluting our environment. This means that our world will get so that we cannot live easily here anymore. We need to keep our land as clean as we need to keep our water. Animals and fish and plants live on our earth too. We must not hurt them in any way. As you take your walk, bring along a big plastic bag for cleanup purposes. Pick up all the trash you see.

Health & Safety: Bring some cod liver oil to class. Let the students smell it. The brave ones can put some on their finger and taste it. Say, There are many fish products that provide health benefits. One old fashioned product is Cod Liver Oil. Cod liver oil is taken from the codfish. Codfish is a fish 2 or 3 feet in length, having a gray back with yellowish spots and a white abdomen. Though not used much anymore, years ago cod liver oil was a household medical cabinet standby. It aids in good nutrition. It was given in the past during the winter months to decrease the need for antibiotics.

NOTES:

Lesson 101

Week 21: Day 1

Activities in this Lesson: Bible Lesson, Arts & Crafts, Social Studies/Science/Outdoor Activity, Language Arts, Phonics, Reading, Writing, Memory Verse, Math, Story Time, Music, Physical Education

Bible Reference: Genesis 1:20-23.

Bible Concept to Present: On the fifth day of Creation, God made flying creatures.

Bible Lesson: With your students, review the days of Creation. Use the Days of Creation Numbers. Ask them to tell you what things were created on each day.

Say, You have done a very good job in telling me what God has created. We know that God made the fish and water creatures on the fifth day of Creation, but He also made something else. Can you guess what it is? Well, let me help you. Let's play a guessing game. The things that God created on day five have feet. (Let the students guess each time.) They have a mouth. They have a special mouth. Their mouth is hard. They wear a pretty coat all the time. Their coat is made of feathers. Continue on until students can guess what God made on the fifth day. You are so right. I am proud of the way you used your mind to decide what God had created.

On the fifth day of Creation, God made all the fish. He also made the flying creatures, including birds, bats, and the "dinosaurs" of the sky, such as pterosaurs (**ter**-uh-sawrs). God filled the heavens with birds. He put birds all over the world. He made some birds to be big and some to be small. He made some to be beautiful colors, and some to be plain. He made each bird very special. He also made birds to lay eggs, so there could be more birds. God placed the birds everywhere. God blessed us very much when He gave us birds.

Multimedia Resources: Listen to the songs "My Favorite Things," "I Know Somebody Who Knows," and "Jesus Gave Me Wings" from the "Bullfrogs and Butterflies: God is Great" CD.

Arts & Crafts: *Bring toilet paper rolls, enough for each student to have two. Also bring in masking tape or duct tape.* Let the students tape their rolls together, making "binoculars." They may color them with poster pens. Or you might have them cover the rolls with black construction paper before taping them together. Let the students use their binoculars for the Social Studies/Science lesson.

Social Studies/Science/Outdoor Activity: Birds are all around us. For Social Studies and Science we suggest you take a walk outdoors to a place where you can watch birds. Let student use their binoculars. Be very still. Comment on the birds you see. Name them if you can and emphasize that birds live everywhere. God placed birds where it is very, very hot. He placed birds where it is very, very cold. God made each bird special for the place He wanted it to live. There is a chapter on Birds in *First Book of Nature* by Usborne.

Language Arts: Different birds make different sounds. Some birds have a high pitched tweet - others make a low sound. Some birds easily learn to talk and some never do. Each bird's song glorifies God. God made the birds to be able to communicate with each other and to praise Him. As you go on your

"Bird Watch Walk," listen to the sounds of birds. Imitate them. Can you and your students identify a bird by its sound alone, without seeing it?

Read the following poem.

The Little Bird

The little bird up in the tree
Sings a song for you and me
He sings all day long
From early dawn,
And ends with an evening song.
I'd like to ask him what he says
When he raises his voice to sing.
I think I know
God's Word tells me so
He's singing praises to the KING.

Multimedia Resources: Listen to the song "The Whistle Song" from "The Music Machine, The Fruit of the Spirit" CD.

Phonics: Teach the initial short sound of Ee. Review the initial sounds of Aa-Dd. Review letter recognition Aa-Zz.

Write several initial short Ee words on the board: elect, elephant, elk, end, enter, etc. Underline the initial letter Ee and say the words. Ask the students for other words that start with the same sound.

Continue to use the "A Was an Apple Pie" poem to review the letters of the alphabet and initial sounds.

Reading: Given a sound and two words, identify the word that begins with the sound. Assemble a simple object or craft following illustrated directions.

Multimedia Resources: Review "Rev-Up for Reading" from the "Rev-Up for Learning" DVD to drill letter recognition and sound. The students should say each letter sound along with the presentation.

Writing: Write one's first name.

Multimedia Resources: Review "Rev-Up for Writing" from the "Rev-Up for Learning" DVD to review the writing of upper- and lowercase letters.

Memory Verse: Matthew 6:26a.

Look at the birds of the air; they do not sow or reap or store away in barns, and yet your heavenly Father feeds them. Matthew 6:26a NIV

Behold the fowls of the air: for they sow not, neither do they reap, nor gather into barns; yet your heavenly Father feedeth them. Matthew 6:26a KJV

Have available four clothespins per student. Make a "clothesline" across one wall with string. Give students their Lesson 101 Memory Verse worksheet. Let them cut out the pretty birds. Glue clothespins on the base of each bird. When dry, use the pins to place birds all along the clothesline. Say the verse several times as you look at the clothesline. Let the students take home Memory Verse Card 16. They will have two weeks to work on this verse.

Math: Teach 3 + 1 = 4. Review the plus (+) sign. Remind the students that it means addition. Addition is putting things together. Review the equal (=) sign. Remind the students that it means equals. When things are put together, addition, it makes more. Have four students come to the front, put three together, a plus sign and the fourth student. Say, "Jane, Sam and Bill are three students and Dick is one student. If we add them together what does that equal?" Have four more students come to the front. Hold the equal sign after Jane, Sam, Bill and Dick and have the four new students stand in a group after the equal sign. Have the students count the number in the new group. Say "three plus one equals, four" and count the four students in the new group. Do this with several groups of students.

$$\text{👥👥👥} + \text{👤} = \text{👥👥👥👤}$$

Do the Lesson 101 Math worksheet. Count the number of objects in the box with the number 0. Trace the number 0 following the proper strokes. Count the objects in each box at the bottom of the page. Circle the number that tells how many are in each set.

Multimedia Resources: View "Rev-Up for Arithmetic" from the "Rev-Up for Learning" DVD to practice number recognition, counting and addition 1-20.

Shapes: Give each student a handful of different shapes. Have them identify each shape and then sort the shapes by color, shape, and size. Can they make a bird from the shapes that you have given to them?

Story Time: Read a story or stories of your choice.

Music: Teach the students "The Birds Upon The Treetop" song from the "Horizons Preschool Music" CD.

Multimedia Resources: This week, listen and sing along to selections from "Bullfrogs and Butterflies: God is My Friend" CD.

Physical Education: Do the "Bird Walk." Place activity-oriented music on the recording device, squat down and walk like a duck. Quack as you do. Imitate other birds' walking, such as the Ostrich. Now, place gliding, serene music on the player and pretend to fly. How would a bird feel while in flight? In your imitation, do not forget to "dive" for food.

Activities in this Lesson: Bible Lesson, Science, Language Arts, Phonics, Reading, Writing, Memory Verse, Math, Shapes, Story Time, Music, Arts & Crafts, Health & Safety, Physical Education

Bible Reference: Genesis 1:20-23.

Bible Concept to Present: God made fish and birds on the same day. Fish and birds are animals, but they are very different.

Bible Lesson: Review yesterday's lesson. On the fifth day, God filled the air and the waters with thousands of kinds of fish and birds. Talk about the features that make birds different from fish.

Science: Show students the picture of the fish, Lesson 102a Resource page, and the birds, Lesson 102b Resource page. Talk about breathing, moving, eating, and skin coverings. This would be a good day to bring in a bird if you or a friend have one at home.

Language Arts: There are many wonderfully illustrated books on birds. *Bring one from the library* and share it with the class. Emphasize how many different kinds of birds there are. Go to the board and write the names of birds that live in your area. Write their names clearly in big letters. Find their pictures in the book.

Phonics: Review the initial short sound of Ee. Review the initial sounds of Aa-Dd. Review letter recognition Aa-Zz.

Do the Lesson 102 Phonics worksheet. The Short Sound of Ee. Review the letter sound with the picture and words on the worksheet. Ask the students for other words that begin with the same sound. Discuss the position of the letters on the guidelines. Give them specific instructions for how the letter should be traced. Trace the letters and say the short sound of Ee. Observe the students as they trace the letters and help them with the letter strokes. If you have the students do one row at a time, the worksheet can be carried over to various parts of the day or another day.

Reading: Given a sound and two words, identify the word that begins with the sound. Assemble a simple object or craft following illustrated directions.

Writing: Write one's first name.

Memory Verse: Review Matthew 6:26a. Today, print the memory verse on rectangular strips of paper, several words to a strip. Clip the verse to the bottom side of the clothesline, with the birds arranged on top. Review the verse. You might learn the verse in three sections.

ONE	Look at the birds of the air;
TWO	they do not sow or reap or store away in barns,
THREE	and yet your Heavenly Father feeds them. Matthew 6:26

Math: Review 3 + 1 = 4. Give the students the dog bones that they cut out previously and a bowl to put them in. Have them place 3 bones in the bowl while saying "three plus one" and have them place another bone in the bowl, "equals" and have them count "one, two, three, four bones in the bowl." Do this several times. Reverse the order and also practice previous addition facts.

Do the Lesson 102 Math worksheet. As they count the images have them say the addition problems. Trace the numbers.

Shapes: Review the triangle, circle, rectangle, square, star, heart, and oval shapes. Talk about simple musical instruments and what shape they come in. cymbals – circle, triangles – triangle, sand blocks – rectangle, wooden blocks – square, maracas – oval, bells – diamond (you know, "diamond ring") If you have access to these instruments the students can play shape music. Pass out the instruments to the class. Each person should have something. Draw the shapes on the board or hold up shape flashcards. As you point to or hold up a shape the students with those instruments can play them until you move to different shape.

Story Time: Read a story or stories of your choice.

Music: Review "The Birds Upon The Treetop."

Multimedia Resources: This week, listen and sing along to selections from "Bullfrogs and Butterflies: God is My Friend" CD.

Arts & Crafts: Go to the Creation Mural and review all of the things that the students have added to each day. Ask, What do we need to add today? Let the students draw and cut out birds to add to the mural. OR if you didn't use the Lesson 97 Arts & Crafts worksheet for the memory verse project, use them for the mural.

Give the students playdough. Let them create their own bird.

Health & Safety: There are some diseases that are spread by birds. Some birds are called "pest birds" because they become irritating to people. Pigeons, starlings, crows, house sparrows, and sea gulls can become nuisance birds. Birds are also carriers of the West Nile Virus, transmitted by mosquito to people. NEVER touch a dead bird. We don't know how or why the bird died. If you accidentally touch a dead bird, wash your hands right away.

Physical Education: Balloon Catch. Balloons, like feathers, are light so that they can easily fly. Give each student a balloon. They will practice throwing the balloon with both hands straight up in the air and then catch it with both hands when in comes down. Have them start by not throwing the balloons too high into the air.

If you have more than three students, let them put themselves in a V formation and "fly." Talk about V formations and the fact that the lead bird leads awhile, and then trades his position to another bird.

Take a walk, and as you are walking, look for the feather of a bird. You will want one feather for each child you are teaching. *Bring gloves to wear when picking up feathers.* Discuss the coloring of the feathers, the weight and the shape. Save and clean the feathers for Language Arts in Lesson 103. (Do not let the students handle the feathers without first cleaning the feathers with an approved solution.) Caution: Because of recent diseases associated with birds it might be better to purchase some feathers at a craft supply store.

NOTES:

Lesson 103

Week 21: Day 3

Activities in this Lesson: Bible Lesson, Social Studies, Science, Language Arts/Arts & Crafts, Phonics, Reading, Writing, Memory Verse, Math, Shapes, Story Time, Music, Physical Education

Bible Reference: Genesis 1:20-23.

Bible Concept to Present: When God made the birds, He made them to live in special places.

Bible Lesson: When God made the birds on the fifth day of Creation, He made them to live on land and He made them to live in special homes. Today, birds live in many places. Some birds only live where it is very hot. Some birds only live where it is very cold. Some birds live where it is warm in the summer, and when their normal habitat gets cold for winter, the birds fly to a warmer place. We call this migration. Many birds migrate. A Mommy bird will migrate from the northern United States to a southern state, and have a baby there. God made that baby so special that, the next year, that baby will go back to the same place where it was born. Nobody tells the baby where to go, it just knows. God has placed within birds instinct, a way to know where to migrate. Instinct is when an animal knows what to do without being taught. They don't have to go to school to learn these things.

Social Studies: Birds live all over the world. A special bird that lives in Canada (show the students on a globe) is the Canada goose (show a picture if you can locate one). The Canada geese begin to fly from Canada to the southern part of the United States every fall. As they fly, they form a V formation. The geese take turns being the leader of the flock as they fly. They fly all day and sometimes stop to rest and eat. They stop to rest at night too. The geese make a special "honk" sound as they fly. Man uses the eggs from geese to eat and their feathers to make down clothes and pillows.

Science: Birds fly through the air to get from one place to another. God gave the birds a very special helper in flying. When God made the bird's feathers, He made them so they were very light. The inside of a feather is hollow. That means it does not have anything in it. Discuss the diagram below with students. Stress that God planned the feather to be a very special help to the bird.

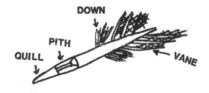

Language Arts/Arts & Crafts: Give each student a feather, either one cleaned from Lesson 102 or one purchased from a craft store. Give the students a weakened mixture of dark paint, and let them "write" numbers or words with the "pen." Explain that this type of pen is called a quill. These kinds of pens were used very often in the days of George Washington, when our country was new. If you know calligraphy, show your students this style of writing. Although they will not be able to imitate it completely, they can have fun trying. In the early 1900s penmanship was highly prized. My grandmother used to tell how the children would get their hands slapped with the ruler if they failed to do a good job. Her expert handwriting remained with her all her life. Stress quality with students. They should be taught to do the best they can do at all times.

Teacher's Guide, Part 2   81

Phonics: Review the initial short sound of Ee. Review the initial sounds of Aa-Dd. Review letter recognition Aa-Zz.

Do the Lesson 103 Phonics worksheet. The Short Sound of Ee. Review the letter sound with the picture and words on the worksheet. Ask the students for other words that begin with the same sound. Give them specific instructions for how the letter should be traced. Allow time for tracing the letters and observe their progress. If you have the students do one row at a time, the worksheet can be carried over to various parts of the day or another day.

Reading: Given a sound and two words, identify the word that begins with the sound. Assemble a simple object or craft following illustrated directions.

Writing: Write one's first name.

Memory Verse: Review Matthew 6:26a. Learn another part of the verse today.

Math: Review 3 + 1 = 4. Review 3 + 1 = 4 by writing the problem on the board. Draw objects over the numbers with + sign between them. Write the = sign and then draw an excess of objects over the answer. Have a student come to the board and circle the correct number of objects to make the addition problem correct. Erase the extra objects and orally say the problem with the class. Repeat several times drawing simple objects such as dots or various shapes. Review previous addition problems if the students need the practice.

Do the Lesson 103a Math worksheet. Count the items and have them say the addition problems. Trace the numbers.

Do the Lesson 103b Math worksheet. Count the number of objects in the box with the number 10. Trace the number 10 following the proper strokes. Count the number of diamonds in each tile. Circle the tile that has 10.

Shapes: Teach the diamond shape. Give each student 2 triangle shapes of the same size. Show them how to put them together to make a diamond shape.

Do the Lesson 103a Shapes worksheet. Have the students trace the diamond.

Do the Lesson 103b Shapes worksheet. Color the diamond shapes, cut them out and paste them on the picture.

Story Time: Read a story or stories of your choice.

Music: Review "The Birds Upon The Treetop."

Multimedia Resources: This week, listen and sing along to selections from "Bullfrogs and Butterflies: God is My Friend" CD.

Physical Education: If you have more than three students, let them put themselves in a V formation and "fly." Talk about V formations and the fact that the lead bird leads awhile, and then trades his position to another bird.

NOTES:

Activities in this Lesson: Bible Lesson, Science, Social Studies, Language Arts, Phonics, Reading, Writing, Memory Verse, Math, Shapes, Story Time, Music, Arts & Crafts, Outdoor Activity, Physical Education, Homework

Bible Reference: Genesis 1:20-23.

Bible Concept to Present: God gave the birds an instinct to know about building their nests.

Bible Lesson: God made birds very smart. He gave them an instinct to know about building their own homes. Birds know how to build bird nests without anyone telling them. Only God could have done that. Birds build nests in trees, but they also build them on building ledges and cliffs.

Science: *It is important that you find an old bird nest and bring it to class.* Wear plastic gloves. With students observing, pull the nest apart, one piece at a time. Arrange the pieces of twigs and string so that you can count them later. Talk about each piece of the nest requiring a trip for the mother or father bird. How many trips did they have to make to build the nest?

Social Studies: Birds are unique in that they can fly. Man has been watching birds since Creation, wondering how to fly like they do. Hundreds of years ago, man tried to attach wings to his arms so that he could fly. But our arms can't move fast enough. Hummingbird wings can beat 100 times a minute, and they can fly 30 miles per hour. In December 2003, we celebrated the 100 year anniversary of the Wright Brothers flight. Wilbur and Orville learned how to use the air to fly, not wings. How many kinds of flying vehicles are there now? Talk about planes, satellites, rockets, balloons, shuttles, and blimps. Let the students talk about any flying they have done.

Language Arts: *Prepare ahead - Get the book Feathers for Lunch, by Lois Elhert, from the library. Using adding machine tape, measure out each bird's wingspan from the list below. Write the name of the bird on each piece of tape.* After reading the book, take out the tape measurements you have prepared ahead of time. Spread them on the floor, taping the ends so they will lie flat. Let the students lie on the floor and compare their "arm span" with the bird's wingspan. Take some time to look at the many birds in the book. Point out birds familiar to your location.

Royal Albatross	11 feet 6 inches	Magpie	3 feet
Andean Condor	10 feet	Crow	17 inches
Trumpeter Swan	9 feet	Robin	15 inches

Phonics: Review the initial short sound of Ee. Review the initial sounds of Aa-Dd. Review letter recognition Aa-Zz.

Have the students brainstorm words that begin or include the letter Ee. Write these words on the board. Model the correct letter formation as you write the letters on the board. The students should practice forming the letter Ee on a blank sheet of paper. Students who are ready can practice copying complete words from the board.

Do the Lesson 104a Phonics worksheet. The Short Sound of Ee. Review the letter sound with the picture and words on the worksheet. Ask the students for other words that begin with the same sound. Trace the letters and say the short sound of Ee. Observe the students as they trace the letters and help them with the letter strokes. If you have the students do one row at a time, the worksheet can be carried over to various parts of the day or another day.

Do the Lesson 104b Phonics worksheet. Trace the diamonds and write the word diamond, stressing the beginning Dd sound.

Reading: Given a sound and two words, identify the word that begins with the sound. Assemble a simple object or craft following illustrated directions.

Writing: Write one's first name.

Memory Verse: Review Matthew 6:26a. Learn another part to the verse today.

Math: Review 3 + 1 = 4. Give each of the students 10 counters. Have them count the objects to make sure that they have 10 objects. Have them make the addition problem with the counters. Have them point to the counters and say the addition problem, drawing the plus and equal sign with their finger between the counters as they say the words. Review previous problems if the students need the practice.

Do the Lesson 104a Math worksheet. Review counting 1-12.

Do the Lesson 104b Math worksheet. As they trace the numbers have them say the addition problems.

Shapes: Review the diamond shape. Have the students glue 4 craft sticks onto paper to make a kite. Glue on a piece of yarn for a string. They can decorate the kite as desired.

Story Time: Read a story or stories of your choice.

Music: Review "The Birds Upon The Treetop."

Multimedia Resources: This week, listen and sing along to selections from "Bullfrogs and Butterflies: God is My Friend" CD.

Arts & Crafts: Give each student long pieces of yarn, beige, gold, yellow, and brown, and some scissors. Let the students glue the yarn on construction paper, making their own bird nests. This is cutting and gluing practice.

Outdoor Activity: Give each student a small piece of yarn. Take a walk outside. Lay the yarn on fence posts or ledges in an area where there are a lot of trees. Birds will find these pieces of yarn and use them in their nests. You might go a distance away from the yarn and watch awhile to see if it is taken by a bird.

Physical Education: Review the Balloon Catch activity. Balloons, like feathers, are light so that they can easily fly. Give each student a balloon. They will practice throwing the balloon with both hands straight up in the air and then catch it with both hands when it comes down. Have them start by not throwing the balloons too high into the air.

Homework: Take home Lesson 104 Homework worksheet today, the Birdwatch activity. Ask the students to bring it back tomorrow.

NOTES:

Lesson 105

Week 21: Day 5

Activities in this Lesson: Bible Lesson, Social Studies, Science, Language Arts, Phonics, Reading, Writing, Memory Verse, Math, Shapes, Story Time, Music, Arts & Crafts, Creative Cooking, Physical Education

Bible Reference: Genesis 1:20-23.

Bible Concept to Present: God made the birds very special to do special things.

Bible Lesson: When God made the birds, He made them very special. Birds are the only creation of God (other than insects and bats) that flies. God made the birds with special feet, too. Some bird's feet have spurs on them to help the birds to protect themselves. Other birds have special claws to help them dig. God made the birds with beaks suited to the type of food they eat, too. Some bird's beaks are very strong and can break branches for their homes. Other bird's beaks are long, suited for gathering nectar from plants. God made the bodies of the birds to be very lightweight, so they can easily fly. God is so wise and wonderful.

Social Studies: Birds are very useful to man. They eat harmful insects; they give us meat, eggs, and feathers for our use. In America, we rarely eat anything but chicken eggs. All birds lay eggs though. Compare the size of an ostrich egg to the size of a hummingbird egg. (See illustration below.) Which egg would make the biggest breakfast? Why are the eggs so different in size?

Comparative (not actual) Sizes

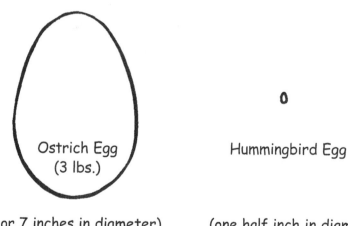

Ostrich Egg
(3 lbs.)

Hummingbird Egg

(6 or 7 inches in diameter)
equivalent to 24 chicken eggs

(one half inch in diameter)

Science: Using Lesson 105 Resource page, discuss with your student the different types of beaks and feet. Identify birds which have the characteristic discussed. An encyclopedia or bird guide on the internet will help you with the identification process.

Language Arts: Use a set of alphabet flashcards for these activities. If your student already knows the alphabet, ask him to place the cards in order. You may permit the student to spell his name or other words he can sound out. Allow some extra time for students to play with the cards. If a student does not know the alphabet, have him spell his name from the cards, following his Name Card. You may also permit him to play with the cards, calling out what letters he does know, or following written guides. On the lower level, this is a matching game, on the upper level, it is reinforcement for knowledge gained and can inspire your students to spell.

Phonics: Blend the sounds Aa-Ee. (Ed, bed, ebb, Deb) Review the initial short sound of Ee. Review the initial sounds of Aa-Dd. Review letter recognition Aa-Zz.

Continue to show the students that letter sounds can combine to make words. Use only the sounds covered so far to make the words. Begin with *eb*. Say the sound of *e*, then the sound of *b*, then combine the two to say *eb*. Next say the *D* sound and add to the *eb* sound to say the word *Deb*. Repeat the process for the other sounds and words.

e	b	eb		e	d		ed
e	bb	ebb		E	d		Ed
D	e	b Deb	b	e	d	bed
			C	e	d	Ced

Some of the words formed in these activities may not be common or real words. They are included because they illustrate blending concepts that may be needed for other words.

Do the Lesson 105 Phonics worksheet. The Short Sound of Ee. Review the letter sound with the picture and words on the worksheet. Ask the students for other words that begin with the same sound. Trace the letters and say the short sound of Ee. Observe the students as they trace the letters and help them with the letter strokes. If you have the students do one row at a time, the worksheet can be carried over to various parts of the day or another day.

Reading: Given a sound and two words, identify the word that begins with the sound. Assemble a simple object or craft following illustrated directions.

Writing: Write one's first name.

Memory Verse: Review Matthew 6:26a. Continue to work on the memory verse. Students should be learning the second line of the verse today.

Math: Review 3 + 1 = 4.

Do the Lesson 105a Math worksheet. Count the number of objects in the box with the number 11. Trace the number 11 following the proper strokes. Count the objects in each box at the bottom of the page. Color the set that shows 11.

Do the Lesson 105b Math worksheet. Circle the correct number of objects to answer the addition problems.

Shapes: Review the diamond shape. Give each student a diamond shape cut from white construction paper. Drop a little paint in the center of each diamond and have the students fold the shape in half to make a design. More than one color of paint can be used.

Do the Lesson 105 Shapes worksheet. Count the diamonds in the picture and color them.

Story Time: Read a story or stories of your student's choice or ones they have brought from home.

Music: Review "The Birds Upon The Treetop."

Multimedia Resources: This week, listen and sing along to selections from "Bullfrogs and Butterflies: God is My Friend" CD.

Arts & Crafts: Hard boil some eggs. Give your students water base markers and let them make egg "faces" on the egg. You may add felt or cloth to dress the egg. Ask students to create a story about the "person" he has made. Students may then peel and eat the egg or take it home.

Creative Cooking: With your help, have the students make an egg dish to share. You will want this to be a simple cooking experience, with the students doing as much of the work as possible.

Physical Education: How would it feel to be an egg? Roll yourself into a ball the shape of an egg. Now pretend to be a little chick pecking its way out. Discuss with the students how the chick would feel coming out into the bright world. Would the air be cold? Would mother hen be warm? Where would you want to be if you were a chick—in the egg or under Mommy Hen's wing?

NOTES:

Activities in this Lesson: Bible Lesson, Social Studies/Science, Language Arts, Phonics, Reading, Writing, Memory Verse, Math, Shapes, Story Time, Music, Arts & Crafts, Physical Education

Bible Reference: Genesis 1:20-23.

Bible Concept to Present: When God made the birds, He made them for man to enjoy.

Bible Lesson: God made each bird very special. I am so happy God made the birds each with their own special kind of beak and special kind of feet. I am glad God made the birds to know how and where to fly to keep warm in the winter. God made each bird for us to enjoy. He made each bird to help us. We enjoy watching the birds. They are so beautiful. They fly from tree to tree. We can watch them peck for worms and drink the sweet fluid a flower makes. Birds help us in many ways. They eat insects that hurt our plants. They give us eggs to eat. They give us soft down feathers to use for pillows and clothing. Birds help us in many ways. God blessed us very much when He made the birds for us to enjoy.

Social Studies/Science: Birds are very beneficial to us. They not only provide many items we use but are enjoyable to watch. We suggest that you take your students to an area where you can watch birds today. If you have an aviary nearby, it would be beneficial to the student's education to observe the many varieties of birds. If you do not have access to an aviary, view what birds you can from the area around your classroom or house. Notice coloring, wing structure, feet, beaks, and habits. Include a review of the types of beaks and feet in this observation period.

Language Arts: Have each of the students describe something that they learned about birds from what has been taught or from what they observed on their walk. Encourage them to use complete sentences.

Phonics: Teach the initial sound of Ff. Review the initial sounds of Aa-Fe. Review letter recognition Aa-Zz.

Write several initial Ff words on the board: fad, fall, fan, far, fat, fed, fib, few, fog, full, fur, etc. Underline the initial letter Ff and say the words. Ask the students for other words that start with the same sound.

Reading: Given a sound and two words, identify the word that begins with the sound. Assemble a simple object or craft following illustrated directions.

Multimedia Resources: Review "Rev-Up for Reading" from the "Rev-Up for Learning" DVD to drill letter recognition and sound. The students should say each letter sound along with the presentation.

Writing: Write one's first name.

Multimedia Resources: Review "Rev-Up for Writing" from the "Rev-Up for Learning" DVD to review the writing of upper- and lowercase letters.

Memory Verse: Review or continue to work on Matthew 6:26. Add the next part to the memory work if students are ready.

Math: Review 3 + 1 = 4. Use the string of Counting Beads or pop beads to review 1 + 1 = 2, 2 + 1 = 3 and 3 + 1 = 4.

Do the Lesson 106a Math worksheet. Count the number of objects in the box with the number 12. Trace the number 12 following the proper strokes. Count the number of diamonds in each tile. Circle the tile that has 12.

Do the Lesson 106b Math worksheet. Count the items and say the addition problem. Trace the correct answer and say the addition problem.

Multimedia Resources: View "Rev-Up for Arithmetic" from the "Rev-Up for Learning" DVD to practice number recognition, counting and addition 1-20.

Shapes: Review the diamond shape. Have the students place silver stars on a diamond shape to make it sparkle.

Do the Lesson 106 Shapes worksheet. Trace the diamonds, count them, and color the picture.

Story Time: Read a story or stories of your choice.

Music: Review the song "The Birds Upon The Treetop." Learn the song "One Little, Two Little, Three Little Birdies." Have the students stand on a rope stretched across the floor like birds on a line. They can flap their arms and switch from one foot to the other, acting like birds as they sing the song.

One Little, Two Little, Three Little Birdies
Tune of Ten Little Indians
by Al Christopherson

One little, two little, three little birdies....
four little, five little, six little birdies...
seven little, eight little, nine little birdies....
ten little birdies on the line.

Multimedia Resources: This week, listen and sing along to selections from "The Amazing Children" CD.

Arts & Crafts: *Bring enough pine cones for each student to have one. Also have peanut butter and string or wire available.* Spread the pine cones with peanut butter and roll them in birdseed. Attach wire or string for a hanger. Place each in a zippered sandwich bag to take home. Make an extra pine cone feeder for tomorrow.

The students should hang the feeders from a tree with the seed low enough that they can observe the birds eating.

Physical Education: Throughout this week, we will be working on gross motor coordination. We suggest you spread the following activities throughout the week.
1. Lie down on a carpeted area and stretch your arms out to your side. With your arm moving up and down (as a bird flies) open and close your legs, keeping all parts of your body flat on the floor.
2. Sitting on the floor, spread your legs, moving them in and out while clapping your hands.
3. Lying on the floor on your back, stretch one leg over your body and point the toe towards the opposite wall. Do this to the count of four and then reverse legs.
4. Practice jumping in rhythm. Jump once with legs together, then hop on one foot and jump with both feet with legs together again. Vary this exercise by seeing how high the children can jump each time.
5. Practice crawling with a right/left order of the hands and knees. (When right hand is forward, the left knee is forward.)

NOTES:

Lesson 107

Activities in this Lesson: Bible Lesson, Language Arts, Phonics, Reading, Writing, Memory Verse, Math, Shapes, Story Time, Music, Creative Cooking, Outdoor Activity/Memory Verse, Physical Education, Catch Up

Bible Reference: Genesis 1:20-23.

Bible Concept to Present: When God made tropical birds He used every color available.

Bible Lesson: Continue teaching about the fifth day of Creation and birds. Tropical birds are the most beautiful birds of all. God made them in bright and gorgeous colors: bright, bright reds and greens and blues and yellows. Try to find a picture of a colorful parrot to show the students. Ask the students to tell you about places where they have seen colorful birds. Many people buy these lovely birds then realize they can't care for them. There are groups of bird lovers that rescue these birds, so that they aren't just released without a home. Tropical Bird Rescue is one group that helps save unwanted birds. If you want the class to get involved or see what they do, go to their web page.

Language Arts: Make a list on the board of bird characteristics. What makes a bird different from other animals? What makes them like other animals? Perhaps you could have them make comparisons between a bird and a dog.

Phonics: Review the initial sound of Ff. Review the initial sounds of Aa-Ee. Review letter recognition Aa-Zz.

Do the Lesson 107 Phonics worksheet. The Sound of Ff. Review the letter sound with the picture and words on the worksheet. Ask the students for other words that begin with the same sound. Discuss the position of the letters on the guidelines. Give them specific instructions for how the letter should be traced. Trace the letters and say the sound of Ff. Observe the students as they trace the letters and help them with the letter strokes. If you have the students do one row at a time, the worksheet can be carried over to various parts of the day or another day.

Reading: Given a sound and two words, identify the word that begins with the sound. Assemble a simple object or craft following illustrated directions.

Writing: Write one's first name.

Memory Verse: Review Matthew 6:26a. Continue to add parts to the verse if not all of it has been learned.

Math: Review 3 + 1 = 4.

Shapes: Review the diamond shape.

Do the Lesson 107 Shapes worksheet. Trace the shapes and draw them freehand.

Story Time: Read a story or stories of your choice.

Music: Review the song "The Birds Upon The Treetop." Review the song "One Little, Two Little, Three Little Birdies." Have the students stand on a rope stretched across the floor, like birds on a line. They can flap their arms and switch from one foot to the other acting like birds as they sing the song.

Multimedia Resources: This week, listen and sing along to selections from "The Amazing Children" CD.

Creative Cooking: Bird Nests – You'll need a large mixing bowl, a large spoon, a small spoon, aluminum foil, and a muffin tin. Cut the foil in squares big enough to cover each muffin cup. Let the students help press the foil down into each cup hole.

> Ingredients:
> 1 cup chocolate chips or white chocolate for candy making
> 1 1/2 cups Chinese noodles
> Jelly beans or M&Ms®

Melt the chocolate chips slowly in a microwave in the large bowl. Add the Chinese noodles. Let the students help stir in the noodles. Scoop a large spoonful of mixture into each muffin cup. Using the small spoon, gently press the "nest" down to form a nest. Place the jelly beans or M&Ms into the nest. Cool and lift the nest out of each cup. Peel off the foil, discuss how the nest looks, and eat the nest and eggs,

Outdoor Activity/Memory Verse: Take the extra bird seed pine cone outside. Hang it in a tree then have the students sit back quietly and watch for the birds to come. Check the yarn, is it all gone? Review the memory verse while you are watching the birds. This verse is a bit long. Students should have it almost memorized at this point. Talk about what the verse means as you watch the birds.

Physical Education: Throughout the week, we will be working on gross motor coordination. We suggest you spread the following activities throughout the week.

1. Lie down on a carpeted area and stretch your arms out to your side. With your arm moving up and down (as a bird flies) open and close your legs, keeping all parts of your body flat on the floor.
2. Sitting on the floor, spread your legs, moving them in and out while clapping your hands.
3. Lying on the floor on your back, stretch one leg over your body and point the toe towards the opposite wall. Do this to the count of four and then reverse legs.
4. Practice jumping in rhythm. Jump once with legs together, then hop on one foot and jump with both feet with legs together again. Vary this exercise by seeing how high the children can jump each time.
5. Practice crawling with a right/left order of the hands and knees. (When right hand is forward, the left knee is forward.)

Catch Up: Do any assignment that you didn't have time for earlier in the month.

NOTES:

Activities in this Lesson: Bible Lesson, Social Studies, Science, Language Arts, Phonics, Reading, Writing, Memory Verse, Math, Shapes, Story Time, Music, Physical Education

Bible Reference: Genesis 1:20-23.

Bible Concept to Present: God created a great variety of birds.

Bible Lesson: When God made the birds, He made each of them to be very different. God made tall, long-legged birds such as the flamingo. The flamingo has a beak like no other bird. It eats its food by placing its head upside down on the bottom of the pond where it lives. Flamingos have a very long neck and long legs. In fact, there is no other bird with such a long neck. Flamingos usually have some pink coloring in their feathers. Isn't it neat God made a pink bird?

God also made some birds that do not fly. The ostrich is a very big bird. God made the ostrich to be able to run very, very fast. The ostrich also has spurs on its legs to kick its enemies. The ostrich is a bird, but the ostrich does not fly. God made the ostrich with feathers to help keep it dry.

Another bird that God made is the tiny, little hummingbird. The hummingbird is a little bird with a very long beak. The hummingbird eats while it is flying backwards. It beats its wings very fast and is actually flying backwards while it is drinking the flower's sweet liquid. Hummingbirds are born with only one feather. They have long beaks, and are very, very tiny when they are born. Their nests are usually close to a good food supply and the mother birds usually only lays two eggs. The babies are black in color when they are born and after awhile they develop one big feather on their back. Later, their down comes in. Hummingbirds are the littlest bird (now living) that God made.

God made many birds. We have only talked about a few of them. I am happy God made so many birds with each different from the other.

Social Studies: On a globe point out to students where you live, and then indicate the location of the birds discussed in the Bible Lesson. Flamingos live in the Caribbean, hummingbirds live all over North and South America, and the ostrich only lives in Africa. Simply name and locate the countries where each live. You do not expect retention of this information. You are introducing concepts that will take root later.

Science: Flamingos live in a water home. They live mainly in the tropics, in shallow water that contains salt and other minerals. These waters also contain algae, the food that flamingos like so well. Algae are a type of a tiny plant that grows in water. Flamingos also eat tiny animals and shrimp. The flamingo's bill makes it so the flamingo can eat the tiny plants and animals in the water without drinking much of the water itself. The flamingo puts its head under the water and turns it upside down, scraping up the food from the bottom of the pond. Its web-like feet stir up animals from their hiding places at the bottom of the pools. All flamingos have some pink on them, but they are not born pink. They are gray when they are born. Both the mother and father care for their young. There is only one egg laid at a time, and the parents take turns sitting on the egg. Both parents can feed the chick. God made the parents to have a special fluid which is produced in the flamingos neck that helps the baby chick to grow strong. The flamingo can fly up to 35 m.p.h. and they often use the water to help them take off. Flamingos are a wonderful bird. Find a picture of a flamingo and show it to your students. Ask students to draw a flamingo.

Language Arts: Some students may have a bird in their home as a pet; others may wish that they could also have a bird for a pet. Have each student describe some of the responsibilities about having a bird as a pet. What things do you have to buy? What supplies are needed? What type of a home do they need? Who is going to care for the bird? Who cleans up the mess? How often do they need to be fed? Will neighbors complain about the noise? Do pet birds need exercise?

Phonics: Blend the sounds Aa-Ff. (fab, fad, fed, Feb.) Review the initial sound of Ff. Review the initial sounds of Aa-Ee. Review letter recognition Aa-Zz.

<u>fa</u>	<u>fe</u>
fab	Feb.
fad	fed

Do the Lesson 108 Phonics worksheet. The sound of Ff. Review the letter sound with the picture on the worksheet. Ask the students for other words that begin with the same sound. Give them specific instructions for how the letter should be traced. Allow time for tracing the letters and observe their progress. If you have the students do one row at a time, the worksheet can be carried over to various parts of the day or another day.

Reading: Given a sound and two words, identify the word that begins with the sound. Assemble a simple object or craft following illustrated directions.

Writing: Write one's first name.

Memory Verse: Continue to review Matthew 6:26a. Work on the entire verse.

Math: Review 3 + 1 = 4. Draw a strip of 10 squares on the board. Under the strip write 3 + 1 =. Have a student come up and color the first three squares, have another student come and color the next square using a different color. Say, "three plus one equals how many squares?" Point to the squares as you say this. Have a student give the answer to the addition problem and have another student write 4 after the = sign if they can. Repeat and review 1 + 1 = 2 and 2 + 1 = 3.

Do the Lesson 108a Math worksheet. Read the number. Count the dots under the number. Draw 0 objects in the counting jar. Trace the number 0 following the proper strokes. The students can color the counting jar.

Do the Lesson 108b Math worksheet. Count the dots in the tiles and trace the numbers.

Shapes: Review the diamond shape.

Do the Lesson 108 Shapes worksheet. Count the diamonds in the picture. Color the large diamonds purple and the small diamonds green. Color the rest of the picture as you wish.

Story Time: Read a story or stories of your choice.

Music: Review the song "The Birds Upon The Treetop." Review the song "One Little, Two Little, Three Little Birdies." Have the students stand on a rope stretched across the floor, like birds on a line. They can flap their arms and switch from one foot to the other acting like birds as they sing the song.

Multimedia Resources: This week, listen and sing along to selections from "The Amazing Children" CD.

Physical Education: Throughout this week, we will be working on gross motor coordination. We suggest you spread the following activities throughout the week.

1. Lie down on a carpeted area and stretch your arms out to your side. With your arm moving up and down (as a bird flies) open and close your legs, keeping all parts of your body flat on the floor.
2. Sitting on the floor, spread your legs, moving them in and out while clapping your hands.
3. Lying on the floor on your back, stretch one leg over your body and point the toe towards the opposite wall. Do this to the count of four and then reverse legs.
4. Practice jumping in rhythm. Jump once with legs together, then hop on one foot and jump with both feet with legs together again. Vary this exercise by seeing how high the children can jump each time.
5. Practice crawling with a right/left order of the hands and knees. (When right hand is forward, the left knee is forward.)

NOTES:

Activities in this Lesson: Bible Lesson, Science, Language Arts, Phonics, Reading, Writing, Memory Verse, Math, Shapes, Story Time, Music, Arts & Crafts, Health & Safety, Field Trip, Physical Education

Bible Reference: Genesis 1:20-23.

Bible Concept to Present: God is awesome! His creation includes over 9,700 species of birds.

Bible Lesson: Review yesterday's lesson. God made a huge variety of birds.

Science: What are some names of birds that God created? Write them on the board in large letters for students to see. Help students with some names so that you end up with at least twenty.

Some examples: blue jay, canary, chicken, crow, dove, duck, goose, hawk, owls, parrot, penguin, pheasant, quail, robin, sparrow, stork, swan, woodpecker. *Find a good picture of a colorful bird. Cut out a copy of the egg from Lesson 109 Resource page. Cut out the bird picture the exact size of the bird egg. Glue the bird picture on a piece of construction paper. Then cut out and glue the egg pieces onto the bird picture, using only a few small drops of glue.* When you show it to the students, open it as if the bird egg was cracking open. Add "Birds: 9,700" to the Facts Poster started in Lesson 97.

Language Arts: Read the story of Henny Penny. This story was written in 1870, a long time ago.

Henny Penny

A hen was picking at a stack of pea-straw when a pea fell on her head, and she thought the sky was falling. And she thought she would go and tell the king about it. And she went, and went, and went, and she met a cock. And he said, "Where are you going this day, Henny-Penny?" And she says, "I'm going to tell the king the sky is falling." And he says, "I'll go with you, Henny-Penny." And they went, and they went, and they went. And they met a duck. And the duck says, "Where are you going this day, Cocky-Locky, Henny-Penny?" "We're going to tell the king the sky is falling." "I'll go with you, Cocky-Locky, Henny-Penny." "Then come along, Ducky-Daddles." And they went, and they went, and they went. And they met a goose. And the goose says, "Where are you going this day, Ducky-Daddles, Cocky-Locky, Henny-Penny?" "We're going to tell the king the sky is falling." And he says, "I'll go with you, Ducky-Daddles, Cocky-Locky, Henny-Penny." "Then come along, Goosie-Poosey," said they. And they went, and they went, and they went, till they came to a wood, and there they met a fox. And the fox says, "Where are you going this day, Goosie-Poosey, Ducky-Daddles, Cocky-Locky, Henny-Penny?" "We're going to tell the king the sky is falling." And he says, "Come along, and I'll show you the road, Goosie-Poosey, Ducky-Daddles, Cocky-Locky, Henny-Penny." And they went, and they went, and they went, till they came to the fox's hole. And he shoved them all in, and he and his young ones ate them all up, and they never got to tell the king the sky was falling.

Was the sky really falling? Did Henny Penny get upset about a small thing and make it into a big thing?

Phonics: Review the blends Aa-Ff with the blend charts. Review the initial sounds of Aa-Ff. Review letter recognition Aa-Zz.

Have the students brainstorm words that begin or include the letter Ff. Write these words on the board. Model the correct letter formation as you write the letters on the board. The students should practice forming the letter Ff on a blank sheet of paper. Students who are ready can practice copying complete words from the board.

Do the Lesson 109 Phonics worksheet. The Sound of Ff. Review the letter sound with the picture and words on the worksheet. Ask the students for other words that begin with the same sound. Trace the letters and say the sound of Ff. Observe the students as they trace the letters and help them with the letter strokes. If you have the students do one row at a time, the worksheet can be carried over to various parts of the day or another day.

Reading: Given a sound and two words, identify the word that begins with the sound. Assemble a simple object or craft following illustrated directions.

Writing: Write one's first name.

Memory Verse: Continue to review Matthew 6:26a. Work on the entire verse.

Math: Review 3 + 1 = 4. Have the students count off steps to practice addition. If they start from a wall or a line they can step toe-to-toe three steps and then step one more. Have them place a bean bag or some marker where their toe ends up. Have them back up to the wall or line and step forward again counting, "one, two, three, four," until their toe is again at the bean bag. Have them say, "three steps plus one step equals four steps." Do the same for 1 + 1 = 2, 2 + 1 = 3.

Do the Lesson 109 Math worksheet. Count each color of blocks in the strip and say the addition problem and count all of the blocks to get the answer. (Ex. "1, 2, two red blocks plus 1 blue block equals, 1, 2, 3 blocks altogether.") Trace the correct number.

Shapes: Review the diamond shape.

Story Time: Read a story or stories of your choice.

Music: Review the song "The Birds Upon The Treetop." Review the song "One Little, Two Little, Three Little Birdies." Sing it forward first and then backwards counting down from ten to one.

Multimedia Resources: This week, listen and sing along to selections from "The Amazing Children" CD.

Arts & Crafts: A Bird in the Nest - You'll need a lot of foot long pieces of string and/or yarn, flour, water, whisk, construction paper, a small balloon for each student, and a bowl for each student.

The flour mixture can be made in the following proportions, depending on class size:

1/4 cup flour	1/2 cup flour	1 cup flour
1 cup water	2 cups water	4 cups water

Mix the flour and water well, using a whisk. Blow up a small balloon for each student. Let the students dip the string/yarn in the paste then wrap around the balloon. They must get the string/yarn wet with paste. Instruct them to wrap and wrap the pieces around and around the balloon, making a little nest. Let the craft dry until tomorrow. More to follow.

Health & Safety: Americans eat a lot of chicken. There are many, many chicken recipes for lunch and dinner. What is your favorite? The eggs we eat are usually chicken eggs. As with all foods, we have to be very careful and keep our cooking area clean when we cook with chicken or eggs. After cutting chicken, the area should be cleaned well with disinfectant. Make sure that every dish and utensil is washed well with soapy water. You will all grow up to be very careful with cleanliness because you learned to wash your hands and your cooking areas when you were young.

Field Trip: If there is an aviary nearby, plan a trip for the class. Allow the students to bring notebooks and draw the birds that they see. Or bring a recording device and help them to record bird calls.

Physical Education: Throughout this week, we will be working on gross motor coordination. We suggest you spread the following activities throughout the week.

1. Lie down on a carpeted area and stretch your arms out to your side. With your arm moving up and down (as a bird flies) open and close your legs, keeping all parts of your body flat on the floor.
2. Sitting on the floor, spread your legs, moving them in and out while clapping your hands.
3. Lying on the floor on your back, stretch one leg over your body and point the toe towards the opposite wall. Do this to the count of four and then reverse legs.
4. Practice jumping in rhythm. Jump once with legs together, then hop on one foot and jump with both feet with legs together again. Vary this exercise by seeing how high the children can jump each time.
5. Practice crawling with a right/left order of the hands and knees. (When right hand is forward, the left knee is forward.)

NOTES:

Lesson 110

Activities in this Lesson: Bible Lesson, Social Studies, Science, Language Arts, Phonics, Reading, Writing, Memory Verse, Math, Shapes, Story Time, Music, Arts & Crafts, Physical Education
Bible Reference: Genesis 1:20-23.
Bible Concept to Present: God made the birds for man to enjoy. We need to care for the gift God has given to us.

Bible Lesson: God gave us such a special gift when He gave birds to us. Each bird God made, He planned for a special purpose. All the birds were given to man to enjoy. Man has the ability to help or hurt birds. God took such great care to make the birds. We should choose to help birds, not hurt them. We can help take care of the birds God made in many ways. We can leave food for them to eat. We can be sure we do not spray the fruit or garden around our homes with anything that would hurt the birds. We can learn to leave their nests alone so that they can raise their babies in safety. God left His special creation, the birds, for us to care for. Let's thank God now for birds and ask Him to help us take care of His gift to us.

Social Studies: A clean environment is important for birds. Some chemical pesticides are a great danger to birds. Your students may not understand pesticides, but if you explain that often people will spray trees to get rid of bugs, and that the spray also hurts birds, children can understand our need to use pesticides that are safe for other animals. Man takes care of birds in many ways. If you live in California, and wish to discuss the efforts to save the California condor, you may do so.

Science: When all of a certain type of birds is wiped out, and there are no more living of that type of bird, we call the bird extinct. Once a bird is extinct, there can never be any more of that type of bird. There are many birds that used to live in our world that no longer are alive. They are extinct. Many things contribute to a bird being extinct, but the greatest enemy to birds is man himself. Many people kill birds for no reason at all. We must be certain that we do not carelessly hurt birds.

Language Arts: Say the finger play poem, "Five Little Birdies."

Five Little Birdies
by Al Christopherson

Five little birdies, pecking on our door, (five fingers on one hand up in the air)
One flew away and then there were four. (other hand bends down one finger)

Four little birdies looking down at me, (four fingers on one hand up in the air)
One flew away and then there were three. (other hand bends down one finger)

Three little birdies said what can we do? (three fingers on one hand up in the air)
One flew away, and then there were two. (other hand bends down one finger)

Two little birdies out to have some fun, (two fingers on one hand up in the air)
One flew away, and there was one. (other hand bends down one finger)

One little birdie sitting in the sun, (one finger on one hand up in the air)
He flew away and then there were none. (other hand bends down one finger)

No little birdies here to play with me, (fist up in the air)
Five little birdies where can they be? (pop up fingers and say poem again)

Phonics: Review the blends. Aa-Ff with the blend charts. Review the initial sounds of Aa-Ff. Review letter recognition Aa-Zz

Add the following words to the flip chart pages of words and review them with the students.

<u>f</u>	<u>a</u>		<u>fa</u>		<u>f</u>	<u>e</u>		<u>fe</u>
f	a	b	fab		F	e	b	Feb
f	a	d	fad		f	e	d	fed

Some of the words formed in these activities may not be common or real words. They are included because they illustrate blending concepts that may be needed for other words.

Do the Lesson 110 Phonics worksheet. The Sound of Ff. Review the letter sound with the picture and words on the worksheet. Ask the students for other words that begin with the same sound. Trace the letters and say the sound of Ff. Observe the students as they trace the letters and help them with the letter strokes. If you have the students do one row at a time, the worksheet can be carried over to various parts of the day or another day.

Reading: Given a sound and two words, identify the word that begins with the sound. Assemble a simple object or craft following illustrated directions.

Writing: Write one's first name.

Memory Verse: Review Matthew 6:26. Your students should have learned this quite well by this time. Let them recite if they want to.

Math: Review 3 + 1 = 4. Give each student 10 pennies to count 1-10. Have the students add pennies to practice the addition facts: 1 + 1 = 2, 2 + 1 = 3, 3 + 1 = 4

Do the Lesson 110a Math worksheet. Read the number. Count the dots under the number. Draw 1 object in the counting jar. Trace the number 1 following the proper strokes. The students can color the counting jar.

Do the Lesson 110b Math worksheet. Count the first group of pennies in the row and say "plus one penny," then count all of the pennies to get the answer. Trace the correct number.

Shapes: Review the diamond shape, make a Bag of Diamonds activity. Decorate a paper bag with diamond shapes. Place a number of diamond shaped cutouts of several sizes and colors into the bag. Also put in some cutouts of other shapes. Have the students sit in a circle of the floor and say, "Today we are going to have a diamond hunt. I will empty the bag of diamonds on the floor and one at a time you can come up and pick a diamond to put back into the bag." After everyone has had one turn ask if there are any diamonds left. Have them describe by color and position where the remaining diamonds are located. Place each diamond as they describe it back into the bag until all of the diamonds have been collected.

Do the Lesson 110 Shapes worksheet. Draw lines to connect the pictures that are the same.

Story Time: Read a story or stories of your student's choice or ones they have brought from home.

Music: Review the song "The Birds Upon The Treetop." Review the song "One Little, Two Little, Three Little Birdies." Sing it forward first and then backwards counting down from ten to one.

Multimedia Resources: This week, listen and sing along to selections from "The Amazing Children" CD.

Arts & Crafts: Give your students paper, glue, and scissors and ask them to make a little bird. They can make it multi-color if they choose. It must be smaller than the "nests" they made yesterday. Instruct them to cut out the birds. They will need help for the next part: tape a piece of string to the top of the bird. Everyone should pop his balloon. You might provide stick pins. Remove the balloon remains from the nests. Slip the birds into the balloon nests, and then tie them to the top of the nests.

Physical Education: Throughout this week, we will be working on gross motor coordination. We suggest you spread the following activities throughout the week.

1.   Lie down on a carpeted area and stretch your arms out to your side. With your arm moving up and down (as a bird flies) open and close your legs, keeping all parts of your body flat on the floor.
2.   Sitting on the floor, spread your legs, moving them in and out while clapping your hands.
3.   Lying on the floor on your back, stretch one leg over your body and point the toe towards the opposite wall. Do this to the count of four and then reverse legs.
4.   Practice jumping in rhythm. Jump once with legs together, then hop on one foot and jump with both feet with legs together again. Vary this exercise by seeing how high the children can jump each time.
5.   Practice crawling with a right/left order of the hands and knees. (When right hand is forward, the left knee is forward.)

NOTES:

Activities in this Lesson: Bible Lesson, Social Studies, Science, Language Arts, Phonics, Reading, Writing, Memory Verse, Math, Shapes, Story Time, Music, Physical Education

Bible Reference: Genesis 1:24-25.

Bible Concept to Present: God made animals on the sixth day of Creation.

Bible Lesson: Review the days of Creation. Use the Days of Creation Numbers. Can you guess what God made on the sixth day? On the sixth day God made animals. I want to read to you from the Bible where it tells about God making animals. (Read reference). God made land animals on the sixth day. He made the dinosaurs, the bunny rabbits, the elephants, and the little mice. God made many different animals on the sixth day of Creation. Could you imagine what our world would be like if we did not have animals? There would be no kitty to love, no puppy with which to play. There would be no tall giraffes. We would have no zoo, because there would be no animals to live in the zoo. Can you name other animals God made on the sixth day of Creation? Let's thank God for each animal that he made. *First Book of Nature*, an Usborne book, has a chapter on animals.

Social Studies: Animals are important to us. Our world would be very empty without animals. Give your students a piece of paper and ask them to draw what they think the world would have looked like before God made animals. On a second piece of paper, ask them to draw what the world looked like after God made the animals.

Science: Animals live on land. We already know that God made life for the oceans and the sky on the fifth day of Creation. But on the sixth day of Creation, God made life to live on the land. Generally, an animal is any living organism that is capable of moving on its own. That is what makes animals different from plant life. Both are alive, but animals move around. The term animal especially refers to four-footed creatures. View pictures in a magazine with your students. Have them generally categorize whether or not the picture contains an animal.

Language Arts: Review the finger play poem, "Five Little Birdies."

Phonics: Teach the initial sound of Gg. Review the initial sounds of Aa-Ff. Review letter recognition Aa-Zz.

Write several initial hard Gg words on the board: gag, gas, gate, get, give, go, got, gull, etc. Underline the initial hard letter Gg and say the words. Ask the students for other words that start with the same sound.

Note: The pace for introducing new letter sounds will pick up beginning with this lesson. Previously an entire week was devoted to learning a single new letter sound. For the remainder of the alphabet, three letter sounds will be covered every two weeks.

Do the Lesson 111 Phonics worksheet. The Sound of Gg. Review the letter sound with the picture and words on the worksheet. Ask the students for other words that begin with the same sound. Discuss the position of the letters on the guidelines. Give them specific instructions for how the letter should be traced. Trace the letters and say the sound of Gg. Observe the students as they trace the letters and help them with the letter strokes.

Reading: Given a sound and two words, identify the word that begins with the sound. Assemble a simple object or craft following illustrated directions.

Multimedia Resources: Review "Rev-Up for Reading" from the "Rev-Up for Learning" DVD to drill letter recognition and sound. The students should say each letter sound along with the presentation.

Writing: Write one's first name.

Multimedia Resources: Review "Rev-Up for Writing" from the "Rev-Up for Learning" DVD to review the writing of upper- and lowercase letters.

Memory Verse: Genesis 1:24a.
And God said, "Let the land produce living creatures according to their kinds: livestock, creatures that move along the ground, and wild animals, each according to its kind." Genesis 1:24a NIV

And God said, Let the earth bring forth the living creature after his kind, cattle, and creeping thing, and beast of the earth after his kind: Genesis 1:24a KJV

Students will have two weeks to learn this verse. It is long. Be sure that they understand all of the words, especially "according to their kinds" and "livestock." Let the students take home Memory Verse Card 17 today.

Math: Teach 4 + 1 = 5. Have groups of students come to the front of the room to demonstrate that 4 + 1 = 5 as has been done in previous lessons. If there are not enough students then demonstrate the concept on the board with drawings or on a table with objects that are the same.

$$\text{人人人人} + \text{人} = \text{人人人人人}$$

Do the Lesson 111 Math worksheet. Read the number. Count the dots under the number. Draw 2 objects in the counting jar. Trace the number 2 following the proper strokes. The students can color the counting jar.

Multimedia Resources: View "Rev-Up for Arithmetic" from the "Rev-Up for Learning" DVD to practice number recognition, counting and addition 1-20.

Shapes: Review the diamond shape. Find diamonds on socks, clothing, sweaters or gift wrap.

Do the Lesson 111 Shapes worksheet. Trace the diamonds and draw lines to connect the pictures that are the same.

Story Time: Read a story or stories of your choice.

Music: Review "One Little, Two Little, Three Little Birdies." Teach the following song to help the students understand how they can help care for animals. Explain that hunting is not wrong. God created animals for man to use but man also has a responsibility to use what God has given wisely. This may also be a good time to talk about gun safety with the students.

In a Cabin in the Woods

In a cabin in the woods (point fingers and make a roof)
A little man by the window stood (peek through hands)
Saw a rabbit hopping by, (hold two fingers up and hop along)
Frightened as can be, (hug arms)
Spoken: Help me ! Help me ! Help he said, (Stretch out arms)
Or the hunter will shoot me dead. (point index finger as gun)
Come little rabbit, come with me, (make gesture with hands)
Happy we shall be. (rock a cradle)
(Act out the words of the song with hands and repeat the song, replacing each section with actions, until the entire song is pantomime.)

Second verse:
Ittybitty cabin in the woods
Ittybitty man by the window stood
Saw an ittybitty rabbit hopping by
Frightened as can be
"Help me, help me, help!" he said
'Fore the hunter shoots me dead
Ittybitty rabbit come inside
Safely to abide

Third verse:
Great big cabin in the woods
Great big man by the window stood
Saw a great big rabbit hopping by,
Frightened as can be
"Help me, help me, help!" he said
'Fore the hunter shoots me dead
Great big rabbit come inside
Safely to abide

On the second verse use a squeaky voice and the same motions, except make them much smaller, such as, instead of petting your hand, use one finger to pet another finger. On the third verse use your deepest, loudest voice and make all the motions bigger; i.e. instead of making the bunny with your fingers, pretend you're actually a giant rabbit hopping around, etc.

Multimedia Resources: This week, listen and sing along to selections from "Nathaniel the Grublet" CD.

Physical Education: Throughout this week, we suggest you concentrate on fine muscle coordination. This is recommended for the kindergartner, and should only be attempted by the preschooler if the child has developed the coordination to do the activities without stress.

1. Taking a square piece of paper, show students how to round off the corners of the paper to form a circle with the use of scissors. The children should follow the directions specifically.

2. Giving students a strip of paper, ask them to fringe the paper with small cuts to form the fringe.

3. Giving the students various colors of construction paper, ask them to make various shapes, such as triangles, squares etc. Although the child may not be able to make them specifically, he should be able to utilize the scissors in a reasonable fashion. Your goal is to observe his fine muscle coordination. If the student cannot do these things do not attempt to teach him to write.

NOTES:

Activities in this Lesson: Bible Lesson, Language Arts, Phonics, Reading, Writing, Memory Verse, Math, Shapes, Story Time, Music, Arts & Crafts, Physical Education, Homework

Bible Reference: Genesis 1:24-25.

Bible Concept to Present: God made so many animals; we could never count them all. He created animals for us to eat.

Bible Lesson: God created things that were more and more complicated in movement as the week went on. There are so many animals; they are almost as numerous as the stars made on the fourth day! God knew that we would need food. First, He created vegetables and fruit. Then He created chickens that give us eggs. He created cows that give us milk. And pigs that give us meat. God knew that we needed certain vitamins and minerals to stay alive, and that we needed to get these nutrients from our food. Draw a simple food chain on the board.

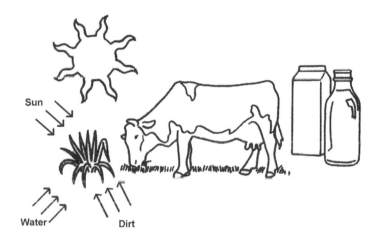

Sunshine
Water   >>> grass > cow > milk > children
Soil

Science: Give each student a small carton of milk. Talk about the properties of milk and what an important food it is for our bodies. Go through the process of milk getting to the store shelves.

Language Arts: The progression of God's Creation is wonderful and amazing. Write this list on the board. Review the days, showing how much God did on each day. How important is the light that God spent an entire day on it?

ONE	Light
TWO	Air - Clouds
THREE	Land - Soil – Rocks - Precious metals – Plants – Grasses – Bushes - Trees
FOUR	Sun – Seasons – Moon – Stars – Planets
FIVE	Fish – All sea creatures – Birds
SIX	Animals – Mammals – ? - ? - ? (We're not done with this day.)

Learn this little poem. Talk about how different all the animals are. How many animals live in a shell but are very different? Turtles, snails, crabs, hermit crabs, clams.

A Snail

He cannot fly, he cannot hop.
He cannot run at all.
But you should see the way he goes
Slowly up the wall.

He cannot skip or race about.
He has one way to go.
And as I watched him I must say
He's good at going slow!

Phonics: Review the initial hard sound of Gg. Review the initial sounds of Aa-Ff. Review letter recognition Aa-Zz.

Do the Lesson 112 Phonics worksheet. The Hard Sound of Gg. Review the letter sound with the picture and words on the worksheet. Ask the students for other words that begin with the same sound. Trace the letters and say the hard sound of Gg. Observe the students as they trace the letters and help them with the letter strokes. If you have the students do one row at a time, the worksheet can be carried over to various parts of the day or another day.

Reading: Given a sound and two words, identify the word that begins with the sound. Assemble a simple object or craft following illustrated directions.

Writing: Write one's first name.

Memory Verse: Review Genesis 1:24a. Divide the verse into phrases and work on the first phrase.

Math: Review 4 + 1 = 5. Give the students the dog bones that they cut out previously and a bowl to put them in. Have them place 4 bones in the bowl while saying "four plus one" and have them place another bone in the bowl, "equals" and have them count "one, two, three, four, five bones in the bowl." Do this several times. Reverse the order and also practice previous addition facts.

Do the Lesson 112a Math worksheet. As they count the images have them say the addition problems and trace the numbers.

Do the Lesson 112b Math worksheet. Instruct the students to draw the shape on the line that completes the pattern. They may need shape patterns to help them with this.

Shapes: Review the diamond shape. Cut out large diamond shapes from construction paper to make a kite. Have the students decorate the kites as they wish. They can color or paste shapes to the kite. Scraps of paper can be used to make a tail.

Story Time: Read a story or stories of your choice.

Music: Review "In a Cabin In the Woods" and "One Little, Two Little, Three Little Birdies."

Multimedia Resources: This week, listen and sing along to selections from "Nathaniel the Grublet" CD.

Arts & Crafts: Return to the Creation Mural. Today we are adding to Day 6. What a lot of things God has made so far. Let the students look at some women's magazines and find pictures of animals, any kind of animals. Have the students cut them out and glue them to the mural, saving room on the top half for people.

Give students playdough. Let them create their favorite animal.

Physical Education: Continue with the fine muscle exercises and evaluation.

Homework: Give the students Lesson 112 Homework worksheet, Drawing Pets. Let them take the page home, and then bring it back tomorrow.

NOTES:

Lesson 113

Activities in this Lesson: Bible Lesson, Social Studies, Science, Language Arts, Phonics, Reading, Writing, Memory Verse/Outdoor Activity, Math, Shapes, Story Time, Music, Arts & Crafts, Physical Education, Homework

Bible Reference: Genesis 1:24-25.

Bible Concept to Present: When God made animals on the sixth day, He made mammals.

Bible Lesson: God made lots of the animals on the sixth day of Creation. He made a special kind of animal. These animals were animals that needed to keep warm. These animals have hair or fur to keep them warm. These animals are born alive. They each need a mommy and a daddy. The mommies feed these animals milk. These animals are called *mammals*. One example of a mammal is a kitten. A kitten needs to be kept warm by its mommy or daddy. A kitten has fur. A kitten drinks milk from its mommy. Can you think of some other examples of mammals? I'm glad God made mammals. God made mammals so we could have pets to love. He made mammals for us to enjoy. Aren't you glad God made mammals?

Social Studies: You know that mammals help us in many ways. When God made mammals He made them for many reasons. Let's think now. What are some reasons why God made mammals? Well, what do mammals possess? They possess fur. (How do we use fur?) They possess milk. (How do we use milk?) They possess meat. (How do we use meat? **Note:** Before the Flood, animals were not to be used for meat. See Genesis 1:29-30. God did not give man permission to eat meat until after the flood. See Genesis 9:3.) Some mammals are very strong. (How do we use their strength?) Now that you have thought about how mammals benefit man, tell students the ways mammals benefit man. Give them paper and pen and have them draw what you have just verbally described. Allow enough time for them to visualize what you have said.

Science: A mammal is an animal that meets the following requirements:
1. Mammals are warm (constant body temperature).
2. Mammals have hair (or fur).
3. Mammals have a mommy and a daddy.
4. Mammals have their babies live.
5. Mammals nurse their babies (live on milk).

Discuss with your students different animals. Include an ape, camel, dog, cat, and zebra. After each animal is mentioned ask students to say "I'm a mammal" if the animal mentioned was a mammal. Now give your students an extended list: horse, pig, duck, snake. Did these animals meet the qualifications listed above? Discuss why or why not.

Language Arts: Sing the song "Old MacDonald Had A Farm" (and on that farm he had mammals). Make the sounds of the mammals on the farm.

Old MacDonald had Some Mammals

Old MacDonald had some mammals
Ee i ee i o
And on his farm he had some cows
Ee i ee i oh
With a moo-moo here
And a moo-moo there
Here a moo, there a moo
Everywhere a moo-moo
Old MacDonald had some mammals
Ee i ee i o

Old MacDonald had some mammals
Ee i ee i o
And on his farm he had some pigs
Ee i ee i o
With an oink-oink here
And an oink-oink there
Here an oink, there an oink
Everywhere an oink-oink
Old MacDonald had some mammals
Ee i ee i o

Add in other mammals like:
    dogs - woof-woof
    sheep - baa-baa
    horses - neigh-neigh

Phonics: Blend the sounds Aa-Gg. (gab, gag, bag, egg, beg, Dag (Meaning day, the Son of Natt or night from Scandinavian mythology.) Review the initial hard sound of Gg. Review the initial sounds of Aa-Ff. Review letter recognition Aa-Zz.

Add the following words to the flip chart pages of words and review them with the students.

g	a		ga		a	g	ag		e	g	eg
g	a	b	gab		b	a	g	bag		e	gg	egg
g	a	g	gag		D	a	g	Dag		b	e	g	beg

Do the Lesson 113 Phonics worksheet. The Hard Sound of Gg. Review the letter sound with the picture and words on the worksheet. Ask the students for other words that begin with the same sound. Give them specific instructions for how the letter should be traced. Allow time for tracing the letters and observe their progress. If you have the students do one row at a time, the worksheet can be carried over to various parts of the day or another day.

Reading: Given a sound and two words, identify the word that begins with the sound. Assemble a simple object or craft following illustrated directions.

- -

Writing: Write one's first name.

Memory Verse/Outdoor Activity: Continue learning Genesis 1:24a. Take a walk. Quote the verse as you walk. Try to observe any animals outside.

Math: Review 4 + 1 = 5. Review 4 + 1 = 5 by writing the problem on the board. Draw objects over the numbers with + sign between them. Write the = sign and then draw an excess of objects over the answer. Have a student come to the board and circle the correct number of objects to make the addition problem correct. Erase the extra objects and orally say the problem with the class. Repeat several times drawing simple objects such as dots or various shapes. Review previous addition problems if the students need the practice.

Do the Lesson 113a Math worksheet. Count the items and say the addition problems. As they trace the numbers have them say the addition problems.

Do the Lesson 113b Math worksheet. Read the number. Count the dots under the number. Draw 3 objects in the counting jar. Trace the number 3 following the proper strokes. The students can color the counting jar.

Shapes: Review triangle, circle, square, rectangle, star, heart, oval, and diamond shapes. We will not be learning any more new shapes this year. These shapes will be reviewed for the next week and then should be reviewed as appropriate for the remainder of the school year. Review shapes by learning the "Shape Song."

Shape Song
Tune of The Farmer in the Dell

A triangle has 3 sides, (hold up 3 fingers)
A triangle has 3 sides,
Up the mountain, (draw in the air)
Down, and back.
A triangle has 3 sides!

A circle's like a ball, (make a circle with thumbs and forefingers)
A circle's like a ball,
Round and round (draw circles in the air)
It never stops.
A circle's like a ball!

A square is like a box, (draw a square in the air)
A square is like a box,
It has four sides, (hold up 4 fingers)
They are the same.
A square is like a box! (draw a square in the air)

A rectangle has 4 sides, (hold up 4 fingers)
A rectangle has 4 sides,
Two are long, and (draw in the air)
Two are short.
A rectangle has 4 sides!

An oval's not quite round, (hold up 1 finger and shake it back and forth to say No!)
An oval's not quite round,
A circle that is all stretched out, (draw oval in the air)
An oval's not quite round.

A star has five points, (hold up 5 fingers)
A star has five points,
In and out and in and out, (draw a zigzag star shape in the air)
A star has five points.

A heart is very sweet, (clasp hands over chest)
A heart is very sweet,
Up and round and back down, (draw up, around and back down with both hands to make a heart shape)
A heart is very sweet.

A diamond has 4 points, (hold up 4 fingers)
A diamond has 4 points,
Two are tight and two are wide (hold up 2 fingers, close them and hold up 2 fingers again)
A diamond has 4 points. (hold up 4 fingers)
> ~ Author Unknown, some verses by Al Christopherson

Do the Lesson 113 Shapes worksheet. Color the diamonds red and the circles green. Color the rest of the picture as you wish.

Story Time: Read a story or stories of your choice.

Music: Review "In a Cabin In the Woods."

Multimedia Resources: This week, listen and sing along to selections from "Nathaniel the Grublet" CD.

Arts & Crafts: Using Lesson 113 Arts & Crafts worksheet, ask your students to color the mammals. Let them cut out the animals on the dotted lines. Place each mammal on a stick and ask him to make the sound of the animal as you present it. This is especially appropriate to the younger child.

Physical Education: After the Memory Verse Walk, let the students pretend to be a mammal. How does the mammal walk? Does it run fast? Is it tall? Attempt to imitate the mammal in its walk, run and habits. This will help students to internalize what they have just learned.

Continue with the fine muscle exercises and evaluation.

Homework: Let the students share their homework page about their pets.

NOTES:

Lesson 114

Activities in this Lesson: Bible Lesson, Science, Language Arts, Phonics, Reading, Writing, Memory Verse, Math, Shapes, Story Time, Music, Physical Education

Bible Reference: Genesis 1:24-25.

Bible Concept to Present: Mammals are very special. There are certain characteristics that are common to most mammals.

Bible Lesson: *Bring a scale to class.* Talk again about mammals. Ask, What makes an animal a mammal? Review the five characteristics discussed: warmth, hair, born alive, need two parents, and feed on milk. Three more points: mammals have four limbs, breathe air, and have a skeleton.

Illustration: Some more fun facts about mammals:
*   There are over 4,000 different types of mammals *

*   Some sources say the smallest mammal in the world is the Pygmy Shrew which only measures 1 1/2 inches from its head to the beginning of its tail. (A shrew is like a mouse) Another source says that the world's smallest mammal is the bumblebee bat of Thailand, weighing less than a penny. Wonder which is correct?

*   The largest mammal is the Blue Whale which is 80-100 feet long. The largest Blue Whales have a heart that weighs about 1,000 pounds! Figure out how much everyone in the room weighs. Use the scale. Compare that to the weight of the Blue Whale's heart.

Science: *Bring a mammal to class today.* Look at the animal you have brought. Ask the class to think about the things we learned about mammals. Go over each of the eight things we learned. See if students can remember what makes an animal a mammal. Point to the mammal and talk about each characteristic.

1.   Mammals are warm (constant body temperature).
2.   Mammals have hair (or fur).
3.   Mammals have a mommy and a daddy.
4.   Mammals have their babies live.
5.   Mammals nurse their babies (live on milk).
6.   Mammals are usually four footed.
7.   Mammals breathe air.
8.   Mammals have a skeleton.

Language Arts: Play a word game. Let the students fill in the blank at the end of each sentence, thinking of a word that rhymes with "whale."

When I am expecting a letter, I run to get the _____. MAIL
Jack and Jill went up the hill to fetch a _____. PAIL
A small animal with a shell, that crawls very, very slowly, is a _____. SNAIL
When it rains and rains and the rain turns into little hard pieces of ice, it is called
_____. HAIL

The police officer caught the man stealing a car, and sent the man to _____.
JAIL

I wanted to hang the picture from the wall, but after I found the hammer, I couldn't find the
_____. NAIL

Old ships are so beautiful. They didn't have a motor, they had a _____. SAIL

Play "Big and Small." Name animals and let the students call out whether they are big or small. Remind them that the Blue Whale is the biggest.

Phonics: Review the blends Aa-Gg with the blend charts. Review the initial sounds of Aa-Gg. Review letter recognition Aa-Zz.

Have the students brainstorm words that begin or include the letter Gg. Write these words on the board. Model the correct letter formation as you write the letters on the board. The students should practice forming the letter Gg on a blank sheet of paper. Students who are ready can practice copying complete words from the board.

Do the Lesson 114 Phonics worksheet. The Hard Sound of Gg. Review the letter sound with the picture and words on the worksheet. Ask the students for other words that begin with the same sound. Trace the letters and say the hard sound of Gg. Observe the students as they trace the letters and help them with the letter strokes. If you have the students do one row at a time, the worksheet can be carried over to various parts of the day or another day.

Reading: Given a sound and two words, identify the word that begins with the sound. Assemble a simple object or craft following illustrated directions.

Writing: Write one's first name.

Memory Verse: The students should have the first part of Genesis 1:24a memorized. Try to move on to the second part.

Math: Review 4 + 1 = 5. Give each of the students 10 counters. Have them count the objects to make sure that they have 10 objects. Have them make the addition problem with the counters. Have them point to the counters and say the addition problem, drawing the plus and equal sign with their finger between the counters as they say the words. Review previous problems if the students need the practice.

Do the Lesson 114 Math worksheet. Trace the numbers and say the addition problem.

Shapes: Review triangle, circle, square, rectangle, star, heart, oval, and diamond shapes with the "Shape Song."

Story Time: Get the book *Stellaluna* from the library. The author is Janell Cannon. Read the book today. It will be used again tomorrow.

Music: Review "In a Cabin In the Woods."

Multimedia Resources: This week, listen and sing along to selections from "Nathaniel the Grublet" CD.

Physical Education: Continue with the fine muscle exercises and evaluation.

NOTES: * http://www.suzy.co.nz/suzysworld/Factpage.asp?FactSheet=107

Activities in this Lesson: Bible Lesson, Social Studies, Science, Phonics, Reading, Writing, Memory Verse, Math, Shapes, Story Time/Science, Music, Arts & Crafts, Physical Education

Bible Reference: Genesis 1: 24-25.

Bible Concept to Present: God made mammals, many different kinds of mammals.

Bible Lesson: God created many kinds of animals on the sixth day. He wanted to show us how much He loved us by giving us many beautiful kinds of animals. He wanted them to all be different in some way so we could tell them apart. When God created mammals, He created mammals that could swim the rivers, streams, and oceans. Some mammals cannot swim at all. He made some mammals able to build their homes in trees. Others live on the ground all of their lives. We should remember that God wants us to enjoy all of the animals.

Social Studies: Men use animals in many ways. Beyond what you discussed last lesson, animals are used to help us. We use dogs to help us protect our property, for pets, for pulling sleds, and for helping the visually handicapped. Today, discuss ways dogs are used with your students. You may also consider the use of horses, camels, or donkeys.

Science: *Bring a large bag of plastic animals to class.* God made some mammals with the ability to be used to carry heavy loads. Each animal God made is special. For example, the camel is sometimes called the "ship of the desert." It is called this because it carries large loads across the desert. The desert is a very hot place, and there is no water for miles and miles. The camel is made by God to use very little water and it can travel for miles and not get thirsty. The camel also has special feet so that the hot sands do not hurt its feet. What do you think is in the hump of the camel's back? Fat, not water! The camel uses the fat in its hump for nourishment when food is scarce. Camels store large amounts of water in their bloodstream. Let the students look at the plastic animals. Arrange them in groups of wild and domestic, fast and slow, jungle, and desert.

Phonics: Teach the initial sound of Hh. Review the initial sounds of Aa-Gg. Review letter recognition Aa-Zz.

Write several initial Hh words on the board: had, ham, hard, hat, hay, her, hid, hit, him, hip, hog, hop, hug, hut, etc. Underline the initial letter Hh and say the words. Ask the students for other words that start with the same sound.

Do the Lesson 115 Phonics worksheet. The Sound of Hh. Review the letter sound with the picture and words on the worksheet. Ask the students for other words that begin with the same sound. Discuss the position of the letters on the guidelines. Give them specific instructions for how the letter should be traced. Trace the letters and say the sound of Hh. Observe the students as they trace the letters and help them with the letter strokes. If you have the students do one row at a time, the worksheet can be carried over to various parts of the day or another day.

Reading: Given a sound and two words, identify the word that begins with the sound. Assemble a simple object or craft following illustrated directions.

Writing: Write one's first name.

Memory Verse: Review the memory verse Genesis 1:24a. Write it on the board. This familiarizes students with the look of the words. Have students close their eyes. Wipe off one or two words. Have the students open their eyes and say the verse. Wipe off the hardest words, so that the easiest words to read are left each time.

Math: Review 4 + 1 = 5.

Do the Lesson 115a Math worksheet. Read the number. Count the dots under the number. Draw 4 objects in the counting jar. Trace the number 4 following the proper strokes. The students can color the counting jar.

Do the Lesson 115b Math worksheet. Count the fruit, add, and trace the answer.

Do the Lesson 115c Math worksheet. Circle the correct number of objects to answer the addition problems.

Shapes: Review triangle, circle, square, rectangle, star, heart, oval, and diamond shapes with the "Shape Song."

Do the Lesson 115 Shapes worksheet. Trace the square frame, color the rectangles orange and the diamonds red. Color the rest as you wish.

Story Time/Science: Read the book *Stellaluna* again. On a piece of poster board, draw a line through the middle horizontally. Write "Birds" on the top section and "Bats" on the bottom section. Say, It seems strange that bats are not birds. In fact, bats are mammals. Let's write down or draw what makes birds and bats different. Use facts from the book on the chart.

Music: Review "In a Cabin In the Woods."

Multimedia Resources: This week, listen and sing along to selections from "Nathaniel the Grublet" CD.

Arts & Crafts: Give the students a piece of paper and ask them to make two pictures, one in which farm animals are illustrated and one in which wild animals are illustrated. You may wish to discuss which animals are which before you ask the students to draw. Label all drawings. Students may look at pictures first.

Let the students use playdough to make animal houses.

Physical Education: Continue with the fine muscle exercises and evaluation.

NOTES:

Activities in this Lesson: Bible Lesson, Social Studies, Science, Language Arts, Phonics, Reading, Writing, Memory Verse, Math, Shapes, Story Time, Music, Arts & Crafts, Physical Education

Bible Reference: Genesis 1:25-26.

Bible Concept to Present: God made mammals to care for their young.

Bible Lesson: God created mammals on the 6th day of Creation. He made the Mommy and Daddy mammal so they could have baby mammals. Every mammal is born alive, with the exception of the platypus and the echidna (i-**kid**-nuh). Their young come from an egg. But God made all the mammals to have babies. God made all the mammal mommies and daddies know that they are to take care of their babies. They know they are to feed them, keep them warm, and love them. Mammals take very good care of their babies. They learned this by instinct. Instinct is when an animal is born knowing they must care for their young. Aren't you glad that your mommy and daddy know how to take care of you? God made your mommy and daddy know they need to take care of you, too. God loves your whole family. He wants you to take care of one another and the animals.

Social Studies: Mammal babies are wonderful to watch. Little kittens, puppies, and bears all are so furry and soft. God created wonderful things when He made mammal babies. It takes a mammal mommy and daddy to have a mammal baby. When God first made mammals He made them to be able to have babies. God could have continued to create every mammal but instead He chose for the mammals to have babies. Mammal babies need to be cared for by their parents. The babies cannot eat the grown-up food their parents eat so God made the mammal mommy to produce milk for the baby. When we drink milk, we are drinking the food God made for a mammal baby. We drink the milk because God gave the cow too much milk for it's baby and the milk is good for us. I am thankful God made special food for the mammal baby.

Science: Both mammal daddies and mommies care for the babies. Although only the mommy can feed the tiny baby, the daddy often helps. Some mammals take turns caring for their young. With other mammals, the mommy takes care of the babies while the daddy mammal brings home the food for them all to eat. God intended for mammals to have both mommies and daddies.

Multimedia Resources: Watch "Gentleness" from the *Character Builders Video Series*.

Language Arts: Tell favorite animal stories or stories about stupid pet tricks. Perhaps someone knows a story about animal survival or a pet that returned home after being gone for several years.

Phonics: Blend the sounds Aa-Hh. (ha, hag, had) Review the initial sound of Gg. Review the initial sounds of Aa-Ff. Review letter recognition Aa-Zz.

Add the following words to the flip chart pages of words and review them with the students.

<u>h</u>   <u>a</u>   <u>ha</u>
h   a   ha
h   a   d   had
h   a   g   hag

Do the Lesson 116a Phonics worksheet. The Sound of Hh. Review the letter sound with the picture and words on the worksheet. Ask the students for other words that begin with the same sound. Give them specific instructions for how the letter should be traced. Allow time for tracing the letters and observe their progress. If you have the students do one row at a time, the worksheet can be carried over to various parts of the day or another day.

Do the Lesson 116b Phonics worksheet. The Sound of Hh. Review the letter sound with the picture and words on the worksheet. Ask the students for other words that begin with the same sound. Give them specific instructions for how the letter should be traced. Allow time for tracing the letters and observe their progress. If you have the students do one row at a time, the worksheet can be carried over to various parts of the day or another day.

Reading: Given a sound and two words, identify the word that begins with the sound. Assemble a simple object or craft following illustrated directions.

Multimedia Resources: Review "Rev-Up for Reading" from the "Rev-Up for Learning" DVD to drill letter recognition and sound. The students should say each letter sound along with the presentation.

Writing: Write one's first name.

Multimedia Resources: Review "Rev-Up for Writing" from the "Rev-Up for Learning" DVD to review the writing of upper- and lowercase letters.

Memory Verse: Genesis 1:24a. Give special attention to the final phrases of the verse.

Math: Review 4 + 1 = 5. Use the string of Counting Beads or pop beads to review 1 + 1 = 2, 2 + 1 = 3, 3 + 1 = 4, and 4 + 1 = 5.

Do the Lesson 116a Math worksheet. Read the number. Count the dots under the number. Draw 5 objects in the counting jar. Trace the number 5 following the proper strokes. The students can color the counting jar.

Do the Lesson 116b Math worksheet. Count the beads and say the addition problem. Trace the correct answer and say the addition problem again.

Multimedia Resources: View "Rev-Up for Arithmetic" from the "Rev-Up for Learning" DVD to practice number recognition, counting and addition 1-20.

Shapes: Review triangle, circle, square, rectangle, star, heart, oval, and diamond shapes with the "Shape Song."

Do the Lesson 116 Shapes worksheet. Color the ovals yellow, the diamonds red, and the rest of the picture as you wish.

Story Time: Read a story or stories of your choice.

Music: Review "In a Cabin In the Woods."

Multimedia Resources: This week, listen and sing along to selections from "The Amazing Miracles" CD.

Arts & Crafts: Mammal babies are quite interesting. On the Lesson 116 Arts & Crafts worksheet are pictures of mammal babies. These are wild animal babies and pet babies. Students need to decide which is which. Ask students to cut out the picture and the color animals. Let them make cages with cut straws.

Find a picture of a porcupine on the Internet and copy it for students. You will need spaghetti noodles, clay (Lesson 14), and two craft sticks per student. Say, Some animals that God made are really weird! We are going to make a porcupine today. Look at this picture. What is unusual about this animal? Would you want to cuddle with them? Everyone take a piece of clay and form it like a potato. Break your spaghetti noodles into pieces and stick them into the clay everywhere on one side. Break the craft sticks in half (teacher might have to help) to make four legs. Stick them into the bottom side of your porcupine. Let your animal dry, then paint on a face.

Physical Education: Go on a lion hunt. To go on a lion hunt, you must prepare carefully. The preparation takes place in the mind of the students. Say, We are going on a lion hunt. Let's get down and be lions. Then continue the hunt, crawling under things, over things, facing many dangers, etc. The trip is your imagination with your body doing the action. This is a type of obstacle course put to a story.

NOTES:

Activities in this Lesson: Bible Lesson, Social Studies, Science/Arts & Crafts, Language Arts/Arts & Crafts, Phonics, Reading, Writing, Memory Verse, Math, Shapes, Story Time, Music, Physical Education

Bible Reference: Genesis 1:24-25.

Bible Concept to Present: God created animals to be wild, domestic, or pets.

Bible Lesson: Continue teaching the scope of the many animals God created on the sixth day. God created wild animals, domestic animals, and animals for pets. He knew exactly what He wanted each animal to do. Man has tried to domesticate some wild animals, but they often remain wild. Wild animals: giraffes, zebras, lions. Domestic animals: cows, horses, pigs. Pets: dogs and cats. Many animals have very strange habits. Explain to the students that birds and fish are animals, too.

Multimedia Resources: Listen to the songs "I Know Somebody Who Knows" from the "Bullfrogs and Butterflies: God is Great" CD and "The Lions Weren't Hungry Last Night" from the "Bullfrogs and Butterflies: God Loves Fun" CD.

Social Studies: *Get a video from the library about baby animals. Preview the video first to be sure it doesn't present an evolutionary explanation for animals. Show the video to the class.*

Science/Arts & Crafts: Have the students make a book today. Keep it simple. Give each of the students three pieces of white paper and one piece of construction paper in their favorite color. Fold all the papers in half. Use a hole punch to punch holes in the fold. Give each student a piece of yarn to tie their book together. Write on the board STRANGE ANIMALS. Let the students copy this to the front of their books. Now they can draw the various strange animals that they learn about. Include any information you have about strange animal habits.

> Elephant teeth can weigh up to ten pounds. Find something that weighs ten pounds and let the students lift it.
> An albatross can glide for six days without beating its wings and it can take a nap while gliding!
> Anglerfish use their tails and fins to crawl around on the ocean floor.
> Zebras can walk when they are 30 minutes old, and run when they are 45 minutes old.
> Llamas hum to communicate.
> Cows have almost 360 degrees of vision. They can almost see behind them without turning their heads.
> One in 5,000 lobsters is born bright blue.
> A snail can sleep for three years.
> A full grown bear can run as fast as a horse.
> The penguin is the only bird that can swim but not fly.
> An ostrich is one of the world's largest land animals, yet its brain is smaller than its eye!

Language Arts/Arts & Crafts: *Bring in some animal books from the library.* Let the students look at all of the pictures. *Cut some green construction paper into leaf shapes.* Instruct students to draw their favorite wild animal on white paper. Let them glue leaves around the picture. Talk about wild animals. How do they have enough to eat? Why don't they make good pets? Do wild animals have to take care of their babies?

Phonics: Review the blends Aa-Hh with the blend charts. Review the initial sounds of Aa-Gg. Review letter recognition Aa-Zz.

Do the Lesson 117 Phonics worksheet. The Sound of Hh. Review the letter sound with the picture and words on the worksheet. Ask the students for other words that begin with the same sound. Trace the letters and say the sound of Hh. Observe the students as they trace the letters and help them with the letter strokes. If you have the students do one row at a time, the worksheet can be carried over to various parts of the day or another day.

Reading: Given a sound and two words, identify the word that begins with the sound. Assemble a simple object or craft following illustrated directions.

Writing: Write one's first name.

Memory Verse: Talk about the memory verse Genesis 1:24a, that it mentions different kinds of animals: livestock, reptiles, and wild animals. Explain "each according to its kind." Birds have baby birds, cows have baby cows, and giraffes have baby giraffes. Work on memorizing the first two parts of the verse today.

Math: Review 4 + 1 = 5.

Do the Lesson 117 Math worksheet. The students may need manipulative shapes to help them complete the patterns.

Shapes: Review triangle, circle, square, rectangle, star, heart, oval, and diamond shapes with the "Shape Song."

Story Time: Get the book *Millions of Cats*, by Wanda Gag, from the library. Read it through once. Set up the recording device. Explain that as you read it through again, everyone can repeat the recurring phrases. Let the students make the different cat sounds, purr, meow, and hiss. Be sure each student has a chance to speak into the recording device. Students will enjoy listening to themselves making cat sounds.

Music: Review "In a Cabin In the Woods."

Multimedia Resources: This week, listen and sing along to selections from "The Amazing Miracles" CD.

Physical Education: "Kitty Wants a Corner." Students are to arrange chairs into a circle, one less chair than students. One student is picked as the kitty. The kitty walks up to any students and asks, "Kitty wants a corner?" The one asked says, "Go see my neighbor" and points to his/her right or left. The kitty goes to one of them and asks again, "Kitty wants a corner?" Again they answer, "Go ask my neighbor" and points right or left. While this continues, at any time, any persons in the circle can (with eye contact, gesture, or movement) change seats with another person in the group. Many can move at a time. The kitty will try to take an empty seat while they are moving. If she/he succeeds, the one left without a seat is the new kitty. Kitty can be angry, plead or ask in any manner but must say the words, "Kitty wants a corner." Usually, the movement happens behind kitty and she/he must concentrate on peripheral vision, as well as keeping the dialogue going. No pushing, shoving or talking to anyone, other than the lines between kitty and the neighbors. This game encourages non-verbal communication and is a great concentration game. It is also great for a warm-up to increase energy.

NOTES:

Activities in this Lesson: Bible Lesson, Social Studies, Science, Science/Arts & Crafts, Language Arts, Phonics, Reading, Writing, Memory Verse, Math, Shapes, Story Time, Music, Physical Education

Bible Reference: Genesis 1:24-25.

Bible Concept to Present: God made each mammal to be special.

Bible Lesson: God made each of the mammals very different. Some of the mammals are very large and move very slow, like the elephant. Some of the mammals can move very quickly, like the cheetah. Some of the mammals were created to be very small. Each of these mammals has a special job to do. The big elephant uses his strength to carry heavy items. The smaller mammals eat termites and destructive insects. God made all these animals to be special and to have special jobs to do. Isn't it neat that God wanted each mammal to be different? Each of us is different too. God wants everything He made to be just the way He made it. You are special, just like all of the mammals are special, too.

Social Studies: Man uses mammals for many things. God knew that we would need big mammals to help us carry items and pull heavy loads. He knew we would need small mammals, like the Pygmy Shrew, to eat insects that hurt us. He knew we would need cats to help get rid of mice. He knew we would need some mammals to simply enjoy. God knew all of this when He made many different mammals. Continue reading books from the library that display a wide variety of mammals. As you view the different mammals, note individual habits, how each affects man, how each differs from others either in size, coloring, etc. Comment on similarities of the mammals also. Your goal is not only observation of differences and similarities, but also to acquaint students with different kinds of mammals in preparation for further study.

Science: More weird animal facts:
        Fastest land animal – Cheetah, runs up to 60 mph
        Smallest mammal – Bumblebee bat, weighs as much as a dime (.07 oz.)
        Largest appetite – Blue whale, can eat 4+ tons of krill a day
        Smallest horse – Falabella of Argentina, 30 inches high at the shoulder
        Heaviest bear – Polar bear, weighs 2,200+ pounds
        Weirdest mammal – Duck-billed platypus, lays eggs

Science/Arts & Crafts: There are many coloring books that contain pictures of animals. Find several that have the best illustrations. If you have a zoo nearby, the gift shop there will have some excellent coloring books. Cut out the pages of animal pictures. Let the students color them. Hang them together on a wall and talk about what students know about each animal. Write on the edges to keep track of what you learn. Emphasize wild versus domestic animals.

Language Arts: Make a pictograph or a bar graph on the board of the numbers of each kind of pets that the students have at home. If 5 students have dogs then draw 5 dogs on the graph. If the students have 10 cats then draw 10 cats on the graph. After you have completed the graph ask the students what information the graph quickly tells them. It may show the most common and the least common pet.

Phonics: Teach the initial short sound of Ii. Review the initial sounds of Aa-Gg. Review letter recognition Aa-Zz.

Write several initial short Ii words on the board: if, ill, iguana, in, ink, it, igloo, etc. Underline the initial short letter Ii and say the words. Ask the students for other words that start with the same sound.

Do the Lesson 118 Phonics worksheet. The Short Sound of Ii. Review the letter sound with the picture and words on the worksheet. Ask the students for other words that begin with the same sound. Discuss the position of the letters on the guidelines. Give them specific instructions for how the letter should be traced. Trace the letters and say the short sound of Ii. Observe the students as they trace the letters and help them with the letter strokes. If you have the students do one row at a time, the worksheet can be carried over to various parts of the day or another day.

Reading: Given a sound and two words, identify the word that begins with the sound. Assemble a simple object or craft following illustrated directions.

Writing: Write one's first name.

Memory Verse: Students should be working on the entire verse Genesis 1:24a by today. What an accomplishment! Plan to reward them tomorrow for their hard work.

Math: Review 4 + 1 = 5. Practice this problem and review the problems: 1 + 1 = 2, 2 + 1 = 3, 3 + 1 = 4, with a strip of squares drawn on the board.

Do the Lesson 118a Math worksheet. Read the number. Count the dots under the number. Draw 6 objects in the counting jar. Trace the number 6 following the proper strokes. The students can color the counting jar.

Do the Lesson 118b Math worksheet. Count the dots in the tiles and trace the numbers to do the addition problems.

Shapes: Review triangle, circle, square, rectangle, star, heart, oval, and diamond shapes with the "Shape Song."

Story Time: Review the book *Millions of Cats*, by Wanda Gag.

Music: Review "In a Cabin In the Woods."

Multimedia Resources: This week, listen and sing along to selections from "The Amazing Miracles" CD.

Physical Education: Review the game Kitty Wants a Corner. This time have the students stand in a circle. The kitty must find an open space on the circle while the others are switching places.

NOTES:

Activities in this Lesson: Bible Lesson, Social Studies, Science, Language Arts, Phonics, Reading, Writing, Memory Verse, Math, Shapes, Story Time, Music, Arts & Crafts, Physical Education, Homework

Bible Reference: Genesis 1:24-25.

Bible Concept to Present: God intentionally made some animals to be our friends.

Bible Lesson: God knew we would love our pets. We thank God for creating them. Certain animals make good pets. God made them to want to cuddle with us and be our friends.

Illustration: *Bring in a different pet today,* different from last week. Talk about how many animals make good pets. How do we care for pets? Are they a responsibility? Write on the board the things we have to do to take care of our pets. God also made baby animals especially cute. What is special about animal babies?

Multimedia Resources: Watch "Responsibility" from the *Character Builders Video Series.*

Social Studies: God didn't make one pet smarter or prettier than another, but people try to do that. There are many, many ways that pets can compete: dog shows, horse races, science fairs, and etc. There are whole books written just on the qualifications for entering a dog show. *Find the movie "Babe" to show to the students.* Even the younger students should love the animal interaction. Plan to show half of the movie today and half tomorrow. It would be fun to have popcorn and lemonade.

Science: There are special doctors just for animals. These doctors are called veterinarians. They have to go to medical school just like other doctors. Some veterinarians specialize in certain kinds of animals. They can be horse doctors or reptile doctors. They work for zoos or horse farms. Some veterinarians specialize in cattle or pigs on farms. Since "veterinarian" is a long word, we call these doctors "vets." When we have pets, we should take them to the vet for check ups and for shots to keep them well. There are some vets that specialize in cats and dogs.

Note: The book, *James Herriot's Treasury for Children,* would be a wonderful accompaniment to this portion of the lesson. The stories and illustrations are very nice. The ISBN # is 978-0-312-08512-4. It can be found in many libraries.

Language Arts: Animals make so many different sounds. The movie "Babe" is funny because the animals talk. We know that animals don't really talk, but how do you think they would sound? What is the funniest sounding animal? Let the students make animal sounds and guess what they are.

Phonics: Review the initial short sound of Ii. Review the initial sounds of Aa-Gg. Review letter recognition Aa-Zz.

Have the students brainstorm words that begin or include the letter Ii. Write these words on the board. Model the correct letter formation as you write the letters on the board. The students should practice forming the letter Ii on a blank sheet of paper. Students who are ready can practice copying complete words from the board.

Do the Lesson 119 Phonics worksheet. The Short Sound of Ii. Review the letter sound with the picture and the words on the worksheet. Ask the students for other words that begin with the same sound. Trace the letters and say the short sound of Ii. Observe the students as they trace the letters and help them with the letter strokes. If you have the students do one row at a time, the worksheet can be carried over to various parts of the day or another day.

Reading: Given a sound and two words, identify the word that begins with the sound. Assemble a simple object or craft following illustrated directions.

Writing: Write one's first name.

Memory Verse: Let the students recite the verse Genesis 1:24a if they want to. Reward all students for working on this long verse.

Math: Review 4 + 1 = 5. Have the students count off steps to practice addition. Review: 1 + 1 = 2, 2 + 1 = 3, 3 + 1 = 4, 4 + 1 = 5.

Do the Lesson 119 Math worksheet. Count each color of blocks in the strip and say the addition problem and count all of the blocks to get the answer. Trace the correct number.

Shapes: Review triangle, circle, square, rectangle, star, heart, oval, and diamond shapes with the "Shape Song." Give each student a set of shapes so they can hold up the shape for each verse of the song.

Story Time: Read a story or stories of your choice.

Music: Review "In a Cabin In the Woods."

Multimedia Resources: This week, listen and sing along to selections from "The Amazing Miracles" CD.

Arts & Crafts: Give the students white construction paper and markers. Let them draw an animal that they would like, one from their imagination.

Physical Education: Play Red Rover. Red Rover starts with two teams on opposite sides of the room. The teams line up, holding hands tightly. Then, someone from one team calls out, "Red Rover, Red Rover, send _____ right over." Then that "_____" person runs over to the line, trying to break up the bond of held-hands between the people. If the bond is broken, that person gets to choose one other person to join their line on the other side. If he/she fails to break through the line, then he/she must join the other team. Each team alternates calling people over until one team has all the people and is declared the winner.

Homework: Send Lesson 119 Homework worksheet home with students. This will help them to be prepared for the zoo trip tomorrow. Your school may also require a release form that must be signed and returned before the students can go on such a trip.

NOTES:

Activities in this Lesson: Bible Lesson, Social Studies/Outdoor Activity, Language Arts/Outdoor Activity, Phonics, Reading, Writing, Memory Verse, Math, Shapes, Story Time, Music, Arts & Crafts/Outdoor Activity, Physical Education/Outdoor Activity

Bible Reference: Genesis 1:24-25.

Bible Concept to Present: God gave us the mammals as a gift. We must care for what God has given.

Bible Lesson: (Teachers Note: We suggest a trip to the zoo today. You may incorporate all subjects while you are at the zoo.) God made the mammals and put them in man's care. By caring for the mammals, we show God how much we appreciate His wonderful gift. We need to take care of the mammals, since they were a gift to us. If we do not take care of what God gave us, we soon will not have it. Sometimes, man is not very nice to the mammals. Sometimes, we don't take care of them. We cut down their homes by cutting down the trees or grasses. We must be careful not to destroy what mammals eat or make their water dirty. When we no longer have a certain kind of animal, we call that animal extinct. We must always take care of animals, not let them become extinct. Teachers Note: If you desire, you may tell about a near extinct mammal, such as the American Bison, who was driven from his home on the prairie because man cut the grass and took over his roaming places.

If you are unable to make a trip to a zoo take an imaginary trip to the zoo. Go on a walk outside and imagine animals in the bushes and up in the trees. Ask them what animal they might see in a particular place. Use a mud puddle for an imaginary lake or pond. What animals could be found around the pond?

Social Studies/Outdoor Activity: These may be taught as you observe each animal. Mention how each mammal helps us, is different from another mammal, or is similar. Notice eye location, nose location, size, type of hoof, etc.

Language Arts/Outdoor Activity: Encourage your student to verbalize about what he sees. You may also play a "Mammal A B C" game. You start by naming a mammal that begins with the letter A - then B - then C etc. with students guessing also. NOTE: If you play this game, keep to the mammals that begin with the short sound of the letter. Long sounds may confuse the child learning phonics.

A Mammals: Aardvarks, Aardwolf, Addax, African Buffalo, African Elephant, African Hunting or Wild Dog, African Lion, African Wild Dog, Agoutis, Albatross/Gooney Bird, American Badger, American Mink, American Porcupine, Anteater, Antelopes, Ape, Arctic Hare, Arctic Wolf, Armadillo, Artic Fox, Artic Hare, Artic Wolf, Asian Elephant, Asian Lion, Aye-Ayes

B Mammals: Baboon, Badgers, Banded Mongoose, Bandicoot, Bats, Beagle, Bears, Beaver, Beluga Whale, Bettongs, Big Brown Bat, Bighorn Sheep, Bilby, Bison, Black Bear, Black Lemur, Black Swan, Black-footed Ferret, Blue Whale, Bobcat, Bobcat, Bongo, Bowhead Whale, Brown Bear, Brown Rat, Buck, Buffalo, African, Bull, Bunny

C Mammals: Camel, Canine Family, Cape Buffalo, Capuchin Monkey, Capybaras, Caracal, Caribou (Reindeer), Cats, Cheetah, Chimpanzee, Chimps & Bonobos, Chinchillas, Chipmunk, Chiru or Tibetan Antelope, Civets, Coatis, Colugos, Cougar/Catamount/Puma/Mountain Lion, Cow, Coyote, Crocodile

D Mammals: Deer, Dhole, Dik Dik, Dingoes, Dog, Dolphins & Porpoises, Donkey, Doracas Gazelle, Duck-billed Platypus, Dugongs, Duiker

E **Mammals:** Eagle, Eastern Chipmunk, Eastern Cougar, Eastern Tarsier, Echidnas, Eland, Elephant, Elephant Seal, Elk, Ermine

F **Mammals:** Fennec Fox, Ferrets, Fin Whale, Fishers, Florida Manatee, Florida Panther, Flying Squirrel, Fox

G **Mammals:** Gaur, Gazelle, Gerbils & Jirds, Giant Anteater, Giant Armadillo, Giant Panda, Gibbon, Gibbons & Siamangs, Giraffe, Goat, Gophers, Gorilla, Gray Wolf/Timber Wolf, Great Panda Bear, Grey Fox, Grey Whale, Grizzly Bear, Groundhog/Woodchuck, Guinea Pig

H **Mammals:** Hairy-tailed Mole, Hamsters, Harp Seal, Hartebeest, Hedgehogs, Hippopotamus, Hoary Marmot, Hooded Seal, Horse, House Mouse, Howler Monkey, Hummingbird, Humpback Whale, Hyena, Hyraxes

I **Mammals:** Ibex, Ibis, Impala, Indian Rhinoceros

J **Mammals:** Jackal, Jackrabbit, Jaguar, Jaguarundi

K **Mammals:** Kangaroo, Kangaroo Rat, Kangaroos, Killer Whale (Orca), Kinkajous, Klipspringer, Koala Bear, Kudu

L **Mammals:** Lamb, Least Weasel, Lemmings, Lemur, Leopards, Lion, Llama, Lorises, Lynx

M **Mammals:** Mali Spiny-Tailed Lizard, Manatee, Maned Wolf, Mangabey, Marmosets & Tamarins, Marmot, Marten, Mediterranean Monk Seal, Meerkats, Mice, Mink, Moles, Mongoose, Monkey, Moose, Mountain Goat, Mountain Gorilla, Mountain Lion/Cougar/Catamount/Puma, Mouse, Muskox, Muskrat

N **Mammals:** Naked Mole Rats, Nilgai, Numbats, Nutria, Nyala

O **Mammals:** Ocelot, Opossums, Orangutan, Orca/Killer Whale, Oryx, Otters, Ox/Oxen

P **Mammals:** Panda Bear, Pangolins, Panther, Pata Monkey, Peary Caribou, Peccary, Pigs & Swine, Pika, Platypus, Polar Bear, Pony, Porcupines, Possum/Opossum, Potoroos, Prairie Dogs, Pronghorn Antelope, Prosimians, Przewalski's Horse, Puma/Catamount/Cougar/Mountain Lion, Puppy, Pygmy Hippopotamus

Q **Mammals:** Quokkas, Quolls

R **Mammals:** Rabbits & Hares, Raccoon, Raccoon Dog, Rats, Red Fox, Red Panda, Red Squirrel, Redtail Monkey, Reindeer, Rhinoceros, Richardson Ground, River Otter

S **Mammals:** Sable Antelope, Sea Lion/Sea Cow, Sea Otter, Seals, Sei Whale, Sheep & Goats, Shrews, Skunk, Sloth, Small-eared Dog, Snow Leopard, Sperm Whale, Spider Monkey, Spotted Hyena, Squirrel, Squirrel Monkey, Star-nosed Mole, Striped Skunk, Sugar Gliders

T **Mammals:** Tamarins, Tanuki, Tapir, Tasmanian Devil, Tasmanian Tiger or Wolf, Tenrecs, Thomson's Gazelle, Tiger, Timber Wolf/Gray Wolf

U **Mammals:** Ungulates (hooved animals)

V **Mammals:** Vancouver Island Marmot, Voles

W **Mammals:** Wallabies, Walrus, Wart Hog, Waterbuck, Weasel, Whales, White Rhinoceros, White Whale, White-faced Monkey, Wild Ass, Wild Yak, Wildebeest, Wolf, Wolverine, Wolves, Wombat, Woodchuck/Groundhog, Woolly Monkey, Wrasse

X **Mammals:** Xenops

Y **Mammals:** Yak

Z **Mammals:** Zebra, Zorilla, Zorro

Phonics: Blend the sounds Aa-Ii. (if, bib, fib, bid, did, hid, big, dig, fig, Bic, hic) Review the initial sounds of Aa-Ii. Review letter recognition Aa-Zz.

Add the following words to the flip chart pages of words and review them with the students. Continue to sound out the individual letters of each word as has been done previously. It may also be helpful for the students to see the words spaced out and spelled out as has been done in previous lessons.

<u>bi</u>	<u>di</u>	<u>fi</u>	<u>hi</u>	<u>if</u>	<u>gi</u>
bib	did	fib	hic	if	gig
Bic	dig	fig	hid		
bid					
big					

Do the Lesson 120a Phonics worksheet. The Short Sound of Ii. Review the letter sound with the picture and words on the worksheet. Ask the students for other words that begin with the same sound. Trace the letters and say the short sound of Ii. Observe the students as they trace the letters and help them with the letter strokes. If you have the students do one row at a time, the worksheet can be carried over to various parts of the day or another day.

Do the Lesson 120b Phonics worksheet. The Short Sound of Ii. Review the letter sound with the picture and words on the worksheet. Ask the students for other words that begin with the same sound. Give them specific instructions for how the letter should be traced. Allow time for tracing the letters and observe their progress. If you have the students do one row at a time, the worksheet can be carried over to various parts of the day or another day.

Reading: Given a sound and two words, identify the word that begins with the sound. Assemble a simple object or craft following illustrated directions.

Writing: Write one's first name.

Memory Verse: Let the students recite the verse Genesis 1:24a if they want to. Reward all students for working on this long verse.

Math: Review 4 + 1 = 5. Give each student 10 pennies to count 1-10. Have the students add pennies to practice the addition facts: 1 + 1 = 2, 2 + 1 = 3, 3 + 1 = 4, 4 + 1 = 5.

Do the Lesson 120a Math worksheet. Read the number. Count the dots under the number. Draw 7 objects in the counting jar. Trace the number 7 following the proper strokes. The students can color the counting jar.

Do the Lesson 120b Math worksheet. Count the first group of pennies in the row and say "plus one penny," then count all of the pennies to get the answer. Trace the correct number.

Shapes: Review triangle, circle, square, rectangle, star, heart, oval, and diamond shapes with the "Shape Song." Give each student a set of shapes so they can hold up the shape for each verse of the song.

Do the Lesson 120 Shapes worksheet. Can the students correctly identify the shapes? The circle will not follow a smooth curve.

Story Time: Read a story or stories of your student's choice or ones they have brought from home.

Music: Review "In a Cabin In the Woods."

Multimedia Resources: This week, listen and sing along to selections from "The Amazing Miracles" CD.

Arts & Crafts/Outdoor Activity: After you view the mammals, have the students draw their favorite, the biggest, the smallest, the prettiest, the one with the longest nose, the one who spends most of it's time in water, the one who is the furriest, etc. Help them to label and date all drawings.

Physical Education: This is completed in the miles you will walk today at the zoo or outside.

ENJOY THE DAY!!!! This style of teaching and integrating subjects while on a field trip is a favorite. Children gain more from a field trip than ten days in the school room. Consider the various ways to utilize field trips. Either use it as we did today, with the integration of subjects, or you may use the field trip to introduce a subject and then use what you saw and what occurred as a conversation starter in the classroom. Another alternative is to use field trips as a review for what you have already studied. Remember: the more the children do and see, the more they remember.

NOTES:

Activities in this Lesson: Bible Lesson, Social Studies, Science, Language Arts, Phonics, Reading, Writing, Memory Verse, Math, Shapes, Story Time, Music, Physical Education, Catch Up

Bible Reference: Genesis 1:24-26.

Bible Concept to Present: When God created the creeping things of the earth, He created reptiles.

Bible Lesson: God made the sun, moon, and stars. He made all plant life and animal life. Review each day of Creation at this time. You can use the Days of Creation Numbers. When God made creeping things of the earth on the sixth day, He made reptiles. A reptile is a cold-blooded creature (contrast this to a mammal which is warm blooded). It relies on the direct sun or heat from its surroundings to warm itself. A reptile creeps or crawls on the ground. If it has legs, its legs are short and stubby. Some examples of reptiles are snakes, alligators, crocodiles, lizards, and turtles. God made all animals different with different needs. God is so wonderful to give us so many different kinds of animals, isn't he?

Multimedia Resources: Listen to the song "It's Time To Let My People Go" from the "Bullfrogs and Butterflies: God is Great" CD.

Social Studies: Reptiles are all around us. Some reptiles live in the desert where it is very, very hot. Others live in and near the water. For example, a turtle could be found near a pond, a river, or in the desert. God made the turtle to carry its own house to protect itself. A crocodile lives near the swamp (explain the word) and helps to eat bugs and snakes. Snakes live everywhere. Some live in water and some live under rocks. Everywhere you go some form of reptile lives nearby. God made the reptiles to be very special.

Science: Reptiles vary in each form, but all have some things in common.
1. Reptiles all either crawl on their belly or have very short stubby legs.
2. Most reptiles have scaly skin such as the skin of a snake.
3. All reptiles must be warmed by the sun. This means that when winter comes, the reptile must hide in the earth or it would freeze. When a warm day comes, the reptiles can be found sunning themselves to get warm again.
4. Reptiles lay eggs to bear young; some give live birth.

Language Arts: Discuss the concept of larger and smaller. Although your students may already have a general idea of comparison, help them to master the concept and to integrate it into their every day language. Gather several items of various sizes. As you pick up an item, tell students that the item is larger than another item you have chosen. Continue to compare items, including students in the discussion. Throughout this week, as you are comparing items, compare each item with something that is larger than the item you are holding and something that is smaller than the item you are holding. Your objective is to introduce the fact that larger and smaller are comparative to the items being discussed.

Phonics: Teach the initial sound of Jj. Review the initial sounds of Aa-Ii. Review letter recognition Aa-Zz.

Write several initial Jj words on the board: jab, Jack, jag, jam, jar, jig, jet, jay, jut, etc. Underline the initial letter Jj and say the words. Ask the students for other words that start with the same sound.

Do the Lesson 121 Phonics worksheet. The Sound of Jj. Review the letter sound with the picture and words on the worksheet. Ask the students for other words that begin with the same sound. Discuss the position of the letters on the guidelines. Give them specific instructions for how the letter should be traced. Trace the letters and say the sound of Jj. Observe the students as they trace the letters and help them with the letter strokes. If you have the students do one row at a time, the worksheet can be carried over to various parts of the day or another day.

Reading: Use a simplified, illustrated telephone listing. Give the beginning sound of a word. Identify the name and sound of the letters in one's name.

Multimedia Resources: Review "Rev-Up for Reading" from the "Rev-Up for Learning" DVD to drill letter recognition and sound. The students should say each letter sound along with the presentation.

Writing: If a computer is available for the students to use, give them an opportunity to type their names using a word processing program. You may provide the Name Plates but the goal is for them to type their names without them. Allow them to type other words or sentences if they are ready to do so. An old typewriter could also be used for this activity.

Try doing Learning Logs. Encourage the students to draw or write about themselves. Some sample topics might be My Pet, My Favorite Reptile, My Favorite School Activity, My Family, or other teacher selected topics. The writing can be invented temporary spellings or dictations to the teacher.

Multimedia Resources: Review "Rev-Up for Writing" from the "Rev-Up for Learning" DVD to review the writing of upper- and lowercase letters.

Memory Verse: Take time for the next two weeks to review the memory verses that the students have learned so far. Genesis 1:1, Genesis 1:3, Genesis 1:6, Genesis 1:10, I Peter 1:24-25, Genesis 8:22, Genesis 1:16, Psalm 90:12, Psalm 89:1, Revelation 22:16, Psalm 148:13, Genesis 1:26, Psalm 48:1, Matthew 6:26a, and Genesis 1:24a.

Math: Teach 5 + 1 = 6. Have groups of students come to the front of the room to demonstrate that 5 + 1 = 6 as has been done in previous lessons. If there are not enough students then demonstrate the concept on the board with drawings or on a table with objects that are the same.

Do the Lesson 121 Math worksheet. Read the number. Count the dots under the number. Draw 8 objects in the counting jar. Trace the number 8 following the proper strokes. The students can color the counting jar.

Multimedia Resources: View "Rev-Up for Arithmetic" from the "Rev-Up for Learning" DVD to practice number recognition, counting and addition 1-20.

Shapes: Review triangle, circle, square, rectangle, star, heart, oval, and diamond shapes with the "Shape Song." Give each student a set of shapes so they can hold up the shape for each verse of the song.

Story Time: Read a story or stories of your choice.

Music: Review "In a Cabin In the Woods."

Multimedia Resources: This week, listen and sing along to selections from "Bullfrogs and Butterflies: I've Been Born Again" CD.

Physical Education: Do the "Reptile Crawl." Get on the ground and crawl like a snake. Hiss like a snake and do snake type things. Do a "Galapagos Walk." Crawl like a turtle, very, very, slow. Be an alligator and snap up a cracker or two. Continue this throughout the week with the variation of music. If you put on fast music, is it hard to crawl slowly?

Catch Up: Do any activities that you have been unable to get completed over the past several days.

NOTES:

Activities in this Lesson: Bible Lesson, Social Studies, Science, Language Arts/Music, Phonics, Reading, Writing, Memory Verse, Math, Shapes, Story Time, Music, Arts & Crafts, Physical Education

Bible Reference: Genesis 1:24-26.

Bible Concept to Present: God made many kinds of reptiles.

Bible Lesson: Review yesterday's lesson, emphasizing that God made even more animals. Facts about reptiles: there are about 250 species of turtles, 25 species of crocodilians, 5,500 species of snakes, 3,000 species of lizards, 130 species of amphibians. Add "Snakes: 5,500" and "Turtles: 250" to the Facts Poster.

Social Studies: *If possible bring a reptile to class.* Look at our reptile friend. Does he have the characteristics we talked about yesterday? How are reptiles different? What did we learn yesterday? Can you cuddle with a reptile, like with a kitten? Will a reptile do what you tell them to, like a dog does?

Science: Go to this web site, if possible, and copy off some of the wonderful pictures of Galapagos island to share with students. http://www.lammerlaw.com/photos/ss25.html The Galapagos Islands are named after the Galapagos Turtle. These islands are unusual because there are many unusual animals that live there that can't be found anywhere else. If you have a computer in your classroom, show students how to look for information. Put "Galapagos islands animals" in a search engine and look at what you find. Be careful of evolutionary comments.

Language Arts/Music: Here is a song that can be used to review the letters and sounds of the alphabet. There is an illustrated book by the same name that is very interesting to look at. The students may just be able to say the letters of the alphabet while you sing the remainder of the song to them. Midi files for this song and many of the songs used in the Horizons Preschool program can be found at the Kids Pages of the National Institute of Environmental Health Sciences website. http://www.niehs.nih.gov/kids/home.htm You can also just make up a tune; the kids will never know the difference.

A, You're Adorable
(The Alphabet Love Song)

(chorus)
"A," you're adorable, "B," you're so beautiful,
"C," you're a cutie full of charms.
"D," you're a darling and "E," you're exciting
And "F," you're a feather in my arms.
"G," you look good to me, "H," you're so heavenly,
"I," you're the one I idolize.
"J," we're like Jack and Jill, "K," you're so kissable,
"L," is the lovelight in your eyes.
"M," "N," "O," "P," I could go on all day.
"Q," "R," "S," "T," alphabetically speaking, you're OK.

U," made my life complete, "V," means you're very sweet,
Double-"U" "X" "Y" "Zee."
It's fun to wander through the alphabet with you
To tell you what you mean to me.
(repeat the chorus)

Words and original music: Buddy Kaye, Fred Wise and Sidney Lippman
Copyright: 1948 Music of the Times Publ. Corp.
Recorded by Perry Como and the Fontane Sisters

Multimedia Resources: This week, listen and sing along to selections from "Bullfrogs and Butterflies: I've Been Born Again" CD.

Phonics: Teach the initial sound of Jj. Review the initial sounds of Aa-Ii. Review letter recognition Aa-Zz.

Do the Lesson 122 Phonics worksheet. The Sound of Jj. Review the letter sound with the picture and words on the worksheet. Ask the students for other words that begin with the same sound. Trace the letters and say the sound of Jj. Observe the students as they trace the letters and help them with the letter strokes. If you have the students do one row at a time, the worksheet can be carried over to various parts of the day or another day.

Reading: Use a simplified, illustrated telephone listing. Give the beginning sound of a word. Identify the name and sound of the letters in one's name.

Writing: Have the students type their names on a computer or with a typewriter.

Memory Verse: Take time these two weeks to review the memory verses that the students have learned so far. Genesis 1:1, Genesis 1:3, Genesis 1:6, Genesis 1:10, I Peter 1:24-25, Genesis 8:22, Genesis 1:16, Psalm 90:12, Psalm 89:1, Revelation 22:16, Psalm 148:13, Genesis 1:26, Psalm 48:1, Matthew 6:26a, and Genesis 1:24a.

Math: Review 5 + 1 = 6. Give the students the dog bones that they cut out previously and a bowl to put them in. Have them place 5 bones in the bowl while saying "five plus one" and have them place another bone in the bowl, "equals" and have them count "one, two, three, four, five, six bones in the bowl." Do this several times. Reverse the order and also practice previous addition facts.

Do the Lesson 122 Math worksheet. As they count the images have them say the addition problems and trace the numbers.

Shapes: Review triangle, circle, square, rectangle, star, heart, oval, and diamond shapes with the "Shape Song." Give each student a set of shapes so he can hold up the shape for each verse of the song.

Story Time: Read a story or stories of your choice.

Arts & Crafts: Let the students add some snakes and lizards to the Creation Mural. They may use poster pens and draw right onto the mural paper. Be sure to save room for man at the top of day six. Make clay, using the recipe on Lesson 14. Let the students help mix the clay. Then have the students make snakes and lizards. Let the clay dry for two days. This craft will be continued in Lesson 124.

Physical Education: Let the students crawl and be reptiles again. Encourage them to be accurate in their enactment.

NOTES:

Activities in this Lesson: Bible Lesson, Social Studies, Science, Language Arts, Phonics, Reading, Writing, Memory Verse, Math, Shapes, Story Time, Music/Language Arts, Arts & Crafts, Physical Education

Bible Reference: Genesis 1:24-26.

Bible Concept to Present: God made many different kinds of reptiles when He created them on the sixth day.

Bible Lesson: When God made reptiles on the sixth day, He made many different kinds of them. God made the snakes. He made some snakes to be big (such as the Boa Constrictor), He made some snakes to be small (Garter Snakes). Because God made snakes to be different from one another, we should know about snakes and which snakes we should never pick up because today some snakes are very, very poisonous.

God made turtles. Turtles are unique because they carry their homes with them. Turtles live in many different places. There are many kinds of turtles, big and little, some that live in water, and some that live on land. Turtles eat vegetables, fish, insects, and crustaceans.

God made alligators and crocodiles. These reptiles live near the swamps. They eat fish, insects, and small animals. They have short legs. There is a difference between alligators and crocodiles. Crocodiles are larger than alligators. Crocodiles are scalier than alligators. They are important to the balance of nature in our world today. God made lizards. Lizards are scaly and often have horns. They live in hot dry places and wet, damp places. Lizards eat insects. Each reptile was made by God and given to us to help us. God knew what He was doing when he made the reptiles.

Social Studies: Reptiles help us in many ways. One of the most important things that they do is keep the harmful insect population down. They eat many insects, that were they not controlled, would harm our food supply and spread disease.

Science: Most reptiles reproduce by laying eggs. Often a reptile will lay its eggs, bury them in the sand and then disappear. They rarely care for their young. The eggs hatch on their own and the babies are on their own to care for themselves. How is this different from most mammals' births?

Try to acquire small pieces of fake fur, leather, feathers, a piece of fish with skin, a snakeskin, and a realistic baby doll. Let the students compare the different types of skin. All mammals have hair, some more than others. Reptiles have scales. Talk about similarities and differences.

Language Arts: Play Name Bingo. Give each student their Name Card and a button or counter. The teacher randomly calls out a letter. If the letter appears in the student's name they should cover the letter with a button. The student who covers all of the letters in their name first is the winner and can shout out their name.

Phonics: Blend the sounds Aa-Jj. (jab, jib, Jif, jig, Jeb, jag) Review the initial sounds of Aa-Jj. Review letter recognition Aa-Zz.

Add the following words to the flip chart pages of words and review them with the students. Continue to sound out the individual letters of each word as has been done previously. It may also be helpful for the students to see the words spaced out and spelled out as has been done in previous lessons.

ja	je	ji
jab	Jeb	jib
jag		Jif
		jig

Do the Lesson 123 Phonics worksheet. The Sound of Jj. Review the letter sound with the picture and words on the worksheet. Ask the students for other words that begin with the same sound. Give them specific instructions for how the letter should be traced. Allow time for tracing the letters and observe their progress. If you have the students do one row at a time, the worksheet can be carried over to various parts of the day or another day.

Reading: Use a simplified, illustrated telephone listing. Give the beginning sound of a word. Identify the name and sound of the letters in one's name.

Writing: Have the students type their names on a computer or with a typewriter.

Memory Verse: Take time these two weeks to review the memory verses that the students have learned so far. Genesis 1:1, Genesis 1:3, Genesis 1:6, Genesis 1:10, I Peter 1:24-25, Genesis 8:22, Genesis 1:16, Psalm 90:12, Psalm 89:1, Revelation 22:16, Psalm 148:13, Genesis 1:26, Psalm 48:1, Matthew 6:26a, and Genesis 1:24a.

Math: Review 5 + 1 = 6. Review 5 + 1 = 6 by writing the problem on the board. Draw objects over the numbers with + sign between them. Write the = sign and then draw an excess of objects over the answer. Have a student come to the board and circle the correct number of objects to make the addition problem correct. Erase the extra objects and orally say the problem with the class. Repeat several times drawing simple objects such as dots or various shapes. Review previous addition problems if the students need the practice.

Do the Lesson 123a Math worksheet. Read the number. Count the dots under the number. Draw 9 objects in the counting jar. Trace the number 9 following the proper strokes. The students can color the bear.

Do the Lesson 123b Math worksheet. Count the items and say the addition problems. As they trace the numbers have them say the addition problems and trace the numbers.

Shapes: Review triangle, circle, square, rectangle, star, heart, oval, and diamond shapes with the song "Sing a Song of Shapes."

Sing a Song of Shapes
Tune of *If We All Will Pull Together*
by Al Christopherson

(Verse 1)
Sing a song of shapes, of shapes, of shapes
O sing a song of shapes, a song of shapes.

We have circles and triangles, (draw the shapes in the air with both hands)
diamonds and rectangles, (draw the shapes in the air with both hands)
O sing a song of shapes, a song of shapes.

(Verse 2)
Sing a song of shapes, of shapes, of shapes
O sing a song of shapes, a song of shapes.

We have ovals and heart shapes, (draw the shapes in the air with both hands)
squares and stars, (draw the shapes in the air with both hands)

O sing a song of shapes, a song of shapes.

Story Time: Read a story or stories of your choice.

Music/Language Arts: Review the *A, You're Adorable* song and book.

Multimedia Resources: This week, listen and sing along to selections from "Bullfrogs and Butterflies: I've Been Born Again" CD.

Arts & Crafts: Do the Lesson 123 Arts & Crafts worksheet. Observe the various colorings of snakes by bringing a library book to class. Give the students crayons and ask them to reproduce the colors of the snakes on the worksheet.

Prepare ahead – Cut out curvy pieces of cardboard or poster board about a foot long, one for each student. Wrap each piece in aluminum foil and tape it on. Have glitter, glue and craft "eyes" available. Give the students their foil "snake." First, tell them to make a pattern on the snake like a snake skin. Bring them glitter and let them shake it all over their glue. Have the students glue on two eyes. Let the snakes dry while you do the science lesson or let dry until tomorrow. Then come back and carefully tap the extra glitter into the trash can.

Physical Education: Repeat the game Red Rover from Lesson 119. Red Rover starts with two teams on opposite sides of the room. The teams line up, holding hands tightly. Then, someone from one team calls out, "Red Rover, Red Rover, send _____ right over." Then that "_____" person runs over to the line, trying to break up the bond of held-hands between the people. If the bond is broken, that person gets to choose one other person to join their line on the other side. If he/she fails to break through the line, then he/she must join the other team. Each team alternates calling people over until one team has all the people and is declared the winner.

NOTES:

Activities in this Lesson: Bible Lesson, Social Studies, Science, Language Arts, Phonics, Reading, Writing, Memory Verse, Math, Shapes, Story Time, Music/Language Arts, Arts & Crafts, Outdoor Activity, Physical Education

Bible Reference: Genesis 1:24-26.

Bible Concept to Present: God made some snakes that are poisonous.

Bible Lesson: God didn't make every animal for us to touch and hold. Some animals are poisonous and must be avoided. In the United States, the coral snake and the rattlesnake, or diamondback, are poisonous. That is why we have to be careful not to touch any snake unless we know what kind it is.

Illustration: Nearly all snakes avoid people and travel away from them. Don't ever chase a snake to pick it up. Since there are 5,500 species of snakes, we can tell that most snakes are NOT dangerous. Always wear long pants and shoes and socks when hiking. If you see a snake, call for an adult. Snakes move slowly so don't panic if you see one.

Social Studies: There aren't many reptiles that Americans normally eat, but when our great grandparents were alive, they ate what they could find because they were hungry. Turtle soup and frog legs were a treat. Snakes are edible. In the southwest, the rattlesnake was considered a delicacy by cowboys and Native Americans. In coastal areas like New Orleans, reptiles are served quite often. Talk about how different foods are eaten in different areas of the country and of the world.

Science: Discuss snakes that are common to your area. Help them learn to recognize common snakes. Most snakes are harmless and they eat rodents, earthworms, slugs, or bugs. Remind your students that when they see a snake they should not panic, unless you are in an area where there are many poisonous snakes. Snakes move slowly and it is not hard to move away from danger. Most people who have been bitten by a snake have been teasing or poking at them, or have accidentally stepped on or very close to them. Do not touch or handle a snake unless you know that it is not poisonous. Given a chance, most snakes will move away rather than pick a fight with something bigger. When you see a snake, leave it alone and it will move away on its own.

Language Arts: Read the Aesop's Fable *The Lion and the Mouse*. Role play by letting the students choose a partner and then take turns acting out the roles of the lion and the mouse after the story is read. The story is about a friendship between an unlikely pair.

The Lion and the Mouse

Once when a Lion was asleep a little Mouse began running up and down upon him; this soon wakened the Lion, who placed his huge paw upon him, and opened his big jaws to swallow him. "Pardon, O King," cried the little Mouse: "forgive me this time, I shall never forget it: who knows but what I may be able to do you a turn some of these days?"

The Lion was so tickled at the idea of the Mouse being able to help him that he lifted up his paw and let him go. Some time after the Lion was caught in a trap, and the hunters who desired to carry him alive to the King, tied him to a tree while they went in search of a wagon to carry him on.

Just then the little Mouse happened to pass by, and seeing the sad plight in which the Lion was, went up to him and soon gnawed away the ropes that bound the King of the Beasts. "Was I not right?" said the little Mouse.

Little friends may prove great friends.

Phonics: Review blends Aa-Jj with the blend charts. Review the initial sounds of Aa-Jj. Review letter recognition Aa-Zz.

Have the students brainstorm words that begin or include the letter Jj. Write these words on the board. Model the correct letter formation as you write the letters on the board. The students should practice forming the letter Jj on a blank sheet of paper. Students who are ready can practice copying complete words from the board.

Do the Lesson 124 Phonics worksheet. The Sound of Jj. Review the letter sound with the picture and words on the worksheet. Ask the students for other words that begin with the same sound. Trace the letters and say the sound of Jj. Observe the students as they trace the letters and help them with the letter strokes. If you have the students do one row at a time, the worksheet can be carried over to various parts of the day or another day.

Reading: Use a simplified, illustrated telephone listing. Give the beginning sound of a word. Identify the name and sound of the letters in one's name.

Writing: Have the students type their names on a computer or with a typewriter.

Memory Verse: Take time these two weeks to review the memory verses that the students have learned so far. Genesis 1:1, Genesis 1:3, Genesis 1:6, Genesis 1:10, I Peter 1:24-25, Genesis 8:22, Genesis 1:16, Psalm 90:12, Psalm 89:1, Revelation 22:16, Psalm 148:13, Genesis 1:26, Psalm 48:1, Matthew 6:26a, and Genesis 1:24a.

Math: Review 5 + 1 = 6. Give each of the students 10 counters. Have them count the objects to make sure that they have 10 objects. Have them make the addition problem with the counters. Have them point to the counters and say the addition problem, drawing the plus and equal sign with their finger between the counters as they say the words. Review previous problems if the students need the practice.

Do the Lesson 124 Math worksheet. As they trace the numbers have them say the addition problems. Have them check the problems with counters.

Shapes: Review triangle, circle, square, rectangle, star, heart, oval, and diamond shapes with the song "Sing a Song of Shapes."

Story Time: Read a story or stories of your choice.

Music/Language Arts: Review the *A, You're Adorable* song and book.

Multimedia Resources: This week, listen and sing along to selections from "Bullfrogs and Butterflies: I've Been Born Again" CD.

Arts & Crafts: Use poster pens to color the snakes and lizards that the students made in Lesson 122. Encourage them to draw little scales of color. Talk about the patterns on snake skin.

Purchase several bags of colorful beads, large enough for the students to string. Also provide pieces of string for each student. Give the students beads and string. Let them make "snakes" out of the beads. Tie the beads at each end to secure.

Outdoor Activity: Talk a walk. Let the students act out what they would do if they saw a snake. Remind them that they would always tell a parent or a teacher. Talk about places that snakes live, under brush or rocks.

Physical Education: Snake Path. Tape arrows, dots, footsteps, squares, triangles, etc. in an area to designate a movement course. Form zigzag, straight and curved lines with the shapes or markers. The students are to follow the markers on the course using a variety of movements, skipping, hopping, crawling, jumping, etc. as they go from start to finish on the course.

NOTES:

Lesson 125

Week 25: Day 5

Activities in this Lesson: Bible Lesson, Social Studies/Science, Language Arts, Phonics, Reading, Writing, Memory Verse, Math, Shapes, Story Time, Music/Language Arts, Arts & Crafts, Physical Education

Bible Reference: Genesis 1:24-26.

Bible Concept to Present: God has given us the reptiles to enjoy and to help us. We must care for them.

Bible Lesson: When God made the reptiles, He made them for us. God took great care to make them. We need to take care of what God has made for us. Reptiles are exposed to water a great deal of the time. We must keep our water supplies clean. Let's think of ways to keep the water supplies clean. Man also hunts reptiles for their skin. It is important that we never kill a reptile unless we need that reptile to help us survive. God has been very good to us by giving us reptiles. He wants us to take care of them. We can thank God for giving us reptiles by taking care of them.

Social Studies/Science: Present a general overview of our ecological system. This can be a simple drawing of a circle. You may use the following illustration to guide your drawing. We suggest you enlarge this for your students.

Language Arts: Play a game of "Guess What I Am?" with students. To begin the game, describe a reptile you have talked about. Give just one description clue. Example: This reptile has a hard shell. If students guess turtle immediately, try to make the clues harder. If students cannot guess after a time, give another clue. Just three clues are allowed. If the student guesses the reptile's name, it will be his turn to give you clues.

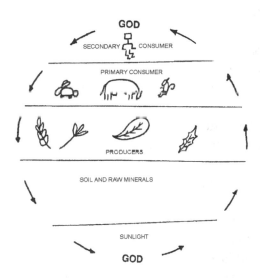

Phonics: Teach the initial sound Kk. Review the initial sounds of Aa-Jj. Review letter recognition Aa-Zz.

Write several initial Kk words on the board: key, kid, kill, kit, king, kiss, etc. Underline the initial letter Kk and say the words. Ask the students for other words that start with the same sound.

Do the Lesson 125 Phonics worksheet. The Sound of Kk. Review the letter sound with the picture and words on the worksheet. Ask the students for other words that begin with the same sound. Discuss the position of the letters on the guidelines. Give them specific instructions for how the letter should be traced. Trace the letters and say the sound of Kk. Observe the students as they trace the letters and help them with the letter strokes. If you have the students do one row at a time, the worksheet can be carried over to various parts of the day or another day.

Reading: Use a simplified, illustrated telephone listing. Give the beginning sound of a word. Identify the name and sound of the letters in one's name.

Writing: Have the students type their names on a computer or with a typewriter.

Memory Verse: Take time these two weeks to review the memory verses that the students have learned so far. Genesis 1:1, Genesis 1:3, Genesis 1:6, Genesis 1:10, I Peter 1:24-25, Genesis 8:22, Genesis 1:16, Psalm 90:12, Psalm 89:1, Revelation 22:16, Psalm 148:13, Genesis 1:26, Psalm 48:1, Matthew 6:26a, and Genesis 1:24a.

Math: Review 5 + 1 = 6.

Do the Lesson 125a Math worksheet. Read the number. Count the dots under the number. Draw 10 objects in the counting jar. Trace the number 10 following the proper strokes. The students can color the counting jar.

Do the Lesson 125b Math worksheet. Circle the correct number of objects to answer the addition problems.

Shapes: Review triangle, circle, square, rectangle, star, heart, oval, and diamond shapes with the song "Sing a Song of Shapes."

Do the Lesson 125 Shapes worksheet. Have the students count the number of each shape and write the answer on the line. They can color the Shape Lady figure as they wish.

Story Time: Read a story or stories of your student's choice or ones they have brought from home.

Music/Language Arts: Review the *A, You're Adorable* song and book.

Multimedia Resources: This week, listen and sing along to selections from "Bullfrogs and Butterflies: I've Been Born Again" CD.

Arts & Crafts: Give the students playdough. Let them make their favorite reptile.

Physical Education: Follow the Leader. Begin by dividing the students into groups of two. Do this activity in a large outdoor area with boundaries where they can and cannot move. The role of the leader is to move in different directions and in a manner that they think a reptile would move. Snakes-crawl, frogs-hop, turtles-all fours, alligator-all fours, include motions of the head that the reptile makes if possible. The follower should follow the leader and do the same movements. After a minute or so, switch the places of the leader and the follower. Remind the students to leave some space between themselves and the leader and to watch out for other teams as they play the game. This activity can be done in open space or on a playground where the equipment becomes part of the challenge to imitate reptile movements.

NOTES:

Activities in this Lesson: Bible Lesson, Social Studies, Science, Language Arts, Phonics, Reading, Writing, Memory Verse, Math, Story Time, Science, Music/Language Arts, Science/Arts & Crafts/Outdoor Activity, Physical Education/Outdoor Activity

Bible Reference: Genesis 1:24-26.

Bible Concept to Present: When God made creeping things on the sixth day, He made insects.

Bible Lesson: God made insects and bugs on the sixth day of Creation. God made every bug in the world. He made the ant, the bee, the lady bug, and all the creepy, crawly beetles. God made an insect to have three main parts to its body and six legs. A spider is not an insect because it has eight legs. God made the insects to help us. He wants us to be glad He made insects.

Multimedia Resources: Listen to the song "God Knows Everything" from "The Music Machine: The Majesty Of God" CD.

Social Studies: Insects are very helpful to man. (Note: Only ten percent of the insect population is harmful to man.) They live near the soil and help to keep air in our soil. They also help to give us food by pollinating (explain word) the plants so they can produce fruit. God blessed us very much when He gave us insects.

Science: An insect must fit the following description: It must have three body parts, six legs, and usually has compound eyes. Consider the bugs around your home. Which is a true insect? We suggest that you begin a collection of insects. If you wish to make a live collection, be sure you know what the insect eats before you catch it. You may also make a mounted insect collection. To do so, prepare a "Bug Jar" in which you place cotton balls soaked in alcohol. Lay a small piece of cloth over the soaked cotton to keep the insects from smashing their body parts. Be certain there is a tight fitting lid to the jar. Capture the insects in the jar. The alcohol will kill them. Then mount them on a piece of cardboard or foam with pins. Label all entries.

Language Arts: Play a "Bug in the Rug" game with your students. Take a small lightweight rug and pretend to have several bugs under it. Pinching your thumb and forefinger together, pretend to take a bug out from under the rug. Examples: The "Hug Bug" - Give your student a hug; The "Laugh Bug" – laugh out loud; The "Dance Bug" – do a little jig. Your students will love the game more if they can make up bug names, too. *First Book of Nature*, an Usborne book, has a chapter on "Creepy Crawlies"... bugs and slugs, spiders and snails.

Multimedia Resources: Watch "Goodness" from the *Character Builders Video Series*.

Phonics: Blend the sounds Aa-Kk. (kid, keg) Review the initial sounds of Aa-Kk. Review letter recognition Aa-Zz.

Add the following words to the flip chart pages of words and review them with the students. Continue to sound out the individual letters of each word as has been done previously. It may also be helpful for the students to see the words spaced out and spelled out as has been done in previous lessons.

ke   ki
keg   kid

Do the Lesson 126a Phonics worksheet. The sound of Kk. Review the letter sound with the picture and words on the worksheet. Ask the students for other words that begin with the same sound. Trace the letters and say the sound of Kk. Observe the students as they trace the letters and help them with the letter strokes. If you have the students do one row at a time, the worksheet can be carried over to various parts of the day or another day.

Do the Lesson 126b Phonics worksheet. The Sound of Kk. Review the letter sound with the picture and words on the worksheet. Ask the students for other words that begin with the same sound. Give them specific instructions for how the letter should be traced. Allow time for tracing the letters and observe their progress. If you have the students do one row at a time, the worksheet can be carried over to various parts of the day or another day.

Reading: Use a simplified, illustrated telephone listing. Give the beginning sound of a word. Identify the name and sound of the letters in one's name.

Multimedia Resources: Review "Rev-Up for Reading" from the "Rev-Up for Learning" DVD to drill letter recognition and sound. The students should say each letter sound along with the presentation.

Writing: Have the students type their names on a computer or with a typewriter.

Multimedia Resources: Review "Rev-Up for Writing" from the "Rev-Up for Learning" DVD to review the writing of upper- and lowercase letters.

Music: Sing and learn "Skeeters And The Bed Bugs" on the "Horizons Preschool Music" CD.

Multimedia Resources: This week, listen and sing along to selections from "Music Machine: The Fruit Of The Spirit" CD.

Memory Verse: Take time these two weeks to review the memory verses that the students have learned so far. Genesis 1:1, Genesis 1:3, Genesis 1:6, Genesis 1:10, I Peter 1:24-25, Genesis 8:22, Genesis 1:16, Psalm 90:12, Psalm 89:1, Revelation 22:16, Psalm 148:13, Genesis 1:26, Psalm 48:1, Matthew 6:26a, and Genesis 1:24a.

Math: Review 5 + 1 = 6. Use the string of Counting Beads or pop beads to review 1 + 1 = 2, 2 + 1 = 3, 3 + 1 = 4, 4 + 1 = 5, and 5 + 1 = 6.

Do the Lesson 126a Math worksheet. Read the number. Count the dots under the number. Draw 11 objects in the counting jar. Trace the number 11 following the proper strokes The students can color the counting jar.

Do the Lesson 126b Math worksheet. Count the beads and say the addition problem. Trace the correct answer and say the addition problem again.

Multimedia Resources: View "Rev-Up for Arithmetic" from the "Rev-Up for Learning" DVD to practice number recognition, counting and addition 1-20.

Shapes: Review triangle, circle, square, rectangle, star, heart, oval, and diamond shapes with the song "Sing a Song of Shapes."

Story Time: Read a story or stories of your choice.

Music/Language Arts: Review the *A, You're Adorable* song and book.

Science/Arts & Crafts/Outdoor Activity: Take a Spider Web Search walk. It might take some time, but find a good spider web. Taking white paper and a can of spray paint, place the paper behind a spider web, and lightly spray the web. The outline of the web should be distinguishable on the paper. Be alert to the direction of the wind when doing this.

Physical Education/Outdoor Activity: We will be taking a "Bug Walk" every day this week. Have the students bring their bug jars. Talk a walk, turning over rocks and leaves to find bugs. Carefully put the bugs in the bug jars and take them back to class for the insect collection. This may be combined with the Spider Search Walk.

NOTES:

Lesson 127

Week 26: Day 2

Activities in this Lesson: Bible Lesson, Science, Language Arts, Phonics, Reading, Writing, Memory Verse, Math, Shapes, Story Time/Arts & Crafts, Music/Language Arts, Music, Arts & Crafts, Creative Cooking, Physical Education/Outdoor Activity

Bible Reference: Genesis 1:24-26.

Bible Concept to Present: God made an unbelievable number of insects on the sixth day.

Bible Lesson: Remind the class about how many animals God made on the sixth day. Then talk about how many insects there are. There are over 900,000 known insects. Scientists guess that there are more unknown insects than are known.

Illustration: Put this on your Facts Poster: "Insects: 900,000" "At any time, it is estimated that there are some 10 quintillion (10,000,000,000,000,000,000) individual insects alive. Certain social insects have large numbers in their nests. An ant nest in Jamaica was calculated to include 630,000 individuals. A South American termite nest was found to have 3 million individuals. Locust swarms are said to hold up to one billion individuals." *

Science: You may choose to make a simple ant farm. Use a large tea jar. Make many pinprick holes in the lid with a nail. Don't make the holes very big. Set a smaller jar, like a well washed pickle jar, inside the large jar. Pack the space between the jars with sand or soil, about 3/4 full. Find some ants and put them on the soil. You could set out a "bait" pan with some sweets in it to attract some ants for the jar. Use a straw to dribble a bit of water right on the edge of the soil, against the glass. Put a few crystals of sugar, drops of honey, or a piece of cookie on the soil. Close the lid of the tea jar. The ants will start making tunnels where the water was dribbled. Students should be able to see the tunnels the ants make. After a week, release the ants outside. Ant farms are also available for purchase.

Continue to work on the insect collection started in Lesson 126.

Language Arts: Purchase the game "Cootie®" for your students. Let them play the game, talking about the body parts of insects.

Phonics: Blend the sounds Aa-Kk. (kid, keg) Review the initial sounds of Aa-Kk. Review letter recognition Aa-Zz.

Have the students brainstorm words that begin or include the letter Kk. Write these words on the board. Model the correct letter formation as you write the letters on the board. The students should practice forming the letter Kk on a blank sheet of paper. Students who are ready can practice copying complete words from the board.

Do the Lesson 127 Phonics worksheet. The Sound of Kk. Review the letter sound with the picture and words on the worksheet. Ask the students for other words that begin with the same sound. Trace the letters and say the sound of Kk. Observe the students as they trace the letters and help them with the letter strokes. If you have the students do one row at a time, the worksheet can be carried over to various parts of the day or another day.

Reading: Use a simplified, illustrated telephone listing. Give the beginning sound of a word. Identify the name and sound of the letters in one's name.

Writing: Have the students type their names on a computer or with a typewriter.

Continue to do Learning Logs. Encourage the students to draw or write about themselves. Some sample topics might be My Pet, My Favorite Reptile, My Favorite School Activity, My Family, or other teacher selected topics. The writing can be invented temporary spellings or dictations to the teacher.

Memory Verse: Take time these two weeks to review the memory verses that the students have learned so far. Genesis 1:1, Genesis 1:3, Genesis 1:6, Genesis 1:10, I Peter 1:24-25, Genesis 8:22, Genesis 1:16, Psalm 90:12, Psalm 89:1, Revelation 22:16, Psalm 148:13, Genesis 1:26, Psalm 48:1, Matthew 6:26a, and Genesis 1:24a. We are taking a review break to prepare for a long memory project coming up in Week 27, Lesson 131.

Math: Review 5 + 1 = 6.

Do the Lesson 127 Math worksheet. The students may need manipulative shapes to help them complete the patterns.

Shapes: Review triangle, circle, square, rectangle, star, heart, oval, and diamond shapes with the song "Sing a Song of Shapes."

Story Time/Arts & Crafts: Make a trip to the library to get some Eric Carle books. Find *The Very Hungry Caterpillar, The Grouchy Ladybug, The Honeybee and the Robber, The Very Busy Spider, The Very Quiet Cricket,* or *The Very Lonely Firefly.* Check out five books, one for each day for the next few days. Let the students draw the bug from the book each day or make the bug with playdough.

Music/Language Arts: Review the *A, You're Adorable* song and book.

Music: Review the "Skeeters And The Bed Bugs" song.

Multimedia Resources: This week, listen and sing along to selections from "Music Machine: The Fruit Of The Spirit" CD.

Arts & Crafts: *Mix some flour and water to make a very thin paste. Provide white string cut into various lengths up to six inches.* Older students may cut their own string. Give each student a small bowl of paste, some pieces of string and a large black piece of construction paper. Say, Today we are spiders. We are going to design our own webs. Dip the string into the glue until it is wet. Then lay it on your paper in a web design.

Creative Cooking: *Bring some round crackers, cream cheese at room temperature, Chinese noodles and sliced olives, both green and black. Provide paper plates and plastic knives for each student.* Let the students spread the cream cheese on the crackers, then make "bugs" with the noodles and olives.

Physical Education/Outdoor Activity: We will be taking a "Bug Walk" every day this week. Have the students bring their bug jars. Take a walk, turning over rocks and leaves to find bugs. Carefully put the bugs in the bug jars and take them back to class for the insect collection.

NOTES: * http://www.si.edu/resource/faq/nmnh/buginfo/bugnos.htm

Activities in this Lesson: Bible Lesson, Social Studies/Science, Science, Language Arts, Phonics, Reading, Writing, Math, Shapes, Story Time/Arts & Crafts, Music, Physical Education/Outdoor Activity

Bible Reference: Genesis 1:24-26.

Bible Concept to Present: When God created insects, He made a diversity of insects.

Bible Lesson: God created insects on the sixth day. We know that all insects have six legs, three body parts, and compound eyes. God made many different kinds of insects. You have collected just some of the different kinds of insects. God knew each insect He made would be needed by us. There are more good insects than harmful ones. Insects help make our world a better place to live. We should thank God for the insects.

Multimedia Resources: Listen to the song "It's Time To Let My People Go" from the "Bullfrogs and Butterflies: God is Great" CD.

Social Studies/Science: Insects are important to man, and used by man for many things. The following insect facts will give your students an idea of the variety and uses of insects.

1. Bees are an insect that is very important to us. Bees drink the sweet liquid from flowers for food. In drinking the liquid, the bees help the flowers to make seeds, which make more flowers or fruit. The bees take the sweet liquid to their hives and from it make honey. We like to eat their honey, too. Bees have three body parts, six legs, and compound eyes like a mirrored disco type ball. They are an insect.

2. The adult silk moth lays eggs. The eggs hatch into silkworms. Each spins a cocoon. The cocoon of the silkworm is used to make silk. (For an explanation, see Lesson 128 Resource page which includes information on how silk fabric is made. This explanation will include the fact of reproduction of the silk worm, an illustration of insect life-cycle, and can be incorporated into the lessons to follow.) The silkworm that makes the beautiful silk is the caterpillar of a kind of moth. The adult moth is white, rather large with black-lined wings. It has a short body with stout legs. Wild silk moths lay their eggs in mulberry trees.

Multimedia Resources: Listen to the song "Bullfrogs And Butterflies" from the "Bullfrogs and Butterflies: God is My Friend" CD.

Science: Weird insect and bug facts:
Fastest insect runner – Cockroach, 3 mph
Fastest insect – Dragonfly, 36 mph
Largest bug – Stick insect, 15 inches long
Longest insect migration – Desert locust, travels about 2,800 miles yearly
Most legs – Millipede, 750 legs
Loudest insect – African cicada, almost as loud as a chain saw

Continue to work on the insect collection started in Lesson 126.

Purchase a small piece of real silk. Let the students feel it. Pull out a strand for each student to hold and feel.

Language Arts: Read one of Eric Carle's books today. Let the students act out the book on the second reading.

Phonics: Teach the initial sound Ll. Review the initial sounds of Aa-Kk. Review letter recognition Aa-Zz.

Write several initial Ll words on the board: lad, lady, lap, last, late, leaf, lay, led, leg, let, lid, lip, log, lop, low, lot, lug, etc. Underline the initial letter Ll and say the words. Ask the students for other words that start with the same sound.

Do the Lesson 128 Phonics worksheet. The Sound of Ll. Review the letter sound with the picture and words on the worksheet. Ask the students for other words that begin with the same sound. Discuss the position of the letters on the guidelines. Give them specific instructions for how the letter should be traced. Trace the letters and say the sound of Ll. Observe the students as they trace the letters and help them with the letter strokes. If you have the students do one row at a time, the worksheet can be carried over to various parts of the day or another day.

Reading: Use a simplified, illustrated telephone listing. Give the beginning sound of a word. Identify the name and sound of the letters in one's name.

Writing: Have the students type their names on a computer or with a typewriter.

Memory Verse: Take time these two weeks to review the memory verses that the students have learned so far. Genesis 1:1, Genesis 1:3, Genesis 1:6, Genesis 1:10, I Peter 1:24-25, Genesis 8:22, Genesis 1:16, Psalm 90:12, Psalm 89:1, Revelation 22:16, Psalm 148:13, Genesis 1:26, Psalm 48:1, Matthew 6:26a, and Genesis 1:24a.

Math: Review 5 + 1 = 6. Practice this problem and review the problems: 1 + 1 = 2, 2 + 1 = 3, 3 + 1 = 4, 4 + 1 = 5, with a strip of squares drawn on the board.

Do the Lesson 128a Math worksheet. Read the number. Count the dots under the number. Draw 12 objects in the counting jar. Trace the number 12 following the proper strokes. The students can color the counting jar.

Do the Lesson 128b Math worksheet. Count the dots in the tiles and trace the numbers. Say the addition problems.

Shapes: Review triangle, circle, square, rectangle, star, heart, oval, and diamond shapes with the song "Sing a Song of Shapes."

Story Time/Arts & Crafts: Read one of Eric Carle's books. Let the students draw the bug from the book or make the bug with playdough.

Music: Review the "Skeeters And The Bed Bugs" song.

Multimedia Resources: This week, listen and sing along to selections from "Music Machine: The Fruit Of The Spirit" CD.

Physical Education/Outdoor Activity: We will be taking a "Bug Walk" every day this week. Have the students bring their bug jars. Take a walk, turning over rocks and leaves to find bugs. Carefully put the bugs in the bug jars and take them back to class for the insect collection.

Activities in this Lesson: Bible Lesson, Science, Social Studies, Language Arts, Phonics, Reading, Writing, Memory Verse, Math, Shapes, Story Time/Arts & Crafts, Music, Arts & Crafts, Physical Education/Outdoor Activity, Homework

Bible Reference: Genesis 1:24-26.

Bible Concept to Present: God made insects and bugs to be amazing creatures.

Bible Lesson: Continue teaching about insects and bugs. We know what an awesome God we have when we realize how many varieties of insects God made on the sixth day. Insects are fascinating creatures. Though we know that insects have six legs, three body parts, and have compound eyes, what a wide variety of styles and sizes God made!

God also made spiders. Spiders are not insects but are one of the bugs God created. Insects have six legs and three body parts. Spiders have eight legs and two body parts. Most have either six or eight eyes. A spider web gets quite dirty so most spiders spin a new web every day. In the web many types of insects are caught that would be harmful to the plants in a garden. God created spiders to keep his Creation working smoothly.

Illustration: Add to the fact poster: "Spiders: 32,000"

Science: Some additional weird insect and bug facts:
    Some ants kidnap other ants and keep them as slaves. Many ants exhibit parental care, carrying food to their larvae, and cleaning and guarding nests.
    Spider's silk is stronger than steel.
    Fireflies light up at night because of a chemical reaction in their abdomen.
    Male bees don't do any work, only the females do the work. Bees are vitally important to us, as they help transfer pollen from plant to plant and tree to tree, keeping our fruit and vegetables producing.
    Ladybugs, a favorite insect, are red and black so that birds will leave them alone.
    The largest insect is the Acteon Beetle from South America. It can be 3 1/2 inches long by 2 inches wide.
    Megaphragma caribea flies that measure 0.17 mm long are probably the smallest known insects in the world.
    The monarch butterfly migrates thousands of miles each year, from Canada to Mexico.

Social Studies: Entomophagists are people who eat insects. In many countries, eating insects is quite common. Some people eat crickets, ants and worms. There are several places on the Internet that provide recipes using insects and insect flour. Sometimes, we eat insects by accident. They don't hurt us, though. Do you think you could ever eat insects?

Language Arts: Learn some poems about bugs. Let the students illustrate the poems if they choose.

Bugs

Big bugs, little bugs, thin bugs, fat.
Creepy, crawling, creepy, crawling, just like that!
Black bugs, brown bugs, green bugs, too.
Leaping, jumping, leaping jumping, right past you!

Hug a Bug

Hug a bug, hug a bug,
But don't ever hug a bee!
It might sting your nose, your hand
Or your knee!

Grasshopper

Hop, hop, hop - my, what strength!
A grasshopper hops twenty times its length.
Hop in the grass or on a single blade,
Hop in the sun or hop in the shade.
Farmer says, "Grasshopper, stay off my crop!"
There goes the grasshopper, hop, hop, hop.

Phonics: Review the initial sound Ll. Review the initial sounds of Aa-Kk. Review letter recognition Aa-Zz.

Have the students brainstorm words that begin or include the letter Ll. Write these words on the board. Model the correct letter formation as you write the letters on the board. The students should practice forming the letter Ll on a blank sheet of paper. Students who are ready can practice copying complete words from the board.

Do the Lesson 129 Phonics worksheet. The Sound of Ll. Review the letter sound with the picture and words on the worksheet. Ask the students for other words that begin with the same sound. Trace the letters and say the sound of Ll. Observe the students as they trace the letters and help them with the letter strokes. If you have the students do one row at a time, the worksheet can be carried over to various parts of the day or another day.

Reading: Use a simplified, illustrated telephone listing. Give the beginning sound of a word. Identify the name and sound of the letters in one's name.

Writing: Have the students type their names on a computer or with a typewriter.

Memory Verse: Take time these two weeks to review the memory verses that the students have learned so far. Genesis 1:1, Genesis 1:3, Genesis 1:6, Genesis 1:10, I Peter 1:24-25, Genesis 8:22, Genesis 1:16, Psalm 90:12, Psalm 89:1, Revelation 22:16, Psalm 148:13, Genesis 1:26, Psalm 48:1, Matthew 6:26a, and Genesis 1:24a.

Math: Review 5 + 1 = 6. Have the students count off steps to practice addition. Review: 1 + 1 = 2, 2 + 1 = 3, 3 + 1 = 4, 4 + 1 = 5, 5 + 1 = 6.

Do the Lesson 129 Math worksheet. Count each color of blocks in the strip and say the addition problem and count all of the blocks to get the answer. Trace the correct number.

Shapes: Review triangle, circle, square, rectangle, star, heart, oval, and diamond shapes with the song "Sing a Song of Shapes."

Story Time/Arts & Crafts: Read one of Eric Carle's books. Let the students draw the bug from the book or make the bug with playdough.

Music: Learn the song about the spider and the water spout.

Itsy, Bitsy Spider

Itsy, bitsy spider went up the water spout.
Down came the rain and washed the spider out!
Out came the sun and dried up all the rain
And the itsy bitsy spider went up the spout again.

Multimedia Resources: This week, listen and sing along to selections from "Music Machine: The Fruit Of The Spirit" CD.

Arts & Crafts: Fingerprint Butterflies - Have stamp pads available in different colors. Let the students put their thumbs or fingers on the stamp pad, then stamp on white paper. Instruct them to stamp two prints or four prints close together, making butterfly wings. Then add antennae and feet with black pens.

Bring paper towel rolls, one for each student. Provide aluminum foil, little eyes, small round Styrofoam balls and pipe cleaners. Cut the Styrofoam balls in half. Paint them black and let them dry. Let the students cover the paper rolls with foil, taping it on, to make the water spout. Cut the pipe cleaners in half. Let the students attach eight spider legs to the Styrofoam balls. Have a hot glue gun set up on the counter, where students can't reach it. Hot glue each spider to the bottom of the water spouts. Hot glue two eyes to the spiders.

Physical Education/Outdoor Activity: We will be taking a "Bug Walk" every day this week. Have the students bring their bug jars. Take a walk, turning over rocks and leaves to find bugs. Carefully put the bugs in the bug jars and take them back to class for the insect collection.

Homework: Take Lesson 129 Homework worksheet on bugs home. Bring the page and a bug back to class tomorrow.

NOTES:

Activities in this Lesson: Bible Lesson, Social Studies, Science, Language Arts, Phonics, Reading, Writing, Memory Verse, Math, Shapes, Story Time/Arts & Crafts, Music, Creative Cooking, Physical Education/Outdoor Activity, Homework

Bible Reference: Genesis 1:24-26.

Bible Concept to Present: Students are introduced to the fact that God made a life cycle for the insects.

Bible Lesson: When God made insects, He made a way for them to have babies, to live their life and to die. Insects lay eggs. The eggs develop into larvae or worms. The worms eat and grow and spin a cocoon. The insect-worm changes into a moth or butterfly. The moth lays eggs and then dies. God planned for all these things to happen so insects would continue to live on this earth. God plans for us to take care of the good insects. We can thank God for insects by taking care of them.

Multimedia Resources: Listen to the songs "Oh Me Oh My," "My Favorite Things," "I Know Somebody Who Knows," and "There's Been a Metamorphosis" from the "Bullfrogs and Butterflies: God is Great" CD.

Social Studies: Review the illustration of the silk worm from Lesson 128 Resource page.

Science: Review the illustration of the silk worm. Finish the insect collection today. Display it in a place where students may study it.

Language Arts: Continue to play "Cootie®." Discuss the body parts of bugs as you play.

Phonics: Blend the sounds Aa-Ll. (lab, lad, lag, led, leg, lid, all, ball, call, fall, gall, hall, bell, Bel, cell, Dell, fell, gel, hell, Kell, ill, Bill, bill, dill, fill, hill, kill, Lil) Review the initial sounds of Aa-Ll. Review letter recognition Aa-Zz.

Add the following words to the flip chart pages of words and review them with the students. Continue to sound out the individual letters of each word as has been done previously. It may also be helpful for the students to see the words spaced out and spelled out as has been done in previous lessons.

la	le	li	al	el	il
lab	led	lid	call	bell	ill
lad	leg	Lil	ball	fell	bill
lag			fall	gel	Bill
			gall	hell	dill
			hall	jell	fill
				Kell	hill
					kill
					Lil

Do the Lesson 130a Phonics worksheet. The sound of Ll. Review the letter sound with the picture and words on the worksheet. Ask the students for other words that begin with the same sound. Trace the letters and say the sound of Ll. Observe the students as they trace the letters and help them with the letter strokes. If you have the students do one row at a time, the worksheet can be carried over to various parts of the day or another day.

Do the Lesson 130b Phonics worksheet. The Sound of Ll. Review the letter sound with the picture and words on the worksheet. Ask the students for other words that begin with the same sound. Give them specific instructions for how the letter should be traced. Allow time for tracing the letters and observe their progress. If you have the students do one row at a time, the worksheet can be carried over to various parts of the day or another day.

Reading: Use a simplified, illustrated telephone listing. Give the beginning sound of a word. Identify the name and sound of the letters in one's name.

Writing: Have the students type their names on a computer or with a typewriter.

Memory Verse: Take time these two weeks to review the memory verses that the students have learned so far. Genesis 1:1, Genesis 1:3, Genesis 1:6, Genesis 1:10, I Peter 1:24-25, Genesis 8:22, Genesis 1:16, Psalm 90:12, Psalm 89:1, Revelation 22:16, Psalm 148:13, Genesis 1:26, Psalm 48:1, Matthew 6:26a, and Genesis 1:24a.

Math: Review 5 + 1 = 6. Give each student 10 pennies to count 1-10. Have the students add pennies to practice the addition facts: 1 + 1 = 2, 2 + 1 = 3, 3 + 1 = 4, 4 + 1 = 5, 5 + 1 = 6.

Do the Lesson 130a Math worksheet. Read the number. Count the dots under the number. Trace the letters for the number word. Draw 0 objects in the counting jar. Trace the number and the number word following the proper strokes. The students can color the counting jar.

Do the Lesson 130b Math worksheet. Count the first group of pennies in the row and say "plus one penny," then count all of the pennies to get the answer. Trace the correct number.

Shapes: Review triangle, circle, square, rectangle, star, heart, oval, and diamond shapes with the song "Sing a Song of Shapes."

Story Time/Arts & Crafts: Read one of Eric Carle's books today. Ask the students which book they liked the best. Let the students draw the bug from the book or make the bug with playdough.

Music: Review "Itsy, Bitsy Spider" and "Skeeters And The Bed Bugs."

Multimedia Resources: This week, listen and sing along to selections from "Music Machine: The Fruit Of The Spirit" CD.

Creative Cooking: *Make sugar cookies cut into ovals or rounds, one for each student. Bring red and/or black frosting. Bring black licorice and black jelly beans. First, let the students frost their cookies to* be either lady bugs, red, or spiders, black. Give them thin strings of licorice for spider legs or black jelly beans for lady bug spots.

Physical Education/Outdoor Activity: We will be taking a "Bug Walk" every day this week. This is the final day. Have the students bring their bug jars. Talk a walk, turning over rocks and leaves to find bugs. Carefully put the bugs in the bug jars and take them back to class for the insect collection.

Homework: Have available as many magnifying glasses as you can obtain. Provide coffee can lids or trays to put the bug on. Did everyone bring a bug to school? Let's look at the bugs through the magnifying glass. Some bugs might have to stay in their jars. Who brought the biggest bug? The smallest bug? Use tweezers to carefully pull the bugs legs and wings out to view.

NOTE: In Week 32 beginning with Lesson 156, we will be making bugs from egg cartons. Now is the time to start saving cardboard egg cartons. You might send a note home, asking parents to save some for you. You will need one cardboard egg carton for every two students.

NOTES:

Lesson 131

Week 27: Day 1

Activities in this Lesson: Bible Lesson, Social Studies, Science, Language Arts, Phonics, Reading, Writing, Memory Verse, Math, Story Time/Arts & Crafts, Music, Arts & Crafts, Health & Safety, Physical Education, Homework

Bible Reference: Gen 1: 26-27.

Bible Concept to Present: On the sixth day of Creation, God made man.

Bible Lesson: Did you know there is only one of you? There is no one else just like you. God made each one of us special. God knew how he wanted us to look, and act. He created each of us so we are all different. He wants all of us to talk to Him. God made you to be happy doing what He wants. God made you to love Him. He loves you, too!

Multimedia Resources: Listen to the song "Me-Raculous!" from "The Amazing Children" CD.

Social Studies: God made each of us different. He made us in His image; but you are one special person. He knew you before you were born. He knows you now. Even though you may have the same color of hair just like your mother or father, you are different inside. You even have the same last name as your mother or father, but you are still different. You are a special person. To compare differences and similarities of students, begin to teach beginning graphing. The students should be able to begin to talk about some of the differences and similarities. Discuss things that make us unique. Emphasize that God gave us our hair color, our eyes, our ears, everything about us. If we make fun of someone because of their ears or their tallness or anything about them, we are ridiculing God. Never laugh at someone because of what he looks like. God wants us to be kind and loving to everyone.

Science: You may make a big graph on the board, with titles on top like "hair color," "eye color," "height," and "ears." Add names to the graph as traits are discussed. Take care not to emphasize a feature that might embarrass a student.

Language Arts: *Bring a mirror* or use a window. We are going to play a "Mirror Talk" game today. We will look in the mirror and see who is there. I see a person in the mirror. That person has _____ color of hair. That person has _____ eyes. (Let the students describe themselves in the mirror.)

Phonics: Teach the initial sound Mm. Review the initial sounds of Aa-Ll. Review letter recognition Aa-Zz.

Write several initial Mm words on the board: mad, make, mall, man, map, Mars, math, May, mid, mill, miss, mob, mop, mud, mug, mutt, etc. Underline the initial letter Mm and say the words. Ask the students for other words that start with the same sound.

Do the Lesson 131 Phonics worksheet. The Sound of Mm. Review the letter sound with the picture and words on the worksheet. Ask the students for other words that begin with the same sound. Discuss the position of the letters on the guidelines. Give them specific instructions for how the letter should be traced. Trace the letters and say the sound of Mm. Observe the students as they trace the letters and help them with the letter strokes. If you have the students do one row at a time, the worksheet can be carried over to various parts of the day or another day.

Reading: Use a simplified, illustrated telephone listing. Give the beginning sound of a word. Identify the name and sound of the letters in one's name.

Multimedia Resources: Review "Rev-Up for Reading" from the "Rev-Up for Learning" DVD to drill letter recognition and sound. The students should say each letter sound along with the presentation.

Writing: Continue to do Learning Logs. Encourage the students to draw or write about themselves. Some sample topics might be My Pet, My Favorite Reptile, My Favorite School Activity, My Family, or other teacher selected topics. The writing can be invented temporary spellings or dictations to the teacher.

Multimedia Resources: Review "Rev-Up for Writing" from the "Rev-Up for Learning" DVD to review the writing of upper- and lowercase letters.

Memory Verse: Psalm 139:14-16.
I praise You because I am fearfully and wonderfully made:
Your works are wonderful, I know that full well.
My frame was not hidden from you when I was made in the secret place …
Your eyes saw my unformed body.
All the days ordained for me were written in Your book
before one of them came to be.
Psalm 139:14-16 NIV

I will praise thee; for I am fearfully and wonderfully made:
marvellous are thy works; and that my soul knoweth right well.
My substance was not hid from thee, when I was made in secret, …
Thine eyes did see my substance, … and in thy book all my members were written, when as yet there was none of them. Psalm 139:14-16 KJV

This long verse may require much repetition, but a four year old or above can learn it. Students will be very proud of doing this. Memorize one section at a time. This verse will be worked on for four weeks. There will be a Memory Verse reminder every day. (You may choose to learn only the first two lines.)

ONE	I praise You because I am fearfully and wonderfully made:
TWO	Your works are wonderful, I know that full well.
THREE	My frame was not hidden from you when I was made in the secret place …
FOUR	Your eyes saw my unformed body.
FIVE	All the days ordained for me were written in Your book before one of them came to be.
SIX	Psalm 139:14-16

Send Memory Verse Card 18 home with students.

Math: Teach 2 - 1 = 1. Have two students come to the front of the room. Count the students. Have one of them return to his seat. Ask the class how many students are still standing at the front of the room after one left. Do this with several groups of two students. Say the problem, "two minus one equals one." An optional way to do this is to hold up a subtraction sign between the first two students and a third that has come to the front. Then as you say the subtraction problem, have the student after the subtraction sign hold a piece of paper with a big X on it in front of him. You can also hold up an equal sign and have one additional student represent the answer to the subtraction problem.

Do the Lesson 131 Math worksheet. Read the number. Count the dots under the number. Trace the letters for the number word. Draw 1 object in the counting jar. Trace the number and the number word following the proper strokes. The students can color the counting jar.

Multimedia Resources: View "Rev-Up for Arithmetic" from the "Rev-Up for Learning" DVD to practice number recognition, counting and addition 1-20.

Story Time: Read a story or stories of your choice.

Music: Review "Itsy, Bitsy Spider" and "Skeeters And The Bed Bugs." Sing and learn "Say To the Lord I Love You" on the "Horizons Preschool Music" CD.

Sing the following song: (To the tune of "If You're Happy and You Know It.")

Put Your Finger
Tune of If You're Happy and You Know It

Put your finger on your nose, on your nose
Put your finger on your nose, on your nose
Put your finger on your nose,
Just watch it as it grows,
Put your finger on your nose, on your nose.

Put your finger on your cheek, on your cheek.
Put your finger on your cheek, on your cheek.
Put your finger on your cheek,
Leave it there about a week.
Put your finger on your cheek, on your cheek.

Put your finger on your chest, on your chest.
Put your finger on your chest, on your chest.
Put your finger on your chest,
Just give it a little rest.
Put your finger on your chest, on your chest.

Put your finger on your belly, on your belly,
Put your finger on your belly, on your belly,
Put your finger on your belly,
Shake it like a bowl of jelly.
Put your finger on your belly, on your belly.

Multimedia Resources: This week, listen and sing along to selections from "Sir Oliver's Song" CD.

Arts & Crafts: *Provide paper plates and poster pens for each student.* We are going to make your face today. Take this paper plate and draw your face on it. Don't forget your eyes. Be sure and color on the right color of hair. Watch the preschool child to see whether eyebrows or eyelashes are added. This can help you tell the maturity of the student. You may even glue on pieces of yarn for the hair if you have yarn available.

Health & Safety: We need to care for the body God gave us. There are lots of good ways we can care for our bodies. We always need to eat good food, keep our bodies clean, exercise our bodies, and give plenty of rest to our bodies. These are all ways to show God we are glad He made us just the way He did. We are special to God so we need to remember to take care of ourselves. Let the students act out in charades healthy ways to care for themselves. Other students can guess what they are doing. Examples: brushing teeth, showering, bathing, eating good food, exercising.

Physical Education: Rock and Roll Relay. Divide the class into two groups for a relay race. On GO the first child runs to the other side of the area where you have put a rocking chair and a ball for each team. The player picks up the ball and sits down on the rocking chair. They should rock back and forth 3 times while holding the ball and then roll the ball to the next player on the team and finally they should go to the end of the line. The next players repeat the procedure until all have had a turn.

Homework: Give the students the Lesson 131 Homework worksheet on Family Traits, to take home. Instruct them to bring it back tomorrow.

NOTES:

Lesson 132

Week 27: Day 2

Activities in this Lesson: Bible Lesson, Social Studies, Science, Language Arts, Phonics, Reading, Writing, Memory Verse, Math, Story Time/Arts & Crafts, Music, Arts & Crafts, Physical Education, Homework, Catch Up

Bible Reference: Genesis 1:26-27.

Bible Concept to Present: We are all different in looks and personality, but God loves us all.

Bible Lesson: Review the days of Creation, briefly mentioning each creation. God's final creation was man. Just like the rest of Creation, God made people to be so very different. But every person can communicate with God in prayer. God tells us that looks aren't what is important, that the heart is what is important.

Multimedia Resources: Listen to the song "Your Heart" from the "Bullfrogs and Butterflies: I've Been Born Again" CD and the song "King Of My Heart" from the "Bullfrogs and Butterflies: God Loves Fun" CD.

Social Studies: *Bring several magazines to class.* Let the students cut out lots of pictures of people, all kinds of people. Glue them to a piece of poster board or a piece of banner paper. Try to have as many different faces as possible, including all races, all sizes. Include babies through senior citizens. Talk about God loving every single one of these people.

Science: God is a fantastic scientist! He made people so that they could make new people. When a mom and dad come together and have a baby, the baby is half of the mom and half of the dad. But some traits can be seen and some can't be seen. If the father has brown eyes and the mother has brown eyes, the baby will probably have brown eyes. The child's height will probably be somewhere in between the two parents. There are many things we get from our parents that can't be seen. Handwriting styles can be inherited, that's what it is called when a trait is passed on to a child. Voices can be inherited. Artistic talent, mathematical talent, all kinds of talents can be inherited. Sometimes families look back at grandparents and great grandparents to find a special trait. Ask, "What did you inherit from your parents?"

Language Arts: Use the student Name Cards and see if the students can arrange them in alphabetical order. Explain to them that things like a phone book have names in alphabetical order. Only be concerned that they arrange the names by the first letter. Mix the cards up and have several students do this activity. It could also be done in pairs or small groups.

Phonics: Review the initial sound Mm. Review the initial sounds of Aa-Ll. Review letter recognition Aa-Zz.

Do the Lesson 132 Phonics worksheet. The Sound of Mm. Review the letter sound with the picture and words on the worksheet. Ask the students for other words that begin with the same sound. Trace the letters and say the sound of Mm. Observe the students as they trace the letters and help them with the letter strokes. If you have the students do one row at a time, the worksheet can be carried over to various parts of the day or another day.

Reading: Use a simplified, illustrated telephone listing. Give the beginning sound of a word. Identify the name and sound of the letters in one's name.

Writing: Continue to do Learning Logs. Encourage the students to draw or write about themselves. Some sample topics might be My Pet, My Favorite Reptile, My Favorite School Activity, My Family, or other teacher selected topics. The writing can be invented temporary spellings or dictations to the teacher.

Memory Verse: Continue working on Psalm 139:14-16. Only work section ONE. Remind students that when we memorize God's word, we are hiding it in our heart to be used in the future. We can take memorized verses with us wherever we go.

      ONE   I praise You because I am fearfully and wonderfully made:

Math: Review 2 - 1 = 1. Give the students the dog bones that they cut out previously and a bowl to put them in. Have them place 2 bones in the bowl while saying "two minus one" and have them take a bone from the bowl, "equals" and have them count "one bone in the bowl." Do this several times. Practice previous addition facts.

Do the Lesson 132a Math worksheet. As they count the images have them say the subtraction and addition problems and trace the numbers.

Do the Lesson 132b Math worksheet. Play the Caterpillar Race Game. This can be done individually or as a class. If doing it together as a class all of the students should finish at the same time if they have added and subtracted correctly. Emphasize that getting to the finish line first is not the most important part of the game. Counting, adding, and subtracting correctly make everyone a winner. Play this game again tomorrow.

Story Time: Read a story or stories of your choice.

Music: Review "Say To the Lord I Love You," "Put Your Finger," "Itsy, Bitsy Spider," and "Skeeters And The Bed Bugs."

Multimedia Resources: This week, listen and sing along to selections from "Sir Oliver's Song" CD.

Arts & Crafts: Let each of the students draw themselves on white paper. Then let them cut around their self portraits and add them to the Creation Mural. We want them to see that they are a part of God's fabulous Creation and the most loved of all.

Homework: Let the students share their homework, talking about different traits in their families.

Physical Education: Put some music on and do exercises to music. Do some jumping jacks then let the students make up their own exercises.

Catch Up: Do any assignment that you didn't have time for earlier in the month.

NOTES:

Activities in this Lesson: Bible Lesson, Social Studies, Science, Language Arts, Phonics, Reading, Writing, Memory Verse, Math, Shapes, Story Time, Music, Arts & Crafts, Physical Education

Bible Reference: Genesis 1:26-27.

Bible Concept to Present: God made man like Himself. We have a soul. Nothing else God created had a soul.

Bible Lesson: The Bible tells us that we are the only creatures that God made that have what we call a soul. Nothing else that God made has a soul. What is a soul? A soul is the way we are inside. It is what makes us different from everyone else. Remember when we talked about no one else being just like you? That is very true. Your soul makes you different from other people. Other people have souls, too. But all of them are different from you. God made us each different, so no two souls are alike. It is our soul that learns to love God and serve him.

Social Studies: Continue graphing the differences and similarities of family members that was started in Lesson 131.

Science: Talk about fingerprints. God gave every single person different fingerprints. Use a stamp pad to print the students fingerprints on a piece of paper comparing thumb to thumb. Let them see how, though similar, their fingerprints are intricately different. Talk about fingerprints being used in crime detection.

Language Arts: Play the Mirror Talk game again, doing several facial expressions to indicate emotions.

Phonics: Blend the sounds Aa-Mm. (am, bam, dam, ham, jam, mad, mag, mall, Meg, Mel, gem, hem, dim, him, Kim, mid, mig, mill) Review the initial sounds of Aa-Mm. Review letter recognition Aa-Zz.

Add the following words to the flip chart pages of words and review them with the students. Continue to sound out the individual letters of each word as has been done previously. It may also be helpful for the students to see the words spaced out and spelled out as has been done in previous lessons.

ma	me	mi	am	em	im
mad	Meg	mid	am	gem	dim
mag	Mel	mig	bam	hem	him
mall		mill	dam	Lem	Kim
			ham		
			jam		

Do the Lesson 133 Phonics worksheet. The Sound of Mm. Review the letter sound with the picture and words on the worksheet. Ask the students for other words that begin with the same sound. Give them specific instructions for how the letter should be traced. Allow time for tracing the letters and observe their progress. If you have the students do one row at a time, the worksheet can be carried over to various parts of the day or another day.

Reading: Use a simplified, illustrated telephone listing. Give the beginning sound of a word. Identify the name and sound of the letters in one's name.

Writing: Continue to do Learning Logs. Encourage the students to draw or write about themselves. Some sample topics might be My Pet, My Favorite Reptile, My Favorite School Activity, My Family, or other teacher selected topics. The writing can be invented temporary spellings or dictations to the teacher.

Memory Verse: Continue working on Psalm 139:14-16. Only work section ONE. Remind students that when we memorize God's word, we are hiding it in our heart to be used in the future. We can take memorized verses with us wherever we go.

 ONE I praise You because I am fearfully and wonderfully made:

Math: Review 2 - 1 = 1. Review 2 - 1 = 1 by writing the problem on the board. Draw objects over the numbers with - sign between them. Make a large X over the object being subtracted. Write the = sign and then draw an excess of objects over the answer. Have a student come to the board and circle the correct number of objects to make the subtraction problem correct. Erase the extra objects and orally say the problem with the class. Repeat several times drawing simple objects such as dots or various shapes. Review previous addition problems if the students need the practice.

Play the Caterpillar Race Game worksheet again. This can be done individually or as a class. If doing it together as a class all of the students should finish at the same time if they have added and subtracted correctly. Emphasize that getting to the finish line first is not the most important part of the game. Counting, adding and subtracting correctly make everyone a winner.

Do the Lesson 133a Math worksheet. Read the number. Count the dots under the number. Trace the letters for the number word. Draw 2 objects in the counting jar. Trace the number and the number word following the proper strokes. The students can color the counting jar.

Do the Lesson 133b Math worksheet. Count the items and say the subtraction or addition problem. As they trace the numbers have them say the subtraction and addition problems.

Shapes: Review triangle, circle, square, rectangle, star, heart, oval, and diamond shapes with the songs "Sing a Song of Shapes" or the "Shapes Song."

Do the Lesson 133 Shapes worksheet. The House of Shapes. Do the color key together with the students and then allow them to color the picture independently following the color key.

Story Time: Get the book *The Little Engine That Could*, by Watty Piper, from the library. We are learning about our personality and how important we are to God. Talk about trying to do our best at all times.

Music: Review "Say To the Lord I Love You," "Put Your Finger on Your Nose," and "Itsy, Bitsy Spider."

Multimedia Resources: This week, listen and sing along to selections from "Sir Oliver's Song" CD.

Arts & Crafts: Obtain a stamp pad, a well-soaped sponge, and paper. Place your student's thumb on the pad so that the thumb is well-inked. Then roll the thumb on a piece of paper to make a print. Permit the student to draw designs in the print.

Make the clay recipe from Lesson 14. Give each student a piece a bit bigger than his hand. Instruct them to press it out into a round piece about 3/4 inch thick. Help the students to gently press their whole hand into the clay, making sure that their hand is inside the edges of the clay. Remind the students that every single person's fingerprints are different. Let the handprints dry. Paint another day.

Physical Education: Block Bowling. You will need 3-5 cardboard boxes for this activity with their tops taped shut. Set up a bowling alley with an area to stack the pins and a line to stand behind when bowling the ball. Begin with 3 boxes and have a student selected as the "pin setter" stack the boxes in any configuration. Line the rest of the students up and have them sit down. The first student in line stands and rolls a ball at the stack of blocks and attempts to knock them down. The "pin setter" collects the ball and takes it to the next player in line. The player who rolled the ball becomes the new "pin setter" and the game continues.

NOTES:

Activities in this Lesson: Bible Lesson, Language Arts/Social Studies, Science, Phonics, Reading, Writing, Memory Verse/Outdoor Activity, Math, Story Time, Music, Arts & Crafts, Creative Cooking, Physical Education

Bible Reference: Genesis 1:26-27.

Bible Concept to Present: God gave people different personalities.

Bible Lesson: God gave people very different looks. He also gave us different personalities. Some people are very quiet. Some are excited and loud. Some people laugh all the time. Some people like to read and some people like to do things. We should be happy with who we are. Being quiet isn't wrong and being noisy isn't wrong. There are different times for everyone to be quiet or everyone to be noisy. But neither is wrong. God loves us very much just the way we are. And God can use each of us and use our different personalities.

Language Arts/Social Studies: Language is very important to people. Only people can talk to one another. Other animals can't use words or their voices to communicate. We use words to talk. It is important to learn a lot of words, so that we can say what we feel. Some feelings show on our face, even when we don't speak. When I say the word, you make your face look like the word. Happy. Sad. Hungry. Mad. Afraid. Excited. Mean. Sleepy. Our face can show how we feel.

Science: Our face is pulled and moved by muscles. Did you know it takes many more muscles to frown than to smile? Everyone frown, really big. That even feels bad, doesn't it? Now everyone smile, really big. Doesn't that make you feel happier? Sometimes, we need to smile even when we don't feel like it because it will help us feel better.

Multimedia Resources: Listen to the song "Smile" from "The Music Machine: The Fruit of the Spirit" CD.

Phonics: Review blends Aa-Mm with the blend charts. Review the initial sounds of Aa-Mm. Review letter recognition Aa-Zz.

Have the students brainstorm words that begin or include the letter Mm. Write these words on the board. Model the correct letter formation as you write the letters on the board. The students should practice forming the letter Mm on a blank sheet of paper. Students who are ready can practice copying complete words from the board.

Do the Lesson 134 Phonics worksheet. The Sound of Mm. Review the letter sound with the picture and words on the worksheet. Ask the students for other words that begin with the same sound. Trace the letters and say the sound of Mm. Observe the students as they trace the letters and help them with the letter strokes. If you have the students do one row at a time, the worksheet can be carried over to various parts of the day or another day.

Reading: Use a simplified, illustrated telephone listing. Give the beginning sound of a word. Identify the name and sound of the letters in one's name.

Writing: Continue to do Learning Logs. Encourage the students to draw or write about themselves. Some sample topics might be My Pet, My Favorite Reptile, My Favorite School Activity, My Family, or other teacher selected topics. The writing can be invented temporary spellings or dictations to the teacher.

Memory Verse/Outdoor Activity: Continue working on Psalm 139:14-16. We are adding section TWO today. Remind students that when we memorize God's word, we are hiding it in our heart to be used in the future. We can take memorized verses with us wherever we go.

ONE	I praise You because I am fearfully and wonderfully made:
TWO	Your works are wonderful, I know that full well.

Let the students walk outside, chanting the memory verse as they walk. Bring a copy of the entire verse so that you can lead them through it all, even if they don't know it yet.

Math: Review 2 - 1 = 1. Give each of the students 10 counters. Have them count the objects to make sure that they have 10 objects. Have them make the subtraction problem with the counters. Have them point to the counters and say the subtraction problem, drawing the minus and equal sign with their finger between the counters as they say the words. Review previous problems if the students need the practice.

Do the Lesson 134 Math worksheet. As they trace the numbers have them say the subtraction and addition problems.

Story Time: Review "The Little Engine That Could." Read a story or stories of your choice.

Music: Review "Say To the Lord I Love You," "Put Your Finger on Your Nose," and "Itsy, Bitsy Spider."

Multimedia Resources: This week, listen and sing along to selections from Sir Oliver's Song CD.

Arts & Crafts: Give the students Lesson 134 Arts & Crafts worksheet, the Gingerbread Man. Instruct the students to put a dot in each eye. Circle the eyebrows. Put an X on each thumb. Circle each foot. Circle the nose. Put an X on the tummy. Continue to name each body part that the students know. Save the picture for Lesson 145.

Creative Cooking: *Mix one box of gingerbread mix and 1/3 cup warm water. Mix well and roll into a ball. Refrigerate.* With the students, roll the dough out on wax paper with a bit of flour to prevent sticking. Cut out with gingerbread girl and boy cookie cutters. Brush lightly with cold water. Bake at 300 degrees for 12-14 minutes. Cool. Decorate with canned frosting if desired.

Physical Education: Repeat the Block Bowling activity. Set up a bowling alley with an area to stack the pins and a line to stand behind when bowling the ball. Begin with 4 or 5 boxes and have a student selected as the "pin setter" stack the boxes in any configuration. Line the rest of the students up and have them sit down. The first student in line stands and rolls a ball at the stack of blocks and attempts to knock them down. The "pin setter" collects the ball and takes it to the next player in line. The player who rolled the ball becomes the new "pin setter" and the game continues.

NOTES:

Activities in this Lesson: Bible Lesson, Social Studies, Science, Language Arts, Phonics, Reading, Writing, Memory Verse, Math, Story Time, Music, Arts & Crafts, Health & Safety, Physical Education

Bible Reference: Genesis 1:26-27.

Bible Concept to Present: God made man from the dust of the earth.

Bible Lesson: God took the dust from the ground and made Adam. Clay is from the ground also, but while man was made from the dirt, we are more than clay men. We have a soul. We breathe. God did not want just a pile of dirt. He wanted someone who could talk to Him and love Him. Man is the most special of God's creations, because we are created in God's image. We are very important to God. Aren't you glad God made you special?

Multimedia Resources: Listen to the song "A Pow-Wow-Wonderful God" from "The Music Machine: The Majesty of God" CD.

Social Studies: Tell students, "You know, I love you just the way you are. You are very special to me. I'm glad God gave you to me." It is very important not to limit your praise to only the times that students fulfill your expectations. Your desire is for the students to get their value from God, to reduce the chances of peer influences affecting your students, and to train them to stand for what they believe. To obtain these goals, you will need to show your student unconditional love and acceptance. This is relayed through praise.

Multimedia Resources: Watch "Love" from the *Character Builders Video Series*.

Science: Dust is made up of several different particles of powdered rocks and humus material. It is the solid matter used in the preparation of making dirt and mud. God made us from the dust of the earth. It keeps us humble to remember that we were first made from dust. "Humble" means not to think too highly of ourselves. Dust is a very lowly material, yet God made people from it. And people are very special to God because they can talk to God and be His friends.

Multimedia Resources: Listen to the song "Friends" from the "Bullfrogs and Butterflies: God is My Friend" CD.

Language Arts: Read the following poem:

> **I Am One**
> Author Unknown
>
> I am one, I am very small
> But I soon will be very tall.
>
> I am two, growing fast that's true
> Someday I'll be just like you.

I am three, learning, loving, growing, showing
What I want to be.

I am four, growing some more.
Soon you will see how big I can be.

I am five, busy as a bee hive
Growing, growing, God has made me alive.

Phonics: Teach the initial sound Nn. Review the initial sounds of Aa-Mm. Review letter recognition Aa-Zz.

Write several initial Nn words on the board: nag, nap, name, Nebraska, need, net, new, nip, nod, North, number, nut, etc. Underline the initial letter Nn and say the words. Ask the students for other words that start with the same sound.

Do the Lesson 135 Phonics worksheet. The Sound of Nn. Review the letter sound with the picture and words on the worksheet. Ask the students for other words that begin with the same sound. Discuss the position of the letters on the guidelines. Give them specific instructions for how the letter should be traced. Trace the letters and say the sound of Nn. Observe the students as they trace the letters and help them with the letter strokes. If you have the students do one row at a time, the worksheet can be carried over to various parts of the day or another day.

Reading: Use a simplified, illustrated telephone listing. Give the beginning sound of a word. Identify the name and sound of the letters in one's name.

Writing: Continue to do Learning Logs. Encourage the students to draw or write about themselves. Some sample topics might be My Pet, My Favorite Reptile, My Favorite School Activity, My Family, or other teacher selected topics. The writing can be invented temporary spellings or dictations to the teacher.

Memory Verse: Continue to work on Psalm 139:14-16, sections ONE and TWO.

Math: Review 2 - 1 = 1.

Do the Lesson 135a Math worksheet. Read the number. Count the dots under the number. Trace the letters for the number word. Draw 3 objects in the counting jar. Trace the number and the number word following the proper strokes. The students can color the counting jar.

Do the Lesson 135b Math worksheet. Count the items. Say the subtraction or addition problem. Circle the correct number of objects to answer the subtraction and addition problems.

Story Time: Read a story or stories of your student's choice or ones they have brought from home.

Music: Review "Say To the Lord I Love You," "Put Your Finger on Your Nose," and "Itsy, Bitsy Spider."

Multimedia Resources: This week, listen and sing along to selections from "Sir Oliver's Song" CD.

Arts & Crafts: *Bring some fine sand or dirt to class.* On a big piece of white construction paper, draw a simple stick man with white glue. Let the students see the white paper with the white glue. Now sprinkle the dirt on it, all over the paper, Talk about God making man with the dust of the ground. Carefully dump the excess dirt into the trash. Show the students the man that was made from dust.

Paint the handprints. Let the students take them home when they are dry.

Health & Safety: We must always keep our bodies clean. We do that by bathing regularly using soap and clean water. We use shampoo to clean our hair and deodorant soap to clean our bodies. We need to be sure we wash all of our bodies. God wants us to keep our bodies clean and smelling good. This shows God we care about the body he made for us.

Physical Education: Walk With Me. This is a follow the leader type activity that is done in a large circle. The first person who is IT begins walking in a very distinct manner around the inside of the circle. (Limp, half-step, zigzag, backwards, sideways, etc.) As the first person "walks" around the circle they invite another person to "_____ Walk With Me around the circle." The second person mimics the "walk" and follows the first person. When the first person gets around to the empty space in the circle they rejoin the circle and the other person begins a new "walk" and invites another person to walk with them around the circle.

NOTES:

Activities in this Lesson: Bible Lesson, Social Studies/Science, Science, Language Arts, Phonics, Reading, Writing, Memory Verse, Math, Story Time, Music, Health & Safety, Physical Education

Bible Reference: Genesis 1:26-27.

Bible Concept to Present: God made us to have cells.

Bible Lesson: God knew exactly what he was doing when He made us. He put within our bodies little structures called cells. These cells do many things for our bodies. One thing they do is help us to grow bigger. I know you want to grow bigger each day, and one way you can do that is to eat good food, so your cells can work right in your body. All living things are made of cells. These cells do all their work without you even feeling anything. Wasn't God great to make cells to work inside of our bodies too?

Social Studies/Science: Explain to your students the various cells in our body, what each type looks like, and how they divide. Lesson 136b Science worksheet illustrates the various cells. Talk about the fact that when cells divide, we grow. Our cells are constantly growing, dividing and dying. Skin cells rub off all the time. When God made our cells, He made them to know what kind of cell they were. Skin cells are always skin cells and they know that they work on the outside of our body. This information is to be introduced only. Retention is not expected.

Do the Lesson 136b Science worksheet. Briefly discuss the layers of the skin. Discuss how cells grow and divide to produce new cells. Discuss the different types of cells. Instruct the students to lightly color the cells on the worksheet with red and purple colors. Set Lesson 136b Science worksheet aside to use again in Lesson 137.

Science: *Bring two clear plastic 8 oz cups, sugar and a package of dry yeast to class.* We are going to conduct an experiment on yeast. Yeast grows as individual cells. Yeast is alive and must have the four requirements for living things. Let the students help set up the experiment.

Make sure the plastic cups are clean. Open the yeast packet and pour half of the yeast into each cup. Add two tablespoons of warm water, not hot, to each cup. Add one teaspoon sugar to each cup. Stir gently. Are the four requirements for life met? Sugar = food. Water. Cup = shelter. Air = in the water and above the water. So the four requirements are met. Now, put one cup on the counter and one in the refrigerator. We will come back later to see what happens.

Go back to see what is happening with the yeast. These yeast cells are living things. Did it make a difference when they were too cold? How fast do they grow? What does yeast smell like? Explain that yeast is used to make bread. It is what makes the bread soft and fluffy. Save the cups for observation over the next several days.

With *another package of dry yeast,* make the yeast/water/sugar mixture again. Pour the yeast liquid into a plastic two liter bottle. Stretch a balloon over the top of the bottle opening. Set the bottle in a bowl of warm water. Watch what happens. As the yeast feeds on the sugar, carbon dioxide is released. This gas makes bubbles; the bubbles pop and fill the balloon.

Give students Lesson 136a Science worksheet. Discuss the basic parts of the yeast cell. Assist the students to color the parts of the yeast cell as is indicated. Share the basic parts of the yeast cell. Instruct students to take the cell picture home and show their families what they learned.

Language Arts: We are going to play a game called "Teacher Says." Teachers say "Teacher says to touch your ear, eye, elbow, knee," etc. This will teach your students awareness of different parts of their body. This will also teach students to listen to your commands.

Sing this song that reviews the body parts. Do motions that fit with the words. Make up additional verses for the other body parts.

Touch Your Finger
Tune of If You're Happy and You Know It
By Al Christopherson

Touch your finger to your ear, to your ear,
Touch your finger to your ear, to your ear.
Touch your finger to your ear, and give a happy cheer,
Touch your finger to your ear, to your ear.

Touch your finger to your knee, to your knee,
Touch your finger to your knee, to your knee.
Touch your finger to your knee, and pinch it like a bee
Touch your finger to your knee, to your knee.

Touch your finger to your foot, to your foot,
Touch your finger to your foot, to your foot.
Touch your finger to your foot, and stomp off all the soot,
Touch your finger to your foot, to your foot.

Touch your finger to your stomach, to your stomach,
Touch your finger to your stomach, to your stomach.
Touch your finger to your stomach, and give a little kick,
Touch your finger to your stomach, to your stomach.

Touch your finger to your hip, to your hip,
Touch your finger to your hip, to your hip.
Touch your finger to your hip, and sail off like a ship,
Touch your finger to your hip, to your hip.

Touch your finger to your nose, to your nose,
Touch your finger to your nose, to your nose.
Touch your finger to your nose, and smell it like a rose,
Touch your finger to your nose, to your nose.

Touch your finger to your eye, to your eye,
Touch your finger to your eye, to your eye.
Touch your finger to your eye, and wave a glad goodbye,
Touch your finger to your eye, to your eye.

Phonics: Blend the sounds Aa-Nn. (an, Ann, ban, can, Dan, fan, Jan, man, Nan, nab, nag, Ben, den, hen, Jen, Ken, Len, men, Ned, Nell, in, bin, din, fin, gin, kin, nib, nil) Review the initial sounds of Aa-Nn. Review letter recognition Aa-Zz.

Add the following words to the flip chart pages of words and review them with the students. Continue to sound out the individual letters of each word as has been done previously. It may also be helpful for the students to see the words spaced out and spelled out as has been done in previous lessons.

an	en	in	na	ne	ni
an	Ben	in	nab	Ned	nib
Ann	den	bin	nag	Nell	nil
ban	hen	din			
Dan	Jen	fin			
fan	Ken	gin			
Jan	Len	kin			
man	men				
Nan					

Do the Lesson 136a Phonics worksheet. The sound of Nn. Review the letter sound with the picture and words on the worksheet. Ask the students for other words that begin with the same sound. Trace the letters and say the sound of Nn. Observe the students as they trace the letters and help them with the letter strokes. If you have the students do one row at a time, the worksheet can be carried over to various parts of the day or another day.

Do the Lesson 136b Phonics worksheet. The Sound of Nn. Review the letter sound with the picture and words on the worksheet. Ask the students for other words that begin with the same sound. Give them specific instructions for how the letter should be traced. Allow time for tracing the letters and observe their progress. If you have the students do one row at a time, the worksheet can be carried over to various parts of the day or another day.

Reading: Use a simplified, illustrated telephone listing. Give the beginning sound of a word. Identify the name and sound of the letters in one's name.

Multimedia Resources: Review "Rev-Up for Reading" from the "Rev-Up for Learning" DVD to drill letter recognition and sound. The students should say each letter sound along with the presentation.

Writing: Continue to do Learning Logs. Encourage the students to draw or write about themselves. Some sample topics might be My Pet, My Favorite Reptile, My Favorite School Activity, My Family, or other teacher selected topics. The writing can be invented temporary spellings or dictations to the teacher.

Multimedia Resources: Review "Rev-Up for Writing" from the "Rev-Up for Learning" DVD to review the writing of upper- and lowercase letters.

Memory Verse: Work on sections ONE and TWO of Psalm 139:14-16. Talk about all of the things we have learned about God's works. What is the most wonderful to your students? Let them share.

  ONE   I praise You because I am fearfully and wonderfully made:
  TWO   Your works are wonderful, I know that full well.

Math: Review 2 - 1 = 1. Use the string of Counting Beads or pop beads to review 1 + 1 = 2, 2 + 1 = 3, 3 + 1 = 4, 4 + 1 = 5, and 2 – 1 = 1.

Do the Lesson 136a Math worksheet. Read the number. Count the dots under the number. Trace the letters for the number word. Draw 4 objects in the counting jar. Trace the number and the number word following the proper strokes. The students can color the counting jar.

Do the Lesson 136b Math worksheet. Count the beads and say the subtraction or addition problem. Trace the correct answer and say the subtraction or addition problem again.

Multimedia Resources: View "Rev-Up for Arithmetic" from the "Rev-Up for Learning" DVD to practice number recognition, counting and addition 1-20.

Story Time: Read a story or stories of your choice.

Music: Review "Put Your Finger on Your Nose" and "Say To the Lord I Love You." Learn the song "If You're Happy and You Know It, Clap Your Hands."

If You're Happy and You Know It, Clap Your Hands

If you're happy and you know it, clap your hands (Clap hands)
If you're happy and you know it, clap your hands
If you're happy and you know it
Then you're face will really show it.
If you're happy and you know it, clap your hands

If you're happy and you know it, stomp your feet (Stomp feet)
If you're happy and you know it, stomp your feet
If you're happy and you know it
Then your face will really show it.
If you're happy and you know it, stomp your feet.

(Continue with different body actions. Try doing two actions at once.)

Multimedia Resources: This week, listen and sing along to selections from "The Story of Little Tree" CD.

This week, watch *The Kingdom Under the Sea* adventure "Return of the King" which is an Easter story.

Health & Safety: Our body is replacing cells all the time. Our skin cells are constantly renewing themselves. That is why we need to be careful and bathe at least every other day. When we use a washcloth, we help our body to get rid of the old cells. When you take a bath, try to rub your entire body with the washcloth, rubbing off the old skin cells and making way for the new skin cells.

Physical Education: Mulberry Bush Hide and Seek. You will need something that serves as short walls behind which the students can hide. Sheets draped over chairs or tables tipped on their sides would provide walls to hide behind. Play some lively music as the students move walking, skipping, etc. in a circular direction behind the walls. When the music stops the students hide by crouching behind the nearest wall. They should be quiet and not touch the walls. The teacher then sings the song, "Round and round the cobbler's bench, The monkey chased the weasel, The monkey thought 'twas all in fun, Pop! Goes the weasel." The students should all jump up from behind the walls at "Pop goes the weasel" to scare the teacher. The teacher chooses another walking movement and starts the procedure again.

NOTES:

Activities in this Lesson: Bible Lesson, Science, Language Arts, Phonics, Reading, Writing, Memory Verse, Math, Story Time, Music, Creative Cooking, Physical Education, Homework

Bible Reference: Genesis 1:26-27.

Bible Concept to Present: Every living thing has cells.

Bible Lesson: God knew that every living thing would be different but the same. Living things have many characteristics in common. Let's review them:
1. Living things need air. They must get air, even if they live under water.
2. Living things need food.
3. Living things need water. Animals will move permanently if their water supply moves.
4. Living things need shelter, some kind of protection.

Social Studies: Each living cell within an organism needs these four things, too. Cells need air and water, food and protection, or they die. Did you know there is a very good example of a cell that we see almost every day?

Science: An egg is a cell. *Bring in several eggs.* Let the students crack them, as that is so much fun. Break the eggs onto a plate. Explain that every living cell is basically like the egg. It has a nucleus, the yolk. It has cytoplasm, the egg white. It has a shell. The drawing on Lesson 137 Resource page is for the teacher's reference. Use it to help explain the very simple facts about the egg cell to the students. Use a straight pin to pull the membrane from the shell pieces to show students. Very slowly pop the yolk, showing that there is a membrane around it. Explain that the shell protects the inside of the egg, just like every cell is protected by its shell. If you brought enough eggs, let each student have his own egg and plate. Give them straight pins to poke the yolk and pull out the membrane. Tell the students to keep their hands out of their mouths while doing this. Clean up everything, including hands, after doing this activity.

Every living thing needs: water, air, food, and shelter. We looked at eggs today. How do you think the egg gets air? Did you know that the egg shell isn't solid, that it has little holes in it? Use your last whole egg. We will do an experiment to see if there are tiny holes in eggshells. Fill a glass container half full with warm water. Place the egg inside. Carefully observe the egg. Does it float or sink? Do you see tiny bubbles? Which part of the egg is giving off bubbles? The bubbles are air escaping out of the egg. There are very tiny holes in the egg shell so that air and water can go in and out. This has to be true, because what happens to an egg if it is left alone in a warm environment? A bird or other animal grows inside. That baby would need air to breathe. So now you know that egg shells have tiny little holes in them for air and water to pass through.

Language Arts: How many cells can you think of? Let's write them on the board. Encourage students to name all the parts of a human or animal body. Explain as you write that all of these body parts have their own cells. Look again at Lesson 136b Science worksheet with the students. Tell them that these are only a very few of the cells that exist.

Phonics: Review blends Aa-Nn with the blend charts. Review the initial sounds of Aa-Nn. Review letter recognition Aa-Zz.

Have the students brainstorm words that begin or include the letter Nn. Write these words on the board. Model the correct letter formation as you write the letters on the board. The students should practice forming the letter Nn on a blank sheet of paper. Students who are ready can practice copying complete words from the board.

Do the Lesson 137 Phonics worksheet. The Sound of Nn. Review the letter sound with the picture and words on the worksheet. Ask the students for other words that begin with the same sound. Trace the letters and say the sound of Nn. Observe the students as they trace the letters and help them with the letter strokes. If you have the students do one row at a time, the worksheet can be carried over to various parts of the day or another day.

Reading: Use a simplified, illustrated telephone listing. Give the beginning sound of a word. Identify the name and sound of the letters in one's name.

Writing: Continue to do Learning Logs. Encourage the students to draw or write about themselves. Some sample topics might be My Pet, My Favorite Reptile, My Favorite School Activity, My Family, or other teacher selected topics. The writing can be invented temporary spellings or dictations to the teacher.

Memory Verse: Continue working on Psalm 139:14-16. Add section THREE today. Remind students that God knew us even before we were born. They are doing a super job. Most adults don't memorize scripture, especially a long section like this.

ONE	I praise You because I am fearfully and wonderfully made:
TWO	Your works are wonderful, I know that full well.
THREE	My frame was not hidden from you when I was made in the secret place ...

Math: Review 2 - 1 = 1.

Make Hand Prints. Paint each student's hand with some paint and have each one make a palm print on a sheet of white paper. Set these aside to dry. They will be used later in Lesson 147 for measuring practice.

Story Time: Read a story or stories of your choice.

Music: Review "If You're Happy and You Know It," "Touch Your Finger," "Put Your Finger," and "Say To the Lord I Love You."

Multimedia Resources: This week, listen and sing along to selections from "The Story of Little Tree" CD.

This week, watch *The Kingdom Under the Sea* adventure "Return of the King" which is an Easter story.

Creative Cooking: If any eggs are still whole, let the students help you poach them. Put them on plates and investigate how they have changed. What happened to the yolks and the whites? Can we ever put the eggs back in the shells? Some things that change can never be put back the way they were. Talk about how many ways you can change an egg.

Physical Education: Repeat the Mulberry Bush Hide and Seek activity. You will need something that serves as short walls behind which the students can hide. Sheets draped over chairs or tables tipped on their sides would provide walls to hide behind. Play some lively music as the students move walking, skipping, etc. in a circular direction behind the walls. When the music stops the students hide by crouching behind the nearest wall. They should be quiet and not touch the walls. The teacher then sings the song, "Round and round the cobbler's bench, The monkey chased the weasel, The monkey thought 'twas all in fun, Pop! Goes the weasel." The students should all jump up from behind the walls at "Pop goes the weasel" to scare the teacher. The teacher chooses another walking movement and starts the procedure again.

Homework: Send home Lesson 137 Homework worksheet. The students will be looking at eggs with their families, and talking about what they learned. The pages don't have to be returned.

NOTES:

Lesson 138

Week 28: Day 3

Activities in this Lesson: Bible Lesson/Social Studies, Science, Language Arts, Phonics, Reading, Writing, Memory Verse, Math, Story Time, Music, Arts & Crafts, Creative Cooking, Physical Education

Bible Reference: Genesis 1:26-27.

Bible Concept to Present: God made us to have skin.

Bible Lesson/Social Studies: Do you think you would look funny if you didn't have any skin? What would hold your bones in place? If you did not have skin you could see inside your body. God wanted to keep our insides all together. He wanted to keep our insides safe. In order to do that, He created skin. Our skin keeps out germs so we don't get sick all of the time.

Social Studies: Did you know God even made people with different colors of skin? It doesn't matter what color your skin is, God loves you so much. We should love everyone, too.

Science: Our skin is our protective bag. To illustrate the skin to your students, use a zip-lock plastic bag and two pieces of bread that have been dampened. In the bag place one piece of bread. Close the zipper on the bag. Leave the other piece of bread out in the open. You might set them outside. Our skin keeps moisture in and dirt out. Just as the bread in the bag stays clean and damp, our internal body organs stay clean and damp inside our skin bag. The piece of bread left out not only dried out but was exposed to contamination. Our skin is composed of seven layers. The cells of the skin are constantly renewing themselves, and skin cells are constantly dying. God made a wonderful "bag" for us to live in.

Bring some clean, dry chicken skin to class. It would be especially great to have a piece of skin for each student. Lay the pieces of skin on paper towels. Let the students observe the skin under a magnifying glass. Ask, What do you see? Can you see hair? Can you see places where there used to be feathers? Is the skin hard or soft? How is chicken skin different from our skin? Let the students look at their own skin with the magnifying glass. Instruct the students to not put their fingers in their mouths after touching the skin. Have the students wash their hands and the table after touching the chicken skin.

Language Arts: We will be doing a "Texture Feel" today. Walk around the classroom or house and discover the different "textures." For example, feel the chairs, wood trim, floors, appliances, and other fixtures in your school room. Talk about soft, hard, rough, and smooth textures.

Phonics: Teach the initial short sound of Oo. Review the initial sounds of Aa-Nn. Review letter recognition Aa-Zz.

Write several initial short Oo words on the board: October, odd, off, offer, ox, ostrich, etc. Underline the initial short letter Oo and say the words. Ask the students for other words that start with the same sound.

Do the Lesson 138 Phonics worksheet. The Short Sound of Oo. Review the letter sound with the picture and words on the worksheet. Ask the students for other words that begin with the same sound. Discuss the position of the letters on the guidelines. Give them specific instructions for how the letter should be traced. Trace the letters and say the short sound of Oo. Observe the students as they trace the letters and help them with the letter strokes. If you have the students do one row at a time, the worksheet can be carried over to various parts of the day or another day.

Reading: Use a simplified, illustrated telephone listing. Give the beginning sound of a word. Identify the name and sound of the letters in one's name.

Writing: Continue to do Learning Logs. Encourage the students to draw or write about themselves. Some sample topics might be My Pet, My Favorite Reptile, My Favorite School Activity, My Family, or other teacher selected topics. The writing can be invented temporary spellings or dictations to the teacher.

Memory Verse: Continue working on sections ONE, TWO, and THREE of Psalm 139:14-16.

Math: Review 2 - 1 = 1. Draw a strip of squares on the board. Write 2 – 1 = under the row of squares. Have a student color two of the squares. Say, "two minus one equals," and have another student erase or cross out one of the squares. Say again while pointing to the squares, "two minus one equals" and have another student give the answer. Review the problems: 1 + 1 = 2, 2 + 1 = 3, 3 + 1 = 4, 4 + 1 = 5, 5 + 1 = 6.

Do the Lesson 138a Math worksheet. Read the number. Count the dots under the number. Trace the letters for the number word. Draw 5 objects in the counting jar. Trace the number and the number word following the proper strokes. The students can color the counting jar.

Do the Lesson 138b Math worksheet. Count the dots in the tiles and trace the numbers for the addition and subtraction problems.

Story Time: Read a story or stories of your choice.

Music: Review "If You're Happy and You Know It," "Touch Your Finger," and "Say To the Lord I Love You."

Multimedia Resources: This week, listen and sing along to selections from "The Story of Little Tree" CD.

This week, watch *The Kingdom Under the Sea* adventure "Return of the King" which is an Easter story.

Arts & Crafts: *Provide finger paint that is washable.* Permit the students to finger paint. If you are able, permit them to toe paint. Remove shoes and socks and have some fun.

Creative Cooking: To reinforce the concept of the short sound of *o* make Hot Dog Octopuses. Cut the bottom 3/4 of a hot dog into 8ths (using vertical cuts). Leave the top 1/4 intact. Boil as you normally would. When done, your student will enjoy a crazy octopus with wavy arms!

Physical Education: Spend some time stretching your skin. Instruct students to stretch as high as possible. Then stretch as wide, then as low. Our skin will stretch as far as we can reach.

NOTES:

Lesson 139

Week 28: Day 4

Activities in this Lesson: Bible Lesson, Science, Language Arts, Phonics, Reading, Writing, Memory Verse, Math, Story Time, Music, Arts & Crafts/Science, Arts & Crafts, Health & Safety, Physical Education

Bible Reference: Genesis 1:26-27.

Bible Concept to Present: God gave us five most amazing gifts: our five senses.

Bible Lesson: With all of the creating that God was doing, He gave animals the most amazing gifts of the five senses. Almost all animals have five senses. Some animals have their five senses in unusual places! But they have them. The five senses alone prove the existence of a loving, intelligent, all knowing creator.

Science: Insects have the five senses, but in some funny places! The sense of touch is highly developed in cockroaches. That is how they can move so fast. Most insects smell with their antennae which stick out of the front or sides of their heads. Aren't you glad our ears don't stick out from the tops of our heads? Insects hear with their bodies, not ears. Some insects have tympanal organs on their bodies for hearing. Remember what a tympani looks like. It is a big kettle drum used by an orchestra. The top of the drum is a large circle made from hide or plastic. The tympanal organs of an insect are large disks used for hearing. The cricket has his "ears" or tympanal organs on his front legs.

Language Arts: Obtain the library book *My Five Senses* by Aliki. Bring a lemon, cinnamon, piece of fur (from Week 25), flashlight, and a bell. After reading the book, test each sense with students, taking turns with everyone. Explain that there are five senses: touching, smelling, seeing, hearing, and tasting.

Play the "Five Senses" game. Call out each sentence and let the students name the senses used. There will be some overlap of answers.

I was walking down the street one day.	TOUCH: feet on street
I stopped and smelled some honeysuckle.	SMELL
When I pulled a flower closer, a thorn poked me.	TOUCH
I looked around and saw that it was a very sunny day.	SIGHT
It was really warm outside, I was hot.	TOUCH
Suddenly, I heard a loud buzzing sound.	HEARING
It was a bee! I could see its little stinger.	SIGHT
I ran away until I couldn't hear it anymore.	HEARING

Phonics: Review the initial short sound of Oo. Review the initial sounds of Aa-Nn. Review letter recognition Aa-Zz.

Have the students brainstorm words that begin or include the letter Oo. Write these words on the board. Model the correct letter formation as you write the letters on the board. The students should practice forming the letter Oo on a blank sheet of paper. Students who are ready can practice copying complete words from the board.

Do the Lesson 139 Phonics worksheet. The Short Sound of Oo. Review the letter sound with the picture and words on the worksheet. Ask the students for other words that begin with the same sound. Trace the letters and say the short sound of Oo. Observe the students as they trace the letters and help them with the letter strokes. If you have the students do one row at a time, the worksheet can be carried over to various parts of the day or another day.

Reading: Use a simplified, illustrated telephone listing. Give the beginning sound of a word. Identify the name and sound of the letters in one's name.

Writing: Continue to do Learning Logs. Encourage the students to draw or write about themselves. Some sample topics might be My Pet, My Favorite Reptile, My Favorite School Activity, My Family, or other teacher selected topics. The writing can be invented temporary spellings or dictations to the teacher.

Memory Verse: Let the students take turns saying the sections of Psalm 139:14-16. If this project seems overwhelming, continue to work on this amount for the next two weeks, don't add the other three parts.

ONE	I praise You because I am fearfully and wonderfully made:
TWO	Your works are wonderful, I know that full well.
THREE	My frame was not hidden from you when I was made in the secret place …

Math: Review 2 - 1 = 1. Have the students count off steps to practice addition and subtraction. For subtraction they should step forward the first number of steps, then backwards one step and place their bean bag. Then they should go back to the starting point and count forward to answer the subtraction problem. Review: 1 + 1 = 2, 2 + 1 = 3, 3 + 1 = 4, 4 + 1 = 5, 5 + 1 = 6.

Do the Lesson 139 Math worksheet. For subtraction count all of the blocks in the strip, then say, "minus one block equals," and count the blocks that are not covered by an X. Trace the correct number. Do the addition problems as before.

Story Time: Read a story or stories of your choice.

Music: Review "If You're Happy and You Know It," "Touch Your Finger," and "Say To the Lord I Love You."

Multimedia Resources: This week, listen and sing along to selections from "The Story of Little Tree" CD.

This week, watch *The Kingdom Under the Sea* adventure "Return of the King" which is an Easter story.

Arts & Crafts/Science: Give students playdough. Say, Everyone has an assignment. With your playdough, make the body part that has to do with smelling, with seeing, with tasting, with hearing, with touch. Wait, oh my, how much of our body has to do with touch? We would have to make a little person, because all of our body has a part in touching. Everyone needs to be touched. That is why hugs are important. Don't you love hugs? Have you heard of a "group hug?" Let's all come together and have a group hug.

Arts & Crafts: *Bring in equal amounts of cinnamon and applesauce. You also need thin wire, wire cutters, cookie cutters or plastic knives.* Let the students measure equal amounts into a bowl and mix well. Add cinnamon or applesauce to make the right consistency. Knead the cinnamon dough. Roll it out to about a 1/2 inch thickness. Let the students cut out shapes with plastic knives or cookie cutters. If you use cookie cutters, they must be simple ones that are just outlines. Cut a piece of wire for each Cinnamon Hanger, about 10 inches long. Poke the wire through the top of each shape. Then let the shapes dry for a week, turning them over every day. When the Cinnamon Hangers are totally dry, careful shape the wires into hangers. Hang in a window and enjoy the scent.

Health & Safety: Not everyone has the use of the five senses. It is not because they don't want to have them. Some people are born without one of the senses. Some people have had an accident that damaged one of the senses. Remember when we learned about Helen Keller? Helen Keller used the senses she did have to make up for the ones that were missing. We should never, ever make fun of people because they can't see or they can't speak. It is never their fault.

Everyone close his eyes. Now I will describe a beautiful sunset. The sky is a very soft pink, with clouds across the horizon. The clouds are touched with gold and purple. The sun is just sinking below the mountain. Now, did you see the sunset? It isn't as much fun or lovely if you can't see it, is it? We have to remember how hard it would be if we couldn't ever see the sunset, but just had to hear about it. That is why we always take care of our eyes, our ears, and our bodies.

Our senses involve openings in our bodies. Our nose, our ears, even our eyes are openings into our bodies. We should never, ever put anything into these openings. Has anyone ever done that? Some children will put beans or clay or other things into their ears or into their noses. Often they have to go to the emergency room to remove the objects. The best way to protect our body is to never put anything in our eyes, our ears, or our noses.

Physical Education: Snowball Throw. Make snowmen from large cardboard circles or draw on banner paper. The students can help you decorate the snowmen. Tape the snowmen to the wall. Make snowballs from plastic grocery bags that have been rolled into balls and taped. Have the students stand behind a line about 5 feet away from the snowman target to throw the snowballs. See if the students can hit different parts of the target.

NOTES:

Activities in this Lesson: Bible Lesson, Science, Social Studies, Language Arts, Phonics, Reading, Writing, Memory Verse, Math, Story Time, Music, Health & Safety, Physical Education

Bible Reference: John 9:1-41.

Bible Concept to Present: Our eyesight is a precious gift from God.

Bible Lesson: Read the story of the blind man ahead of time. Retell it to your students in your own words. Jesus was a miracle healer. He often healed a person that was damaged in one of his five senses. Sometimes people are born blind, like the man in the Bible account. We don't know why. Jesus said that it wasn't because this man was bad. It was to glorify God. When Jesus healed the man, God was glorified because it was a miracle. What do you think it was like when the man could see for the first time?

Science: Show students Lesson 140 Resource page, the diagram of the eye. Talk about the miracle of the eye. God uses light entering the eye to enable us to see. Remember when we learned about reflected light? Light that is reflected off of an object goes into our eyes and lets us see. Trace the path of light on the diagram, from outside into the brain.

Give students a paper towel tube. Instruct them to hold the tube up to their right eye and hold their left hand up beside the tube. Keep both eyes open. What happens? It looks like there is a hole in the hand! One eye is seeing the hand and one eye is seeing the hole through the tube. Our eyes put together what they are each seeing.

Social Studies: There are many ways to help those that have lost their sight. Remember when we learned about Braille, the system of writing for the blind? Who can remember how the blind can read Braille? There are also many audiobooks available, so that the blind can listen to books.

One wonderful help for someone that is blind is a guide dog. There are special places, like Guide Dogs for the Blind in San Rafael, California, that train dogs for special duty. The dogs learn how to guide a blind person through traffic and to work and wherever they want to go. Families around the office location raise puppies for the company. The puppy raisers have certain rules they have to follow in raising the puppy. When the dog is a year old, he is taken to the Guide Dogs for the Blind location and tested to see if he can be a guide dog. Not every dog raised for this is accepted. If you want to learn more, go to this website: http://www.guidedogs.com/

Language Arts: One wonderful advantage to having sight is reading. You are all learning to read. Books will become a big part of your life. But there are many, many ways we use reading other than books. How do you shop for groceries? How do you know the contents of the cans? How do you drive a car and follow directions? How do you play a computer game? Reading is very important and necessary to everyone. Try to do your best as you learn to read.

Phonics: Blend the sounds Aa-Oo. (bob, Bob, cob, fob, job, lob, mob, odd, bod, cod, God, mod, nod, bog, cog, dog, fog, hog, jog, log, mom, on, Bonn, con, Don, Jon, Lon) Review the initial sounds of Aa-Oo. Review letter recognition Aa-Zz.

Add the following words to the flip chart pages of words and review them with the students. Continue to sound out the individual letters of each word as has been done previously. It may also be helpful for the students to see the words spaced out and spelled out as has been done in previous lessons.

ob	od	og	om	on
bob	odd	bog	mom	on
Bob	bod	cog		Bonn
cob	cod	dog		con
fob	God	fog		Don
job	mod	hog		Jon
lob	nod	jog		Lon
mob		log		

bo	co	do	fo	go	ho
bob	cob	dog	fob	gob	hog
Bob	cod	Don	fog	God	
bod	cog				
bog	con				
Bonn					

jo	lo	mo	no
job	lob	mob	nod
jog	log	mod	
Jon	Lon	mom	

Do the Lesson 140a Phonics worksheet. The Short Sound of Oo. Review the letter sound with the picture and words on the worksheet. Ask the students for other words that begin with the same sound. Trace the letters and say the short sound of Oo. Observe the students as they trace the letters and help them with the letter strokes. If you have the students do one row at a time, the worksheet can be carried over to various parts of the day or another day.

Do the Lesson 140b Phonics worksheet. The Short Sound of Oo. Review the letter sound with the picture and words on the worksheet. Ask the students for other words that begin with the same sound. Give them specific instructions for how the letter should be traced. Allow time for tracing the letters and observe their progress. If you have the students do one row at a time, the worksheet can be carried over to various parts of the day or another day.

Reading: Use a simplified, illustrated telephone listing. Give the beginning sound of a word. Identify the name and sound of the letters in one's name.

Writing: Continue to do Learning Logs. Encourage the students to draw or write about themselves. Some sample topics might be My Pet, My Favorite Reptile, My Favorite School Activity, My Family, or other teacher selected topics. The writing can be invented temporary spellings or dictations to the teacher.

Memory Verse: For those trying to memorize all six parts of Psalm 139:14-16, add part FOUR today. Write the four sections on poster board. Though some students can't read all of the words, it will still help them focus.

ONE	I praise You because I am fearfully and wonderfully made:
TWO	Your works are wonderful, I know that full well.
THREE	My frame was not hidden from you when I was made in the secret place …
FOUR	Your eyes saw my unformed body.

Math: Review 2 - 1 = 1. Give each student 10 pennies to count 1-10. Have the students add and subtract pennies to practice the facts: 1 + 1 = 2, 2 + 1 = 3, 3 + 1 = 4, 4 + 1 = 5, 5 + 1 = 5, 2 – 1 = 1.

Do the Lesson 140a Math worksheet. Read the number. Count the dots under the number. Trace the letters for the number word. Draw 6 objects in the counting jar. Trace the number and the number word following the proper strokes. The students can color the counting jar.

Do the Lesson 140b Math worksheet. For subtraction count all of the pennies in the row, then say, "minus one penny equals," and count the pennies that are not covered by an X. Trace the correct number. Do the addition as before.

Story Time: Read a story or stories of your student's choice or ones they have brought from home.

Music: Review "If You're Happy and You Know It," "Touch Your Finger," and "Say To the Lord I Love You."

Multimedia Resources: This week, listen and sing along to selections from "The Story of Little Tree" CD.

This week, watch *The Kingdom Under the Sea* adventure "Return of the King" which is an Easter story.

Health & Safety: *Bring in a pair of glasses. A child's size would be great. Also bring in some contact lenses.* Sometimes our eyes don't work right. We can see but not clearly. We are so fortunate that glasses are available. Let me show you these glasses. The lenses in the glasses help the lenses in our eyes to adjust and see clearly. Do any of you wear glasses? Does anyone want to try these on? When children get older, they can wear contact lenses. These are tiny little circles of lenses that fit right onto the eye. Show the students on the diagram where the contact lenses would fit on the eye.

Try arranging for an eye test for students. Often eyesight problems go undetected for many years in children. You can devise a simple test by printing block letters on poster board, sitting the students six feet away and testing one eye at a time.

Physical Education: Play "Blind Man's Bluff" outside or inside. Tie a scarf around one student's head, over his eyes. Make sure the play area is clear of objects and toys. Spin the student around five times. All the other students run to hide. When the spinning is done, the teacher yells, "Stop!" All students must stop where they are. "It" roams around, blindfolded, trying to find the other students. "It" may yell "blind man" at any time and the other students must answer "bluff." The first person tagged is "It" the next time.

NOTES:

Lesson 141

Week 29: Day 1

Activities in this Lesson: Bible Lesson, Social Studies/Science, Science, Science/Physical Education, Language Arts, Phonics, Reading, Writing, Memory Verse/Physical Education, Math, Story Time, Music, Health & Safety, Physical Education

Bible Reference: Proverbs 20:12.

Bible Concept to Present: Our hearing is a precious gift from God. God's works are wonderful. We must treasure them.

Bible Lesson: Ears that hear and eyes that see... the Lord has made them both. Proverbs 20:12. Our amazing God gave us the gift of hearing. What is interesting is that He tells us people can hear but not understand. They can hear but not act.

Arrange with a student ahead of time not to respond to instructions from you. Give him some simple commands that he completely ignores. After a few minutes, explain that the student was hearing but not acting on what he heard. Many people hear the Word and hear the gospel, but they don't believe. They don't act on it. It is the same as having sight but being blind to truth.

Illustration: What we hear stays with us. When you hear or see something, like a movie, it stays with you. It is in your brain. You can't get it out. We must take care of the gifts of sight and hearing. We must be careful about what we put into our brain, through our eyes and our ears. That is why there are some movies and there is some music that we shouldn't hear. Things we see and hear stay with us for years. That is why we obey God and only watch and listen to things that are pure, things that are just, things that are good.

Multimedia Resources: Listen to the song "Make a Noise" from the "Bullfrogs and Butterflies: God Loves Fun" CD.

Social Studies/Science: Play a variety of CDs: classical music, children's music, animal sounds, etc. Talk about the wonderful gift of being able to hear music and voices. What kind of music is your favorite? Use Lesson 141 Resource page to trace the flow of sound from outside the ear into the inner ear of the drawing.

Science: *Bring a package of Styrofoam 8 oz cups to class. Cut the bottoms out of a few of them.* Play some lively music. Instruct students to put cups over each ear. Does it make a difference? Now put cups over your ears that have the bottoms cut out. What was different?

Do the Lesson 141 Science worksheet. Have the students circle things that can be heard.

Science/Physical Education: Sit one student in a chair in the middle of the room. Blindfold him with a scarf. Give other students or the teacher the film canister/rice shakers. When the teacher points at a student, he shakes his canister. See how many times the blindfolded student can point to the sound. Let everyone have a turn in the chair.

Language Arts: Much of our lives is surrounded by the sound of voices. Hearing a loved one's voice can soothe and comfort us. We can tell someone's voice just by listening to it. Some voices are high pitched, some are low. Our voices are made by our vocal chords in our throat. The chords vibrate to make sounds. People are the only living things with speech ability. We can talk or sing to communicate with one another.

This is a great privilege given to us. The most amazing part is that we can talk to God and He hears us. God always hears us.

Sit one student in a chair in the middle of the room. Blindfold him with a scarf. Point to one of the students and have him ask, "Can you guess who is speaking?". See how many times the blindfolded student can name the person who spoke. Let everyone have a turn in the chair.

Phonics: Teach the initial sound of Pp. Review the initial sounds of Aa-Oo. Review letter recognition Aa-Zz.

Write several initial Pp words on the board: pad, page, pan, paper, pants, Pat, pay, pen, pep, pig, pill, pin, pit, pod, pop, put, etc. Underline the initial letter Pp and say the words. Ask the students for other words that start with the same sound.

Do the Lesson 141 Phonics worksheet. The Sound of Pp. Review the letter sound with the picture and words on the worksheet. Ask the students for other words that begin with the same sound. Discuss the position of the letters on the guidelines. Give them specific instructions for how the letter should be traced. Trace the letters and say the sound of Pp. Observe the students as they trace the letters and help them with the letter strokes. If you have the students do one row at a time, the worksheet can be carried over to various parts of the day or another day.

Reading: Begin to use invented phonetic spelling in writing. Indicate the number of phonemes (1 - 3) heard in a real or nonsense word.

Multimedia Resources: Review "Rev-Up for Reading" from the "Rev-Up for Learning" DVD to drill letter recognition and sound. The students should say each letter sound along with the presentation.

Writing: Continue to do Learning Logs. Encourage the students to draw or write about themselves. Some sample topics might be My Pet, My Favorite Reptile, My Favorite School Activity, My Family, or other teacher selected topics. The writing can be invented temporary spellings or dictations to the teacher.

Teach your students how to write their home addresses and phone numbers. Do this by creating tracing sheets for each student. This can be easily done on a computer by using an outline font or a gray rather than a black color for the font. Only attempt this activity if your students are ready.

Multimedia Resources: Review "Rev-Up for Writing" from the "Rev-Up for Learning" DVD to review the writing of upper- and lowercase letters.

Memory Verse/Physical Education: Continue working on the four parts of Psalm 139:14-16 today. Combine the memory work with some physical education. Do jumping jacks to the verse.

Math: Teach 3 - 1 = 2. Have three students come to the front of the room. Count the students. Have one of them return to his seat. Ask the class how many students are still standing at the front of the room after one left. Do this with several groups of three students. Say the problem, "three minus one equals two." An optional way to do this is to hold up a subtraction sign between the first three students and a fourth that you have asked to come to the front. Then as you say the subtraction problem, have the student after the subtraction sign hold a piece of paper with a big X on it in front of him. You can also hold up an equal sign and have two additional students represent the answer to the subtraction problem.

Do the Lesson 141 Math worksheet. Read the number. Count the dots under the number. Trace the letters for the number word. Draw 7 objects in the counting jar. Trace the number and the number word following the proper strokes. The students can color the counting jar.

Multimedia Resources: View "Rev-Up for Arithmetic" from the "Rev-Up for Learning" DVD to practice number recognition, counting and addition 1-20.

Story Time: Read a story or stories of your choice.

Music: Review "If You're Happy and You Know It" and "Touch Your Finger."

Multimedia Resources: This week, listen and sing along to selections from "The Story of Little Tree" CD.

This week, watch *The Kingdom Under the Sea* adventure "Return of the King" which is an Easter story.

Health & Safety: *Bring a hearing aid to class.* If you don't have access to one, print a picture of one from the Internet. Explain to the students that when people have trouble hearing, they might wear a hearing aid. This little device can help people to hear correctly. Though we are never to put anything in our ears, it is alright to use one of these aids. Let the students look at and touch the hearing aid.

Schedule a hearing test for your students if your school does not do this on a regular basis. It is important that difficulties be identified early so that parents and teachers can help the students with any problems.

Physical Education: Play the game Captain, May I? or Teacher, May I? This game illustrates the importance of hearing. Set up a goal line and a starting line. The player who is "Captain" stands at the goal line. The "Captain" addresses one player at a time to "Take one giant step" or "Take 5 baby steps" or "Skip three steps," etc. That player must remember to say "Captain, May I?" and wait for permission before he can advance. If the player forgets to ask permission first, he must return to the starting line. The Captain then addresses another player on the line and continues until one player finally reaches the goal line. That player then becomes the "Captain."

NOTES:

Activities in this Lesson: Bible Lesson, Science, Language Arts, Phonics, Reading, Writing, Memory Verse, Math, Story Time, Music, Arts & Crafts, Outdoor Activity, Physical Education

Bible Reference: Daniel 3:27.

Bible Concept to Present: Our sense of smell is a precious gift from God.

Bible Lesson: After God made so many wonderful smells for our world, He had to allow us to smell them so he gave us smelling. He made such a wide variety of smells, good, bad, and ugly. Sometimes the smell of something is a warning to us. God protects us in ways we don't even think about. God gave almost every living thing an odor.

Multimedia Resources: Listen to the song "Goodness" from "The Music Machine: The Fruit of the Spirit" CD and the song I Know Somebody Who Knows from the "Bullfrogs and Butterflies: God is Great" CD.

Social Studies: We smell different things all day long. Doesn't it smell good when our dinner is cooking? The sense of smell helps us to taste things. Our sense of smell is also important to our memory. Certain smells can bring back memories of past meals, holidays, and experiences. We scent our homes with different smells because we like them. We sometimes forget that smell is a gift from God.

Science: *Bring in many different scents for the students to smell.* Spices, soap, pine branch, cookies, perfume, peanut butter, popcorn, tuna fish, dry mustard, cocoa, talcum powder, etc. Put the items in a small plastic container that has been covered with aluminum foil. Poke a hole in the foil with a pencil for the students to smell through. Let the students smell each one, deciding if they like the smell or not. Be sure to bring some things that smell bad.

Language Arts: When something burns in a fire, it smells like smoke. Our verse is part of a Bible account in Daniel. Review the story in Daniel 3. Tell the story to the students in your own words. Emphasize the obedience of Shadrach, Meshach, and Abednego and that, beyond the miracle of their survival, God put a shining stamp of grace on the miracle when the three don't even smell of smoke when they come out of the fire.

Multimedia Resources: Get the video "Rack, Shack and Benny," a Veggie Tales® movie by Big Idea. Or watch "Obedience" from the *Character Builders Video Series*. After watching the video, talk about obedience. Listen to the song "Never Seen Nothing Like That" from "The Amazing Miracles" CD.

Phonics: Review the initial sound of Pp. Review the initial sounds of Aa-Oo. Review letter recognition Aa-Zz.

Do the Lesson 142 Phonics worksheet. The Sound of Pp. Review the letter sound with the picture and words on the worksheet. Ask the students for other words that begin with the same sound. Trace the letters and say the sound of Pp. Observe the students as they trace the letters and help them with the letter strokes. If you have the students do one row at a time, the worksheet can be carried over to various parts of the day or another day.

Reading: Begin to use invented phonetic spelling in writing. Indicate the number of phonemes (1 - 3) heard in a real or nonsense word.

Writing: Continue to do Learning Logs. Encourage the students to draw or write about themselves. Some sample topics might be My Pet, My Favorite Reptile, My Favorite School Activity, My Family, or other teacher selected topics. The writing can be invented temporary spellings or dictations to the teacher.

Teach your students how to write their home addresses and phone numbers. Do this by creating tracing sheets for each student. This can be easily done on a computer by using an outline font or a gray rather than a black color for the font. Only attempt this activity if your students are ready.

Memory Verse: Review Psalm 139:14-16. How are students doing? Even if they are struggling to memorize, keep them going over the verse. Get some stickers and hand them out for each section of the verse that is memorized.

Math: Review 3 - 1 = 2. Give the students the dog bones that they cut out previously and a bowl to put them in. Have them place 3 bones in the bowl while saying "three minus one" and have them take a bone from the bowl, "equals" and have them count "one, two bones in the bowl." Do this several times. Practice previous addition and subtraction facts.

Do the Lesson 142 Math worksheet. As they count the images have them say the subtraction and addition problems and trace the numbers.

Story Time: Read a story or stories of your choice.

Music: Review "If You're Happy and You Know It" and "Touch Your Finger."

Multimedia Resources: This week, listen and sing along to selections from "The Story of Little Tree" CD.

This week, watch *The Kingdom Under the Sea* adventure "Return of the King" which is an Easter story.

Arts & Crafts: *Bring in cinnamon, paper plates, and thin ribbon.* Let the students paint a design in tacky glue on the plate. Then let them shake cinnamon all over the glue. After the glue sets, pour off the excess cinnamon. Punch a hole in the plate and put the ribbon in it for a hanger.

Outdoor Activity: Take a "Scent Walk." Walk and find as many different scents as possible. Bring samples back to class. Then smell the scents brought back and talk about remembering the walk by the scents.

Physical Education: Repeat the game Captain, May I? or Teacher, May I? This game illustrates the importance of hearing. Set up a goal line and a starting line. The player who is "Captain" stands at the goal line. The "Captain" addresses one player at a time to "Take one giant step" or "Take 5 baby steps" or "Skip three steps," etc. That player must remember to say "Captain, May I?" and wait for permission before he can advance. If the player forgets to ask permission first, he must return to the starting line. The Captain then addresses another player on the line and continues until one player finally reaches the goal line. That player then becomes the "Captain."

NOTES:

Lesson 143

Activities in this Lesson: Bible Lesson, Science, Social Studies, Language Arts, Phonics, Reading, Writing, Memory Verse, Math, Story Time, Music, Arts & Crafts, Physical Education

Bible Reference: Ps 19:9-11 "sweeter also than honey," Ps 34:8 "Taste and see that the Lord is good."

Bible Concept to Present: Our sense of taste is a precious gift from God. We are fearfully and wonderfully made.

Bible Lesson: God is enthusiastic about His Creation. He enjoys the sweet savor of a sweet spirit. He made our lives rich and pleasant. Our tongue is where God put taste buds so that we could taste things. Taste buds can be destroyed. If we eat food that is too hot, it can kill our taste buds. They take several months to be replaced. Medicines and age can hinder our ability to taste. That is why older people can't taste things as well as they used to in their youth. Your taste buds are all over your tongue.

Our smell is also tied to our taste of things. God made our bodies to be perfectly balanced and work together.

Multimedia Resources: Listen to the song "Goodness" from "The Music Machine: The Fruit of the Spirit" CD.

Science: *Bring apples and onions to class.* Cut up the apples into bite size pieces but don't let the students see them. Also cut the onion in half. One at a time, have students close their eyes. Give them a bite of the apple while you hold the onion under their noses. Did they taste apple or onion?

Do a taste and guess test. Gather a number of items that taste very different but don't use anything that is unpleasant. Use small items that can be swallowed without chewing or cut them up into very small pieces. Use items like salt, juices, sugar, green pepper, ketchup, lemon juice, apple, cinnamon, pickle juice, milk, mustard, maple syrup, peanut butter, honey, miniature marshmallows, jam, drink powder, gelatin powder, etc. Seat the students in a circle and have them put on blindfolds. Place a sample of a food on the first player's tongue and see if he can guess what it is. If he guesses incorrectly, continue to give the next players the same item until it is guessed correctly. Put just a drop of the liquids on their tongues with an eyedropper or the tip of a spoon. After something is guessed correctly, give the next player a new taste. Repeat the foods to see if they can do a better job of guessing the second time around.

Social Studies: The sense of taste is an important part of our life. Family get-togethers include food, usually traditional foods that we enjoy together. Talk about the foods we share when we are at family gatherings and holidays. What are some favorites? They are favorites because of their taste. Some of us like sweet foods, some like spicy foods. Plan an evening potluck or family meal. Encourage families to bring their traditional family favorites.

Something to do at home: Plan a family dinner, allowing your student to choose the menu. Prepare family favorites that the children remember from holidays or special events. Say a prayer thanking God for the sense of taste.

Language Arts: Get the book *Bread and Jam for Frances* by Russell Hoban (1993). All Frances, the badger, will eat is bread and jam. She won't even taste anything else. What is mother badger to do? *Gregory, the Terrible Eater* by Mitchell Sharmat (1980) and *Oliver's Fruit Salad* by Vivian French (1998) are also good choices.

Phonics: Blend the sounds Aa-Pp. (pad, pan, cap, gap, lap, map, nap, pap, pen, ped, peg, pen, pep, dip, hip, Kip, lip, nip, pig, pill, pin, pip, pod, pog, hop, lop, mop, pop) Review the initial sounds of Aa-Pp. Review letter recognition Aa-Zz.

Add the following words to the flip chart pages of words and review them with the students. Continue to sound out the individual letters of each word as has been done previously. It may also be helpful for the students to see the words spaced out and spelled out as has been done in previous lessons.

ap	ep	ip	op	pa	pe	pi	po
cap	pep	dip	hop	pad	ped	pig	pod
gap		hip	lop	pan	peg	pill	pog
lap		kip	mop		pen	pin	
map		lip	pop				
pap		nip					

Do the Lesson 143 Phonics worksheet. The sound of Pp. Review the letter sound with the picture and words on the worksheet. Ask the students for other words that begin with the same sound. Give them specific instructions for how the letter should be traced. Allow time for tracing the letters and observe their progress. If you have the students do one row at a time, the worksheet can be carried over to various parts of the day or another day.

Reading: Begin to use invented phonetic spelling in writing. Indicate the number of phonemes (1 - 3) heard in a real or nonsense word.

Writing: Continue to do Learning Logs. Encourage the students to draw or write about themselves. Some sample topics might be My Pet, My Favorite Reptile, My Favorite School Activity, My Family, or other teacher selected topics. The writing can be invented temporary spellings or dictations to the teacher.

Teach your students how to write their home addresses and phone numbers. Do this by creating tracing sheets for each student. This can be easily done on a computer by using an outline font or a gray rather than a black color for the font. Only attempt this activity if your students are ready.

Memory Verse: Today we add the fifth part of Psalm 139:14-16. Concentrate just on the fifth line today. Write the fifth line on the board. Using a small strip of construction paper, tape it over a word, then say the line together. Do this several times.

ONE	I praise You because I am fearfully and wonderfully made:
TWO	Your works are wonderful, I know that full well.
THREE	My frame was not hidden from you when I was made in the secret place …
FOUR	Your eyes saw my unformed body.
FIVE	All the days ordained for me were written in Your book before one of them came to be.

Math: Review 3 - 1 = 2. Review 3 - 1 = 2 by writing the problem on the board. Draw objects over the numbers with - sign between them. Make a large X over the object being subtracted. Write the = sign and then draw an excess of objects over the answer. Have a student come to the board and circle the correct number of objects to make the subtraction problem correct. Erase the extra objects and orally say the problem with the class. Repeat several times drawing simple objects such as dots or various shapes. Review previous addition and subtraction problems if the students need the practice.

Do the Lesson 143a Math worksheet. Read the number. Count the dots under the number. Trace the letters for the number word. Draw 8 objects in the counting jar. Trace the number and the number word following the proper strokes. The students can color the counting jar.

Do the Lesson 143b Math worksheet. Count the items and say the subtraction or addition problem. As they trace the numbers have them say the subtraction and addition problems.

Story Time: Read a story or stories of your choice.

Music: Review some of the songs from the "Horizons Preschool Music" CD. Let the students choose the songs.

Multimedia Resources: This week, listen and sing along to selections from "The Story of Little Tree" CD.

This week, watch *The Kingdom Under the Sea* adventure "Return of the King" which is an Easter story.

Arts & Crafts: Give the students white construction paper and poster pens. Let them draw whatever foods are their favorites. If you have read any of the books listed in Language Arts, let them draw from one of the stories.

Physical Education: Play the game Drop the Handkerchief. The students form a circle and join hands. One person, who is IT, walks around the outside of the circle chanting/singing the rhyme below and then drops the handkerchief at the end of the song behind one of the students in the circle. The person who is IT runs around the circle in one direction; the other person picks up the handkerchief and runs around the circle in the opposite direction. They race to see who can get back to the empty space in the circle first. The loser is the next person who is IT and the game continues.

A Tisket, A Tasket

A tisket, a tasket,
A green and yellow basket,
I wrote a letter to my love
And on my way I dropped it,
I dropped it, I dropped it,
And on my way I dropped it.
A little girl/boy, picked it up
And put it in her/his pocket.

NOTES:

Activities in this Lesson: Bible Lesson, Social Studies/Science, Language Arts, Phonics, Reading, Writing, Memory Verse, Math, Story Time, Music, Arts & Crafts/Science, Physical Education

Bible Reference: Genesis 1:26-27.

Bible Concept to Present: God made a way for us to enjoy what He made by giving us the sense of touch which is part of our nervous system. The sense of touch is a precious gift from God.

Bible Lesson: We enjoy seeing the great things God has made. We enjoy hearing the birds and the pleasant sounds around us. We also can smell wonderful smells. But, God made us with a sense of touch, too. It is a wonderful feeling to touch a soft blanket when we are cold, or to feel the touch of our Moms' hands when we feel afraid. God wants us to enjoy his Creation. He gave us hands with nerves in them, so we can feel with them. Our body has the sense of touch all over it. This is so we can enjoy all of the things God knew we would want to touch.

Multimedia Resources: Listen to the song "My Hands Belong To You" from the "Bullfrogs and Butterflies: God is My Friend" CD.

Social Studies/Science: Have your students gently pinch themselves. The sense of touch and feeling is provided by the nervous system of our body. The nervous system is like many little wires that run throughout our body. They are all interconnected with the brain. When we get hurt, it is the nervous system that sends messages to the brain and we either cry or say "ouch." If we did not have these wonderful messengers called nerves, we could not feel anything. You would not know if you hurt. You would not know how nice and soft something feels.

To reinforce the concept of nerves, have students create a "Feel Box." A soda pop flat will work well. Let the students write their names in the bottom. Place objects that are soft, hard, rough, smooth, etc. Stress that it is our nerves which tell us how something feels.

Do a touch and guess test. Gather a number of items that feel distinctive when touched. Put each item into a separate paper bag that has been laid flat on a table. Use items like cotton, string, wax, ice cube, steel wool, pennies, fake fur, sponge, sand paper, etc. Have all of the students go through a line and place their hand into the first bag to feel the item. After all have touched the item see if they can guess what it is. Continue touching the contents of one bag at a time until all items have been touched. This could also be done in teams where one team selects items from the room for the other group to touch and guess.

Language Arts: Review the "Texture Feel," Lesson 138.

Phonics: Review blends Aa-Pp with the blend charts. Review the initial sounds of Aa-Pp. Review letter recognition Aa-Zz.

Have the students brainstorm words that begin or include the letter Pp. Write these words on the board. Model the correct letter formation as you write the letters on the board. The students should practice forming the letter Pp on a blank sheet of paper. Students who are ready can practice copying complete words from the board.

Do the Lesson 144 Phonics worksheet. The Sound of Pp. Review the letter sound with the picture and words on the worksheet. Ask the students for other words that begin with the same sound. Trace the letters and say the sound of Pp. Observe the students as they trace the letters and help them with the letter strokes. If you have the students do one row at a time, the worksheet can be carried over to various parts of the day or another day.

Reading: Begin to use invented phonetic spelling in writing. Indicate the number of phonemes (1 - 3) heard in a real or nonsense word.

Writing: Continue to do Learning Logs. Encourage the students to draw or write about themselves. Some sample topics might be My Pet, My Favorite Reptile, My Favorite School Activity, My Family, or other teacher selected topics. The writing can be invented temporary spellings or dictations to the teacher.

Teach your students how to write their home addresses and phone numbers. Do this by creating tracing sheets for each student. This can be easily done on a computer by using an outline font or a gray rather than a black color for the font. Only attempt this activity if your students are ready.

Memory Verse: Continue to review Psalm 139:14-16.

Math: Review 3 - 1 = 2. Give each of the students 10 counters. Have them make the subtraction problem with the counters. Have them point to the counters and say the subtraction problem, drawing the minus and equal sign with their finger between the counters as they say the words. Review previous problems if the students need the practice.

Do the Lesson 144 Math worksheet. As they trace the numbers have them say the subtraction and addition problems.

Story Time: Read a story or stories of your choice.

Music: Review "If You're Happy and You Know It" and "Touch Your Finger."

Multimedia Resources: This week, listen and sing along to selections from "The Story of Little Tree" CD.

This week, watch *The Kingdom Under the Sea* adventure "Return of the King" which is an Easter story.

Arts & Crafts/Science: Give each student a magnifying glass, paper and markers. Instruct them to look at their skin under the magnifying glass and draw it on their paper. What do they see as part of their skin? Though we have nerves throughout our bodies, our skin is the biggest part of the sense of touch.

Play Finger Print Match Up. Discuss the special pictures that we have on the ends of our fingers. Let the students examine the ends of their fingers with a magnifying glass. Give each student two index cards and have them write their name on the front of one card and on the back of the other. Make thumb prints for each student on the front sides of the two cards. When you have two sets of cards for each student mix them up and lay them out on a table. Let each student try to find their matching cards.

Physical Education: Play the game Drop the Handkerchief again. The students form a circle and join hands. One person who is IT runs or walks around the outside of the circle and then drops the handkerchief behind one of the students in the circle. The person who is IT continues to run around the circle in one direction; the other person picks up the handkerchief and runs around the circle in the opposite direction. They race to see who can get back to the empty space in the circle first. The loser is the next person who is IT and the game continues.

NOTES:

Activities in this Lesson: Bible Lesson/Social Studies, Science/Creative Cooking, Science, Language Arts, Phonics, Reading, Writing, Memory Verse, Math, Story Time, Music, Arts & Crafts, Physical Education

Bible Reference: Genesis 1:26-27.

Bible Concept to Present: God made us to have bones.

Bible Lesson/Social Studies: Wouldn't we look silly if we didn't have any bones in our bodies? How would we stand up? We would be just like jelly. God created us with bones to help our skin stay in shape. The bones we have make us strong. We would not be able to walk, run, or play if our bones were made of soft material. God made our bones hard, so we could walk, run, and play. Some people are made with bigger bones than others. Some people have small bones. There are lots of bones in our bodies. They all have special jobs to do. For example, your spine is a bone, and it holds your back and neck up. I'm glad God made us with hard bones, aren't you?

Science/Creative Cooking: The bones in our bodies are made of cells. Without bones, our bodies would be like a piece of Jell-O®. The bones help our body to move. To illustrate what we would be like without bones, make a recipe of sugar free gelatin in which you have added extra gelatin. The added gelatin will stabilize the mix so you may use cookie cutters. Obtain a gingerbread man cookie cutter and cut the gelatin into the shape of a man. This is how we would be if we did not have bones. Our bones are very important for us. You may show your students a picture of a skeleton. They do not need to retain any information about the bones, except that they exist and help us move. Encourage students to feel their wrists and fingers, to feel the bones.

Sugar free products are very good, especially sugar free Jell-O®. Most of the time, children can't tell the difference. Don't tell them about the difference ahead of time.

Science: *Get some big bones from the meat market. Boil off any meat.* Bring them to class and talk about how bones work. Talk about the strength of bones and eating right for strong bones by drinking milk and eating cheese. Our bones make blood cells inside the center of the bones. If the butcher will cut one lengthwise, you can show students the inside of the bone. Explain that this is where blood cells are made in our body. Put this bone in a freezer and save it for Lesson 152.

Language Arts: Bring a floppy rag doll to class to explain how someone would look without bones. Talk about the joints in the body, places where bones join together. Muscles join bones together so that we can bend, walk and move. Our joints move in different ways. Have the students bend their elbows and compare that movement to the many directions they can move their head with the joints that are in their necks. Have them move one part of their body and describe the motion as up and down, around in a circle, side to side, and so on.

Phonics: Teach the initial sound of Qq. Review the initial sounds of Aa-Pp. Review letter recognition Aa-Zz.

Write several initial Qq words on the board: quack, quail, quarter, quart, quick, quill, quilt, quiz, etc. Underline the initial letter Qq and say the words. Ask the students for other words that start with the same sound.

Do the Lesson 145 Phonics worksheet. The Sound of Qq. Review the letter sound with the picture and words on the worksheet. Ask the students for other words that begin with the same sound. Discuss the position of the letters on the guidelines. Give them specific instructions for how the letter should be traced. Trace the letters and say the sound of Qq. Observe the students as they trace the letters and help them with the letter strokes. If you have the students do one row at a time, the worksheet can be carried over to various parts of the day or another day.

Reading: Begin to use invented phonetic spelling in writing. Indicate the number of phonemes (1 - 3) heard in a real or nonsense word.

Writing: Continue to do Learning Logs. Encourage the students to draw or write about themselves. Some sample topics might be My Pet, My Favorite Reptile, My Favorite School Activity, My Family, or other teacher selected topics. The writing can be invented temporary spellings or dictations to the teacher.

Teach your students how to write their home addresses and phone numbers. Do this by creating tracing sheets for each student. This can be easily done on a computer by using an outline font or a gray rather than a black color for the font. Only attempt this activity if your students are ready.

Memory Verse: Work on the entire memory verse Psalm 139:14-16 today. Give students paper and crayons. Let them draw the most wonderful thing God made for them. Tell them they are a wonderful part of your life.

ONE	I praise You because I am fearfully and wonderfully made:
TWO	Your works are wonderful, I know that full well.
THREE	My frame was not hidden from you when I was made in the secret place ...
FOUR	Your eyes saw my unformed body.
FIVE	All the days ordained for me were written in Your book before one of them came to be.

Math: Review 3 - 1 = 2.

Do the Lesson 145a Math worksheet. Read the number. Count the dots under the number. Trace the letters for the number word. Draw 9 objects in the counting jar. Trace the number and the number word following the proper strokes. The students can color the counting jar.

Do the Lesson 145b Math worksheet. Trace the numbers and say the subtraction or addition problems.

Story Time: Read a story or stories of your student's choice or ones they have brought from home.

Music: Review favorite songs learned this year.

Multimedia Resources: This week, listen and sing along to selections from "The Story of Little Tree" CD.

This week, watch *The Kingdom Under the Sea* adventure "Return of the King" which is an Easter story.

Arts & Crafts: Let the students use playdough to make some bones. Use the bones you brought for Science as models.

Bring in slices of cheese and plastic knives. Give the students the picture of the gingerbread man, Lesson 134 Arts & Crafts worksheet. Also give them a plastic knife and a piece of sandwich cheese. Let the students cut the cheese into strips and lay them on the gingerbread man as bones. Talk about how our bodies have bones everywhere.

Physical Education: Ride tricycles. Lay out a path for them to follow as they ride tricycles. This could be done with cones or markers in a parking lot. Wide space with room to pass would be excellent. A few small inclines or hills will help with muscle development. Stress that banging into another student is not acceptable. To help teach safety habits the students should wear helmets and knee and elbow pads.

NOTES:

Lesson 146

Activities in this Lesson: Bible Lesson/Social Studies, Science, Language Arts/Music, Phonics, Reading, Writing, Memory Verse, Math, Story Time, Music, Arts & Crafts, Health & Safety, Creative Cooking, Physical Education

Bible Reference: Genesis 1:26-27.

Bible Concept to Present: God gave us muscles.

Bible Lesson/Social Studies: God gave us bones. He put skin over our bones. He knew we needed something to help us move our bones. He gave us muscles. We use our muscles everyday just to get out of bed. We use our muscles to walk, run, work and play. God wants you to do all of these activities, so He gave you muscles to use. We need to take care of our muscles by exercising every day. We should be thankful that our muscles are strong enough to use.

Science: Our muscles are strong, rope-like fibers, which work together in pairs. They work very much like a rubber band. To illustrate muscles, permit your students to stretch a rubber band back and forth. Muscles work in pairs. When one muscle is stretched out, the other one is contracted. Illustrate this to your students. You may also note the illustration of the cells of the muscle on Lesson 146 Resource page. Give students rubber bands and let them stretch them. Explain that this is like what happens to our muscles.

Bring in a can of vegetables, one for each student. Say, Our muscles can work well until they get tired. They need lots of nourishment and rest. Let's see what happens when our muscles get tired. Everyone hold a can of vegetables out in front of themselves with both hands. Try to hold the can as long as possible. How do your muscles feel? Are they beginning to hurt? After a time, we can't hold something out any longer. Our muscles need to rest. If we exercise our muscles every day, we can use them longer and longer. They are strengthened.

Language Arts/Music: Today the students will consider how their muscles will help them do things they enjoy. On the wall, tape a large piece of paper. Give the students colored pens or crayons, play music and have your students color or draw to the rhythm of the music. Use both slow and fast music. Place emphasis on how the hand muscles help do the art work.

Phonics: Because the letter Uu has not been covered, blends with Qq will be covered later. Review blends Aa-Pp with the blend charts. Review the initial sounds of Aa-Qq. Review letter recognition Aa-Zz.

Do the Lesson 146a Phonics worksheet. The sound of Qq. Review the letter sound with the picture and words on the worksheet. Ask the students for other words that begin with the same sound. Trace the letters and say the sound of Qq. Observe the students as they trace the letters and help them with the letter strokes. If you have the students do one row at a time, the worksheet can be carried over to various parts of the day or another day.

Do the Lesson 146b Phonics worksheet. The Sound of Qq. Review the letter sound with the picture and words on the worksheet. Ask the students for other words that begin with the same sound. Give them specific instructions for how the letter should be traced. Allow time for tracing the letters and observe their progress. If you have the students do one row at a time, the worksheet can be carried over to various parts of the day or another day.

Reading: Begin to use invented phonetic spelling in writing. Indicate the number of phonemes (1 - 3) heard in a real or nonsense word.

Multimedia Resources: Review "Rev-Up for Reading" from the "Rev-Up for Learning" DVD to drill letter recognition and sound. The students should say each letter sound along with the presentation.

Writing: Continue to do Learning Logs. Encourage the students to draw or write about themselves. Some sample topics might be My Pet, My Favorite Reptile, My Favorite School Activity, My Family, or other teacher selected topics. The writing can be invented temporary spellings or dictations to the teacher.

Continue to have your students work on writing their home addresses and phone numbers if you have chosen to do this activity.

Multimedia Resources: Review "Rev-Up for Writing" from the "Rev-Up for Learning" DVD to review the writing of upper- and lowercase letters.

Memory Verse: Today, we add the sixth part of Psalm 139:14-16, the reference! All week, we will work on the entire verse. Explain how important the reference is. Show students the verses in the Bible. Remind them that no one can take away God's Word that they have memorized.

ONE	I praise You because I am fearfully and wonderfully made:
TWO	Your works are wonderful, I know that full well.
THREE	My frame was not hidden from you when I was made in the secret place …
FOUR	Your eyes saw my unformed body.
FIVE	All the days ordained for me were written in Your book before one of them came to be.
SIX	Psalm 139:14-16

Math: Review 3 - 1 = 2. Use the string of Counting Beads or pop beads to review 1 + 1 = 2, 2 + 1 = 3, 3 + 1 = 4, 4 + 1 = 5, 2 – 1 = 1, and 3 – 1 = 2.

Do the Lesson 146a Math worksheet. Read the number. Count the dots under the number. Trace the letters for the number word. Draw 10 objects in the counting jar. Trace the number and the number word following the proper strokes. The students can color the counting jar.

Do the Lesson 146b Math worksheet. Count the beads and say the subtraction problem. Trace the correct answer and say the subtraction problem again.

Multimedia Resources: View "Rev-Up for Arithmetic" from the "Rev-Up for Learning" DVD to practice number recognition, counting and addition 1-20.

Story Time: Read a story or stories of your choice.

Music: Learn the following song to the tune of Twinkle, Twinkle Little Star.

I'M MADE OUT OF HINGES
Tune of Twinkle, Twinkle Little Star

I'm made out of hinges
I can bend this way and that (Bend to one side, and then the other)
Twist and turn and bend way down
My muscles help me move around
God has made me very strong
I'll be big before too long.
            Carol McSpadden Sheldon

Multimedia Resources: This week, listen and sing along to selections from "Music Machine: All About Love" CD.

Arts & Crafts: Give the students colored construction paper and scissors. Let them cut out triangles, rectangles, circles and squares. Remind them that it is the muscles in their hands that enable their fingers to move. Have the students hold up their shapes while the other students or the teacher calls out what shape it is.

Health & Safety: We need to exercise our bodies. Although Physical Education has been included in the curriculum, everyone needs to develop a regular routine of physical exercise. We suggest the following:
1. Take daily walks with your students. These not only increase cardiovascular capacities, they increase the child's awareness for God's beauty in nature.
2. Incorporate an aerobic exercise period two to three times a week.
3. Games such as volleyball, football or baseball are excellent.

Creative Cooking: Four year olds are still learning to control the muscles in their fingers. Helping with cooking is a good way to exercise their muscles. Juicing fruit, mashing fruits and vegetables, measuring, grinding and beating are all good exercises. Always remind students to wash their hands. Don't be afraid of a little mess. Let the students help clean up. Have the students pantomime the steps to the recipe several times before actually doing the recipe. Try this new recipe:

Fruity Pizza

English muffins, cut in half and toasted
American or jack cheese
Various fruits cut into chunks

Let the students place a piece of cheese on their muffin half, then arrange some fruit on top.

Place the muffins on a cookie sheet and bake at 325 degrees until the cheese melts. Enjoy this healthy snack.

Physical Education: Ride tricycles. Lay out a path for them to follow as they ride tricycles. This could be done with cones or markers in a parking lot. Wide space with room to pass would be excellent. A few small inclines or hills will help with muscle development. Stress that banging into another student is not acceptable. To help teach safety habits the students should wear helmets and knee and elbow pads.

Lesson 147

Activities in this Lesson: Bible Lesson, Science, Social Studies/Outdoor Activity, Language Arts, Phonics, Reading, Writing, Memory Verse, Math, Story Time, Music, Arts & Crafts, Health & Safety, Physical Education

Bible Reference: Genesis 1:26-27.

Bible Concept to Present: God cares for us. He made sure that the important parts of our body were protected by bone.

Bible Lesson: Our ribs and our skull protect us. Our abdominal muscles also protect us. God is a God of protection. Throughout the Bible, He tells us not to be afraid, to trust Him for everything. We can trust Him that we are fearfully and wonderfully made, and that He protected us in His Creation of us.

Multimedia Resources: Watch "Honesty" from the *Character Builders Video Series*.

Science: Look at the picture of the skeleton, Lesson 147 Resource page. Show students the rib cage. See how the ribs surround the important heart and lungs? Look at the skull. The brain is completely encased in bone. If possible, obtain a skeleton kit from a craft store and put it together with the students. It will help their retention if they can touch and see a model skeleton.

Social Studies/Outdoor Activity: Take a walk. See how many things you can find that are protected by something. There are some if you look. A transformer box. A house or field with a fence. A tree trunk with bark. A dog with a doghouse. A house. A car. Talk about how these things are made to protect what is inside.

Language Arts: Long before there were rulers, people could measure things: a cubit is the length from the elbow to the fingertips, a span is the measure of your outspread fingers, a fathom measures your out-stretched arms, and a pace is a walking step. Use your own cubit to find some measures in the classroom. How many cubits long is a table or a bookshelf? Look for something in the room that is the same size as your cubit. What is it? Guess how many cubits long the teacher's desk is and then measure it to check. Does it matter who does the measuring? Have a student with a short arm and one with a long arm measure the desk. Are the measurements the same? A span is the measure of your spread out fingers. How many spans wide is your table? What is something in the room that is the same size as a span? Draw a line on a sheet of paper to show the size of your span. What is something in the room that is the same size as your fathom, the length of your outstretched arms? How many fathoms long is the board? Also measure a few things in the room by paces.

Get the book *Dem Bones* by Bob Barner, Chronicle Books, 1996. It includes the song we all used to sing as children about how our bones are put together.

Phonics: Review blends Aa-Pp with the blend charts. Review the initial sounds of Aa-Qq. Review letter recognition Aa-Zz.

Have the students brainstorm words that begin or include the letter Qq. Write these words on the board. Model the correct letter formation as you write the letters on the board. The students should practice forming the letter Qq on a blank sheet of paper. Students who are ready can practice copying complete words from the board.

Do the Lesson 147 Phonics worksheet. The Sound of Qq. Review the letter sound with the picture and words on the worksheet. Ask the students for other words that begin with the same sound. Trace the letters and say the sound of Qq. Observe the students as they trace the letters and help them with the letter strokes. If you have the students do one row at a time, the worksheet can be carried over to various parts of the day or another day.

Reading: Begin to use invented phonetic spelling in writing. Indicate the number of phonemes (1 - 3) heard in a real or nonsense word.

Writing: Continue to do Learning Logs. Encourage the students to draw or write about themselves. Some sample topics might be My Pet, My Favorite Reptile, My Favorite School Activity, My Family, or other teacher selected topics. The writing can be invented temporary spellings or dictations to the teacher.

Continue to have your students work on writing their home addresses and phone numbers if you have chosen to do this activity.

Memory Verse: Review Psalm 139:14-16. The students are almost done working on this long memory project. Plan a special treat for the end of the week, rewarding all students. They worked hard on it, whether they could memorize it all or not.

Math: Review 3 - 1 = 2.

Take out the Hand Prints made in Lesson 137. The students will use non-standard units of measurement to measure the length of their hands. Pass out buttons, paper clips, craft sticks, etc. and have the students measure the length of their hands. They will be able to share and compare their lengths with others in the class. This activity will be repeated in Lesson 157.

Story Time: Read a story or stories of your choice.

Music: Review "I'm Made Out of Hinges." Sing the old "Dry Bones" spiritual, put your hand on the bone as the song is sung.

DRY BONES

Dem bones, dem bones, dem dry bones
Dem bones, dem bones, dem dry bones
Dem bones, dem bones, dem dry bones
Oh hear the word of the Lord!

Ezekiel connected dem dry bones
Ezekiel connected dem dry bones
Ezekiel connected dem dry bones
Oh hear the word of the Lord!

(tune ascends in half steps)
The toe bone connected foot bone
The foot bone connected ankle bone
The ankle bone connected leg bone

The leg bone connected knee bone
The knee bone connected thigh bone
The thigh bone connected hip bone
The hip bone connected back bone
The back bone connected shoulder bone
The shoulder bone connected neck bone
The neck bone connected head bone
Oh hear the word of the Lord!

Dem bones, dem bones gon-na walk a-roun'
Dem bones, dem bones gon-na walk a-roun'
Dem bones, dem bones gonna walk aroun'
Oh hear the word of the Lord!

Disconnect dem bones, dem dry bones
Disconnect dem bones, dem dry bones
Disconnect dem bones, dem dry bones
Oh hear the word of the Lord!

(tune descends in half steps)
The head bone connected to the neck bone,
The neck bone connected to shoulder bone
The shoulder bone connected to the back bone
The back bone connected to the hip bone
The hip bone connected to the thigh bone
The thigh bone connected to the knee bone
The knee bone connected to the leg bone

Multimedia Resources: This week, listen and sing along to selections from "Music Machine: All About Love" CD.

Arts & Crafts: Give the students colored paper pieces, white paper, and tacky glue. Instruct them to cut the paper pieces into "bone" strips then glue the "bones" onto the white paper, making a skeleton.

Health & Safety: Continue to exercise your bodies with daily walks, days of aerobic exercise and ball games.

Physical Education: Ride tricycles with traffic control signs. Add STOP signs, students holding traffic lights, and other signs to the tricycle course for the students to obey as they ride. To help teach safety habits the students should wear helmets and knee and elbow pads.

NOTES:

Activities in this Lesson: Bible Lesson/Social Studies, Science, Language Arts, Phonics, Reading, Writing, Memory Verse, Math, Story Time, Music, Arts & Crafts, Health & Safety, Homework

Bible Reference: Genesis 1:26-27.

Bible Concept to Present: God made a way for our bodies to use the food we eat.

Bible Lesson/Social Studies: God has made our bodies so special, hasn't He? He made us so our stomachs would get hungry. He knew we would use our muscles to work and play, and then we would need food to help us work and play some more. God arranged our bodies so that after we ate the food, it made us feel stronger. He made our bodies in such a way that we can get rid of the food particles we don't need. Why do you think God made everything work together inside of us? I think it is because He knows just what we need. Don't you?

Science: The digestive system is one of God's miracles. Using Lesson 148a Resource page, a picture of the digestive system of the human body, trace an article of food through the digestive system. The journey begins with food being placed into our mouth. The teeth chew up the food. It is important to chew your food well, so the rest of the body can do its work easily. The chewed food goes down the esophagus, which is a muscle-like tube which squeezes the food into the stomach. In the stomach the food is mixed with chemicals that help to break the food into little pieces. The food goes into the large intestine which continues to break the food down. In the large and small intestines, the nutrients of the food are absorbed into the blood, and the waste materials are eliminated from the body.

Language Arts: *Bring food from each food group or buy a bag of plastic food.* Introduce your students to the basic food groups by having them categorize their meals on the MyPlate chart. There is a master copy for the teacher Lesson 148b Resource page and one for each student on Lesson 148 Language Arts worksheet. Make a large food chart on a piece of poster board, copying Lesson 148b Resource page. Parents will help the child keep a record of everything eaten for several days. Take out the foods you have brought. Lay the poster board chart on a table. Let the students put the food pieces on the correct section of the chart. Mix up the foods and let the students do this several times.

Phonics: Teach the initial sound of Rr. Review the initial sounds of Aa-Qq. Review letter recognition Aa-Zz.

Write several initial Rr words on the board: rabbit, rag, rail, rain, rake, ran, rat, read, real, rectangle, red, rest, rig, ring, ride, rib, rip, rob, rub, run, rut, etc. Underline the initial letter Rr and say the words. Ask the students for other words that start with the same sound.

Do the Lesson 148 Phonics worksheet. The Sound of Rr. Review the letter sound with the picture and words on the worksheet. Ask the students for other words that begin with the same sound. Discuss the position of the letters on the guidelines. Give them specific instructions for how the letter should be traced. Trace the letters and say the sound of Rr. Observe the students as they trace the letters and help them with the letter strokes. If you have the students do one row at a time, the worksheet can be carried over to various parts of the day or another day.

Reading: Begin to use invented phonetic spelling in writing. Indicate the number of phonemes (1 - 3) heard in a real or nonsense word.

Writing: Continue to do Learning Logs. Encourage the students to draw or write about themselves. Some sample topics might be My Pet, My Favorite Reptile, My Favorite School Activity, My Family, or other teacher selected topics. The writing can be invented temporary spellings or dictations to the teacher.

Continue to have your students work on writing their home addresses and phone numbers if you have chosen to do this activity.

Memory Verse: Review Psalm 139:14-16.

Math: Review 3 - 1 = 2. Draw a strip of squares on the board. Write 3 – 1 = under the row of squares. Have a student color three of the squares. Say, "three minus one equals," and have another student erase or cross out one of the squares. Say again while pointing to the squares, "three minus one equals" and have another student give the answer. Review the problems: 1 + 1 = 2, 2 + 1 = 3, 3 + 1 = 4, 4 + 1 = 5, 5 + 1 = 6, 2 - 1 = 1.

Do the Lesson 148a Math worksheet. Read the number. Count the dots under the number. Trace the letters for the number word. Draw 11 objects in the counting jar. Trace the number and the number word following the proper strokes. The students can color the counting jar.

Do the Lesson 148b Math worksheet. Count the dots in the tiles and trace the numbers.

Story Time: Get the book *Oliver's Milk Shake* by Vivian French, 2000.

Music: Review "Dry Bones" and "I'm Made Out of Hinges."

Multimedia Resources: This week, listen and sing along to selections from "Music Machine: All About Love" CD.

Arts & Crafts: *You'll need a box of instant pudding and milk.* Mix a box of instant pudding using one-half of the milk required. Let it thicken. Let the students finger paint with the pudding on a large piece of freezer paper. Students may lick their fingers after completing the project, or during!

Health & Safety: We need to eat properly. Children in America ingest a tremendous amount of sugars and preservatives. Talk to your students about eating properly. Encourage them to eat foods that are good for them. Vegetarian meals are a wonderful, healthy experience for students and families. Talk to students about encouraging their families to eat one vegetarian dinner each week.

Continue to exercise your bodies with daily walks, days of aerobic exercise, and ball games.

Physical Education: Play the game Ducks Fly. In this game the students face the leader who tells them what to do. They then copy the actions of the leader. The leader will say "ducks fly" and flap his arms. The other students should also flap their arms. The leader gives other instructions, cats meow, cows moo, dogs bark, etc. but the leader also tries to trick the players by saying things like, "horses baa" where the players should remain motionless or quiet until the leader gives the correct instruction.

Homework: After the students look at the MyPlate chart on the Lesson 148 Language Arts worksheet, let them take it home. Also send home the Lesson 148 Homework worksheet. Students will keep track of what they eat for a week.

Lesson 149

Week 30: Day 4

Activities in this Lesson: Bible Lesson, Science, Social Studies, Language Arts, Phonics, Reading, Writing, Memory Verse, Math, Shapes, Story Time, Music, Arts & Crafts, Health & Safety, Physical Education, Homework

Bible Reference: Genesis 1:26-27.

Bible Concept to Present: God gave us teeth. First we have baby teeth, and then we have adult teeth.

Bible Lesson: God gave most animals teeth. Why do you think we need teeth? Much of our food needs to be crunched to go into our stomach.

Science: *Bring a set of dentures to class. Your dentist might let you borrow a set.* Let the students handle the teeth. These teeth are big. Why are they so much bigger than your teeth? You all have baby teeth. You will be losing your "baby teeth" soon. New, bigger teeth will replace them. When we get bigger, we need bigger teeth to crunch up our food. Has anyone lost a tooth yet?

Social Studies: There are doctors that only take care of teeth. They are called dentists. Everyone needs to go to the dentist regularly. Some people are afraid of the dentist because they don't want anyone working in their mouth. If you learn to go to the dentist when you are young, you will go to the dentist as an adult. And if you go regularly, you won't get as many cavities. Cavities are places on teeth that become sick.

Language Arts: We don't think of it often, but our teeth also help us to talk. Say the word "think." Where was your tongue? When we make the "TH" sound, we use our teeth. How about the "T" sound? Say the word "teacher." Did you use your teeth? Sometimes our teeth aren't straight. It can affect our speech and our eating. Many children get braces when they are old enough. Braces straighten our teeth by pulling and tightening them with tiny wires over several years of time. Do any of you know someone with braces? Do they like the braces?

Use the MyPlate chart, Lesson 148b Resource page, to classify the foods that the students had for lunch today. Have them name a food and see if they can correctly classify it.

Phonics: Review the initial sound of Rr. Review the initial sounds of Aa-Qq. Review letter recognition Aa-Zz.

Have the students brainstorm words that begin or include the letter Rr. Write these words on the board. Model the correct letter formation as you write the letters on the board. The students should practice forming the letter Rr on a blank sheet of paper. Students who are ready can practice copying complete words from the board.

Do the Lesson 149 Phonics worksheet. The Sound of Rr. Review the letter sound with the picture and words on the worksheet. Ask the students for other words that begin with the same sound. Trace the letters and say the sound of Rr. Observe the students as they trace the letters and help them with the letter strokes. If you have the students do one row at a time, the worksheet can be carried over to various parts of the day or another day.

Reading: Begin to use invented phonetic spelling in writing. Indicate the number of phonemes (1 - 3) heard in a real or nonsense word.

Writing: Continue to do Learning Logs. Encourage the students to draw or write about themselves. Some sample topics might be My Pet, My Favorite Reptile, My Favorite School Activity, My Family, or other teacher selected topics. The writing can be invented temporary spellings or dictations to the teacher.

Continue to have your students work on writing their home addresses and phone numbers if you have chosen to do this activity.

Memory Verse: Review Psalm 139:14-16. Hurrah! Four weeks is a long time. Has the memory project gone well? Tell students that they will have a treat tomorrow to reward them for all of their hard work. Plan a Memory Party for tomorrow. Have cupcakes or cookies. If you have a punch bowl, it makes it so much more festive to have punch served from a punch bowl. Bring balloons for the students to blow up and hit back and forth. Review all of the verses learned so far this year. Let the students recite if they choose.

Math: Review 3 - 1 = 2. Have the students count off steps to practice addition and subtraction. For subtraction they should step forward the first number of steps, then backwards one step and place their bean bag. Then they should go back to the starting point and count forward to answer the subtraction problem. Review: 1 + 1 = 2, 2 + 1 = 3, 3 + 1 = 4, 4 + 1 = 5, 5 + 1 = 6, 2 - 1 = 1, 3 - 1 = 2.

Do the Lesson 149 Math worksheet. For subtraction, count all of the blocks in the strip, then say, "minus one block equals," and count the blocks that are not covered by an X. Trace the correct number. Do the addition problems as before.

Shapes: Review the rectangle shape.

Do the Lesson 149 Shapes worksheet. Trace the rectangle and then trace the word rectangle. Emphasize the initial Rr sound in rectangle.

Story Time: Review the book *Oliver's Milk Shake*. Check out *Junie B. First Grader: Toothless Wonder* by Barbara Park from the library. This is a great story about Junie B. and her experience of losing a tooth. She is the first one in her class to do so.

Music: Review "Dry Bones" and "I'm Made Out of Hinges."

Multimedia Resources: This week, listen and sing along to selections from "Music Machine: All About Love" CD.

Arts & Crafts: Make the clay recipe from Lesson 14. Put some peppermint or vanilla flavoring in the clay. Give each student a ball of clay a little smaller than a golf ball. Flatten the ball a little bit. Carefully guide them as they put it in their mouth and bite down gently. Tell them to open wide and remove the clay. Let the students look at the impression of their teeth. Let the impressions dry. Explain that our teeth are like fingerprints. An impression of our teeth is unique to us just like our fingerprints are unique.

Health & Safety: *If possible, bring each student a new toothbrush. Ask your dentist for a chart showing how to brush teeth correctly.* We have learned that our bodies have to be kept clean to be healthy. Sometimes it is hard work to keep our bodies clean. We have to remember a lot of things to do each day. We need to take baths. We need to wash our face. We also need to brush our teeth every morning and every night. Show the students the chart on brushing, or explain good brushing. Let them use their new toothbrushes to practice brushing properly.

One way to take care of our teeth is to eat good food. The worst food for teeth is candy, especially candy that sticks to our teeth or between our teeth. Candy should be a treat, not a daily food. Sugared sodas are also bad for our teeth.

Find out if anyone in the class has lost a tooth yet.

Continue to exercise your bodies with daily walks, days of aerobic exercise, and ball games.

Physical Education: Continue to play the game Ducks Fly. In this game the students face the leader who tells them what to do. They then copy the actions of the leader. The leader will say "ducks fly" and flap his arms. The other students should also flap their arms. The leader gives other instructions, cats meow, cows moo, dogs bark, etc. but the leader also tries to trick the players by saying things like, "horses baa" where the players should remain motionless or quiet until the leader gives the correct instruction.

Homework: Have students take the Lesson 149 Homework worksheet home today on which each will draw his favorite food. They will bring in a favorite food tomorrow. Each student will tell where his food goes on the MyPlate chart.

NOTES:

Activities in this Lesson: Bible Lesson/Social Studies, Science, Language Arts, Phonics, Reading, Writing, Memory Verse, Math, Story Time, Music, Outdoor Activity, Health & Safety, Physical Education

Bible Reference: Genesis 1:26-27.

Bible Concept to Present: God made a way for us to breathe.

Bible Lesson/Social Studies: Take a deep breath. Now let it go. God gave us lungs so we could breathe in and out. God wants us to help keep our air clean so we can breathe fresh air. We use our noses to breathe the air in and out.

God made our noses close to our lungs so they would work together. It would be funny to have your nose down on your foot, wouldn't it? The air would have to go up to your lungs and then down to your foot to go out again. How silly!!! God knew exactly where he wanted to put our lungs and how to make our breath flow through them.

Illustration: God made sure that we would always breathe. Our body automatically breathes for us. Did you tell your body to breathe in the last minute? No, your body did it for you. If you try to stop breathing, your body won't let you. Let's try an experiment. Everyone stop breathing for as long as you can. Hold your breath. See, we can't stop breathing for very long, can we? Our body is designed to keep working, even when we are playing or sleeping.

Science: *Bring in a package of large balloons and a small bottle. Bring in enough sponge pieces for each student to have one.* The lungs are like sponges. They absorb the air which travels from our nose, down the trachea and into the lungs. The lungs also break down the oxygen into smaller bits and pass the oxygen into the blood, where it is taken through the entire body. To illustrate, give the students sponges and let them play in water, soaking the water and then squeezing the water out. Explain that the same effect happens with air in the lungs. The lungs also move in and out when we breathe, much like a balloon that is filled with air.

Breathe in and let the students observe the filling of your lungs with air as illustrated by your chest moving out. Breathe out and note the chest move in, just as a balloon loses its air. Let the students blow on the balloons then let out the air.

Take the cover off from the small bottle and show the students how air (really water) fills the little bottle when it is held under water. This would be a good time to remind the students about safety around water. If your lungs get full of water like the little bottle there is no way that your lungs can get air. Remind the students that they should never go swimming unless an adult is there to watch them. They are also old enough to alert an adult when someone younger gets near or into the water when an adult is not there to watch. The best thing the students can do about water safety is to learn how to swim. Perhaps there is a program available in the area that you can send information home about where the students can learn to swim.

Language Arts: Continue to categorize the food groups and graph them on your food chart. Play the game with the pieces of food.

Phonics: Blend the sounds Aa-Rr. (rag, ram, ran, rap, red, rib, rid, rig, rill, rim, rip, Rob, rod, Ron) Review the initial sounds of Aa-Rr. Review letter recognition Aa-Zz.

Add the following words to the flip chart pages of words and review them with the students. Continue to sound out the individual letters of each word as has been done previously. It may also be helpful for the students to see the words spaced out and spelled out as has been done in previous lessons.

ra	re	ri	ro
rag	red	rib	rob
ram		rid	rod
ran		rig	Ron
rap		rill	
		rim	
		rip	

Do the Lesson 150a Phonics worksheet. The sound of Rr. Review the letter sound with the picture and words on the worksheet. Ask the students for other words that begin with the same sound. Trace the letters and say the sound of Rr. Observe the students as they trace the letters and help them with the letter strokes. If you have the students do one row at a time, the worksheet can be carried over to various parts of the day or another day.

Do the Lesson 150b Phonics worksheet. The Sound of Rr. Review the letter sound with the picture and words on the worksheet. Ask the students for other words that begin with the same sound. Give them specific instructions for how the letter should be traced. Allow time for tracing the letters and observe their progress. If you have the students do one row at a time, the worksheet can be carried over to various parts of the day or another day.

Reading: Begin to use invented phonetic spelling in writing. Indicate the number of phonemes (1 - 3) heard in a real or nonsense word.

Writing: Continue to do Learning Logs. Encourage the students to draw or write about themselves. Some sample topics might be My Pet, My Favorite Reptile, My Favorite School Activity, My Family, or other teacher selected topics. The writing can be invented temporary spellings or dictations to the teacher.

Continue to have your students work on writing their home addresses and phone numbers if you have chosen to do this activity.

Memory Verse: Review Psalm 139:14-16. Have a party at the end of the day! As the focus of the party, let the students recite their verse. This should be volunteers only. You might make a special award for those that learned the entire verse. A fold of ribbon attached by a safety pin makes a nice reward. Another nice reward is a visit to an ice cream shop or a mall.

Math: Review 3 - 1 = 2. Give each student 10 pennies to count 1-10. Have the students add and subtract pennies to practice the facts: 1 + 1 = 2, 2 + 1 = 3, 3 + 1 = 4, 4 + 1 = 5, 5 + 1 = 5, 2 – 1 = 1, 3 – 1 = 2.

Do the Lesson 150a Math worksheet. Read the number. Count the dots under the number. Trace the letters for the number word. Draw 12 objects in the counting jar. Trace the number and the number word following the proper strokes. The students can color the counting jar.

Do the Lesson 150b Math worksheet. For subtraction, count all of the pennies in the row, then say, "minus one penny equals," and count the pennies that are not covered by an X. Trace the correct number. Do the addition as before.

Story Time: Read a story or stories of your student's choice or ones they have brought from home.

Music: Review *Dry Bones* and *I'm Made Out of Hinges*.

Multimedia Resources: This week, listen and sing along to selections from *Music Machine, All About Love* CD.

Outdoor Activity: Take a walk. Make this a breathing walk. As you all walk in line, say, "Out, in, out, in." Everyone marches, breathing in, then out. This will make students very aware of their breathing.

Health & Safety: Sit on the floor with the students, with your legs extended in front of your body and your arms beside you. Take a deep breath in and as you do, lift your arms above your head. As you let out the deep breath, drop your arms back to your sides again. Do this several times. You and your students will feel very relaxed.

Physical Education: Ring Toss. Play a game similar to horse shoes with rope rings and stakes or cones. Rings can be made by gluing the ends of a short length of 1/2 inch rope into a PVC coupler with construction adhesive.

NOTES:

Lesson 151

Week 31: Day 1

Activities in this Lesson: Bible Lesson/Social Studies, Science, Language Arts, Phonics, Reading, Writing, Memory Verse, Math, Story Time, Music, Arts & Crafts, Outdoor Activity, Health & Safety, Physical Education

Bible Reference: Genesis 1:26-27.

Bible Concept to Present: God made a way for our blood to circulate.

Bible Lesson/Social Studies: Did you know God has made a way for our bodies to keep warm? He put within us a heart. The heart is a muscle that pumps blood all through our body. The blood goes through tubes in our body called vessels and veins so we can keep warm all over. If we did not have blood, we would not be alive. It is a miracle the way that God made us to have blood all through our bodies. Look at your hand. You will see veins in them, filled with blood. The blood in our body system keeps us healthy. It keeps us alive. We need to thank God that He created us the way He did.

Science: *Borrow a stethoscope. Most nurses or health care workers have one.* Our heart is a muscle. It works day and night. It pumps blood to other parts of the body, and accepts blood from other parts of the body. Without the heart we could not live. Our heart is not shaped like a valentine. It looks very different. Use Lesson 151 Resource page, the picture of the heart and show it to your students. The heart is an organ of the body. The heart never stops beating while you are living. It is a wonderful gift from God. Trace with your finger the flow of blood, into the heart then out of the heart. Let the students listen to their heartbeats.

If you are adventurous, *get a cow heart from the butcher.* Have them cut the heart right down the middle, so that the four chambers can be seen. This seems yucky, but will be a fantastic learning experience for the students. Use tweezers to pull up the valves and vessels. Be prepared to answer questions.

Language Arts: Continue to categorize the food groups and graph them on your food chart. Play the game with the pieces of food.

Phonics: Teach the initial sound of Ss. Review the initial sounds of Aa-Rr. Review letter recognition Aa-Zz.

Write several initial Ss words on the board: sad, safe, sag, salt, sand, sat, self, send, sell, set, sew, side, sign, sin, sing, sip, six, sit, sod, son, south, spell, spot, star, sub, suds, Sunday, etc. Underline the initial letter Ss and say the words. Ask the students for other words that start with the same sound.

Do the Lesson 151 Phonics worksheet. The Sound of Ss. Review the letter sound with the picture and words on the worksheet. Ask the students for other words that begin with the same sound. Discuss the position of the letters on the guidelines. Give them specific instructions for how the letter should be traced. Trace the letters and say the sound of Ss. Observe the students as they trace the letters and help them with the letter strokes. If you have the students do one row at a time, the worksheet can be carried over to various parts of the day or another day.

Reading: Begin to use invented phonetic spelling in writing. Indicate the number of phonemes (1 - 3) heard in a real or nonsense word.

Multimedia Resources: Review "Rev-Up for Reading" from the "Rev-Up for Learning" DVD to drill letter recognition and sound. The students should say each letter sound along with the presentation.

Writing: Continue to do Learning Logs. Encourage the students to draw or write about themselves. Some sample topics might be My Pet, My Favorite Reptile, My Favorite School Activity, My Family, or other teacher selected topics. The writing can be invented temporary spellings or dictations to the teacher.

Continue to have your students work on writing their home addresses and phone numbers if you have chosen to do this activity.

Multimedia Resources: Review "Rev-Up for Writing" from the "Rev-Up for Learning" DVD to review the writing of upper- and lowercase letters.

Memory Verse: Take time this week to review some of the memory verse favorites that the students have learned so far. Genesis 1:1, Genesis 1:3, Genesis 1:6, Genesis 1:10, I Peter 1:24-25, Genesis 8:22, Genesis 1:16, Psalm 90:12, Psalm 89:1, Revelation 22:16, Psalm 148:13, Genesis 1:26, Psalm 48:1, Matthew 6:26a, Genesis 1:24a, and Psalm 139:14-16.

Math: Teach 4 - 1 = 3. Have four students come to the front of the room. Count the students. Have one of them return to his seat. Ask the class how many students are still standing at the front of the room after one left. Do this with several groups of four students. Say the problem, "four minus one equals three." An optional way to do this is to hold up a subtraction sign between the first four students and a fifth that you have asked to come to the front. Then as you say the subtraction problem, have the student after the subtraction sign hold a piece of paper with a big X on it in front of him. You can also hold up an equal sign and have three additional students represent the answer to the subtraction problem.

$$\text{👥👥👥👥} - \text{👥} = \text{👥👥👥}$$

Multimedia Resources: View "Rev-Up for Arithmetic" from the "Rev-Up for Learning" DVD to practice number recognition, counting and addition 1-20.

Story Time: Read a story or stories of your choice.

Music: Review "Dry Bones" and "I'm Made Out of Hinges."

Multimedia Resources: This week, listen and sing along to selections from "Bullfrogs and Butterflies: God Loves Fun" CD.

Arts & Crafts: Give the students yellow, orange, red, and green construction paper and scissors. Let them cut out their favorite vegetables and fruit. They may glue them onto a piece of white paper as a food collage.

Outdoor Activity: If the weather is warm enough, go outside and play with a garden hose. Put kinks in the hose and see what happens. Talk about our blood vessels being similar to lots of hoses in our body. If we get a kink or blockage in a vessel, the blood won't flow through, just like the water won't flow through the hose.

Health & Safety: Continue your physical exercise program. You should be walking farther each day. Walk quickly in order to work your heart muscle and cardiovascular system. People don't have to do strenuous exercise to stay healthy. Walking is actually one of the best ways to strengthen your heart and your body. And walking is free and easy to do. Whenever you have a short trip to make, walk instead of riding in the car.

Physical Education: Ring Toss. Play a game similar to horse shoes with rope rings and stakes or cones. Rings can be made by gluing the ends of a short length of 1/2 inch rope into a PVC coupler with construction adhesive.

NOTES:

AOP's Commitment to Quality—Tell us how we are doing

As a publisher dedicated to providing high quality educational materials we invite you to tell us how we are doing. Please visit our website at www.aop.com to give us your comments, concerns, and/or compliments concerning Horizons Preschool. Contact information can be found in the support area for Horizons at the AOP website.

Activities in this Lesson: Bible Lesson, Science, Social Studies, Language Arts, Phonics, Reading, Writing, Memory Verse, Math, Shapes, Story Time, Music, Arts & Crafts, Health & Safety, Physical Education

Bible Reference: Genesis 1:26-27.

Bible Concept to Present: If we look at only one small part of God's Creation, our blood, we are still awed by the intricacy and majesty of God's Creation.

Bible Lesson: The more we study our body, the more we are in awe of a Loving, Magnificent Creator! In studying blood and the way blood works, we are without words to express the miracle. There is a wonderful book called *Fearfully and Wonderfully Made* by Phillip Yancey and Paul Brand. This is an adult book, but every teacher and every Christian should read it. Dr. Brand worked with lepers in India for many years. His insights into the human body and how it works are touching and humbling. He then compares the human body to the body of Christ. You will be able to share excitement from the book with your students.

Multimedia Resources: Listen to the song "The Majesty Of God" from "The Music Machine: The Majesty of God" CD.

Science: Many of the bones in our body are hollow. Remind them of the bone that you looked at in Lesson 145. If you saved it in a freezer, bring it out again for the students to look at. The outsides are very strong but the inside of the bone contains bone marrow. This marrow makes our red and white blood cells. Just as we all have work to do; our blood cells have work to do. In fact, every cell in our body has work to do. Red blood cells carry oxygen throughout our body. White blood cells fight germs and disease. Use Lesson 152 Resource sheet to illustrate these concepts. When a white blood cell finds an enemy, a bacteria or a germ, it eats it. That is its job. Have any of you played Pac Man™? The white blood cells are similar to the Pac Man™, hurrying around our body, eating up all of the bad germs.

We also have one more major element of our blood called platelets. The platelets are tiny, colorless little things in our blood that are very sticky. Their job, remember, everything has a job, is to stop bleeding. When we get a cut, platelets rush to the wound and start sticking together, clogging it up. They clog up the wound so much that blood can't escape any more. Platelets are very important to us.

Social Studies: Blood is very unique in that we can give blood to one another. Did you know that? Everyone has a different blood type. Most of us are type O. There are also types A, B, and AB. AB blood types can only give blood to other AB's, but O blood types can give blood to anyone. When you are grown up, you can go to a blood donation center and give blood. This is a good way to be a helper to others. Hospitals use blood when people have surgeries or have had an accident.

Language Arts: Share the poem below with students. Let the students write a poem about a blood cell.

My Body
Author Unknown

My body is healthy.
My blood is strong.
My cells do work
The whole day long.

If germs I get,
The white will fight!
They keep a watch
Through day and night.

The reds work hard
To carry air
Through my lungs
To everywhere!

Phonics: Review the initial sound of Ss. Review the initial sounds of Aa-Rr. Review letter recognition Aa-Zz.

Do the Lesson 152 Phonics worksheet. The Sound of Ss. Review the letter sound with the picture and words on the worksheet. Ask the students for other words that begin with the same sound. Trace the letters and say the sound of Ss. Observe the students as they trace the letters and help them with the letter strokes. If you have the students do one row at a time, the worksheet can be carried over to various parts of the day or another day.

Reading: Begin to use invented phonetic spelling in writing. Indicate the number of phonemes (1 - 3) heard in a real or nonsense word.

Writing: Continue to do Learning Logs. Encourage the students to draw or write about themselves. Some sample topics might be My Pet, My Favorite Reptile, My Favorite School Activity, My Family, or other teacher selected topics. The writing can be invented temporary spellings or dictations to the teacher.

Continue to have your students work on writing their home addresses and phone numbers if you have chosen to do this activity.

Memory Verse: Take time this week to review some of the memory verse favorites that the students have learned so far. Genesis 1:1, Genesis 1:3, Genesis 1:6, Genesis 1:10, I Peter 1:24-25, Genesis 8:22, Genesis 1:16, Psalm 90:12, Psalm 89:1, Revelation 22:16, Psalm 148:13, Genesis 1:26, Psalm 48:1, Matthew 6:26a, Genesis 1:24a, and Psalm 139:14-16.

Math: Review 4 - 1 = 3. Give the students the dog bones that they cut out previously and a bowl to put them in. Have them place 4 bones in the bowl while saying "four minus one" and have them take a bone from the bowl, "equals" and have them count "one, two, three bones in the bowl." Do this several times. Practice previous addition and subtraction facts.

Do the Lesson 152 Math worksheet. As they count the images have them say the subtraction problems and trace the numbers.

Shapes: Review the square shape.

Do the Lesson 152 Shapes worksheet. Trace the square and then trace the word square. Emphasize the initial Ss sound in square.

Story Time: Read a story or stories of your choice.

Music: Review "Dry Bones" and "I'm Made Out of Hinges."

Multimedia Resources: This week, listen and sing along to selections from "Bullfrogs and Butterflies: God Loves Fun" CD.

Arts & Crafts: Using red, white, and pink construction paper, instruct the students to first cut the piece of pink paper in half lengthwise. Now have them cut some small red circles and some larger white circles. Let them glue the circles on the pink "vessel" using five red circles for every one white circle. This is a blood vessel, with white and red cells. Talk about what kind of work is done by each cell.

Give the students playdough. Use the picture of the blood cells on Lesson 152 Resource page. Have the students make blood cells. Remind them that red blood cells are round, smooth, and indented. White blood cells are prickly and odd shaped.

Health & Safety: There are certain foods that make healthy blood. We should be eating these foods often during the week. Meat, fish, eggs, poultry, and nuts build white cells. Green leafy vegetables, breads, cereals, bananas, oranges, eggs, and nuts build red blood cells. Strawberries, potatoes, citrus fruits, and broccoli build strong blood vessels. Ask students to raise their hand if they have eaten any of these in recent days.

Continue to exercise your bodies with daily walks, days of aerobic exercise and ball games.

Physical Education: Swing on a swing by pumping the legs. Preschool children should be able to maintain their own momentum on a swing by pumping their legs.

NOTES:

Lesson 153

Week 31: Day 3

Activities in this Lesson: Bible Lesson/Social Studies, Science, Language Arts, Phonics, Reading, Writing, Memory Verse, Math, Story Time, Music, Arts & Crafts, Health & Safety, Physical Education, Homework

Bible Reference: Genesis 1:26-27.

Bible Concept to Present: God made us with a brain to be able to think and reason.

Bible Lesson/Social Studies: It is very important that you think about everything before you do it. But how do we think? God gave us a brain so we could learn, so we could reason. Your brain is inside your skull bone. Feel your head through your hair. Feel the bumps in your skull bone? Remember, your skull protects your brain. Without your brain you would not be able to listen and think about this story. You would not even know what is being said. Our brain is a miracle that God made. Without it, you would not be alive. God knew the brain would help us love Him and think about Him. The best thing we can do with our brain is talk to God and memorize His Word!

Science: Our brain is a very important part of our body. It does not weigh very much, and it is made of very soft tissue, yet the brain does many wonderful things in the body. It is responsible for the messages sent to the nerves, the thoughts you think, your ability to move, and keeping the heart beating. Everything that is done within the human body is dependent upon the brain. Show your students a drawing of the brain, Lesson 153 Resource page. God knew how important the brain would be to us. He put it inside a very strong bone, the skull.

Language Arts: Play the game "I'm Thinking."
For example, say:
      I'm thinking of a body part that beats. HEART
      I'm thinking of a body part that covers and protects my whole body. SKIN
      I'm thinking of a body part that is deep inside, helping me stand up. BONES
      I'm thinking of a body part that thinks and tells the rest of my body what to do. BRAIN
      I'm thinking of a body part that pulls and moves my bones. MUSCLES

Phonics: Blend the sounds Aa-Ss. (sac, sad, sag, Sal, Sam, sap, sass, sell, Sid, sin, sip, sob, sod, sog, son, sop, gas, lass, Mass, pass, Bess, less, mess, hiss, kiss, miss, sis, boss, loss, moss, Ross) Review the initial sounds of Aa-Ss. Review letter recognition Aa-Zz.

Add the following words to the flip chart pages of words and review them with the students. Continue to sound out the individual letters of each word as has been done previously. It may also be helpful for the students to see the words spaced out and spelled out as has been done in previous lessons.

as	es	is	os	sa	se	si	so
as	Bess	his	boss	sac	sell	Sid	sob
gas	less	kiss	loss	sag		sin	sod
lass	mess	miss	moss	Sal		sip	sog
Mass		sis	Ross	sap			son
pass				sass			sop
sass							

Do the Lesson 153 Phonics worksheet. The sound of Ss. Review the letter sound with the picture on the worksheet. Ask the students for other words that begin with the same sound. Give them specific instructions for how the letter should be traced. Allow time for tracing the letters and observe their progress. If you have the students do one row at a time, the worksheet can be carried over to various parts of the day or another day.

Reading: Begin to use invented phonetic spelling in writing. Indicate the number of phonemes (1 - 3) heard in a real or nonsense word.

Writing: Continue to do Learning Logs. Encourage the students to draw or write about themselves. Some sample topics might be My Pet, My Favorite Reptile, My Favorite School Activity, My Family, or other teacher selected topics. The writing can be invented temporary spellings or dictations to the teacher.

Continue to have your students work on writing their home addresses and phone numbers if you have chosen to do this activity.

Memory Verse: Take time this week to review some of the memory verse favorites that the students have learned so far. Genesis 1:1, Genesis 1:3, Genesis 1:6, Genesis 1:10, I Peter 1:24-25, Genesis 8:22, Genesis 1:16, Psalm 90:12, Psalm 89:1, Revelation 22:16, Psalm 148:13, Genesis 1:26, Psalm 48:1, Matthew 6:26a, Genesis 1:24a, and Psalm 139:14-16.

Math: Review 4 - 1 = 3. Review 4 - 1 = 3 by writing the problem on the board. Draw objects over the numbers with - sign between them. Make a large X over the object being subtracted. Write the = sign and then draw an excess of objects over the answer. Have a student come to the board and circle the correct number of objects to make the subtraction problem correct. Erase the extra objects and orally say the problem with the class. Repeat several times drawing simple objects such as dots or various shapes. Review previous addition and subtraction problems if the students need the practice.

Do the Lesson 153 Math worksheet. Count the items and say the subtraction problem. As they trace the numbers have them say the subtraction problems.

Talk about safety when riding a bike, rollerblading, skate boarding or similar activities. It is important that a helmet be worn to add to the protection that the skull provides for the brain. Brain injuries are often permanent so it is important that we do our best to protect our heads.

Story Time: Read a story or stories of your choice.

Music: Review all of the songs learned from the "Horizons Preschool Music" CD and any other song learned so far.

Multimedia Resources: This week, listen and sing along to selections from "Bullfrogs and Butterflies: God Loves Fun" CD.

Arts & Crafts: Ask the students to create a drawing of their family. Check this drawing for body parts added. If the student fails to add a body part, it is an indication that the student is not aware of that part of the body. Don't get too analytical about the picture, though. Children progress in stages in art, in which they are normally aware of different parts of the body and will interpret them in pictures.

Health & Safety: Continue to exercise your bodies with daily walks, days of aerobic exercise, and ball games.

Physical Education: Swing on a swing by pumping the legs. Preschool children should be able to maintain their own momentum on a swing by pumping their legs.

Homework: It has been one week since you sent home the Lesson 148 Homework worksheet where the students were to keep track of what they ate for a week. Have some students share about this activity.

NOTES:

Activities in this Lesson: Bible Lesson, Science, Social Studies, Language Arts, Phonics, Reading, Writing, Memory Verse, Math, Story Time, Music, Arts & Crafts, Health & Safety, Outdoor Activity/Physical Education

Bible Reference: Genesis 1:26-27.

Bible Concept to Present: Our human body is amazing! Nothing can match its workings.

Bible Lesson: God makes all things to work together for good, including our bodies! Every body system is dependent upon the rest of the body to function correctly.

Multimedia Resources: Listen to the song "Me-Raculous!" from "The Amazing Children" CD.

Science: This project will take all morning. Cut out a big piece of banner paper, longer than the student. Cut one for each student. Let the student lie on the floor, on the paper. Outline his body with a marker. Tape or staple the student's double to the wall. Students will now review what they have learned about the body. One by one, discuss the main body parts: heart, lungs, brain, some bones, eyes, ears, nose, mouth, esophagus, stomach. You will be amazed at how much the student remembers! After talking about each body part, one by one, hand out construction paper, glue sticks, and scissors. Instruct the student to cut out that body part. So, for example, as you discuss the heart and its functions then have each student cut out a heart. Take the hearts to the body outlines and glue them on. Help students glue them in the approximately correct location. Do this with each body part that you have studied. Let the students share facts that they remember.

Play Simon Says using phrases such as touch your ears, touch your ankle, touch your chin, touch you nose, etc.

Social Studies: Some facts about our bodies:
    Everyone is color blind at birth.
    More than half of our bones are in our hands and feet.
    Our heart will beat an average of 3,000,000,000 times.
    Food will travel to your stomach even if you eat standing on your head.
    Skin is the largest body organ.
    The average adult has 100 trillion cells. That is 100,000,000,000,000,000.
        http://www.education-world.com/a_lesson/lesson065.shtml

Language Arts: Get "Where's God When I'm Scared," a Veggie Tales® video from Big Idea. God is with us, whoever we are, wherever we are.

Phonics: Review blends Aa-Ss with the blend charts. Review the initial sounds of Aa-Ss. Review letter recognition Aa-Zz.

Have the students brainstorm words that begin or include the letter Ss. Write these words on the board. Model the correct letter formation as you write the letters on the board. The students should practice forming the letter Ss on a blank sheet of paper. Students who are ready can practice copying complete words from the board.

Do the Lesson 154 Phonics worksheet. The Sound of Ss. Review the letter sound with the picture and words on the worksheet. Ask the students for other words that begin with the same sound. Trace the letters and say the sound of Ss. Observe the students as they trace the letters and help them with the letter strokes. If you have the students do one row at a time, the worksheet can be carried over to various parts of the day or another day.

Reading: Begin to use invented phonetic spelling in writing. Indicate the number of phonemes (1 - 3) heard in a real or nonsense word.

Writing: Continue to do Learning Logs. Encourage the students to draw or write about themselves. Some sample topics might be My Pet, My Favorite Reptile, My Favorite School Activity, My Family, or other teacher selected topics. The writing can be invented temporary spellings or dictations to the teacher.

Continue to have your students work on writing their home addresses and phone numbers if you have chosen to do this activity.

Memory Verse: Take time this week to review some of the memory verse favorites that the students have learned so far. Genesis 1:1, Genesis 1:3, Genesis 1:6, Genesis 1:10, I Peter 1:24-25, Genesis 8:22, Genesis 1:16, Psalm 90:12, Psalm 89:1, Revelation 22:16, Psalm 148:13, Genesis 1:26, Psalm 48:1, Matthew 6:26a, Genesis 1:24a, and Psalm 139:14-16.

Math: Review 4 - 1 = 3. Give each of the students 10 counters. Have them make the subtraction problem with the counters. Have them point to the counters and say the subtraction problem, drawing the minus and equal sign with their finger between the counters as they say the words. Review previous problems if the students need the practice.

Do the Lesson 154 Math worksheet. As they trace the numbers have them say the subtraction problems.

Story Time: Read a story or stories of your choice.

Music: Review "Dry Bones."

Multimedia Resources: This week, listen and sing along to selections from "Bullfrogs and Butterflies: God Loves Fun" CD.

Arts & Crafts: Photograph your students doing a project together. This will not only build memories for you as a teacher, but will help your students build happy memories with their sibling or classmates. Use a whole roll of film one day, taking pictures of projects and playtime. Bring the prints to class and let the students chose one to take home. Put the others on a poster on the wall.

Health & Safety: Continue to exercise your bodies with daily walks, days of aerobic exercise, and ball games.

Outdoor Activity/Physical Education: Do you know we can think better when we wake up our brain cells? Here is how to wake up our brain: first, touch your right hand to your left shoulder. Tap your shoulder several times. Now touch your left hand to your right shoulder. Tap that shoulder several times. Crossing hands over and touching the other side of our body wakes up our brain as will any kind of movement or physical activity.

Do some vigorous outdoor movements. Teacher calls out the movement, student's brain hears and responds, students then do the movement. Run. Do a somersault. Walk. Skip. Twirl and spin. Hold hands and spin. Reach for the sky. We are fearfully and wonderfully made full well.

NOTES:

Lesson 155

Week 31: Day 5

Activities in this Lesson: Bible Lesson, Language Arts, Phonics, Reading, Writing, Memory Verse, Math, Story Time, Music, Arts & Crafts, Health & Safety, Physical Education

Bible Reference: Genesis 1:26-27.

Bible Concept to Present: God made each of us special. This is individuality.

Bible Lesson: We are all different. There is no one else like you. Each one of us is special. God did not want two people to be the same. He wanted each of us to be different. We may come from the same family, and have some of the same traits, but we are each an individual. What if you were exactly like me? You would do everything that I do. You would act just like me. You would think just like me. If the world had the same people in it, it would be a boring world. God wanted us to be different. That is why He made you special. You are the only one like you alive. God loves you just the way you are.

Multimedia Resources: Watch "Love" from the *Character Builders Video Series*.

Language Arts: Review and play "Mirror Talk" from Lesson 131.

Pass out a few teddy bear shaped cookies or grahams to the students. As you call out specific body parts the students can nibble those parts.

Phonics: Teach the initial sound of Tt. Review the initial sounds of Aa-Ss. Review letter recognition Aa-Zz.

Write several initial Tt words on the board: tab, table, tag, tail, take, tall, tan, tank, tap, tar, tell, tent, tick, tie, tip, time, toast, today, toe, tongue, tool, top, toss, toy, etc. Underline the initial letter Tt and say the words. Ask the students for other words that start with the same sound.

Do the Lesson 155 Phonics worksheet. The Sound of Tt. Review the letter sound with the picture and words on the worksheet. Ask the students for other words that begin with the same sound. Discuss the position of the letters on the guidelines. Give them specific instructions for how the letter should be traced. Trace the letters and say the sound of Tt. Observe the students as they trace the letters and help them with the letter strokes. If you have the students do one row at a time, the worksheet can be carried over to various parts of the day or another day.

Reading: Begin to use invented phonetic spelling in writing. Indicate the number of phonemes (1 - 3) heard in a real or nonsense word.

Writing: Continue to do Learning Logs. Encourage the students to draw or write about themselves. Some sample topics might be My Pet, My Favorite Reptile, My Favorite School Activity, My Family, or other teacher selected topics. The writing can be invented temporary spellings or dictations to the teacher.

Continue to have your students work on writing their home addresses and phone numbers if you have chosen to do this activity.

Memory Verse: Take time this week to review some of the memory verse favorites that the students have learned so far. Genesis 1:1, Genesis 1:3, Genesis 1:6, Genesis 1:10, I Peter 1:24-25, Genesis 8:22, Genesis 1:16, Psalm 90:12, Psalm 89:1, Revelation 22:16, Psalm 148:13, Genesis 1:26, Psalm 48:1, Matthew 6:26a, Genesis 1:24a, and Psalm 139:14-16.

Math: Review 4 - 1 = 3.

Do the Lesson 155 Math worksheet. Count the items. Say the subtraction or addition problem. Circle the correct number of objects to answer the problem.

Story Time: Read a story or stories of your student's choice or ones they have brought from home.

Music: Learn the songs "The B-i-b-l-e" and "Read Your Bible."

The B-I-B-L-E

The B-I-B-L-E
Yes, that's the book for me;
I stand alone on the Word of God:
The B-I-B-L-E
—Author unknown

Read Your Bible

(1)   Read your Bible, pray everyday,
        pray every day, pray everyday.
        Read your Bible, pray every day,
        and you'll grow, grow, grow.
        and you'll grow, grow, grow.
        and you'll grow, grow, grow.
        Read your Bible, pray every day,
        and you'll grow, grow, grow.

(2)   Neglect your Bible, forget to pray
        forget to pray, forget to pray;
        neglect your Bible, forget to pray
        and you'll shrink, shrink, shrink.
        and you'll shrink, shrink, shrink.
        and you'll shrink, shrink, shrink.
        neglect your Bible, forget to pray
        and you'll shrink, shrink, shrink.

(3)　Read your Bible, pray everyday,
　　　pray every day, pray everyday.
　　　Read your Bible, pray every day,
　　　and you'll grow, grow, grow.
　　　and you'll grow, grow, grow.
　　　Read your Bible, pray every day,
　　　and you'll grow, grow, grow.
　　　　　　—Author unknown

Verse 1. Begin in a squatting position holding hands out in front indicating a book, then switching to hands folding as in prayer as you sing. Slowly stand while singing "grow, grow, grow."

Verse 2. Wipe hands against each other, then wave hands to the side. Slowly return to squatting position as you sing "shrink, shrink, shrink."

Verse 3. Repeat motions for verse 1.

Multimedia Resources: Listen to the song "Bible Medley" from "The Amazing Book" CD. This week, listen and sing along to selections from "Bullfrogs and Butterflies: God Loves Fun" CD.

Arts & Crafts: Give the students a variety of pieces of construction paper you have saved. Give them white paper, scissors, and glue. Instruct them to make their own face, with eye color, hair color, and skin color all unique to them. Remind them that every single face will be different.

Health & Safety: Play a physical team game with your students today. Let them pick the game. It could be baseball, football, Frisbee, or whatever they want. Remind the students that everyone runs differently, kicks differently and throws differently. Some students are better at sports than others. Some are better at art or math.

Physical Education: Soda Bottle Bowling. Set up a bowling alley with one liter soda or water bottles and a softball. A little water or sand in the bottles will make them more stable to set up, but don't use so much that they become difficult to tip over with the ball. At one end of the lane, mark spots for the pins with tape or chalk, and at the other end a baseline that the thrower should not cross when rolling the ball. Select a rolling distance and a number of pins of up to ten that fits the ability of your students. The students will be making an underhand throw where they reach back and swing forward while keeping their arm close to their bodies. The ball should be released at a low level so that it doesn't bounce. Have groups of two to three students be the pinsetters while a similar group is bowling, and then switch positions. Several bowling stations will keep the students busy and active.

NOTES:

Activities in this Lesson: Bible Lesson, Social Studies, Phonics, Reading, Writing, Memory Verse, Math, Story Time, Music, Arts & Crafts, Health & Safety, Physical Education

Bible Reference: Luke 14:28-30.

Bible Concept to Present: God was finished. He started something unbelievably complex and varied, and He finished it.

Bible Lesson: God's Creation was done by the sixth day. So He rested on the seventh. We need to get in the habit of finishing what we start. God gives us several examples, including the lesson in Luke 14:28-30 about the builder. Share the story with the students.

Social Studies: How important is it to finish something? It is so easy to start things, but much harder to finish them. What things have we started in our class this year? We started the Creation Mural. Did we finish it? Didn't it feel wonderful to finish the mural? It helps us to remember all that we have learned this year. Everyone sometimes starts a project but doesn't finish it. But we can't make that a habit in our life. We need to learn to finish what we start, just like God finished His Creation. Let's pray to God, asking Him to help us be "finishers."

Science: When you look at nature it is clear that God completed His Creation. Birds have wings so they can fly, beaks so they can gather food, feet so they can sit in the trees, feathers to keep them warm, eyes so they can see and ears so they can hear each other singing. They are complete animals; everything works together so that they can be birds. Fish have gills so that they can breathe under the water, fins so they can swim in the water, scales that protect their skin, eyes so they can see and a mouth and teeth so they can catch food. Fish are complete animals; everything works together so that they can be fish. God finished His work; the animals have all the things that they need to live on the earth.

Language Arts: It is important to finish sentences when we say something. Practice talking in complete sentences. You can give the start to a sentence and then choose a student to both repeat and finish the sentence. As another activity pick out items in the room and have a student say a complete sentence that uses the word.

Phonics: Blend the sounds Aa-Tt. (Ted, tell, ten, Tess, tic, tiff, till, Tim, tin, tip, tab, tac, Tad, tag, Tam, tan, tap, tip, Todd, Tom top, toss, tot, at, bat, cat, fat, hat, mat, pat, sat, rat, sat, bet, let, met, net, pet, set, it, bit, fit, hit, kit, lit, mitt, nit, pit, sit, cot, dot, got, hot, jot, lot, not, pot, rot, tot) Review the initial sounds of Aa-Tt. Review letter recognition Aa-Zz.

Add the following words to the flip chart pages of words and review them with the students. Continue to sound out the individual letters of each word as has been done previously. It may also be helpful for the students to see the words spaced out and spelled out as has been done in previous lessons.

ta	te	ti	to	at	et	it	ot
tab	Ted	tiff	Todd	bat	bet	bit	dot
tac	tell	till	Tom	cat	get	fit	got
Tad	ten	Tim	top	fat	let	hit	hot
tag	Tess	tin	toss	hat	met	kit	jot
Tam		tip	tot	Nat	net	lit	lot
tan				pat	pet	mitt	not
tap				rat	set	nit	pot
				sat		pit	rot
						sit	tot

Do the Lesson 156a Phonics worksheet. The sound of Tt. Review the letter sound with the picture and words on the worksheet. Ask the students for other words that begin with the same sound. Trace the letters and say the sound of Tt. Observe the students as they trace the letters and help them with the letter strokes. If you have the students do one row at a time, the worksheet can be carried over to various parts of the day or another day.

Do the Lesson 156b Phonics worksheet. The Sound of Tt. Review the letter sound with the picture and words on the worksheet. Ask the students for other words that begin with the same sound. Give them specific instructions for how the letter should be traced. Allow time for tracing the letters and observe their progress. If you have the students do one row at a time, the worksheet can be carried over to various parts of the day or another day.

Reading: Begin to use invented phonetic spelling in writing. Indicate the number of phonemes (1 - 3) heard in a real or nonsense word.

Multimedia Resources: Review "Rev-Up for Reading" from the "Rev-Up for Learning" DVD to drill letter recognition and sound. The students should say each letter sound along with the presentation.

Writing: Continue to do Learning Logs. Encourage the students to draw or write about themselves. Some sample topics might be My Pet, My Favorite Reptile, My Favorite School Activity, My Family, or other teacher selected topics. The writing can be invented temporary spellings or dictations to the teacher.

Continue to have your students work on writing their home addresses and phone numbers if you have chosen to do this activity.

Multimedia Resources: Review "Rev-Up for Writing" from the "Rev-Up for Learning" DVD to review the writing of upper- and lowercase letters.

Memory Verse: Genesis 2:2.
By the seventh day God had finished the work He had been doing so... He rested ... Genesis 2:2 NIV

And on the seventh day God ended his work which he had made; and he rested... Genesis 2:2 KJV

God finally had a day of rest. Talk about the verse, making sure the students understand all of it, especially "finished." Give students Memory Verse Card 19 to take home.

Math: Review 4 - 1 = 3. Use the string of Counting Beads or pop beads to review 1 + 1 = 2, 2 + 1 = 3, 3 + 1 = 4, 4 + 1 = 5, 2 – 1 = 1, 3 – 1 = 2 and 4 – 1 = 3.

Do the Lesson 156 Math worksheet. Count the beads and say the subtraction problem. Trace the correct answer and say the subtraction problem again.

Do the Lesson 156 Math/Phonics/Shapes worksheet. Connect the dots to make the drawing. Identify the shapes found in the drawing. The students can color the drawing.

Multimedia Resources: View "Rev-Up for Arithmetic" from the "Rev-Up for Learning" DVD to practice number recognition, counting and addition 1-20.

Story Time: Read a story or stories of your choice.

Music: Review the songs "The B-i-b-l-e" and "Read Your Bible."

Multimedia Resources: This week, listen and sing along to selections from "Music Machine: Benny's Biggest Battle."

Arts & Crafts: *Bring in the cardboard egg cartons you have been saving. Cut them in half before class time. Also provide two bug eyes per student, glue, pipe cleaners, scissors and construction paper. Say, Every one of us is so different. We studied about all of God's Creation, including bugs. Is anyone in here afraid of bugs? Even some adults are afraid of bugs. We each have different bugs that bother us. Today, we're going to make a Fun Bug Friend. It is to help us remember that most bugs are our friends and won't hurt us. Our bug is going to look like a centipede. That is a long bug with lots of legs.*

Give each student one half of a cardboard egg carton, cut lengthwise. Have students turn the "bug" over. Cut out thin strips of colored construction paper. Glue each piece across one egg section with tacky glue. When turned back over, these pieces will look like lots of legs. Glue the eyes onto the first egg section. Cut small pieces of pipe cleaner and stick into the first section for antennae. Students may color their Fun Bug Friend with poster pens.

Health & Safety: Continue to exercise your bodies with daily walks, days of aerobic exercise and ball games.

Physical Education: Repeat the Soda Bottle Bowling game. Set up a bowling alley with one liter soda or water bottles and a softball. A little water or sand in the bottles will make them more stable to set up, but don't use so much that they become difficult to tip over with the ball. At one end of the lane, mark spots for the pins with tape or chalk, and at the other end a baseline that the thrower should not cross when rolling the ball. Select a rolling distance and a number of pins of up to ten that fits the ability of your students. The students will be making an underhand throw where they reach back and swing forward while keeping their arm close to their bodies. The ball should be released at a low level so that it doesn't bounce. Have groups of two to three students be the pinsetters while a similar group is bowling, and then switch positions. Several bowling stations will keep the students busy and active.

NOTES:

Activities in this Lesson: Bible Lesson, Social Studies, Science, Language Arts, Phonics, Reading, Writing, Memory Verse, Math, Shapes, Story Time, Music, Arts & Crafts, Health & Safety, Physical Education

Bible Reference: Genesis 1:26-27.

Bible Concept to Present: God will give each of us a special job to do. He has a plan for us.

Bible Lesson: God knew you were going to be born before you were born. He planned for you all along. He wanted you to have a place in this world, and He has a special job for you to do. We are learning how to be what God wants us to be. I have a special job to do. That job is to tell you about God and to love you. Your job right now is to listen and to learn how much God loves you, and how much you can love Him.

Social Studies: Remember when we talked about the fact that we were all different? Because you are different from everyone else, you will also do your special job differently from everyone else. We all have talents but my talents are different than yours. Some children can be good piano players; others have no musical ability at all. Think about all the talents God has given you. How can you use them for Him?

Science: God made each of us to have different talents. Our brains work to help us decide which talents are our best. Talk with students about our talents. Though they are young, they can still understand talents. Often God uses something we like to do. What are some things the students like to do? Painting? Running? Numbers? Take care of animals? Take care of people? Talk to them about ways God can use our talents and our skills. Most famous people with amazing talents knew when they were as young as five years old what they wanted to do with their life. They had a passion for something from their early years.

Language Arts: Start a "Secret Angels" project today. Explain to the students that they have jobs every day they must do, such as sharpening pencils or watering plants. You also have jobs you must do each day. For the next week each student will be a "Secret Angel" by doing someone else's job without them knowing who did it. Just one job each day is enough. Little acts of kindness like doing a chore, leaving a treat on someone's desk, or hanging up a jacket are things that can be done. Don't let the person know that you have been his secret angel. The element of surprise is fun for the whole group. You may want to draw names from a hat so that everyone has a "Secret Angel" during this project. Names could be drawn everyday to keep the "Secret Angels" moving around to different people. There might even be an opportunity for some to be a "Secret Angel" to someone outside of the class. Students can be "Secret Angels" at any time for the rest of the year.

Multimedia Resources: Watch "Kindness" from the *Character Builders Video Series*.

Phonics: Review blends Aa-Tt with the blend charts. Review the initial sounds of Aa-Tt. Review letter recognition Aa-Zz.

Have the students brainstorm words that begin or include the letter Tt. Write these words on the board. Model the correct letter formation as you write the letters on the board. The students should practice forming the letter Tt on a blank sheet of paper. Students who are ready can practice copying complete words from the board.

Do the Lesson 157 Phonics worksheet. The Sound of Tt. Review the letter sound with the picture and words on the worksheet. Ask the students for other words that begin with the same sound. Trace the letters and say the sound of Tt. Observe the students as they trace the letters and help them with the letter strokes. If you have the students do one row at a time, the worksheet can be carried over to various parts of the day or another day.

Reading: Begin to use invented phonetic spelling in writing. Indicate the number of phonemes (1 - 3) heard in a real or nonsense word.

Writing: Continue to do Learning Logs. Encourage the students to draw or write about themselves. Some sample topics might be My Pet, My Favorite Reptile, My Favorite School Activity, My Family, or other teacher selected topics. The writing can be invented temporary spellings or dictations to the teacher.

Continue to have your students work on writing their home addresses and phone numbers if you have chosen to do this activity.

Memory Verse: Review Genesis 2:2. Write the verse on the board. Point to each word as you say the verse. Have students take turns saying the words.

Math: Review 4 - 1 = 3.

Take out the Hand Prints made in Lesson 137. The students will use non-standard units of measurement to measure the length of their hands. Pass out buttons, paper clips, craft sticks, etc. and have the students measure the length and width of their hands. They will be able to share and compare their lengths and widths with others in the class.

Shapes: Review the triangle shape.

Do the Lesson 157 Shapes worksheet. Trace the triangle and then trace the word triangle. Emphasize the initial Tt sound in triangle.

Story Time: Read the book *The Berenstain Bears and Too Much Junk Food* by Jan and Stan Berenstain.

Music: Review the songs "The B-i-b-l-e" and "Read Your Bible."

Multimedia Resources: This week, listen and sing along to selections from "Music Machine: Benny's Biggest Battle."

Arts & Crafts: Make a little "This is Me" book. Fold two sheets of paper in half and staple with a cover cut from construction paper. Let the students write or draw something on each page that is unique to them. Instruct them to draw the hat of the occupation that is their favorite. One page might be devoted to family and another page to pets.

Health & Safety: Continue to exercise your bodies with daily walks, days of aerobic exercise, and ball game

Physical Education: Pathway Dribble. Set up a path with jump ropes or tape. The students will be dribbling a ball with their feet, soccer ball fashion, on the path from start to finish. On GO, the first student will begin at the START line and dribble the ball to the END line by using only their feet. They will then pick up the ball and bring it to the next student in line. Encourage them to use both the inside and outside of their feet. A ball that is a little flat will be easier for the children to control. This dribbling activity can also be done as a relay game across an open area.

NOTES:

Lesson 158

Week 32: Day 3

Activities in this Lesson: Bible Lesson, Social Studies, Language Arts, Phonics, Reading, Writing, Memory Verse, Math, Music, Story Time, Arts & Crafts, Outdoor Activity, Health & Safety, Physical Education

Bible Reference: Genesis 1:26-27.

Bible Concept to Present: Every person will work at something. God gave us many abilities and talents to help us work. He expects us to be good workers.

Bible Lesson: Men and women in the Bible had many jobs. In a few days we will talk more about the sons of Adam and Eve, Cain and Abel. Cain was a farmer who planted seeds and raised plants. His brother Abel was a shepherd who watched the sheep. Moses was a shepherd; remember the story of the burning bush where God appeared to Moses. Moses was out in the desert taking care of sheep when God appeared to him. Ruth gathered grain in the field of Boaz for food. David was a shepherd boy when he took 5 stones from the brook and went to face the giant Goliath. Joseph, Jesus' father was a carpenter. Peter, James, and John were fishermen. Paul was a tentmaker. All of these people had jobs that they did. God had all of them do special things for him. God had given them all the ability to be good workers. It didn't matter what kind of work they did.

Science: Many jobs are made easier by tools that people have been able to make. Some of these tools have taken many years and much work to make. Can you imagine a kitchen without a refrigerator, without hot water, without a stove to cook food on, without a toaster, without a microwave, without a blender, or without a coffee pot? All of these things make it easier to store and prepare food. Can you imagine not having a lawn mower to mow the grass, not having tools to work in the garden, not having electric drills and saws to build things with and not having tools to work on the car? Tools help us to do many things and make work easier. Many jobs require special tools. Can you name some special tools that your mom or dad uses to do their work?

Social Studies: Bring some items that students can use to pretend occupations. There are many inexpensive kits that would be fun to have in the classroom. Doctor kit, nurse kit, construction kit, builder kit, cooking set, baby doll and clothes, dishes, any kind of toy that permits occupational play. Let the students play at different occupations. For a more detailed lesson, set up a little town in the classroom. Let the students paint cardboard boxes to represent the fire station, the police station, the hospital, the restaurant, the home and whatever occupation location they choose. Provide hats for each area. Let the students pretend to be workers in those occupations.

Language Arts: Get the book *Mike Mulligan and His Steam Shovel*, by Virginia Lee Burton, from the library. Written in 1939, this classic can still teach about workers. Talk about the sounds that machines make. What sounds did Mary Anne make? What are some other sounds of work being done?

Continue with the "Secret Angel" project started in Lesson 157.

Phonics: Teach the initial short sound of Uu. Review the initial sounds of Aa-Tt. Review letter recognition Aa-Zz.

Write several initial short Uu words on the board: ugly, under, understand, etc. Underline the initial short letter Uu and say the words. Ask the students for other words that start with the same sound.

Do the Lesson 158 Phonics worksheet. The Short Sound of Uu. Review the letter sound with the picture and words on the worksheet. Ask the students for other words that begin with the same sound. Discuss the position of the letters on the guidelines. Give them specific instructions for how the letter should be traced. Trace the letters and say the sound of Uu. Observe the students as they trace the letters and help them with the letter strokes. If you have the students do one row at a time, the worksheet can be carried over to various parts of the day or another day.

Reading: Begin to use invented phonetic spelling in writing. Indicate the number of phonemes (1 - 3) heard in a real or nonsense word.

Writing: Continue to do Learning Logs. Encourage the students to draw or write about themselves. Some sample topics might be My Pet, My Favorite Reptile, My Favorite School Activity, My Family, or other teacher selected topics. The writing can be invented temporary spellings or dictations to the teacher.

Continue to have your students work on writing their home addresses and phone numbers if you have chosen to do this activity.

Memory Verse: Review Genesis 2:2. Write the words of the verse on cards. Have the students put the cards in order.

Math: Review 4 - 1 = 3. Practice this problem and review the problems: 1 + 1 = 2, 2 + 1 = 3, 3 + 1 = 4, 4 + 1 = 5, 5 + 1 = 6, 2 - 1 = 1, 3 - 1 = 2, with a strip of squares drawn on the board.

Do the Lesson 158 Math worksheet. Count the dots in the tiles and trace the numbers.

Story Time: Review the book *The Berenstain Bears and Too Much Junk Food*. Read a story or stories of your choice.

Music: Review the songs "The B-i-b-l-e" and "Read Your Bible."

Multimedia Resources: This week, listen and sing along to selections from "Music Machine: Benny's Biggest Battle." Listen to the song "His Story" from "The Amazing Book" CD and the song "David" from "The Amazing Children" CD.

Arts & Crafts: *Cut out large circles of light colored construction paper, one for each student. Draw one line with black marker from the center out to the edge.* Say, Workers wear many different hats. What hats can you think of that workers wear? Fire fighters, police officers, construction workers, nurses, baseball players, football players, airline pilots, soldiers, there are many. First, decorate your hat. You may color it to be any kind of workers hat that you like. With your scissors, cut the line carefully to the center of the circle. Teacher, staple the hats, overlapping the cut line to make a pyramid/cone type hat. Staple pieces of string or ribbon on each side of the hat. Let the students wear their hats and pretend to be workers.

Outdoor Activity: Take a "Litter Bug Walk" with the litter bags. Say, We have been workers all year, picking up litter in our yard. Work can be fun and good exercise, as well as something worth doing. Consider making your square block or a portion of the school campus an adopted area. Assign students to be Litter Bug Cadets. Take regular walks around your block with litter bags. If you are in a rural area, choose a stretch of road as your adopted area.

Health & Safety: Continue to exercise your bodies with daily walks, days of aerobic exercise, and ball games.

Physical Education: Pathway Dribble. Set up a path with jump ropes or tape. The students will be dribbling a ball with their feet, soccer ball fashion, on the path from start to finish. On GO, the first student will begin at the START line and dribble the ball to the END line by using only their feet. They will then pick up the ball and bring it to the next student in line. Encourage them to use both the inside and outside of their feet. A ball that is a little flat will be easier for the children to control. This dribbling activity can also be done as a relay game across an open area.

NOTES:

Activities in this Lesson: Bible Lesson, Social Studies/Science, Language Arts, Phonics, Reading, Writing, Memory Verse, Math, Story Time, Music, Arts & Crafts, Health & Safety, Physical Education

Bible Reference: Genesis 1:26-27.

Bible Concept to Present: We are responsible for caring for God's wonderful gift.

Bible Lesson: God has been so good to us. He has given us everything we could ever need or want. It is really a miracle that He made us as He did. Because God took so much time to make us, don't you think we should give something to Him? It is very important to take care of our bodies, minds and souls. God doesn't want us to waste anything that He has given us. He wants you to use your brains, muscles and whole body for Him. We belong to God. We must do what He wants us to do.

Social Studies/Science: It is important to keep our bodies clean and safe. We should never put anything into or on our bodies that would harm them. The items that we clean with are not to be played with or eaten. Poisonous substances found in the home like bleach, kitchen cleanser, and furniture polish are harmful to our body. We must never play with medicines that belong to anyone, as they could make us very sick. Only take medicine or pills given to you by a parent or grandparent. Prescription medicine only helps the person that the doctor has given it to; it may be harmful to anyone else who takes it. We belong to God. We must take care of ourselves. Let's all make a promise right now that we will never drink anything or take any pill that our parents don't know about. If another student gives you something to eat that you don't recognize make sure that you show it to an adult first before you eat it. We will never put smoke into our lungs by smoking cigarettes.

Language Arts: *Bring some detergents, medicines, and some good food to class.* Ask your students, in the form of a game, what should be eaten. Be sure and keep an eye on the detergents. This will help make the poisons vs. good food theme a reality.

Continue with the "Secret Angel" project started in Lesson 157.

Phonics: Review the initial short sound of Uu. Review the initial sounds of Aa-Tt. Review letter recognition Aa-Zz.

Have the students brainstorm words that begin or include the letter Uu. Write these words on the board. Model the correct letter formation as you write the letters on the board. The students should practice forming the letter Uu on a blank sheet of paper. Students who are ready can practice copying complete words from the board.

Do the Lesson 159 Phonics worksheet. The Short Sound of Uu. Review the letter sound with the picture and words on the worksheet. Ask the students for other words that begin with the same sound. Trace the letters and say the short sound of Uu. Observe the students as they trace the letters and help them with the letter strokes. If you have the students do one row at a time, the worksheet can be carried over to various parts of the day or another day.

Reading: Begin to use invented phonetic spelling in writing. Indicate the number of phonemes (1 - 3) heard in a real or nonsense word.

Writing: Continue to do Learning Logs. Encourage the students to draw or write about themselves. Some sample topics might be My Pet, My Favorite Reptile, My Favorite School Activity, My Family, or other teacher selected topics. The writing can be invented temporary spellings or dictations to the teacher.

Continue to have your students work on writing their home addresses and phone numbers if you have chosen to do this activity.

Memory Verse: Genesis 2:2 God rested. How do you think He rested? What did he do? What day is our seventh day of rest? Review the verse several times.

Math: Review 4 - 1 = 3. Have the students count off steps to practice addition and subtraction. Review: 1 + 1 = 2, 2 + 1 = 3, 3 + 1 = 4, 4 + 1 = 5, 5 + 1 = 6, 2 − 1 = 1, 3 − 1 = 2, 4 − 1 = 3.

Do the Lesson 159 worksheet. For subtraction count all of the blocks in the strip, then say, "minus one block equals," and count the blocks that are not covered by an X. Trace the correct number.

Story Time: Read a story or stories of your choice.

Music: Review the songs "The B-i-b-l-e" and "Read Your Bible."

Multimedia Resources: This week, listen and sing along to selections from "Music Machine: Benny's Biggest Battle."

Arts & Crafts: Give the students playdough. Have them make their favorite foods.

Health & Safety: *Have frozen waffles and a toaster available.* There are so many things to remember about caring for our bodies. Most of these things must become good habits, things we do without thinking about it each time. We brush our teeth. We take a bath. We eat good food. It is very important to eat breakfast every day. What does breakfast mean? It means to "break" our "fast." A fast is a time of not eating. What fast are we breaking when we eat breakfast? Yes, the fast of sleeping for nine or ten hours. Do you know eating breakfast can help us live longer? It has been proven by research that people that eat breakfast live a lot longer than those who don't eat breakfast.

Breakfast can be any kind of food. What is important is that we eat breakfast, whatever food we choose. Give students paper and poster pens and let them draw some of their favorite breakfast foods. Check to see if anyone draws a waffle. Fix everyone a waffle. Let the students see how good the waffles taste without any butter or syrup. They make a good snack, too.

Continue to exercise your bodies with daily walks, days of aerobic exercise, and ball games.

Physical Education: Kick Hard. In this activity the students will be kicking a rubber playground ball to see how far they can kick it. Do this activity in an open, grassy area where you have set up a kicking line and a few cones out in the field for target distances. The students will be kicking for distance, so don't tell them to aim for any target. Have each student place the ball on the ground behind the kicking line and then back up one step before stepping forward to kick the ball. The student should retrieve the ball and give it to the next person in line. After they have practiced the skill of kicking far, ask them to take several steps back and run to the ball and kick it.

NOTES:

Lesson 160

Week 32: Day 5

Activities in this Lesson: Bible Lesson, Science/Field Trip, Language Arts/Field Trip, Language Arts, Phonics, Reading, Writing, Memory Verse, Math, Story Time, Music, Arts & Crafts, Physical Education

Bible Reference: Colossians 4:14 and Luke 8:43.

Bible Concept to Present: God heals in many ways. He often uses doctors and hospitals to do His work.

Bible Lesson: One of the Bible writers was a doctor. He was called Luke the Physician. The verse from Colossians tells us this fact. Also, the verse from Luke tells us that there were many doctors during the time of Jesus. Luke traveled with Paul and saw him tortured and imprisoned for sharing Christ. Luke probably helped Paul many times as his doctor. God can use a doctor if He chooses to do so. God can use medicine or anything He wants to use, or God can cure a health problem with no doctor or medicine. We should never hesitate to use whatever help is available to us.

Illustration: Today we're going to visit a wonderful place of medicine and healing, the hospital. Arrange with the hospital ahead of time for a tour. Get parents to help if you have a big class. Plan to visit several areas of the hospital then go to a park for a picnic.

Science/Field Trip: Visit the hospital by areas to help students understand and remember. Be sure to visit the baby nursery. Ask ahead for someone to show you what doctors use to help with healing: casts, crutches, stethoscope, beds, etc.

Language Arts/Field Trip: Get the students talking through their field trip. Make them aware of areas of the hospital they are visiting.

Language Arts: Have a discussion about the field trip. Why would you like to be a doctor? Why not? Would you like to work in a hospital? Have any of you been a patient in a hospital? What was it like?

Continue with the "Secret Angel" project started in Lesson 157.

Phonics: Blend the sounds Aa-Uu. (up, bud, bug, bum, bun, bus, but, cub, cud, cuff, cup, cut, dub, dud, dug, dull, full, fun, fuss, gull, gum, gun, Gus, gut, hub, huff, hug, hull, hum, hut, jug, jut, lug, mud, muff, mug, mull, mum, mutt, nub, null, nut, pub, pug, pup, puss, rub, rug, rum, run, rut, sub, sum, sun, sup, tub, tuff, tug) Now that Uu has been covered and Qq always walks with Uu, you can also blend the words for Qq. (quell, quill, quit) Review the initial sounds of Aa-Uu. Review letter recognition Aa-Zz.

Add the following words to the flip chart pages of words and review them with the students. Continue to sound out the individual letters of each word as has been done previously. It may also be helpful for the students to see the words spaced out and spelled out as has been done in previous lessons.

bu	cu	du	fu	gu	hu	mu	nu	pu
bud	cub	dub	full	gull	hub	mud	nub	pub
bug	cud	dud	fun	gum	huff	muff	null	pug
bum	cup	dug	fuss	gun	hug	mug	nut	pun
bun	cut	dull		Gus	hull	mull		pup
bus				gut	hut	mum		puss
but						mutt		

ru	su	tu	up	qu
rub	sub	tub	up	quell
rug	sud	tuff		quill
run	sum	tug		quit
rat	sun			
	sup			

Do the Lesson 160a Phonics worksheet. The Short Sound of Uu. Review the letter sound with the picture and words on the worksheet. Ask the students for other words that begin with the same sound. Trace the letters and say the short sound of Uu. Observe the students as they trace the letters and help them with the letter strokes. If you have the students do one row at a time, the worksheet can be carried over to various parts of the day or another day.

Do the Lesson 160b Phonics worksheet. The Short Sound of Uu. Review the letter sound with the picture and words on the worksheet. Ask the students for other words that begin with the same sound. Give them specific instructions for how the letter should be traced. Allow time for tracing the letters and observe their progress. If you have the students do one row at a time, the worksheet can be carried over to various parts of the day or another day.

Reading: Begin to use invented phonetic spelling in writing. Indicate the number of phonemes (1 - 3) heard in a real or nonsense word.

Writing: Continue to do Learning Logs. Encourage the students to draw or write about themselves. Some sample topics might be My Pet, My Favorite Reptile, My Favorite School Activity, My Family, or other teacher selected topics. The writing can be invented temporary spellings or dictations to the teacher.

Continue to have your students work on writing their home addresses and phone numbers if you have chosen to do this activity.

Memory Verse: Review Genesis 2:2. Review again with the word cards.

Math: Review 4 - 1 = 3. Give each student 10 pennies to count 1-10. Have the students add and subtract pennies to practice the facts: 1 + 1 = 2, 2 + 1 = 3, 3 + 1 = 4, 4 + 1 = 5, 5 + 1 = 5, 2 − 1 = 1, 3 − 1 = 2, 4 − 1 = 3.

Do the Lesson 160 Math worksheet. For subtraction count all of the pennies in the row, then say, "minus one penny equals," and count the pennies that are not covered by an X. Trace the correct number.

Story Time: Read a story or stories of your student's choice or ones they have brought from home.

Music: When students return from the hospital, spend some time in rest. Play some restful music.

Multimedia Resources: This week, listen and sing along to selections from "Music Machine: Benny's Biggest Battle."

Arts & Crafts: While it is fresh in their minds, let the students have crayons and white paper and draw some of the things they saw at the hospital.

Physical Education: Repeat the Kick Hard activity. In this activity the students will be kicking a rubber playground ball to see how far they can kick it. Do this activity in an open, grassy area where you have set up a kicking line and a few cones out in the field for target distances. The students will be kicking for distance, so don't tell them to aim for any target. Have each student place the ball on the ground behind the kicking line and then back up one step before stepping forward to kick the ball. The student should retrieve the ball and give it to the next person in line. After they have practiced the skill of kicking far, ask them to take several steps back and run to the ball and kick it.

NOTES:

Activities in this Lesson: Bible Lesson, Social Studies/Science, Language Arts, Phonics, Reading, Writing, Memory Verse, Math, Story Time, Music, Arts & Crafts, Physical Education

Bible Reference: Genesis 2:1-4.

Bible Concept to Present: Students are introduced to the seventh day of Creation.

Bible Lesson: On the sixth day of Creation, God looked at all He had made, and was very happy. God looked at all of the heavens and the earth and saw how beautiful it all was. He looked at the water and saw how much we would need it. He saw the flowers and trees He had made and was very pleased. He enjoyed watching the fish swim in the water and the birds fly around in the sky. God looked at the ground and saw all of the creeping and crawling creatures. He was glad He had made them. God was the happiest when He looked and saw man walking around. Adam was the first man's name. God had been very, very busy. After looking at all these things, God rested on the seventh day to give us an example of six days of work and one day of rest. God did not create anything else. He was done with all of His work and was very happy with all He had made.

Multimedia Resources: Listen to the song "God Is Forever" from "The Music Machine: The Majesty of God" CD.

Social Studies/Science: God worked very hard to make everything for us. When we work very hard, we become tired. When we become tired, that is our body telling us we need rest. There are several ways to rest your body. You may rest by sitting very still for a few minutes. Sometimes a nap during the day is a very good idea. At night, our body takes a long rest. We should get at least eight hours of rest at night. God made everything in six days, and on the seventh day, He rested.

Language Arts: Do the following action rhyme with your students.

We Are Going To Bed
Author Unknown

We are going to bed. (Lay forefinger on thumb)
Down on the pillow we lay our head.
We will wake up (Fingers opening eyes)
To a new day (Circle formed with arms for sun)
Ready for work and ready for play. (Raking motion, batting motion.)

Continue with the "Secret Angel" project started in Lesson 157. Have the students share about things that someone must have done for them.

Phonics: Teach the initial sound of Vv. Review the initial sounds of Aa-Uu. Review letter recognition Aa-Zz.

Write several initial Vv words on the board: vacation, valentine, valley, value, vane, van, veil, vein, vat, vase, vent, Venus, Vermont, vest, vet, view, violin, vitamin, voice, vowel, vulture, etc. Underline the initial letter Vv and say the words. Ask the students for other words that start with the same sound.

Do the Lesson 161 Phonics worksheet. The Sound of Vv. Review the letter sound with the picture and words on the worksheet. Ask the students for other words that begin with the same sound. Discuss the position of the letters on the guidelines. Give them specific instructions for how the letter should be traced. Trace the letters and say the sound of Vv. Observe the students as they trace the letters and help them with the letter strokes. If you have the students do one row at a time, the worksheet can be carried over to various parts of the day or another day.

Reading: Give the beginning sound of a spoken word.

Multimedia Resources: Review "Rev-Up for Reading" from the "Rev-Up for Learning" DVD to drill letter recognition and sound. The students should say each letter sound along with the presentation.

Writing: Continue to do Learning Logs. Encourage the students to draw or write about themselves. Some sample topics might be My Pet, My Favorite Reptile, My Favorite School Activity, My Family, or other teacher selected topics. The writing can be invented temporary spellings or dictations to the teacher.

Continue to have your students work on writing their home addresses and phone numbers if you have chosen to do this activity.

Multimedia Resources: Review "Rev-Up for Writing" from the "Rev-Up for Learning" DVD to review the writing of upper- and lowercase letters.

Memory Verse: Review Genesis 2:2. Walk around the room chanting the verse. Sing the verse to "Yankee Doodle."

> By the seventh day
> God had finished
> the work He had been doing
> so...He rested...
> Genesis 2:2

Math: Teach 5 - 1 = 4. Have five students come to the front of the room. Count the students. Have one of them return to his seat. Ask the class how many students are still standing at the front of the room after one left. Do this with several groups of five students. Say the problem, "five minus one equals four." An optional way to do this is to hold up a subtraction sign between the first five students and a sixth that you have asked to come to the front. Then as you say the subtraction problem, have the student after the subtraction sign hold a piece of paper with a big X on it in front of him. You can also hold up an equal sign and have four additional students represent the answer to the subtraction problem.

$$\text{👫👫👫👫👫} - \text{👤} = \text{👫👫👫👫}$$

Multimedia Resources: View "Rev-Up for Arithmetic" from the "Rev-Up for Learning" DVD to practice number recognition, counting and addition 1-20.

Story Time: Introduce a chapter book today. Tell students they will be having a time of rest while you read a chapter each day. Choose a book with relatively short chapters: *The Tale of Peter Rabbit* by Beatrix Potter, *Frog and Toad Are Friends* by Arnold Lobel, *A Bear Called Paddington* by Michael Bond, *Winnie the Pooh* by A. A. Milne, *The Boxcar Children* by Gertrude Chandler Warner, any of the *Little House on the Prairie* books by Laura Ingalls Wilder, *Mr. Popper's Penguins* by Richard Atwater, *Sarah Plain & Tall* & its sequel, *Skylark,* by Patricia MacLachlan, or *Black Beauty* by Anna Sewell. All of these are good choices.

Music: Sing "The Wake-up Song" from the "Horizons Preschool Music" CD.

This week, listen and sing along to selections from a CD of your choice.

Arts & Crafts: Go to the Creation Mural. Review all of the days of Creation as you look at the mural. Let the students decide what to put on the seventh day. Remind them of all the art supplies they have available. Perhaps they might each draw a picture of God resting. Or they could draw things that help us rest, like pillows, glasses of milk or music.

On the seventh day, God was finished with His Creation. What an awesome Creation it is! Make something with playdough that is your favorite part of Creation.

Physical Education: Throw Far. In this activity the students will be throwing a tennis ball overhand to see how far they can throw it. Do this activity in an open, grassy area where you have set up a throwing line and a few cones out in the field for target distances. The students will be throwing for distance, so don't tell them to aim for any target. Have each student stand behind the throwing line, hold the ball in their throwing hand, bend their elbow and hold the ball behind their head, step forward with the opposite foot and throw the ball as hard as they can. The student should retrieve the ball and give it to the next person in line.

NOTES:

Lesson 162

Week 33: Day 2

Activities in this Lesson: Bible Lesson, Social Studies/Science, Language Arts, Phonics, Reading, Writing, Memory Verse, Math, Story Time, Music, Arts & Crafts, Health & Safety, Physical Education

Bible Reference: Genesis 2:1-4.

Bible Concept to Present: Nothing else was created after the sixth day of Creation.

Bible Lesson: God had worked so very hard. He was ready to rest. He had created everything in our world. He needed a time to look back at the work He had done. So on the seventh day He took a rest. He did not create anything else after the sixth day of Creation. He saw that all was very good that He had made. He knew He didn't need to make anything more. He was all done with His work. When we are finished with all of our work, it is nice to rest too, isn't it? God made the night time for a rest time.

Illustration: God meant for us to follow His lead and have times of rest. How do we feel if we don't get our rest? Do we feel grumpy? Did you know even machinery runs better if it has a day of rest? Sometimes our "day of rest," Sunday, becomes the busiest day of the week. We need to try to keep it restful and peaceful. Our physical body needs this rest and our mind needs this rest. Even our family needs the rest.

Multimedia Resources: Listen to the song "Yodel Song" from "Sir Oliver's Song" CD.

Social Studies/Science: Our body works very hard during the day. Even when you run and play your body works very hard. Think how hard your heart has to pump in order to keep you running and playing each day. When we rest at night our bodies slow down. It is during the night that our heart does not beat as fast, our breathing becomes slowed, and we rest our muscles. Proper growth cannot take place without proper rest.

Language Arts: Have the student draw himself in bed. Discuss the aspects of taking our favorite objects to bed with us for comfort and the fact that Jesus, our best friend, is always with us to comfort us. The following poem may also be used.

Teddy Bear

Teddy Bear, Teddy Bear turn around.
Teddy Bear, Teddy Bear touch the ground.
Teddy Bear, Teddy Bear show your shoes,
Teddy Bear, Teddy Bear that will do.
Teddy Bear, Teddy Bear climb the stairs,
Teddy Bear, Teddy Bear say your prayers.
Teddy Bear, Teddy Bear turn out the light,
Teddy Bear, Teddy Bear say good night.
... Author Unknown

Conclude the "Secret Angel" project started in Lesson 157. Encourage the students to continue to be "Secret Angels" for the rest of the school year. This will help them to think about the needs of others.

Phonics: Review the initial sound of Vv. Review the initial sounds of Aa-Uu. Review letter recognition Aa-Zz.

Do the Lesson 162 Phonics worksheet. The Sound of Vv. Review the letter sound with the picture and words on the worksheet. Ask the students for other words that begin with the same sound. Trace the letters and say the sound of Vv. Observe the students as they trace the letters and help them with the letter strokes. If you have the students do one row at a time, the worksheet can be carried over to various parts of the day or another day.

Reading: Give the beginning sound of a spoken word.

Writing: Continue to do Learning Logs. Encourage the students to draw or write about themselves. Some sample topics might be My Pet, My Favorite Reptile, My Favorite School Activity, My Family, or other teacher selected topics. The writing can be invented temporary spellings or dictations to the teacher.

Continue to have your students work on writing their home addresses and phone numbers if you have chosen to do this activity.

Memory Verse: Review Genesis 2:2. Practice the memory verse. Let the students make up a tune.

Math: Review 5 - 1 = 4. Give the students the dog bones that they cut out previously and a bowl to put them in. Have them place 5 bones in the bowl while saying "five minus one" and have them take a bone from the bowl, "equals" and have them count "one, two, three, four bones in the bowl." Do this several times. Practice previous addition and subtraction facts.

Do the Lesson 162 Math worksheet. As they count the images have them say the subtraction problems and trace the numbers.

Story Time: Have a time of rest and read the chapter book you have chosen.

Music: Review "The Wake Up Song."

This week, listen and sing along to selections from a CD of your choice.

Arts & Crafts: *Bring in several different kinds of dry noodles.* Let the students glue the noodles on construction paper with tacky glue in their own design.

Health & Safety: Teach your students a skill that can easily be done while resting, such as praying. Enjoy some quiet time with your students. A rest time is important each day.

Physical Education: Repeat the Throw Far activity. In this activity the students will be throwing a tennis ball overhand to see how far they can throw it. Do this activity in an open, grassy area where you have set up a throwing line and a few cones out in the field for target distances. The students will be throwing for distance, so don't tell them to aim for any target. Have each student stand behind the throwing line, hold the ball in their throwing hand, bend their elbow and hold the ball behind their head, step forward with the opposite foot and throw the ball as hard as they can. The student should retrieve the ball and give it to the next person in line.

NOTES:

Activities in this Lesson: Bible Lesson, Science/Music, Social Studies/Music, Language Arts/Music, Phonics, Reading, Writing, Memory Verse, Math, Story Time, Music, Arts & Crafts, Creative Cooking, Physical Education, Catch Up

Bible Reference: Psalm 95:1-3.

Bible Concept to Present: Music is a precious gift from God.

Bible Lesson: Thank you, God, for music. When God made the world, He made music. We don't know when God made music, but whales sing beautiful songs and birds sing. When God made man, He gave him vocal chords so that he could sing.

Multimedia Resources: Watch "Joy" from the *Character Builders Video Series*.

Illustration: Music can be very simple. Music can be unbelievably complicated. Sing a simple song from the "Horizons Preschool Music" CD. Then play a classical piece like the "Hallelujah Chorus" by George Frideric Handel. Share with students that Handel was a Christian. The words for The Messiah are from scripture in the Bible. Most of the "Hallelujah Chorus" is from Revelation 19. Handel barely ate or slept for 24 days to write this musical work.

Explain that music can lift our spirits, help us relax, help us celebrate and even celebrate our patriotism! "The Star-Spangled Banner," our country's national anthem, stirs our hearts and makes us proud to be Americans. Sing "The Star-Spangled Banner" for or with the students.

The Star Spangled Banner

O say, can you see, by the dawn's early light,
What so proudly we hail'd at the twilight's last gleaming?
Whose broad stripes and bright stars, thro' the perilous fight,
O'er the ramparts we watch'd, were so gallantly streaming?
And the rockets' red glare, the bombs bursting in air,
Gave proof thro' the night that our flag was still there.
O say, does that star-spangled banner yet wave
O'er the land of the free and the home of the brave?

Science/Music: *Bring in a set of eight glasses. Also have water, a measuring cup and teaspoons available.* Using the measuring cup, fill the glasses with increments of 1/8 cup of water: 1/8 cup in the first glass, 1/4 cup in the second glass, 3/8 cup in the third glass, and so on. This will give you eight glasses that will play eight notes. Hit the glasses lightly with the round part of the teaspoon. Test the glasses to be sure you have the eight notes: do, re, mi, fa, so, la, ti, do. Add drops of water if needed. Let the students play songs. You can put slips of paper under each cup numbered one through eight. Test the sounds and write down the order of any tune you make.

Obtain an audio recording of whale songs from the Internet or a library. There might be other animal sounds available, but the whales actually sing. Lie on the floor and listen to the whale's song. Talk about music. Talk about resting.

Social Studies/Music: Invite a musician to come and play for your students today. If you don't know any musicians, ask your choir director at church. Choir members often play instruments. Make it a special day and include your visitor at lunch time. Students might make a special lunch treat.

Language Arts/Music: If possible, get the book *First Book of Music* by Emma Danes, Usborne, 1993, or find another book at the library explaining very basic music theory. The Usborne book is out of print but you might be able to find a used copy. *Collect musical instruments from friends and parents.* Ask students to bring in any instruments they have at home. Let the students handle the instruments.

Phonics: Blend the sounds Aa-Vv. (Val, van, vat, Venn, vet, vid, vim, Von, vow) Review the initial sounds of Aa-Vv. Review letter recognition Aa-Zz.

Add the following words to the flip chart pages of words and review them with the students. Continue to sound out the individual letters of each word as has been done previously. It may also be helpful for the students to see the words spaced out and spelled out as has been done in previous lessons.

va	ve	vi	vo
Val	Venn	vid	Von
van	vet	vim	vow
vat			

Do the Lesson 163 Phonics worksheet. The sound of Vv. Review the letter sound with the picture on the worksheet. Ask the students for other words that begin with the same sound. Give them specific instructions for how the letter should be traced. Allow time for tracing the letters and observe their progress. If you have the students do one row at a time, the worksheet can be carried over to various parts of the day or another day.

Reading: Give the beginning sound of a spoken word.

Writing: Continue to do Learning Logs. Encourage the students to draw or write about themselves. Some sample topics might be My Pet, My Favorite Reptile, My Favorite School Activity, My Family, or other teacher selected topics. The writing can be invented temporary spellings or dictations to the teacher.

Continue to have your students work on writing their home addresses and phone numbers if you have chosen to do this activity.

Memory Verse: Review Genesis 2:2. Say the verse several times during the school day.

Math: Review 5 - 1 = 4. Review 5 - 1 = 4 by writing the problem on the board. Draw objects over the numbers with - sign between them. Make a large X over the object being subtracted. Write the = sign and then draw an excess of objects over the answer. Have a student come to the board and circle the correct number of objects to make the subtraction problem correct. Erase the extra objects and orally say the problem with the class. Repeat several times, drawing simple objects such as dots or various shapes. Review previous addition and subtraction problems if the students need the practice.
Do the Lesson 163 Math worksheet. Count the items and say the subtraction problem. As they trace the numbers have them say the subtraction problems.

Story Time: Have a time of rest and read the chapter book you have chosen.

Music: Review "The Wake-up Song."

This week, listen and sing along to selections from a CD of your choice.

Creative Cooking: Make a special treat for the visiting musician.

> **Fancy Pretzels**
> Ingredients: Pretzels, large or small; candy melts, dark and white chocolate; candy sprinkles; coconut; chopped nuts
> Melt the candy melts as the package suggests. A microwave makes it easy. Let the students dip the pretzels halfway into the chocolate, then into one of the toppings. Lay them on wax paper to set. Serve on a pretty tray.

Physical Education: Rhythm Sticks. Play some different types of music and have the students move using the ribbon sticks made in Lesson 24. Have the children move their hands and arms from left to right and back and forth in a high arching motion like a windshield wiper on a car. Move hands and arms in large circles, in front, to the sides, and overhead. Make back and forth motions in front, to the sides and overhead. Make casting motions like you would with a fishing pole. Use various locomotor skills such as skipping, hopping, galloping, giant steps, walking backwards, walking sideways, hopping on one foot, etc.

Catch Up: Do any assignment that you didn't have time for earlier in the month.

NOTES:

Lesson 164

Week 33: Day 4

Activities in this Lesson: Bible Lesson, Science, Social Studies, Science, Language Arts, Phonics, Reading, Writing, Memory Verse, Math, Story Time, Music, Arts & Crafts/Outdoor Activity, Physical Education

Bible Reference: Psalm 19:1, Psalm 69:34, Psalm 89:5 & 6.

Bible Concept to Present: We love God and the world He gave us.

Bible Lesson: We love God's Creation! God's world is so interesting and fun, we would never be able to explore it all. Life is wonderful. We should love life and enjoy it. When we live a life of joy, others will ask us where we get our happiness. Then we can share with them about God and His love for everyone.

Multimedia Resources: Listen to the song "God Likes Fun" from the "Bullfrogs and Butterflies: God Loves Fun" CD.

Science: We love interesting science! The science of magnetism is very interesting. *Bring a compass to class. Bring some magnets to class. One for each student would be best.* Let the students go around the room testing materials to see if the magnet will attach. What kind of materials do magnets attract? Our earth is like a giant magnet. All magnets point to the north. That is what makes a compass work. Take a walk outside and play the "Compass Game." Tell students which direction to walk and how many steps. Let them use a compass to guide them. It is thought that birds use the earth's magnetism to help them in migration routes.

Social Studies: We love to follow directions! We are all left handed or right handed. Raise your hand if you are left handed. Raise your hand if you are right handed. We all have a left side and a right side. Raise your left arm. Raise your right arm. Point to the left then to the right. When we look at a compass, north is straight ahead. East is to the right. South is behind us. West is to the left. Instruct students to stand at the front of the class. Tell them different directions to step. Preschool children need to know left and right. Some of the students are ready to learn north, south, east, and west.

Multimedia Resources: Watch "Faith" from the *Character Builders Video Series*.

Science: We love watching things grow! God planned for His Creation to continue by giving plants seeds and giving animals babies. But we can grow some plants without a seed. You will need carrot tops and water. Cut carrot tops to about 1/2 inch. Cut the greens off right where they start. Set the carrot top in a saucer. Keep water in the saucer for several weeks. Watch the carrots to see what happens. This experiment may also be done with potatoes or yams. Sweet potato plants grow very well and are beautiful.

We all love bubbles! Provide each student with a jar of bubbles. Go outside and blow bubbles. Ask, What is in the bubbles? Our air. What is holding up the bubbles? The outside air.

Language Arts: We just love videos! Get "Dave and the Giant Pickle," a Veggie Tales® video from Big Idea. We are all special and created for God's purpose, no matter our size, our age, or what we look like. Dave (representing David from the Bible) thought he was too small to accomplish anything, but with God's help, he was a giant slayer.

Phonics: Review blends Aa-Vv with the blend charts. Review the initial sounds of Aa-Vv. Review letter recognition Aa-Zz.

Have the students brainstorm words that begin or include the letter Vv. Write these words on the board. Model the correct letter formation as you write the letters on the board. The students should practice forming the letter Vv on a blank sheet of paper. Students who are ready can practice copying complete words from the board.

Do the Lesson 164 Phonics worksheet. The Sound of Vv. Review the letter sound with the picture and words on the worksheet. Ask the students for other words that begin with the same sound. Trace the letters and say the sound of Vv. Observe the students as they trace the letters and help them with the letter strokes. If you have the students do one row at a time, the worksheet can be carried over to various parts of the day or another day.

Reading: Give the beginning sound of a spoken word.

Writing: Continue to do Learning Logs. Encourage the students to draw or write about themselves. Some sample topics might be My Pet, My Favorite Reptile, My Favorite School Activity, My Family, or other teacher selected topics. The writing can be invented temporary spellings or dictations to the teacher.

Continue to have your students work on writing their home addresses and phone numbers if you have chosen to do this activity.

Memory Verse: Review Genesis 2:2. Review again with the words cards.

Math: Review 5 - 1 = 4. Give each of the students 10 counters. Have them make the subtraction problem with the counters. Have them point to the counters and say the subtraction problem, drawing the minus and equal sign with their finger between the counters as they say the words. Review previous problems if the students need the practice.

Do the Lesson 164 Math worksheet. As they trace the numbers have them say the subtraction problems.

Story Time: We love for our teacher to read to us! Have a time of rest and read the chapter book you have chosen.

Music: Review "The Wake-up Song."

This week, listen and sing along to selections from a CD of your choice.

Arts & Crafts/Outdoor Activity: Everyone loves butterflies! Let's make a butterfly friend that we can clip to a curtain or pillow. Each student needs a piece of white paper towel, watercolors, tacky glue, a spring type clothespin, and a pipe cleaner. Let the students paint with the watercolors on the paper towel, watching the colors spread. Make the "wings" as bright as possible. Let dry while the students walk outside to find some butterflies.

The students will need help with the next step: Fold the paper towel like an accordion or fan. Pinch the towel in the middle. Put drop of tacky glue inside the clip of the clothespin. Then clip the towel inside the space. The clothespin is the butterfly's body. Wrap the pipe cleaner around the top end of the clothespin, stretching out the ends for antennae. Draw two little eyes on the end, between the antennae.

Physical Education: Repeat the Rhythm Sticks activity. Play some different types of music and have the students move using the ribbon sticks made in Lesson 24. Have the children move their hands and arms from left to right and back and forth in a high arching motion like a windshield wiper on a car. Move hands and arms in large circles, in front, to the sides, and overhead. Make back and forth motions in front, to the sides and overhead. Make casting motions like you would with a fishing pole. Make a tornado by spinning around and moving the ribbon high and low. Gallop like a horse by holding the ribbon on your back and gallop around the area. Use various locomotor skills such as skipping, hopping, galloping, giant steps, walking backwards, walking sideways, hopping on one foot, etc.

NOTES:

Activities in this Lesson: Bible Lesson, Social Studies/Science, Science, Language Arts, Phonics, Reading, Writing, Memory Verse, Math, Story Time, Music, Arts & Crafts, Physical Education

Bible Reference: Genesis 2:1-4.

Bible Concept to Present: God was happy with what He had made.

Bible Lesson: When God finished His work, He looked at it all and was very pleased. He could see that what He had created was very good. Have you ever drawn a picture, or made something of which you were very proud? God was very proud of His work. He was very happy that everything was finished, and that it was working the way He wanted it to. Think how happy God must have been when He saw Adam taking care of the animals. And think how happy God was when He saw Adam and Eve enjoying the Garden of Eden. He was very pleased that He could create something for man to enjoy. He has created the whole world for us to enjoy. Let's thank God right now for all of the things He has made. He is a wonderful God, isn't He?

Multimedia Resources: Listen to the song "God Is Good" from "The Music Machine: The Majesty of God" CD.

Social Studies/Science: Have you ever finished a big project? It felt really good. You were tired so you sat down to rest. Well, God does not get tired, but the Bible says He rested on the seventh day. He was so pleased with His Creation, He rested in His work. Did you know rest can take many forms? It may take the form of sleep, a time in which our entire body rests. It may take the form of sitting with quiet activities such as reading, listening to CDs, or doing a favorite hobby. However you prefer to rest, the rest is very important to your body. Your body needs a rest period of at least eight hours each night.

Sometimes it is hard to get to sleep at night. We are having so much fun, we don't want to stop. But rest and sleep are very important to our health. What are some things we can do to get ready to sleep? Give students white paper and crayons. Let them draw the things that you talk about. Mention having a glass of milk, reading or being read to, brushing our teeth, brushing our hair, taking a bath, singing, praying, listening to music, etc. We should try to have a pattern to the way we go to sleep at night, doing the same things every night.

Science: Water the carrot tops. Have they changed? (See Lesson 164)

Language Arts: Repeat "Teddy Bear" poem from Lesson 162.

Phonics: Teach the initial sound of Ww. Review the initial sounds of Aa-Vv. Review letter recognition Aa-Zz.

Write several initial Ww words on the board: wag, wagon, waist, walk, wall, walrus, want, war, warm, wash, wasp, waste, watch, water, wax, we, wear, web, wed, week, well, wide, wig, will, win, wind, winter, wolf, won, wood, Washington, Wyoming, etc. Underline the initial letter Ww and say the words. Ask the students for other words that start with the same sound.

Do the Lesson 165 Phonics worksheet. The Sound of Ww. Review the letter sound with the picture and words on the worksheet. Ask the students for other words that begin with the same sound. Discuss the position of the letters on the guidelines. Give them specific instructions for how the letter should be traced. Trace the letters and say the sound of Ww. Observe the students as they trace the letters and help them with the letter strokes. If you have the students do one row at a time, the worksheet can be carried over to various parts of the day or another day.

Reading: Give the beginning sound of a spoken word.

Writing: Continue to do Learning Logs. Encourage the students to draw or write about themselves. Some sample topics might be My Pet, My Favorite Reptile, My Favorite School Activity, My Family, or other teacher selected topics. The writing can be invented temporary spellings or dictations to the teacher.

Continue to have your students work on writing their home addresses and phone numbers if you have chosen to do this activity.

Memory Verse: Review Genesis 2:2. Students should be done working on this verse. Let them recite.

Math: Review 5 - 1 = 4.

Do the Lesson 165 Math worksheet. Circle the correct number of objects to answer the subtraction problems.

Story Time: Have a time of rest and read the chapter book you have chosen.

Music: Review "The Wake-up Song."

This week, listen and sing along to selections from a CD of your choice.

Arts & Crafts: *Bring in small envelopes, cotton, and Psalms 56:3 printed on paper for each student.* Say, There are times when we have trouble sleeping because we are nervous or afraid. Something in our dark bedroom makes us worried. But there is nothing in our bedroom at night that isn't there in the daytime. Our imagination makes us think there is something there. We can pray and trust God to help us be calm and sleep. God gave us the Bible to help us not be afraid. Give each student an envelope, several pieces of cotton and the verse. Let the students decorate the paper if they want to. Put the paper and the cotton inside the envelope and seal the envelope. Instruct the students to put the envelope under their pillow. They will always have God's promise nearby if they get afraid in the night.

Physical Education: Frogs on a Log. Find a sturdy bench or make a balance beam by placing cement or wood blocks under a two by four for this activity. The students will be standing on the balance beam and will maintain their balance as they jump and land on the ground. Have five students get on the balance beam at a time and read the Five Speckled Frogs rhyme below. On the cue from the poem the students will jump off the beam one at a time until there are no students on the beam.

FIVE LITTLE SPECKLED FROGS

Five little speckled frogs,
Sitting on a speckled log
Eating a most delicious fly
Yum! Yum!
One jumped into the pool
Where it was nice and cool
Then there were four little speckled frogs
Glub! Glub!

Four little speckled frogs,
Sitting on a speckled log
Eating a most delicious fly
Yum! Yum!
One jumped into the pool
Where it was nice and cool
Then there were three little speckled frogs
Glub! Glub!

Three little speckled frogs,
Sitting on a speckled log
Eating a most delicious fly
Yum! Yum!
One jumped into the pool
Where it was nice and cool
Then there were two little speckled frogs
Glub! Glub!

Two little speckled frogs,
Sitting on a speckled log
Eating a most delicious fly
Yum! Yum!
One jumped into the pool
Where it was nice and cool
Then there was one little speckled frog
Glub! Glub!

One little speckled frog,
Sitting on a speckled log
Eating a most delicious fly
Yum! Yum!
One jumped into the pool
Where it was nice and cool
Then there were no little speckled frogs
Glub! Glub!

NOTES:

Lesson 166

Activities in this Lesson: Bible Lesson, Social Studies, Science, Language Arts, Phonics, Reading, Writing, Memory Verse, Math, Story Time, Music, Arts & Crafts, Physical Education

Bible References: Genesis 2:5-20; 1:29-31.

Bible Concept to Present: God made a special home for Adam. It had rules. Adam had work to do.

Bible Lesson: Do you remember the man's name in our last lesson? He was the very first man that God created. Yes, you are right. His name was Adam. Adam had to have a place to live, just like you do. God made Adam a home. It was a beautiful garden. The name of that garden was Eden. There were flowers and trees all around the garden. The animals that God had made roamed free in that garden. There were blue streams running through the garden. Adam was to take care of his new home. He gave each kind of animal a name. He took care of them. Can we think of an animal name for every letter of the alphabet? That is only twenty six animals. Adam had to name many, many more kinds of animals!

Social Studies: Although your student will already recognize his house as his home, teaching on the home is very important to children of this age. They need to know that their home is personal, that it is a special blessing from God. Discuss how unique each home is and how it is something that was created for us as a place to be loved and cared for. You may need to reassure your student that his home will always be there for him. In this day, children are introduced to divorce at a young age. If any of your students have been exposed to this concept, they may be fearful that their home will not be the same some day. Reassure them that God will always take care of them, wherever they are.

Multimedia Resources: Watch "Confidence" from the *Character Builders Video Series.*

Science: Water the carrot tops. Have they changed? (See Lesson 164)

Language Arts: Do the following finger activity with your students.

Two Little Houses

Two little houses across the street. (Clench fists.)
Open the doors, and two friends meet. (Open fists, Hold up 2 fingers.)
Saying, "How do you do?" (Point two forefingers together)
"How do you do?"
"It's nice sunny weather."
"Let's go to church together."

Phonics: Blend the sounds Aa-Ww. (wad, wag, watt, web, wed, well, wet, wig, will, win, wit) Review the initial sounds of Aa-Ww. Review letter recognition Aa-Zz.

Add the following words to the flip chart pages of words and review them with the students. Continue to sound out the individual letters of each word as has been done previously. It may also be helpful for the students to see the words spaced out and spelled out as has been done in previous lessons.

<u>wa</u>	<u>we</u>	<u>wi</u>
wad	web	wig
wag	wed	will
watt	well	win
		wit

Do the Lesson 166a Phonics worksheet. The sound of Ww. Review the letter sound with the picture and words on the worksheet. Ask the students for other words that begin with the same sound. Trace the letters and say the sound of Ww. Observe the students as they trace the letters and help them with the letter strokes. If you have the students do one row at a time, the worksheet can be carried over to various parts of the day or another day.

Do the Lesson 166b Phonics worksheet. The Sound of Ww. Review the letter sound with the picture and words on the worksheet. Ask the students for other words that begin with the same sound. Give them specific instructions for how the letter should be traced. Allow time for tracing the letters and observe their progress. If you have the students do one row at a time, the worksheet can be carried over to various parts of the day or another day.

Reading: Give the beginning sound of a spoken word.

Multimedia Resources: Review "Rev-Up for Reading" from the "Rev-Up for Learning" DVD to drill letter recognition and sound. The students should say each letter sound along with the presentation.

Writing: Continue to do Learning Logs. Encourage the students to draw or write about themselves. Some sample topics might be My Pet, My Favorite Reptile, My Favorite School Activity, My Family, or other teacher selected topics. The writing can be invented temporary spellings or dictations to the teacher.

Continue to have your students work on writing their home addresses and phone numbers if you have chosen to do this activity.

Multimedia Resources: Review "Rev-Up for Writing" from the "Rev-Up for Learning" DVD to review the writing of upper- and lowercase letters.

Memory Verse: Proverbs 17:17a.
A friend loves at all times. Proverbs 17:17a NIV

A friend loveth at all times. Proverbs 17:17a KJV

This verse is always a favorite and one that students will love. Talk about what "at ALL times" means: good times and bad, grouchy days and happy days. Give the students Memory Verse Card 20 to take home.

Math: Review 5 - 1 = 4. Use the string of Counting Beads or pop beads to review 1 + 1 = 2, 2 + 1 = 3, 3 + 1 = 4, 4 + 1 = 5, 2 – 1 = 1, 3 – 1 = 2, 4 – 1 = 3, and 5 – 1 = 4.

Do the Lesson 166 Math worksheet. Count the beads and say the subtraction problem. Trace the correct answer and say the subtraction problem again.

Multimedia Resources: View "Rev-Up for Arithmetic" from the "Rev-Up for Learning" DVD to practice number recognition, counting and addition 1-20.

Story Time: Have a time of rest and read the chapter book you have chosen.

Music: Review "The Wake-up Song." Teach the following song to the tune of "London Bridge is Falling Down."

> **God Has Given Me a Home**
> Tune of London Bridge is Falling Down
>
> God has given my home to me
> Home to me.
> Home to me.
> God has given my home to me.
> How I love Him.
>
> I will do my work each day.
> Work each day.
> Work each day.
> I will do my work each day.
> It's just for Him.

This week, listen and sing along to selections from a CD of your choice.

Arts & Crafts: Give your students toothpicks or straws, paper, and tacky glue and have them make a picture of their home. Instruct them to include a special room where they like to spend time.

Physical Education: Repeat the Frogs on a Log activity. Find a sturdy bench or make a balance beam by placing cement or wood blocks under a two by four for this activity. The students will be standing on the balance beam and will maintain their balance as they jump and land on the ground. Have five students get on the balance beam at a time and read the Five Speckled Frogs rhyme below. On the cue from the poem the students will jump off the beam one at a time until there are no students on the beam. Vary the activity by asking the students to jump as high as they can, as far as they can, or from one foot as they jump from the beam to the floor.

NOTES:

Activities in this Lesson: Bible Lesson, Social Studies/Science, Science, Science/Arts & Crafts/Outdoor Activity, Language Arts, Phonics, Reading, Writing, Memory Verse, Math, Story Time, Music, Arts & Crafts, Physical Education, Homework

Bible Reference: Genesis 2:5-20; 1:29-31.

Bible Concept to Present: God had rules for Adam's nice home. Adam could eat any of the food in the garden, but from the Tree of the Knowledge of Good and Evil, he could not eat.

Bible Lesson: Adam had been given a very nice home in which to live. Adam did not have to go out each day and work for his food. It was provided for him by God. God told Adam he could eat any food from the garden, but he could not eat from the Tree of Knowledge of Good and Evil. That was a rule that God had set down. What if we didn't have any rules in our homes? Our house would always be messy, because it would be no one's job to pick up what he had dropped. Meals would not be prepared on time. I don't think we would be very happy, do you? God wants us to have rules in our home, too. He wants us to be a loving and happy family.

Social Studies/Science: Every home has rules to live by. In fact, everywhere you go, there are rules. There are rules for driving, rules for walking, rules for shopping in a store, rules for school, and rules for your home. It should be possible for students to go through an entire day without breaking a rule. In other words, our homes should be livable without children constantly getting into trouble. Send home the Lesson 167 Homework worksheet. Students will be talking with their families about family rules. Every family has rules, whether spoken or unspoken. Sometimes, they need to be more spoken. It is presumed that children know the rules, when they don't.

Science: Water the carrot tops. Have they changed? (See Lesson 164)

Science/Arts & Crafts/Outdoor Activity: *Bring in a cookie sheet. Fill it with sand or soil.* Take a walk and get twigs and leaves to make a Garden of Eden. Let all students take part. Say, God gave Adam and Eve a lovely garden to live in. It had a left side and a right side. From the center of the garden, you could walk north, south, east, or west. Practice learning directions, using the garden.

Language Arts: Students need to learn good working habits from a young age. Talk to students about doing a job. What does it take to do a job? What about helping by taking out the trash? What do we do first? Find the trash and make sure it is tied. Second, make sure we can carry it. Then take it to the right place. Make sure it is in the trash can. Lastly, make sure the trash can lid is on tightly. Every step of a job is important. Kids might think it would be great not to have any jobs to do. But how would that prepare them for life? Talk to them about life, and the fact that life means doing some work as well as playing.

Phonics: Review blends Aa-Ww with the blend charts. Review the initial sounds of Aa-Ww. Review letter recognition Aa-Zz.

Have the students brainstorm words that begin or include the letter Ww. Write these words on the board. Model the correct letter formation as you write the letters on the board. The students should practice forming the letter Ww on a blank sheet of paper. Students who are ready can practice copying complete words from the board.

Do the Lesson 167 Phonics worksheet. The Sound of Ww. Review the letter sound with the picture and words on the worksheet. Ask the students for other words that begin with the same sound. Trace the letters and say the sound of Ww. Observe the students as they trace the letters and help them with the letter strokes. If you have the students do one row at a time, the worksheet can be carried over to various parts of the day or another day.

Reading: Give the beginning sound of a spoken word.

Writing: Continue to do Learning Logs. Encourage the students to draw or write about themselves. Some sample topics might be My Pet, My Favorite Reptile, My Favorite School Activity, My Family, or other teacher selected topics. The writing can be invented temporary spellings or dictations to the teacher.

Continue to have your students work on writing their home addresses and phone numbers if you have chosen to do this activity.

Memory Verse: Review Proverbs 17:17a. Discuss the things that a friend might do for someone else.

Math: Review 5 - 1 = 4.

Create an AB pattern by placing the students in boy/girl order. Do other patterns with hair color, eye color, height, etc. After all students who fit the pattern have been placed ask them what would come next if there were more students.

Story Time: Have a time of rest and read the chapter book you have chosen.

Music: Review "God Has Given Me a Home" and "The Wake-up Song."

This week, listen and sing along to selections from a CD of your choice.

Arts & Crafts: Give the students the Lesson 167 Arts & Crafts worksheet. Let them use crayons or markers to paint the picture of the Garden of Eden.

Physical Education: Rolling Along. Play a game similar to bowling where the students roll a ball toward a target. For this game have them sit on the floor and push the ball with both hands to roll it at the target. The targets can be cones, bowling pins, soda bottles, hula hoops, etc. After they roll the ball at the target they should stand up to retrieve the ball and reset the target for the next student.

Homework: Give the students the Lesson 167 Homework worksheet to take home. They will talk with their families about home rules. It doesn't have to be returned.

NOTES:

Activities in this Lesson: Bible Lesson, Social Studies/Science, Science, Language Arts, Phonics, Reading, Writing, Memory Verse/Outdoor Activity, Math, Story Time, Music, Arts & Crafts, Physical Education

Bible Reference: Genesis 2:5-20; 1:29-31.

Bible Concept to Present: God gave Adam the job of naming all of the animals, birds, and beasts.

Bible Lesson: God had made all of the animals, but He wanted Adam to take care of them. He wanted Adam to feel responsible for them. He knew Adam needed a job to do. So He told Adam to name the animals. How would you like that job? Do you think Adam looked at the pig and thought; "This animal eats everything in sight, so it must be a pig?" I think it was very easy for Adam to name everything. I think God helped put the names of the animals in Adam's mind so he could quickly name all of them. At any rate, Adam did a very good job. He named all of the creeping, crawling beasts. He named all of the birds. He had a name picked out for everything that was made. I think Adam was a friend to the animals, don't you? God had given Adam a big job to do and he had done it. Adam finished the job.

Social Studies/Science: Every person in our home must share the work. There are things that each person can do, regardless of age.

> Note from one of the authors: At the age of two, our children were responsible for picking up their own toys, by three they were beginning to learn to make their beds, and at four, dusting and kitchen clean up began. As I write this, our oldest child is almost eight, and is a gigantic help to me. She can vacuum, dust, scrub the kitchen floor, do laundry, clean a room, and cook. She didn't acquire these skills immediately. I gradually led her from one step to another. She is not required to do all of these skills every day, but she knows how.

There should be jobs that each student must accomplish each day. You may desire to keep a chart of work accomplished, and reward students for some of the harder jobs. Now is the time to begin a battle plan for training the child to be a good worker.

In our modern world, it is appalling how little some children learn about cooking and cleaning. There are teenagers who literally can not boil an egg. They have never cleaned a bathroom. They have a terrible work ethic. Through this year, you have been teaching and preparing your students to be good workers. First, they will be good workers at school and in their homes. Then they will be good workers in the workplace. Ultimately, they will be good workers for God. Don't be afraid to stretch their limits. Please don't, as I have often seen, keep them from cooking because they might make a mess. Messes can be cleaned up, but the opportunity to teach won't come again. Have a "Spring Cleaning" day, making the season whatever season you are in. Take some time to dust and clean, letting students help with everything.

Science: Water the carrot tops. Have they changed? (See Lesson 164)

Language Arts: Get a baby name book from the library. Let the students look at the baby names. They will, of course, want to see their own. Talk about how hard it is to name a baby. What names do they like? Remember, Adam had to name thousands of animals! What a job that was. I'll bet he was glad that God was helping him.

Phonics: Teach the initial and ending sound of Xx. Review the initial sounds of Aa-Ww. Review letter recognition Aa-Zz.

Write several initial and final Xx words on the board: ax, fax, fox, box, sox, wax, max, Xerox, X ray, xylophone, etc. Underline the initial and final letter Xx and say the words. Ask the students for other words that start with the same sound.

Do the Lesson 168 Phonics worksheet. The Sound of Xx. Review the letter sound with the picture and words on the worksheet. Two sounds for Xx will be covered. Ask the students for other words that begin with the same sound. Discuss the position of the letters on the guidelines. Give them specific instructions for how the letter should be traced. Trace the letters and say the sound of Xx. Observe the students as they trace the letters and help them with the letter strokes. If you have the students do one row at a time, the worksheet can be carried over to various parts of the day or another day.

Reading: Give the beginning sound of a spoken word.

Writing: Continue to do Learning Logs. Encourage the students to draw or write about themselves. Some sample topics might be My Pet, My Favorite Reptile, My Favorite School Activity, My Family, or other teacher selected topics. The writing can be invented temporary spellings or dictations to the teacher.

Continue to have your students work on writing their home addresses and phone numbers if you have chosen to do this activity.

Memory Verse/Outdoor Activity: Review Proverbs 17:17a. Work on the verse for this week. Take a Memory Verse walk. Walk around the yard or grounds, saying the memory verse.

Math: Review 5 - 1 = 4. Practice this problem and review the problems: 1 + 1 = 2, 2 + 1 = 3, 3 + 1 = 4, 4 + 1 = 5, 5 + 1 = 6, 2 - 1 = 1, 3 – 1 = 2, 4 – 1 = 3, with a strip of squares drawn on the board.

Do the Lesson 168 Math worksheet. Count the dots in the tiles and trace the numbers.

Story Time: Have a time of rest and read the chapter book you have chosen.

Music: Review "God Has Given Me a Home."

This week, listen and sing along to selections from a CD of your choice.

Arts & Crafts: Let your students draw a picture of themselves performing a task. Give them some ideas as to what jobs they have done. The advanced student will be able to include tools. This will help you realize the student's true feelings regarding their jobs.

Physical Education: Review the Rolling Along activity. Play a game similar to bowling where the students roll a ball toward a target. For this game have them sit on the floor and push the ball with both hands to roll it at the target. The targets can be cones, bowling pins, soda bottles, hula hoops, etc. After they roll the ball at the target they should stand up to retrieve the ball and reset the target for the next student.

NOTES:

Lesson 169

Week 34: Day 4

Activities in this Lesson: Bible Lesson, Social Studies, Science, Language Arts, Phonics, Reading, Writing, Memory Verse, Math, Story Time, Music, Arts & Crafts, Physical Education

Bible Reference: Genesis 2:20b–25

Bible Concept to Present: God saw that there was a need in Adam's life. Adam needed a helper, a friend.

Bible Lesson: God looked around and saw all the wonderful things He had created. Adam looked around and saw all the beautiful things God had made. He enjoyed being with the animals but he needed someone he could talk to. He needed someone who would talk back to him. Remember, man is the only animal that can talk to communicate.

Every one of us needs friends. God looked at Adam and knew he was lonely. God did not see a friend anywhere in the garden for Adam. God wanted to make Adam happy. Adam needed a friend with whom to share all of his thoughts. He needed a friend to play with the animals with him. You need friends to play with too, don't you? God wants us to have happy friendships.

Multimedia Resources: Listen to the song "Friends" from the "Bullfrogs and Butterflies: God is My Friend" CD.

Social Studies: We need friends. If we did not have friends, we would not have anyone to tell our "secrets." A friend is a very special person. A friend can be our age, younger than we are or older. It is okay to have lots of friends. Friends are people we can talk to when we are sad or when we are happy. We would be lonely without friends. We need to be good friends to other people. We need to help other people and show them how to be good friends.

Science: Water the carrot tops. Is something starting to grow?

Language Arts: Have students verbalize what friendship is. Read the poem below to your students.

Friends
Author Unknown

A friend is someone
Just like you
Someone who knows me
And loves me, too.

A friend plays games
And doesn't care who wins
Someone who can always
Make me grin.

A friend helps clean a mess
That we've made together
And plays with me
In all kinds of weather.

Good friends are hard to find
I thank God you're a friend of mine.

Phonics: Review the beginning and ending sound of Xx. Review the initial sounds of Aa-Ww. Review letter recognition Aa-Zz.

Have the students brainstorm words that begin or include the letter Xx. Write these words on the board. Model the correct letter formation as you write the letters on the board. The students should practice forming the letter Xx on a blank sheet of paper. Students who are ready can practice copying complete words from the board.

Do the Lesson 169 Phonics worksheet. The Sound of Xx. Review the letter sound with the picture and words on the worksheet. Two sounds for Xx will be covered. Ask the students for other words that begin with the same sound. Trace the letters and say the sound of Xx. Observe the students as they trace the letters and help them with the letter strokes. If you have the students do one row at a time, the worksheet can be carried over to various parts of the day or another day.

Reading: Give the beginning sound of a spoken word.

Writing: Continue to do Learning Logs. Encourage the students to draw or write about themselves. Some sample topics might be My Pet, My Favorite Reptile, My Favorite School Activity, My Family, or other teacher selected topics. The writing can be invented temporary spellings or dictations to the teacher.

Continue to have your students work on writing their home addresses and phone numbers if you have chosen to do this activity.

Memory Verse: Review Proverbs 17:17a. Student should have this one memorized, it is an easy one. Talk about how important friends are to our life. Some of the students will be friends thirty years from now.

Math: Review 5 - 1 = 4. Have the students count off steps to practice addition and subtraction. Review: 1 + 1 = 2, 2 + 1 = 3, 3 + 1 = 4, 4 + 1 = 5, 5 + 1 = 6, 2 – 1 = 1, 3 – 1 = 2, 4 – 1 = 3, 5 – 1 = 4.

Do the Lesson 169 Math worksheet. For subtraction count all of the blocks in the strip, then say, "minus one block equals," and count the blocks that are not covered by an X. Trace the correct number.

Story Time: Get the book *Stone Soup* by Marcia Brown. Talk about friends. What happened to the soup? Did everyone have to work together?

Have a time of rest and read the chapter book you have chosen.

Music: Review "God Has Given Me a Home."

This week, listen and sing along to selections from a CD of your choice.

Arts & Crafts: *Bring in toilet paper tubes and cut them into one inch pieces. Buy some fake jewels from the craft store. Give each student several pieces of the tube.* Have tacky glue, brushes, and paints available. Say, Today we will make Friendship Bracelets. Paint your bracelet first. Then glue some jewels on the top. After they dry, you may give them to a friend. Make one for yourself, too. Tell your students you would like them to color a picture from a coloring book, thinking of a friend to send it to. Encourage neatness. Let the students fold their pictures and put them in an envelope. Send a note home with the envelope, encouraging parents to mail it, letting the student know that the friend will receive it. Whether the friend remembers to thank your student is immaterial. The concept to present is giving without getting.

Cut up cardboard egg cartons into four pieces. Each student will have a section of three little egg cups. Make the clay recipe from Lesson 14, adding green food coloring. Students may help make the clay. Students need enough clay to put a piece in each of the three sections. Also provide three craft sticks per student. Give the students white construction paper, colored markers and scissors.

First, let the students put a round piece of clay unto each cup the size of a 1" ball. Now have the students make and color three flowers. Their flowers should be about 2" round. Cut them out, then color the other side. Using the markers, color the craft sticks green. Glue the flowers onto the craft sticks with tacky glue. Stick the craft sticks down into the clay. This is a love gift to give to a friend, a neighbor or a grandparent.

Physical Education: Tree Tag. Set up some hula hoops in an area that has an outside boundary. A rope could be placed around the area to serve as a boundary. The hula hoops should be about an arm's length apart. In the game the people who are in the hoops are the trees and they try to tag the other students who are moving between the hoops with their branches (arms). When a tree tags another person they have to shout, "You are a tree," and the two students then switch places. Pick enough students to be trees so that there is one in each of the hoops. The rest of the students are to move in-between the hoops using any locomotor skill that they wish, walking, running, skipping, hopping, galloping, etc. Students inside the hoops can move in anyway that they wish. Students moving outside of the hoops need to watch out for the other players moving between the hoops.

NOTES:

Activities in this Lesson: Bible Lesson, Social Studies, Science, Language Arts, Phonics, Reading, Writing, Memory Verse, Math, Story Time, Music, Arts & Crafts, Creative Cooking, Physical Education

Bible Reference: Genesis 2:20b-25.

Bible Concept to Present: Eve was created from Adam as a special helper. God made Eve to be very special.

Bible Lesson: God saw that Adam needed a friend. God decided to make Adam a friend. He put Adam into a deep sleep. Then he took a rib from Adam's side and made Eve. Eve was a woman. She was a good friend to Adam. She was made to be a helper to Adam. Adam was so happy to have a friend. He was very pleased that God would make him a special friend like Eve. God wants us to have special friend-ships.

Multimedia Resources: Listen to the song "Always Be True" from "Sir Oliver's Song" CD.

Social Studies: Just as Eve was given to Adam as a special helper, we can be a special helper to our friends too. God gives us friends as special helpers. Friends help other friends. When a friend needs something, we are glad to share with him. We are special helpers to our friends. We could think of some friends right now.

Science: In Lesson 128 we talked about bees and how they help flowers produce seeds. The bees are special helpers to plants. Ask the students for other examples where one animal or plant is a special helper to another.

Water the carrot tops. Is something starting to grow?

Language Arts: Continue with the poem "Friends." (Lesson 169)

Phonics: Blend the sounds of Aa-Xx. (ax, fax, lax, Max, pax, rax, sax, tax, wax, Zax, dex, hex, kex, Lex, Rex, sex, Tex, vex, fix, Kix, mix, nix, pix, six, box, cox, fox, gox, lox, ox, pox, sox, vox, lux, tux) Review the initial sounds of Aa-Xx. Review letter recognition Aa-Zz.

Add the following words to the flip chart pages of words and review them with the students. Continue to sound out the individual letters of each word as has been done previously. It may also be helpful for the students to see the words spaced out and spelled out as has been done in previous lessons.

<u>ax</u>	<u>ex</u>	<u>ix</u>	<u>ox</u>	<u>ux</u>
ax	dex	fix	box	lux
fax	hex	Kix	cox	tux
lax	kex	mix	fox	
Max	Lex	nix	gox	
pax	Rex	pix	lox	
rax	sex	six	ox	
sax	Tex		pox	
tax	vex		sox	
wax			vox	
Zax				

Do the Lesson 170a Phonics worksheet. The sound of Xx. Review the letter sound with the picture and words on the worksheet. Two sounds for Xx will be covered. Ask the students for other words that begin with the same sound. Trace the letters and say the sound of Xx. Observe the students as they trace the letters and help them with the letter strokes. If you have the students do one row at a time, the worksheet can be carried over to various parts of the day or another day.

Do the Lesson 170b Phonics worksheet. The Sound of Xx. Review the letter sound with the picture and words on the worksheet. Two sounds for Xx will be covered. Ask the students for other words that begin with the same sound. Give them specific instructions for how the letter should be traced. Allow time for tracing the letters and observe their progress. If you have the students do one row at a time, the worksheet can be carried over to various parts of the day or another day.

Reading: Give the beginning sound of a spoken word.

Writing: Continue to do Learning Logs. Encourage the students to draw or write about themselves. Some sample topics might be My Pet, My Favorite Reptile, My Favorite School Activity, My Family, or other teacher selected topics. The writing can be invented temporary spellings or dictations to the teacher.

Continue to have your students work on writing their home addresses and phone numbers if you have chosen to do this activity.

Memory Verse: Review Proverbs 17:17a. Let the students recite their verse today.

Math: Review 5 - 1 = 4. Give each student 10 pennies to count 1-10. Have the students add and subtract pennies to practice the facts: 1 + 1 = 2, 2 + 1 = 3, 3 + 1 = 4, 4 + 1 = 5, 5 + 1 = 5, 2 – 1 = 1, 3 – 1 = 2, 4 – 1 = 3, 5 – 1 = 4.

Do the Lesson 170 Math worksheet. For subtraction count all of the pennies in the row, then say, "minus one penny equals," and count the pennies that are not covered by an X. Trace the correct number.

Story Time: Read a story or stories of your student's choice or ones they have brought from home.

Music: Review "God Has Given Me a Home."

This week, listen and sing along to selections from a CD of your choice.

Arts & Crafts: Make a Friendship Mural. Staple a big piece of banner paper to the wall. Allow the students to draw and write anything and everything they can think of about being a friend. Examples: friends' names; flowers given to friends; hearts for love; swings for playing together; holding hands; telephone for calling one another. If they choose, the students may use cut out magazine pictures.

Creative Cooking: Make the cookies below as a class project. Let each student take some home in a zippered sandwich bag to give to a friend. Explain that a grandparent or sibling can also be their best friend. It is their decision.

Friendship Cookies

1- 18.25 ounce box cake mix
1/2 cup vegetable oil
2 eggs
Optional: 2 cups of chocolate chips, coarsely chopped semi-sweet chocolate, white chocolate chips, peanut butter chips, butterscotch chips, raisins, coconut, toasted-coarsely chopped nuts

Preheat oven to 350 degrees F. Lightly grease cookie sheet(s). Mix together cake mix, vegetable oil and eggs in a large bowl. Stir in optional ingredients. Make little balls with the dough and put on the cookie sheets. Bake for 8 to 10 minutes. Remove from pan and cool on wire cooling racks.

Physical Education: Repeat the Tree Tag activity. Set up some hula hoops in an area that has an outside boundary. A rope could be placed around the area to serve as a boundary. The hula hoops should be about an arm's length apart. In the game the people who are in the hoops are the trees and they try to tag the other students who are moving between the hoops with their branches (arms). When a tree tags another person they have to shout, "You are a tree," and the two students then switch places. Pick enough students to be trees so that there is one in each of the hoops. The rest of the students are to move in-between the hoops using any locomotor skill that they wish, walking, running, skipping, hopping, galloping, etc. Students inside the hoops can move in anyway that they wish. Students moving outside of the hoops need to watch out for the other players moving between the hoops.

NOTES:

Activities in this Lesson: Bible Lesson, Social Studies, Science, Language Arts, Phonics, Reading, Writing, Memory Verse, Math, Story Time, Music, Arts & Crafts, Outdoor Activity, Physical Education

Bible Reference: Genesis 2:20b-25.

Bible Concept to Present: Eve was to obey what God said just as Adam was to obey what God said.

Bible Lesson: God had made a special friend and helper for Adam. That friend and helper was Eve. Eve became Adam's wife. Eve had rules to obey in her new home just as Adam did. Eve was to obey all the rules that God had made, just as Adam did. She was to help Adam. She was to help Adam obey the rules in their home. They were supposed to do just what God told them to do. We will find out in a later lesson just how much Adam and Eve did not obey the rules.

Social Studies: The rules of God must be obeyed by all in the family. God is the head of the home. Dad must obey God. Mom must obey God and the children must obey God. Illustrate with personal experiences ways in which your students must obey God and ways in which you obey God. It is God's plan for men and women to become husband and wife. Go to the board and list suggestions that students make for being a good husband or a good wife. Write "Husband" on one side and "Wife" on the other. Encourage students to realize that someday they will be a husband or a wife. They will be a good mate by being a kind, considerate person from a young age. Show them that many of the good qualities they listed involve kindness.

Multimedia Resources: Watch "Kindness" from the *Character Builders Video Series*.

Science: Remember to water the carrot tops. They should be growing greens by now.

Language Arts: Talk about how hard it was to remember to obey outside playing the game. Everything has rules, even games. Games wouldn't be fun without rules. Write on the board. Let the students tell you some of the rules they have in their home and the consequences of not obeying them. It is good to have students verbalize what they think the rules are. Are the rules they have at home the same as the rules for the classroom?

Phonics: Teach the initial sound of Yy. Review the initial sounds of Aa-Xx. Review letter recognition Aa-Zz.

Write several initial Yy words on the board: yak, yam, yap, yard, yarn, yawn, yea, year, yell, yellow, yes, yet, yip, yoke, you, your, yo-yo, yucca, Yukon, etc. Underline the initial letter Yy and say the words. Ask the students for other words that start with the same sound.

Do the Lesson 171 Phonics worksheet. The Sound of Yy. Review the letter sound with the picture and words on the worksheet. Ask the students for other words that begin with the same sound. Discuss the position of the letters on the guidelines. Give them specific instructions for how the letter should be traced. Trace the letters and say the sound of Yy. Observe the students as they trace the letters and help them with the letter strokes. If you have the students do one row at a time, the worksheet can be carried over to various parts of the day or another day.

Reading: Give the beginning sound of a spoken word.

Multimedia Resources: Review "Rev-Up for Reading" from the "Rev-Up for Learning" DVD to drill letter recognition and sound. The students should say each letter sound along with the presentation.

Writing: Continue to do Learning Logs. Encourage the students to draw or write about themselves. Some sample topics might be My Pet, My Favorite Reptile, My Favorite School Activity, My Family, or other teacher selected topics. The writing can be invented temporary spellings or dictations to the teacher.

Continue to have your students work on writing their home addresses and phone numbers if you have chosen to do this activity.

Multimedia Resources: Review "Rev-Up for Writing" from the "Rev-Up for Learning" DVD to review the writing of upper- and lowercase letters.

Memory Verse: Romans 3:23.
For all have sinned and fall short of the glory of God. Romans 3:23 NIV

For all have sinned, and come short of the glory of God; Romans 3:23 KJV

Introduce the new verse. Be sure that the students understand all of the words. This is another verse that will stay with them through their whole lifetime. Give the students Memory Verse Card 21 to take home.

Math: Teach 6 - 1 = 5. Have six students come to the front of the room. Count the students. Have one of them return to his seat. Ask the class how many students are still standing at the front of the room after one left. Do this with several groups of six students. Say the problem, "six minus one equals five." An optional way to do this is to hold up a subtraction sign between the first six students and a seventh that you have asked to come to the front. Then as you say the subtraction problem, have the student after the subtraction sign hold a piece of paper with a big X on it in front of him. You can also hold up an equal sign and have five additional students represent the answer to the subtraction problem.

Multimedia Resources: View "Rev-Up for Arithmetic" from the "Rev-Up for Learning" DVD to practice number recognition, counting and addition 1-20.

Story Time: Read a story or stories of your choice.

Music: Review "God Has Given Me a Home."

This week, listen and sing along to selections from a CD of your choice.

Arts & Crafts: Provide the students with red, blue, and yellow paints and a big piece of white construction paper. Remember when we learned about primary colors? Paint with the three primary colors today and see if you can make purple, green and orange. What combinations do we use? Blue and yellow make green. Red and yellow make orange. Blue and red make purple.

Do the Lesson 171 Arts & Crafts worksheet. Use crayons to color the shapes to show how colors mix.

Outdoor Activity: Go outside and play "Teacher, May I?" The teacher tells students to do something as a group. If they forget to ask, "Teacher, may I?" they have to step out. See who last the longest. Tell them to do things like jump, skip, step to the right, touch their toes, etc.

Physical Education: Rumble and Tumble. For the remainder of the year have the students work on some basic tumbling moves beginning with the log roll, crab walk, forward roll, and front straddle roll. Also have them learn how to balance on a beam and swing on a low bar.

To do a log roll, have the students lie on a mat and then roll sideways to the right, and then return rolling to the left (hips and shoulders should rotate at the same time).

To do a crab walk, have your students sit on the floor and lean back on their hands. Have them keep their feet flat on the floor. Then have them lift their bottoms off the floor and try moving sideways as crabs do.

To do a forward roll, start in a squat position with hands in front. Tuck your head to your knees and chin to your chest. Raise your bottom. Start to roll. The back of your head or the top part of your shoulders are the only parts that touch the mat. Stay in a ball. End in the same position you start.

To do a front straddle roll, start by standing at the end of the mat in a straddle position (legs apart). Place the hands on the mat between the legs. Tuck the chin to the chest and roll forward. Remain straddled and keep the hands between the legs. On the up rise keep the head down towards the mat and push hard with the hands and arms back to a straddle stand.

NOTES:

Activities in this Lesson: Bible Lesson, Social Studies, Science, Language Arts, Phonics, Reading, Writing, Memory Verse, Math, Story Time, Social Studies, Language Arts

Bible Reference: Genesis 3.

Bible Concept to Present: Adam and Eve chose to disobey the rule God had given them.

Bible Lesson: Adam and Eve continued to live very happily in the Garden of Eden. They could eat from any tree or plant that they wanted to, except the one tree called the Tree of Knowledge of Good and Evil. One day Eve was tempted by Satan to try the fruit from that tree. She even convinced Adam to taste of the fruit. After they had eaten from that tree, they knew they had done something wrong. The Bible says that they hid from God. God found them and was very unhappy that they had broken the one rule of their home. God does not want us to break His rules either. God calls this sin.

Anytime one of God's rules is broken, it is called sin. Adam and Eve had to feel bad about breaking God's rule. When we break a rule, we should feel bad, too. When we break a rule, we have to have some sort of discipline given to us so that we will remember not to sin again. God was very unhappy that Adam and Eve had broken His rule. Anytime we disobey, God is not happy with us. He still loves us, but He is not happy.

Many things changed after Adam and Eve disobeyed God. Adam and Eve had to leave that beautiful garden because they had sinned. Adam had to work every day now, instead of just playing with the animals. God also decided that since Adam sinned, He would cause man to die. Man could not live forever from then on. Eve would try to take over Adam's responsibilities. She would bear children in pain (optional to present). Adam and Eve's lives changed very much when they sinned. We must always remember to love God enough and try not to do wrong things.

Multimedia Resources: Listen to the song "Nathaniel's Song" from the "Nathaniel the Grublet" CD.

Social Studies: *Print the five laws below on poster board.* All of us sin. Sin is disobeying God's rules. God gave us specific rules to obey. The following is a list of just some of the rules God has given us.
1. Love God and put Him first.
2. Never say words that make fun of God's name.
3. Always tell the truth.
4. Never take anything that does not belong to you.
5. Always obey your parents.

God set these rules so we do not hurt ourselves and others. We should always obey God, and then we don't have to worry about hurting God if we disobey Him. God is not happy with us when we break his rules. He will punish those that sin. If we love God, as He loves us, we will not sin. When Adam and Eve sinned, things changed. They could no longer live in their beautiful home God had made for them. They no longer talked with God every day. A very special friendship between them and God was ruined. When we sin, we hurt other people.

Adam and Eve had to leave their lovely garden. They had to move. Many of us have had to move. It is a big job and can be very stressful. What do we need to do when we move? We have to stop the phone and electricity. We have to tell our friends our new address after learning it! We have to pack up our things in boxes, very carefully so that they won't break. Our old house has to be thoroughly cleaned. We rent a truck or van and move all of our things to our new home. Then when we get there, we have to do everything over again but backwards. Unpacking all of the boxes. Signing up for the phone and electric service. Cleaning our new house. One of the hardest parts is making new friends. Sometimes, we have to go to a new school. Have any of you ever had to do that? Have you ever moved? Give students crayons and paper. Instruct them to draw some work they would have to do if the family moved. Draw a moving van. Draw boxes.

Science: Water the carrot tops. Is something starting to grow?

Language Arts: Give each student two paper plates. Instruct them to make one paper plate a child's face and one paper plate a parent's face. Do some role playing with the students acting out the part of parents. Let the students trade being parent and child, holding the plate faces up in front of their face. Set limits on the time spent doing this. Give the students specific punishments (non-physical) which they can enforce for disobedience. Carefully explain the circumstances in which discipline should take place. You should role-play the normal behavior of children.

Read the following poem to students.

God Sees Me

God sees me in all that I do. (Point to eyes)
God hears me in all that I say. (Point to ears)
God knows me in all that I think. (Point to head)
God, help me to obey. (Hands outstretched)
Carol McSpadden Sheldon

Multimedia Resources: Watch the "Obedience" video from the *Character Builders Video Series*.

Phonics: Review the initial sound of Yy. Review the initial sounds of Aa-Xx. Review letter recognition Aa-Zz.

Do the Lesson 172 Phonics worksheet. The Sound of Yy. Review the letter sound with the picture and words on the worksheet. Ask the students for other words that begin with the same sound. Trace the letters and say the sound of Yy. Observe the students as they trace the letters and help them with the letter strokes. If you have the students do one row at a time, the worksheet can be carried over to various parts of the day or another day.

Reading: Give the beginning sound of a spoken word.

Writing: Continue to do Learning Logs. Encourage the students to draw or write about themselves. Some sample topics might be My Pet, My Favorite Reptile, My Favorite School Activity, My Family, or other teacher selected topics. The writing can be invented temporary spellings or dictations to the teacher.

Continue to have your students work on writing their home addresses and phone numbers if you have chosen to do this activity.

Memory Verse: Review Romans 3:23. Students might not fully understand this verse, but it is very important to the Christian life. Go over the verse several times.

Math: Review 6 - 1 = 5. Give the students the dog bones that they cut out previously and a bowl to put them in. Have them place 6 bones in the bowl while saying six minus one" and have them take a bone from the bowl, "equals" and have them count "one, two, three, four, five bones in the bowl." Do this several times. Practice previous addition and subtraction facts.

Do the Lesson 172 Math worksheet. As they count the images have them say the subtraction problems and trace the numbers.

Story Time: Read a story or stories of your choice.

Music: Review "God Has Given Me a Home."

This week, listen and sing along to selections from a CD of your choice.

Arts & Crafts: Give the students crayons and paper. Instruct them to draw some work they would have to do if the family moved. Draw a moving van. Draw boxes.

Physical Education: Rumble and Tumble. For the remainder of the year have the students work on some basic tumbling moves beginning with the log roll, crab walk, forward roll, and front straddle roll. Also have them learn how to balance on a beam and swing on a low bar.

To do a log roll, have the students lie on a mat and then roll sideways to the right, and then return rolling to the left (hips and shoulders should rotate at the same time).

To do a crab walk, have your students sit on the floor and lean back on their hands. Have them keep their feet flat on the floor. Then have them lift their bottoms off the floor and try moving sideways as crabs do.

To do a forward roll, start in a squat position with hands in front. Tuck your head to your knees and chin to your chest. Raise your bottom. Start to roll. The back of your head or the top part of your shoulders are the only parts that touch the mat. Stay in a ball. End in the same position you start.

To do a front Straddle Roll start by standing at the end of the mat in a straddle position (legs apart). Place the hands on the mat between the legs. Tuck the chin to the chest and roll forward. Remain straddled and keep the hands between the legs. On the up rise keep the head down towards the mat and push hard with the hands and arms back to a straddle stand.

NOTES:

Lesson 173

Week 35: Day 3

Activities in this Lesson: Bible Lesson, Social Studies, Science, Language Arts, Phonics, Reading, Writing, Memory Verse, Math, Story Time, Music, Arts & Crafts, Health & Safety, Physical Education

Bible Reference: Genesis 3.

Bible Concept to Present: God wants us to follow His directions. We also need to follow the world's directions when they involve our safety.

Bible Lesson: God was disappointed in Adam and Eve but He still loved them very much. God loves us when we obey and He loves us when we do wrong. He just wants us to obey because we will be happier and safer if we obey. All of God's rules for us are for our own good and protection.

Multimedia Resources: Listen to the song "Risky Game" from the "Nathaniel the Grublet" CD.

Illustration: When Adam and Eve disobeyed God, they needed some clothes to wear. God made them clothes from animal skins. An innocent animal had to die so that its skin could clothe Adam and Eve. (Draw a corollary between this and the death of Jesus on the cross.) We need clothes to keep us warm and protected. Today we're making a vest. *Provide each student with a large brown grocery bag. Cut out a neck hole in the bottom of the bag. Cut out arm holes in the sides of the bag, at the bottom end. Cut down the middle of one big side, right down to the neck hole. Turn the bag upside down, it's a vest! Staple ribbons to each side of the neck cutout, as a tie.* Let the students color their vests with drawings of things that God created: stars, sun, animals, bugs, etc.

Social Studies: Use Lesson 173 Resource page to show students some signs. Say, Our country has a vast system of rules and laws that we must follow. There is usually a sign to go with each rule. We see signs every day. Look at some of these signs. What do they tell us? Where do we see these signs? We have been learning left and right, north, south, east, and west. Often, street signs tell us to "Turn Left" or "Stay to the Right." Continue to learn directions. Say, The next time you are driving in a car, look around and count the signs.

Science: Take out the plastic animals used in Lesson 115. Label a piece of poster board with North, South, East, and West on the edges. Allow students to play with the animals, moving them in different directions. Say, Move the horse to the far north. Move the elephant to the center. Continue practicing all of the directions, including left and right.

Water the carrot tops. Is something starting to grow?

Language Arts: Watch "Josh and the Big Wall," a Veggie Tales® video by Big Idea. Sometimes we might not understand God's directions, but we must follow them anyway. God's directions to Joshua seemed really dumb. But Joshua trusted God, and God did what He promised.

Phonics: Blend the sounds Aa-Yy. (yak, yam, yap, yell, yen, yet, yip) Review the initial sounds of Aa-Yy. Review letter recognition Aa-Zz.

Add the following words to the flip chart pages of words and review them with the students. Continue to sound out the individual letters of each word as has been done previously. It may also be helpful for the students to see the words spaced out and spelled out as has been done in previous lessons.

ya	ye	yi
yak	yell	yip
yam	yen	
yap	yet	

Do the Lesson 173 Phonics worksheet. The sound of Yy. Review the letter sound with the picture on the worksheet. Ask the students for other words that begin with the same sound. Give them specific instructions for how the letter should be traced. Allow time for tracing the letters and observe their progress. If you have the students do one row at a time, the worksheet can be carried over to various parts of the day or another day.

Reading: Give the beginning sound of a spoken word.

Writing: Practice writing the numbers 911 with the Lesson 173 Writing worksheet.

Continue to have your students work on writing their home addresses and phone numbers if you have chosen to do this activity.

Memory Verse: Review Romans 3:23. Write the verse words on slips of construction paper. Hide the words around the room. Instruct the students to find the words by giving them directions, and then have them arrange the strips in the correct order.

Math: Review 6 - 1 = 5. Review 6 - 1 = 5 by writing the problem on the board. Draw objects over the numbers with - sign between them. Make a large X over the object being subtracted. Write the = sign and then draw an excess of objects over the answer. Have a student come to the board and circle the correct number of objects to make the subtraction problem correct. Erase the extra objects and orally say the problem with the class. Repeat several times drawing simple objects such as dots or various shapes. Review previous addition and subtraction problems if the students need the practice.

Do the Lesson 173 Math worksheet. Count the items and say the subtraction problem. As they trace the numbers have them say the subtraction problems.

Story Time: Read a story or stories of your choice.

Music: Review favorite songs learned this year.

This week, listen and sing along to selections from a CD of your choice.

Arts & Crafts: *Provide one cardboard paper towel roll center per student. Cut out green, yellow, and red 3" circles, one of each color per student. Glue the circles to the paper roll, making a traffic light. Make sure they are in correct order. Talk about traffic lights and why we need to stop or go exactly* as they tell us. Let the students walk around the room. Call out, "Red light" and hold up one of their lights. After they stop, say, "Green light." Repeat as they enjoy the activity.

Copy a large telephone keypad onto a sheet of paper and give one to each of the students. Have them press their fingers on an ink pad and then dial 911 on the keypad. This makes a lasting reminder of what 911 looks like on a telephone.

Health & Safety: *Have a real phone or play phone available.* Say, One day you might have to follow directions in an emergency. There have been times when young children saved their parents or a friend by doing the right thing. We have a phone emergency system called 911. Have any of you heard of that? We are going to practice calling 911. Use the phone to let each student try calling 911. Instruct them to say their name clearly and give their address. Practice answering any of the questions that a police dispatcher might ask. Remind them that they are to never dial 911 unless it is a real emergency. The dispatcher can tell where the call has been made from and will send the police over to check to see if everything is OK. This is a waste of a policeman's time and may hinder him from getting to a real emergency.

Physical Education: Rumble and Tumble. For the remainder of the year have the students work on some basic tumbling moves beginning with the log roll, crab walk, forward roll, and front straddle roll. Also have them learn how to balance on a beam and swing on a low bar.

NOTES:

Activities in this Lesson: Bible Lesson, Social Studies, Science, Language Arts, Phonics, Reading, Writing, Memory Verse, Math, Shapes, Story Time, Music, Arts & Crafts, Health & Safety, Physical Education

Bible Reference: Genesis 4:1-16.

Bible Concept to Present: Cain and Abel were brothers with different jobs to do. They were to help one another.

Bible Lesson: After Adam and Eve left the garden, Eve had a baby boy named Cain. Cain grew up to be a farmer. His job was to get the ground ready for planting the crops. He was a very good farmer. Soon, another little boy was born to Adam and Eve. His name was Abel. He grew up to be a shepherd. He was a very good shepherd. Cain and Abel were brothers. Our brothers and sisters should be special to us. They will always be an important part of our lives.

Social Studies: God gives us brothers and sisters so we have someone to share with. It is very important to remember that we do not have to be the same as our brother or sister. We need to remember that they are different people than we are, but that they are special. We can learn to share and get along with other people by sharing and loving our brother or sister. We should not argue or fight with them. God wants us to love them, not hurt them.

Multimedia Resources: Watch "Sharing" from the *Character Builders Video Series*.

Science: The carrot tops should be growing greenery. Isn't it amazing that a piece of vegetable can start growing again? The carrots may be disposed of after class.

Language Arts: Have your students finish open-ended sentences with you. Example: "I like my brother when he _____." Do several of these statements. Let the students verbalize their feelings regarding their siblings. Try to work with negative feelings, too. This activity may work better with an older preschool child.

Phonics: Review blends Aa-Yy with the blend charts. Review the initial sounds of Aa-Yy. Review letter recognition Aa-Zz.

Have the students brainstorm words that begin or include the letter Yy. Write these words on the board. Model the correct letter formation as you write the letters on the board. The students should practice forming the letter Yy on a blank sheet of paper. Students who are ready can practice copying complete words from the board.

Do the Lesson 174 Phonics worksheet. The Sound of Yy. Review the letter sound with the picture and words on the worksheet. Ask the students for other words that begin with the same sound. Trace the letters and say the sound of Yy. Observe the students as they trace the letters and help them with the letter strokes. If you have the students do one row at a time, the worksheet can be carried over to various parts of the day or another day.

Reading: Give the beginning sound of a spoken word.

Writing: Continue to do Learning Logs. Encourage the students to draw or write about themselves. Some sample topics might be My Pet, My Favorite Reptile, My Favorite School Activity, My Family, or other teacher selected topics. The writing can be invented temporary spellings or dictations to the teacher.

Continue to have your students work on writing their home addresses and phone numbers if you have chosen to do this activity.

Memory Verse: Review Romans 3:23. Work on memorizing the verse.

Math: Review 6 - 1 = 5. Give each of the students 10 counters. Have them make the subtraction problem with the counters. Have them point to the counters and say the subtraction problem, drawing the minus and equal sign with their finger between the counters as they say the words. Review previous problems if the students need the practice.

Do the Lesson 174 Math worksheet. As they trace the numbers have them say the subtraction problems.

Shapes: Do the Lesson 174 Shapes worksheet. Review the names of the shapes and draw lines to match the shapes that are the same.

Story Time: Read a story or stories of your choice.

Music: Review favorite songs learned this year.

Multimedia Resources: Listen to the song "His Story" from "The Amazing Book" CD and the song "David" from "The Amazing Children" CD. This week, listen and sing along to selections from a CD of your choice.

Arts & Crafts: Let the students draw pictures of their families. Classroom teachers, remember that many families today are blended. Students may have half sibling and step siblings. Students that are the only child in their family can draw their parents and themselves as a family. Talk about every family being different but loving and important to our lives.

Health & Safety: Continue to role play dialing and making a 911 call. Remind the students that they should never dial 911 as a prank. In many cities the police are dispatched to the place where the call was made to check that everything is OK. It is possible that someone who is very sick could die by their carelessness. Write the word EMERGENCY on the board and list things that are emergencies where 911 should be called.

Physical Education: Rumble and Tumble. For the remainder of the year have the students work on some basic tumbling moves beginning with the log roll, crab walk, forward roll, and front straddle roll. Also have them learn how to balance on a beam and swing on a low bar.

NOTES:

Activities in this Lesson: Bible Lesson, Social Studies, Language Arts, Phonics, Reading, Writing, Memory Verse, Math, Story Time, Music, Arts & Crafts, Health & Safety, Physical Education, Homework

Bible Reference: Genesis 4:1-16.

Bible Concept to Present: God wants to be our best friend. We have a way to talk to Him every day.

Bible Lesson: God made Adam and Eve to have fellowship and friendship with Him. Though He hates it that they sinned, He made a way to fix the problem of their sin. We sin whenever we break one of God's rules. (Consider using the Ten Commandments as a way to show children what God expects of them.) Just like your parents must punish you when you disobey, God must punish everyone who sins. He wants to have a relationship with us, so He did something very special for us. Jesus came to earth and lived His entire life without ever sinning—even once! Then, even though He had done nothing wrong, Jesus was punished for our sins and died on a cross. Jesus was placed in a grave, but rose from the dead to show that He conquered death. We can all have a right relationship with God if we repent (are sorry for and turn from our sins) and trust that Jesus' death saves us from our disobedience to God. Though we sin, God loves us and wants to talk with us every day. We can talk to God, just like we talk to our parents or our friends, by praying to Him. (Consider using the booklet "How Can I Become a Child of God?" available at www.answersingenesis.org/go/good-news.)

Multimedia Resources: Listen to the song "Diamond In The Rough" from the "Bullfrogs and Butterflies: God Loves Fun" CD.

Illustration: We can talk to God, or "pray," in many ways. Here are some verses about prayer:

I Kings 18:42	Daniel 6:10	Exodus 9:29
Joshua 5:14	Ezra 9:6	Jonah 2:1
Matthew 26:39	Acts 9:40	Nehemiah 8:6

Choose a few of these verses to read to your students from the NIV or other easily understood Bible version. How do we pray? Did you notice that some people in the Bible prayed on their knees, others standing up? Some people lay face down on the ground in awe of God. We can pray before sleeping, before eating or any time we want to. God always hears our prayers.

Social Studies: You can tell God how you feel by talking to Him. God has been so good to you. You can tell God you love Him and thank Him for all of the good things He gives you. Another way to be a friend to God would be to do what He wants you to do. If we can show God how much we love Him by obeying Him, that will show God that we want to be friends. Let's pray to God right now, thanking Him for all He has given us. Let the students pray sentence prayers, only if they want to. Never force a child to pray out loud.

Science: We talk to God by speaking to him in prayer. What are some of the ways that we can communicate with other people? Speaking, gestures, letters, Email, television, radio, newspapers, magazines, telephones, cell phones and signs are some examples that can be listed. Talk about the advantages and disadvantages of each form of communication. Do all of these work all of the time like our communication with God can work?

Language Arts: Teach students A.C.T.S. They are young, but can understand the concept.

    A = Adore
    C = Confess
    T = Thanks
    S = Stuff Needed

Explain this simple ACT of prayer. First, we tell God how much we love and ADORE Him. Then, CONFESS anything wrong we have done that day. THANK God for everything He does for us. Lastly, ask God for NEEDS and desires. Especially needs of others. Let the students take home the Lesson 175a Homework worksheet.

Read the following verse to your students.

> **Special Friends**
> Author Unknown
>
> I have a special friend
> A friend who loves me
> A friend who needs me
> My friend is God.
>
> I have a special friend
> One I can talk to
> One who hears me
> My friend is God.
>
> I have a special friend
> I listen to Him
> I love Him
> My friend is God.

Phonics: Teach the initial sound of Zz. Review the initial sounds of Aa-Yy. Review letter recognition Aa-Zz.

Write several initial Zz words on the board: zebra, zero, zest, zigzag, zillion, zinc, zip, Zip Code, zipper, zoo, zoom, zucchini, etc. Underline the initial letter Zz and say the words. Ask the students for other words that start with the same sound.

Do the Lesson 175 Phonics worksheet. The Sound of Zz. Review the letter sound with the picture and words on the worksheet. Ask the students for other words that begin with the same sound. Discuss the position of the letters on the guidelines. Give them specific instructions for how the letter should be traced. Trace the letters and say the sound of Zz. Observe the students as they trace the letters and help them with the letter strokes. If you have the students do one row at a time, the worksheet can be carried over to various parts of the day or another day.

Reading: Give the beginning sound of a spoken word.

Writing: Continue to do Learning Logs. Encourage the students to draw or write about themselves. Some sample topics might be My Pet, My Favorite Reptile, My Favorite School Activity, My Family, or other teacher selected topics. The writing can be invented temporary spellings or dictations to the teacher.

Continue to have your students work on writing their home addresses and phone numbers if you have chosen to do this activity.

Memory Verse: Review Romans 3:23. Finish the verse today. Let the students recite.

Math: Review 6 - 1 = 5.

Do the Lesson 175 Math worksheet. Circle the correct number of objects to answer the subtraction problems.

Story Time: Read a story or stories of your choice or one the students have brought from home.

Music: Review favorite songs learned this year.

This week, listen and sing along to selections from a CD of your choice.

Arts & Crafts: *Go to a ceramics or craft shop and purchase little praying hands, one for each student. Purchase gold or silver paint made for ceramics. Let the students paint their praying hands.* Encourage them to take them home or to their room and put them on the nightstand. The little prayer reminder will help them remember to say their prayers, talking to God each morning and each night.

Buy some magnetic strips, available at craft stores. Also purchase a sheet of foam board. Cut the foam board into squares, about three inch square, one for each student. An artist's blade works best. Cut the magnetic strip into two inch pieces, one for each student. Give each student a foam board square, a magnetic strip and colored markers. Let the students write "ACTS" on their square. Give them the magnetic strip and help them remove the backing paper and stick the magnet onto their foam board square. They now have a prayer reminder refrigerator magnet to take home.

Health & Safety: Continue to role play dialing and making a 911 call. Have several types of non-working phones available for them to practice with. Remind the students that they should never dial 911 as a prank. Continue to brainstorm for events that would be emergencies.

Physical Education: Rumble and Tumble. For the remainder of the year have the students work on some basic tumbling moves beginning with the log roll, crab walk, forward roll, and front straddle roll. Also have them learn how to balance on a beam and swing on a low bar.

Homework: Send home the Lesson 175b Homework worksheet, a request for family pictures. The students will be sharing the pictures next week in Lesson 177.

Activities in this Lesson: Bible Lesson, Social Studies, Language Arts, Phonics, Reading, Writing, Memory Verse, Math, Story Time, Music, Arts & Crafts, Physical Education

Bible Reference: Genesis 6-9.

Bible Concept to Present: Noah was a man who obeyed God, even when everyone else laughed at him.

Bible Lesson: After Adam and Eve sinned, sin was always in the world. The world was getting to be a very bad place to live. The beautiful place that God had made in the beginning was no longer beautiful. People didn't want to obey God any more. This was making God very sad. He looked down and saw how bad people were acting.

God could only find one man on the earth that was acting good and obeying God. This man's name was Noah. Noah loved God very much. The Bible says, "Noah walked with God." He was a good man with a good family. God told Noah that He was going to get rid of all the bad in the world. God told Noah to build a very big boat. Noah did what God said. Noah started building, and as he was building, he told other people that God was going to make it rain for a very long time. The Bible says that Noah was a preacher of righteousness. Do you know what the people did? They laughed at Noah. They made fun of him. But Noah and his family went ahead and kept building the big boat, and telling people that God loved them. Noah was a brave man, don't you think?

Multimedia Resources: Watch "Faith" from the *Character Builders Video Series*. Listen to the song "Noah" from the "Bullfrogs and Butterflies: God is My Friend" CD. Listen to the song "A Story-Telling Book" from "The Amazing Book" CD or "The Amazing Sing Along" DVD. Listen to the song "Water, Water" from "The Amazing Miracles" CD or "The Amazing Sing Along" DVD.

Social Studies: When people laugh at us, it makes us feel bad, doesn't it? Noah was laughed at a lot but he didn't care. He knew he wanted to obey God. We must obey God's rules even if our friends laugh at us. We should never laugh at anyone else. It hurts their feelings. God wants us to love other people. He wants us to tell other people that God loves them, too. Sometimes, we don't tell others about God's love because we are afraid they will laugh at us. But we should tell them anyway.

Science: God has created natural laws (rules) that cannot be avoided. If you throw a rock straight up over your head you risk getting hit in the head by the rock. Whatever is thrown up into the air must always come back down. Toss a ball up in the air to illustrate this law. These natural laws cannot be avoided. Discuss or demonstrate some other natural laws that cannot be avoided like the action-reaction law.

Language Arts: Sit in a circle on the floor and brainstorm with your students on ways they can tell their friends about God. One way is to invite a friend for lunch or dinner, and show that friend how to pray to God before eating. Or invite a friend to church or Vacation Bible School. The best way is to invite a friend to church and PICK THEM UP. Arrange the time and have your family give them a ride.

Phonics: Blend the sounds Aa-Zz. (zag, zap, Zed, Zek, zig, zip, zit, biz, fizz, wiz, Oz, coz) Review the initial sounds of Aa-Zz. Review letter recognition Aa-Zz.

Add the following words to the flip chart pages of words and review them with the students. Continue to sound out the individual letters of each word as has been done previously. It may also be helpful for the students to see the words spaced out and spelled out as has been done in previous lessons.

<u>za</u>	<u>ze</u>	<u>zi</u>	<u>iz</u>	<u>oz</u>
zag	Zed	zig	biz	Oz
zap	Zek	zip	fizz	coz
		zit	wiz	

Do the Lesson 176a Phonics worksheet. The sound of Zz. Review the letter sound with the picture and words on the worksheet. Ask the students for other words that begin with the same sound. Trace the letters and say the sound of Zz. Observe the students as they trace the letters and help them with the letter strokes. If you have the students do one row at a time, the worksheet can be carried over to various parts of the day or another day.

Do the Lesson 176b Phonics worksheet. The Sound of Zz. Review the letter sound with the picture and words on the worksheet. Ask the students for other words that begin with the same sound. Give them specific instructions for how the letter should be traced. Allow time for tracing the letters and observe their progress. If you have the students do one row at a time, the worksheet can be carried over to various parts of the day or another day.

Reading: Give the beginning sound of a spoken word.

Multimedia Resources: Review "Rev-Up for Reading" from the "Rev-Up for Learning" DVD to drill letter recognition and sound. The students should say each letter sound along with the presentation.

Writing: Continue to do Learning Logs. Encourage the students to draw or write about themselves. Some sample topics might be My Pet, My Favorite Reptile, My Favorite School Activity, My Family, or other teacher selected topics. The writing can be invented temporary spellings or dictations to the teacher.

Continue to have your students work on writing their home addresses and phone numbers if you have chosen to do this activity.

Multimedia Resources: Review "Rev-Up for Writing" from the "Rev-Up for Learning" DVD to review the writing of upper- and lowercase letters.

Memory Verse: Review verses from weeks 1 through 8 today.
Genesis 1:1, Genesis 1:3, Genesis 1:6, Genesis 1:10, and I Peter 1:24-25

Math: Review 6 - 1 = 5. Use the string of Counting Beads or pop beads to review 1 + 1 = 2, 2 + 1 = 3, 3 + 1 = 4, 4 + 1 = 5, 2 – 1 = 1, 3 – 1 = 2, 4 – 1 = 3, 5 – 1 = 4, and 6 – 1 = 5.

Do the Lesson 176 Math worksheet. Count the beads and say the subtraction problem. Trace the correct answer and say the subtraction problem again.

Multimedia Resources: View "Rev-Up for Arithmetic" from the "Rev-Up for Learning" DVD to practice number recognition, counting and addition 1-20.

Story Time: Read a story or stories of your choice.

Music: Review favorite songs learned this year.

This week, listen and sing along to selections from a CD of your choice.

Arts & Crafts: *Bring a package of craft sticks to class. A home improvement store will have wood pieces of pine and cedar, among others. Bring some samples to class.* On a big piece of cardboard or poster board, outline a big boat, similar to the ark on Lesson 176 Resource page. Let the students take turns gluing the craft sticks on the ark, making it look like a wooden ship. Explain that the ark was made of gopher wood. Gopher wood was probably the cypress tree, widely available in Noah's time. It also might have been pine or cedar. Look at the wood samples. Are these woods strong? Would they resist water? See if they will float. Perhaps Noah used some pitch or tar on the seams of the ark.

Physical Education: Rumble and Tumble. For the remainder of the year have the students work on some basic tumbling moves beginning with the log roll, crab walk, forward roll, and front straddle roll. Also have them learn how to balance on a beam and swing on a low bar.

NOTES:

Activities in this Lesson: Bible Lesson, Social Studies/Homework, Social Studies, Language Arts, Phonics, Reading, Writing, Memory Verse, Math, Story Time, Music, Arts & Crafts, Outdoor Activity, Physical Education

Bible Reference: Genesis 5:18-24; Hebrews 11:5.

Bible Concept to Present: Noah's family believed in God and obeyed Him. Noah was blessed with a Godly heritage.

Bible Lesson: Noah had a family. God included Noah's family in his plan of salvation for mankind. Noah had three sons: Shem, Ham and Japheth. Noah taught his family about God. Noah's sons were married. Their wives and their mother were included in the salvation of the ark.

Illustration: Noah's family had a Godly heritage. Perhaps Noah's family had worshiped together. They talked about a loving God. They would have heard stories about the Garden of Eden and the Creation. Methuselah was Noah's grandfather. Isn't that a long name? Methuselah probably knew Adam and talked to him about the Creation and the Creator. Methuselah's father was Enoch. Enoch was a man that "walked with God." What a precious Godly heritage, passed down from Enoch to Methuselah to Lamech to Noah. We can thank God that we have someone who cares enough about us to want us to learn about God. Each student can thank God that they are here, learning about the Bible and a loving God.

Multimedia Resources: Listen to the song "Noah" from the "Bullfrogs and Butterflies: God is My Friend" CD. Listen to the song "A Story-Telling Book"from "The Amazing Book" CD or "The Amazing Sing Along" DVD. Listen to the song "Water, Water" from "The Amazing Miracles" CD or "The Amazing Sing Along" DVD.

Social Studies/Review Homework: Let the students share their family pictures, brought in as a homework project. Touch on the Godly heritage of each student, being careful not to hurt any feelings if there is no belief in God in the student's past. If you have a family tree of your family, bring it to share with students.

Something to do at home: Make a family tree on poster board with whatever pictures you have. If there is a Godly heritage in your family, trace it for your children. Many times, we presume that our children know about our past when they do not. In my family, I wanted so much to know how my grandparents met for a heritage photo album. Five of their children are still alive, so I was sure that one of them would know. Not one of the five had any idea about how their parents met. Don't presume. Talk about family histories, triumphs and failures.

Social Studies: Noah preached to his neighbors for 120 years before the flood. God made sure that everyone had a chance to change and live a Godly life. 120 years is a long time. Cut a piece of poster board into two lengthwise pieces. Make a very simple timeline of the past fifty years. Leave a big space at the end for all of the student's birth dates. Put your birth date in the correct spot. Add a few dates that students might have heard about: World War II; man on the moon 1969; the millennium

2000; September 11, 2001. Show students what a long time fifty years is, yet Noah preached and worked on the ark for 120 years!

Science: Give the students a perspective of how large the ark was that Noah built. The ark was 75 feet wide, 450 feet long and 45 feet tall (or larger). Find a large open area outside where you can pace off the length and width of the ark. Use a helium balloon on a string to show how tall the ark was. Take the students on a Walk Around the Ark by walking the approximate perimeter of the ark.

Language Arts: This song has been around a long time. It is lots of fun.

Rise and Shine

The Lord said to Noah there's gonna be a floody floody
Lord said to Noah there's gonna be a floody floody
Get my children (clap) out of the muddy muddy
Children of the Lord.

> CHORUS
> So rise and shine and give God the glory glory
> Rise and shine and give God the glory glory
> Rise and shine and (clap) give God the glory glory
> Children of the Lord.

The Lord said to Noah you're gonna build an arky arky
Lord said to Noah you're gonna build an arky arky
Build it out of (clap) hickory barky barky
Children of the Lord.
CHORUS

The animals, they came on they came on by twosies twosies
Animals, they came on they came on by twosies twosies
Elephants and (clap) kangaroozies roozies
Children of the Lord.
CHORUS

It rained and poured for forty daisies daisies
Rained and poured for forty daisies daisies
Drove old Noah (clap)almost crazy crazy
Children of the Lord.
CHORUS

The sun came out and dried up the landy landy
Sun came out and dried up the landy landy
Everything was (clap) fine and dandy dandy
Children of the Lord.
CHORUS

Phonics: Review blends Aa-Zz with the blend charts. Review the initial sounds of Aa-Zz. Review letter recognition Aa-Zz.

Have the students brainstorm words that begin or include the letter Zz. Write these words on the board. Model the correct letter formation as you write the letters on the board. The students should practice forming the letter Zz on a blank sheet of paper. Students who are ready can practice copying complete words from the board.

Do the Lesson 177 Phonics worksheet. The Sound of Zz. Review the letter sound with the picture and words on the worksheet. Ask the students for other words that begin with the same sound. Trace the letters and say the sound of Zz. Observe the students as they trace the letters and help them with the letter strokes. If you have the students do one row at a time, the worksheet can be carried over to various parts of the day or another day.

Reading: Give the beginning sound of a spoken word.

Writing: Continue to do Learning Logs. Encourage the students to draw or write about themselves. Some sample topics might be My Pet, My Favorite Reptile, My Favorite School Activity, My Family, or other teacher selected topics. The writing can be invented temporary spellings or dictations to the teacher.

Continue to have your students work on writing their home addresses and phone numbers if you have chosen to do this activity.

Memory Verse: Review verses from weeks 9 through 14 today.
Genesis 8:22, Genesis 1:16, Psalm 90:12, and Psalm 89:1

Math: Review 6 - 1 = 5.

Instruct the students to create an AB pattern with counters, buttons beans, etc. Do other patterns AAB, ABB, AAAB, etc. How many groups of patterns can they create with the items you have given them?

Story Time: Read a story or stories of your choice.

Music: Review favorite songs learned this year.

This week, listen and sing along to selections from a CD of your choice.

Arts & Crafts: Give each student some playdough. Let them fashion their own arks.

Outdoor Activity: We have been working on Horizons Preschool for 36 weeks! What a lot of things we have learned together. Let's take a walk outside and see if any of our plants are still growing. How many things did we look at outside? Are the birds still in the trees? Are the rocks still lying there, waiting for the sun's shadow?

Physical Education: Rumble and Tumble. For the remainder of the year have the students work on some basic tumbling moves beginning with the log roll, crab walk, forward roll, and front straddle roll. Also have them learn how to balance on a beam and swing on a low bar.

NOTES:

Activities in this Lesson: Bible Lesson, Social Studies, Science, Language Arts, Phonics, Reading, Writing, Memory Verse, Math, Story Time, Music, Arts & Crafts, Physical Education

Bible Reference: Genesis 6-9.

Bible Concept to Present: God took care of Noah. God's promises are for us, too, as they were for Noah.

Bible Lesson: Noah finally got the big boat finished. That boat was called an ark. God had decided to get rid of the bad people on the earth, so Noah and his family went to live in the ark. It began to rain. And it rained for 40 day and 40 nights. That is a very long time. The boat began to float and Noah, his family, and all the animals Noah had saved from the rain were saved. God had told Noah to save two of every "unclean" animal and seven of every "clean" animal.

Everyone in the ark was safe. Everyone outside of the ark died. Soon the rain stopped. After a time, Noah opened the ark, and saw a beautiful rainbow in the sky. This was God's promise that He would never let the earth flood everywhere again. Noah was very happy that he had obeyed God. His family was safe. The animals were safe. God would take care of them forever. He will take care of us forever, too.

Multimedia Resources: Listen to the song "Noah" from the "Bullfrogs and Butterflies: God is My Friend" CD. Listen to the song "A Story-Telling Book" from "The Amazing Book" CD or "The Amazing Sing Along" DVD. Listen to the song "Water, Water" from "The Amazing Miracles" CD or "The Amazing Sing Along" DVD.

Multimedia Resources: Watch "Peace" from the *Character Builders Video Series*.

Illustration: There are many inexpensive Noah's Ark sets available with animals. Use a set to demonstrate God calling the animals into the ark. Explain that only God could have helped Noah get lions and ducks and snakes and mice all into the ark safely. This was all a part of God's plan. God provided a way for righteousness to survive with Noah and his family. It is very important that we worship God together with our family. Noah's sons, Shem, Ham and Japheth, all survived with Noah on the ark. Noah's wife and his daughters-in-law also were on the ark. Let the students play and re-enact the story with the ark and animals. (**Note:** Many pictures and models of the ark show an overloaded boat that makes the biblical account look like a mythical children's story. Avoid using misleading pictures of the ark that show animals sticking out of a tiny ark. Answers in Genesis offers paper models to the scale of the biblical dimensions at www.answersbookstore.com.)

Social Studies: Do you know what a promise is? A promise is giving your word that you will do something. God gave His word to Noah that God would not get rid of the earth by lots of rain again. God told Noah this through an arch of colors. That arch was called a rainbow. We will make a rainbow today. I know you will make a beautiful one, just like God did for Noah.

Science: After the flood, the world God created was changed very much. The mountains and valleys had changed. Our world, as we know it now, is not like the world God created. It is a world that tells the story of the flood. God destroyed the people of Noah's day because they did not obey Him. Our world tells about the flood in its fossil record. Explain and show to your students, if possible, a fossil. Students may be very interested in the study of dinosaurs. We suggest you teach this from a Creationist viewpoint. See Job 40:15-24 for a Biblical description of the dinosaur.

(Teachers Note: Many Natural History museums will have some dinosaur bones. These are proof of God's Creation. The Institute for Creation Research or Answers in Genesis has lots of great books on the dinosaurs. Call them or visit their Website for more information.)

Language Arts: Read the following poem to your students.

God Made the World

When God made our world
A long time ago,
He created many animals.
He has said it was so.

He made the dinosaur
Huge and tall.
He made the mouse
Smallest of all.

He made the world
In which they were to live.
And then He made man,
So He would have someone to give
The wonderful gift He had made.

Adam and God became friends,
And Adam's children knew no end
To the blessings God had in store for them.

One day they decided
To disobey their Heavenly Father.
They would do as they wished.
Obeying was too much bother.

So they did what they wanted.
To Noah they did not heed.
They laughed at the boat
God said Noah would need.

When the rain came down upon the earth,
The people requested a boat to ride.
But God had shut the door to the ark
And no man could open it wide.

After the flood was over
God sent a wonderful sign.
A rainbow in the sky announced
His promise to mankind.

The world would never be flooded again.
The rainbow still is there.
A promise of God's wonderful love,
A promise of His care.
        .... Rebecca McSpadden Avery

Phonics: Review blends Aa-Zz with the blend charts. Review the initial sounds of Aa-Zz. Review letter recognition Aa-Zz. Finish up the phonics work for the year. Congratulate the students on their progress in reading.

Reading: Give the beginning sound of a spoken word.

Writing: Continue to do Learning Logs. Encourage the students to draw or write about themselves. Some sample topics might be My Pet, My Favorite Reptile, My Favorite School Activity, My Family, or other teacher selected topics. The writing can be invented temporary spellings or dictations to the teacher.

Continue to have your students work on writing their home addresses and phone numbers if you have chosen to do this activity.

Memory Verse: Review memory verses from weeks 15 through 20 today.
Genesis 1:16, Revelation 22:16, Psalm 148:13, Genesis 1:26, and Psalm 48:1

Math: Review 6 - 1 = 5. Practice this problem and review the problems: 1 + 1 = 2, 2 + 1 = 3, 3 + 1 = 4, 4 + 1 = 5, 5 + 1 = 6, 2 - 1 = 1, 3 – 1 = 2, 4 – 1 = 3, 5 – 1 = 4, with a strip of squares drawn on the board.

Do the Lesson 178a Math worksheet. Color and cut out the pictures. Paste the items that should go above the water and paste what should go below the water.

Do the Lesson 178b Math worksheet. Count the dots in the tiles and trace the numbers.

Story Time: Read a story or stories of your choice.

Music: Review "Rise and Shine" (Language Arts). Learn the "God Put A Rain Cloud in the Sky" song from "Horizons Preschool Music" CD.

This week, listen and sing along to selections from a CD of your choice.

Arts & Crafts: Provide colored markers, crayons, glue, glitter and a large piece of paper. As a treat, you may give each student a piece of white poster board. Let the students spend as much time as they desire making a beautiful rainbow.

Physical Education: Rumble and Tumble. For the remainder of the year have the students work on some basic tumbling moves beginning with the log roll, crab walk, forward roll, and front straddle roll. Also have them learn how to balance on a beam and swing on a low bar.

NOTES:

Activities in this Lesson: Bible Lesson, Science, Language Arts, Phonics, Reading, Writing, Memory Verse, Math, Story Time, Music, Arts & Crafts, Creative Cooking, Physical Education

Bible Reference: Genesis 6-9.

Bible Concept to Present: God had to have brought the animals to Noah. Think of how many animals there are. Noah couldn't have gone all over the world collecting them. God must have helped.

Bible Lesson: Some facts about the ark
> The ark was made of gopher wood.
> It was about 450 feet long. A football field is 300 feet long.
> It was about 75 feet wide.
> It was about 45 feet high.
> It was shaped like a fat house. It had three floors filled with rooms.
> It had one window and one door.
> Noah and his family were in the ark seven days before the rain started.

So who shut the door when Noah and his family were all inside? God did! "The animals going in were male and female of every living thing, as God had commanded Noah. Then the LORD shut him in." Genesis 7:16.

Multimedia Resources: Listen to the song "Noah" from the "Bullfrogs and Butterflies: God is My Friend" CD. Listen to the song "A Story-Telling Book" from "The Amazing Book" CD or "The Amazing Sing Along" DVD. Listen to the song "Water, Water" from "The Amazing Miracles" CD or "The Amazing Sing Along" DVD.

Social Studies: The world after the flood would have been a very lonely place. The only people were Noah and his family and two of every animal. Noah would not have had any neighbors or friends to visit. There would not have been any friends for the children to play with. Any houses or buildings would have been destroyed by the flood. Noah and his family would have been starting over from scratch. Ask the students to imagine what they would do if they did not have a building to live in, no playground toys to play on, no stores to get supplies from and no other people to ask for help. God gave Noah the knowledge to live in the world during this time.

Science: What happened to Noah's ark? The Bible tells us that Noah and his family landed with the ark in the mountains of Ararat. This was probably in a country that today is called Turkey. The problem is whether the ark would have survived all of this time. It is logical that Noah and his family had to use the ark as shelter for some time. They might then have used the gopher wood to build new homes or wagons. This website is sponsored by scientists that are trying to find Noah's ark, if it exists. http://www.noahsarksearch.com/

Language Arts: Rent or check out from the library the video "Fantasia 2000," a Disney release. Set the video to show "Pomp and Circumstance," set to the Noah's Ark story. This is a very touching cartoon portrayal of the Noah's Ark voyage.

Phonics: Review blends Aa-Zz with the blend charts. Review the initial sounds of Aa-Zz. Review letter recognition Aa-Zz. Finish up the phonics work for the year. Congratulate the students on their progress in reading.

Reading: Give the beginning sound of a spoken word.

Writing: Continue to do Learning Logs. Encourage the students to draw or write about themselves. Some sample topics might be My Pet, My Favorite Reptile, My Favorite School Activity, My Family, or other teacher selected topics. The writing can be invented temporary spellings or dictations to the teacher.

Continue to have your students work on writing their home addresses and phone numbers if you have chosen to do this activity.

Memory Verse: Review verses from weeks 21 through 35 today.
Matthew 6:26, Genesis 1:24, Psalm 139:14-16, Genesis 2:2, Proverbs 17:17a, and Romans 3:23

Math: Review 6 - 1 = 5. Have the students count off steps to practice addition and subtraction.
Review: 1 + 1 = 2, 2 + 1 = 3, 3 + 1 = 4, 4 + 1 = 5, 5 + 1 = 6, 2 – 1 = 1, 3 – 1 = 2, 4 – 1 = 3, 5 – 1 = 4, 6 = 1 = 5.

Do the Lesson 179 Math worksheet. For subtraction count all of the blocks in the strip, then say, "minus one block equals," and count the blocks that are not covered by an X. Trace the correct number.

Story Time: Read the book *The Honey Makers* by Gail Gibbons (1997).

Music: Review "Rise and Shine" (Language Arts) and "God Put A Rain Cloud in the Sky."

This week, listen and sing along to selections from a CD of your choice.

Arts & Crafts: *Choose one large table in the room to decorate for tomorrow's party. Cover the table with white freezer paper, taping the corners.* Outline a huge rainbow on the paper, making six striped areas in the center of the table. Lightly pencil in the correct colors in order from the middle: purple, blue, green, yellow, orange, red. Outline a grass level at the end of the table and paint it with a wash of green water color. Paint the other end of the table with a wash of blue water color to represent the sky. Let dry overnight. Students will love helping with this project.

Creative Cooking: Ever wonder how much food Noah had to take on the ark? He had to have enough for eight adults and all of the animals, for almost a year! He surely brought lots of dried foods and nuts. Today we're going to make some Trail Mix, something that Noah could have brought on the ark. Save the treat for tomorrow's party.

Noah's Trail Mix

Let the students help mix together in a big bowl any of these ingredients: popcorn, pretzels, raisins, sunflower seeds, almonds, walnuts, pecans or coconut. You may also add wheat or rice chex type cereal.

Physical Education: Rumble and Tumble. For the remainder of the year have the students work on some basic tumbling moves beginning with the log roll, crab walk, forward roll, and front straddle roll. Also have them learn how to balance on a beam and swing on a low bar.

Activities in this Lesson: Arts & Crafts, Creative Cooking

CONGRATULATIONS! What a lot of wonderful work you have done! Think about all of the things you have learned this year. If the Creation Mural is still available, post it where everyone can see it. Put up the rainbow art that students made.

Arts & Crafts: Decorate the Rainbow Table. Give the students markers and instruct them to draw flowers, a sun, birds, bugs or anything they remember about God's Creation. Show them the colors of the rainbow and let them color the stripes.

Invite parents to the party. Ask them to bring a snack to share.

Find paper plates and cups in a rainbow design, to match the centerpiece table.

Give each student a reward in a rainbow design: a key chain, eraser, sucker, pencil, bookmark, or coloring book.

Invite the students to share any memory verses they can remember. This is for volunteers only.

Go to the Creation Mural and let the students talk about each day of Creation and all that they learned.

Arts & Crafts: Cut up many colors of construction paper into various sizes and shapes. Divide the pieces of paper into little cups for each student. Give the students a piece of white construction paper and glue sticks. Let them glue the little pieces of colored paper in the white piece to make a "stained glass" design to Praise God for His creation.

Creative Cooking:
> Pour the Noah's Trail Mix into small cups to serve.
> Make punch: Pour a cold two liter bottle of lime soda
> and a cold can of punch into a punch bowl.
> Add scoops of rainbow sherbet and some ice.
> Serve rainbow sherbet.

AOP's Commitment to Quality—Tell us how we are doing

As a publisher dedicated to providing high quality educational materials we invite you to tell us how we are doing. Please visit our website at www.aop.com to give us your comments, concerns, and/or compliments concerning Horizons Preschool. Contact information can be found in the support area for Horizons at the AOP website.

314

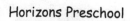

316

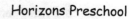

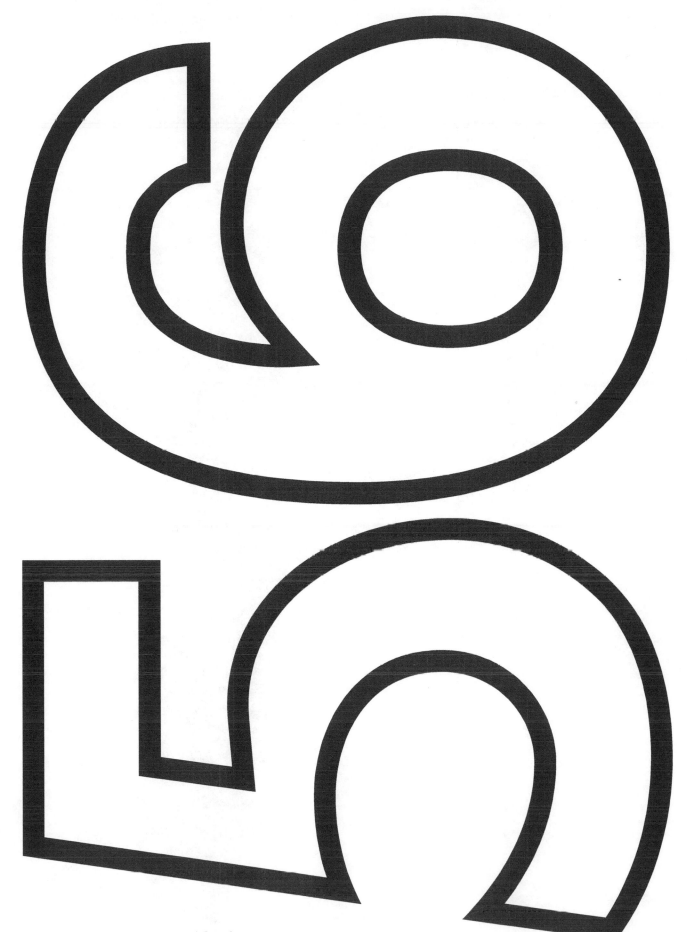

318